SPQR

Also by Mary Beard

Laughter in Ancient Rome
The Roman Triumph
Confronting the Classics
Pompeii: The Life of a Roman Town
It's a Don's Life
All in a Don's Day
The Parthenon
The Colosseum (with Keith Hopkins)

SPQR

A HISTORY OF ANCIENT ROME

MARY BEARD

LIVERIGHT PUBLISHING CORPORATION

A Division of W. W. Norton & Company

Independent Publishers Since 1923

New York · London

For information about permission to reproduce selections from this book,
write to Permissions, Liveright Publishing Corporation, a division of
W. W. Norton & Company, Inc., 500 Fifth Avenue, New York, NY 10110

For information about special discounts for bulk purchases, please contact
W. W. Norton Special Sales at specialsales@wwnorton.com or 800-233-4830

Manufacturing by RR Donnelley Westford
Production manager: Anna Oler

ISBN 978-0-87140-423-7

Liveright Publishing Corporation
500 Fifth Avenue, New York, N.Y. 10110
www.wwnorton.com

W. W. Norton & Company Ltd.
Castle House, 75/76 Wells Street, London W1T 3QT

1 2 3 4 5 6 7 8 9 0

CONTENTS

·

MAPS

·

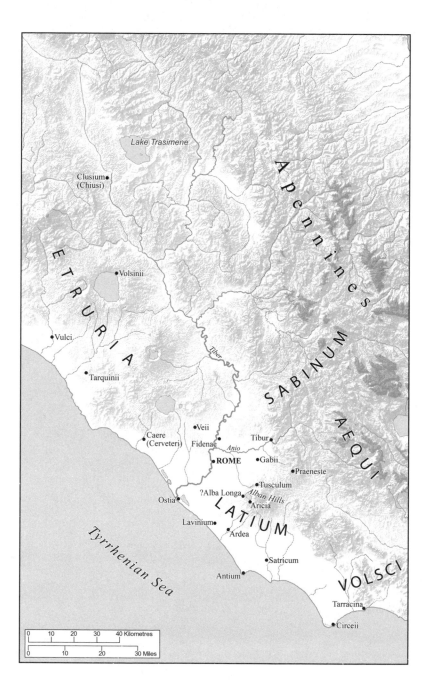

Lake Trasimene

Clusium
(Chiusi)

E T R U R I A

A p e n n i n e s

Volsinii

Tiber

Vulci

S A B I N U M

Tarquinii

A E Q U I

Veii

Caere
(Cerveteri)   Fidenae   Tibur

Anio

•ROME   •Gabii

Praeneste

Tusculum

Ostia   ?Alba Longa   Alban Hills
          Aricia

Lavinium   L A T I U M

Ardea

Tyrrhenian Sea

Satricum

Antium

V O L S C I

Tarracina

Circeii

| 0 | 10 | 20 | 30 | 40 Kilometres |
| 0 | 10 | 20 | 30 Miles |

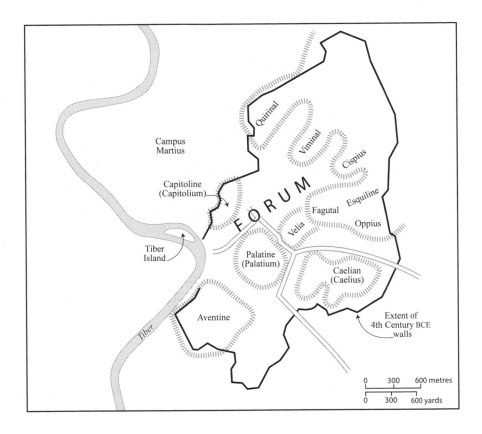

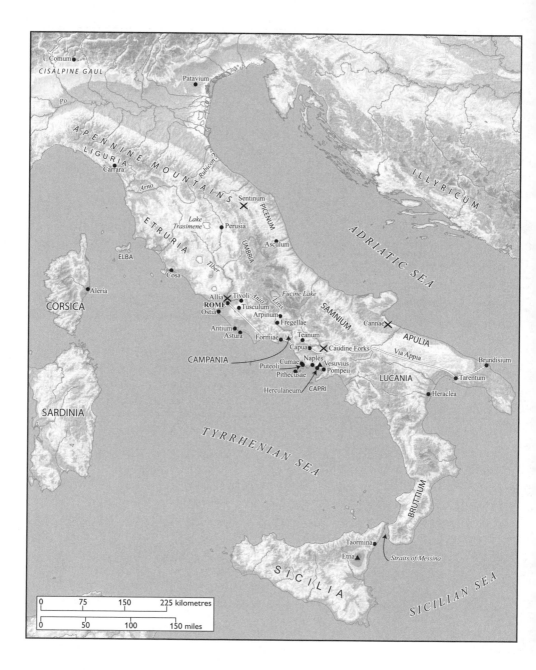

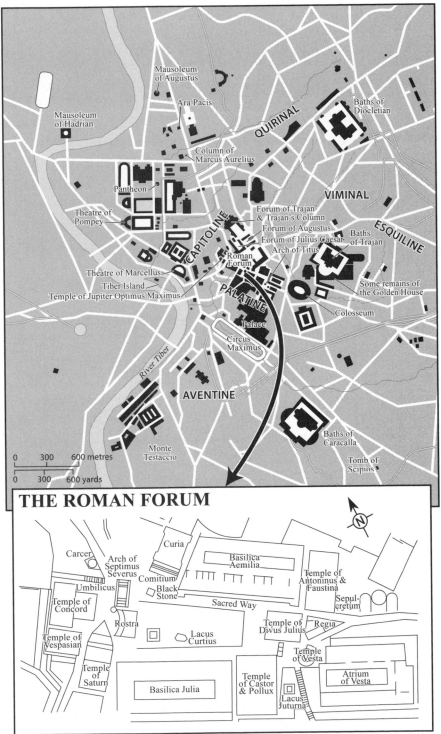

THE ROMAN FORUM

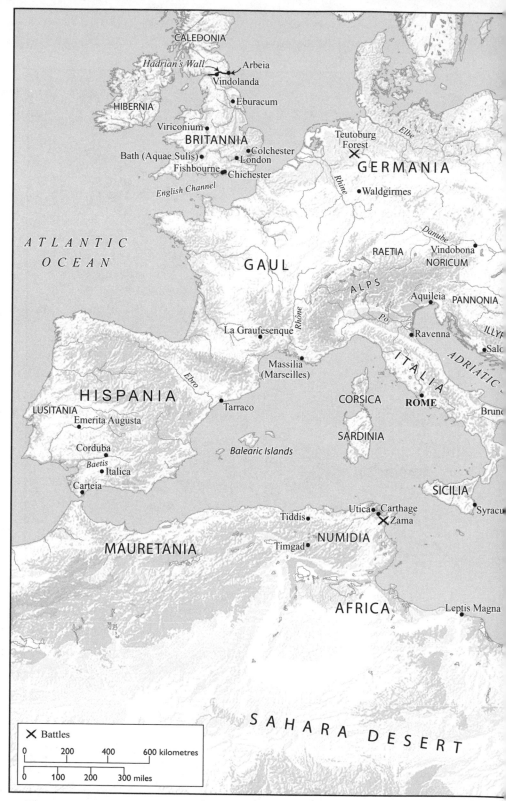

CALEDONIA

Hadrian's Wall — Arbeia
Vindolanda

HIBERNIA

Eburacum

Viriconium

BRITANNIA

Bath (Aquae Sulis) • Colchester
London
Fishbourne • Chichester

English Channel

GERMANIA

Teutoburg
Forest
✗

Rhine

Elbe

• Waldgirmes

ATLANTIC
OCEAN

GAUL

RAETIA

Danube

Vindobona
NORICUM

ALPS

Rhône

Aquileia
PANNONIA

Po

ILLY

• Ravenna

ADRIATIC

• Sal

La Graufesenque

Massilia
(Marseilles)

ITALIA

HISPANIA

Ebro

• Tarraco

CORSICA

ROME

Brund

LUSITANIA

Emerita Augusta

SARDINIA

• Corduba
Baetis • Italica

Carteia

Balearic Islands

SICILIA

Utica • Carthage • Syracu
• Tiddis ✗ Zama

MAURETANIA

• Timgad

NUMIDIA

AFRICA

Leptis Magna

S A H A R A   D E S E R T

✗ Battles

0   200   400   600 kilometres

0   100   200   300 miles

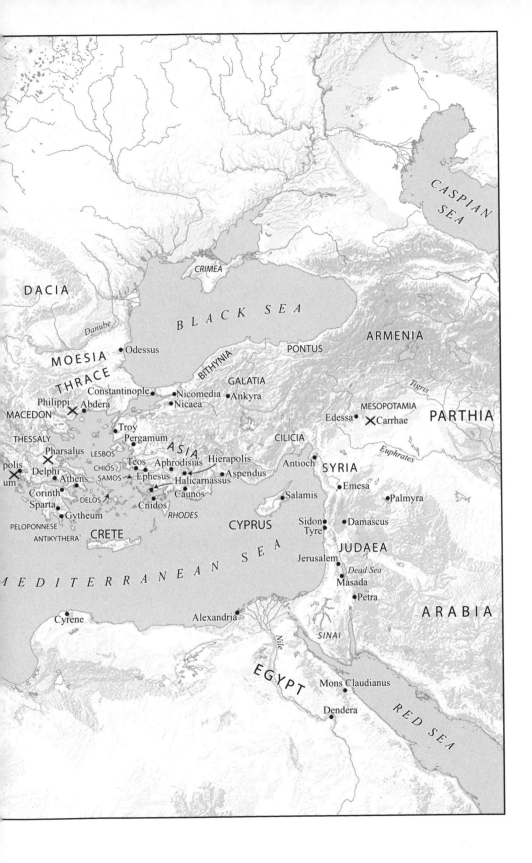

PROLOGUE

·

THE HISTORY OF ROME

ANCIENT ROME IS important. To ignore the Romans is not just to turn a blind eye to the distant past. Rome still helps to define the way we understand our world and think about ourselves, from high theory to low comedy. After 2,000 years, it continues to underpin Western culture and politics, what we write and how we see the world, and our place in it.

The assassination of Julius Caesar on what the Romans called the Ides of March 44 BCE has provided the template, and the sometimes awkward justification, for the killing of tyrants ever since. The layout of the Roman imperial territory underlies the political geography of modern Europe and beyond. The main reason that London is the capital of the United Kingdom is that the Romans made it the capital of their province Britannia – a dangerous place lying, as they saw it, beyond the great Ocean that encircled the civilised world. Rome has bequeathed to us ideas of liberty and citizenship as much as of imperial exploitation, combined with a vocabulary of modern politics, from 'senators' to 'dictators'. It has loaned us its catchphrases, from 'fearing Greeks bearing gifts' to 'bread and circuses' and 'fiddling while Rome burns' – even 'where there's life there's hope'. And it has prompted laughter, awe and horror in more or less equal measure. Gladiators are as big box office now as they ever were. Virgil's great epic poem on the foundation of Rome, the *Aeneid*, almost certainly found more readers in the twentieth century CE than it did in the first century CE.

Yet the history of ancient Rome has changed dramatically over the past fifty years, and even more so over the almost 250 years since Edward Gibbon wrote *The Decline and Fall of the Roman Empire*, his idiosyncratic historical experiment that began the modern study of Roman history in the English-speaking world. That is partly because of the new ways of looking at the old evidence, and the different questions we choose to put to it. It is a dangerous myth that we are better historians than our predecessors. We are not. But we come to Roman history with different priorities – from gender identity to food supply – that make the ancient past speak to us in a new idiom.

There has also been an extraordinary array of new discoveries – in the ground, underwater, even lost in libraries – presenting novelties from antiquity that tell us more about ancient Rome than any modern historian could ever have known before. We now have a manuscript of a touching essay by a Roman doctor whose prize possessions had just gone up in flames, which resurfaced in a Greek monastery only in 2005. We have wrecks of Mediterranean cargo ships that never made it to Rome, with their foreign sculpture, furniture and glass destined for the houses of the rich, and the wine and olive oil that were the staples of everyone. As I write, archaeological scientists are carefully examining samples drilled from the ice cap of Greenland to find the traces, even there, of the pollution produced by Roman industry. Others are putting under the microscope the human excrement found in a cesspit in Herculaneum, in southern Italy, to itemise the diet of ordinary Romans as it went into – and out of – their digestive tracts. A lot of eggs and sea urchins are part of the answer.

Roman history is always being rewritten, and always has been; in some ways we know more about ancient Rome than the Romans themselves did. Roman history, in other words, is a work in progress. This book is my contribution to that bigger project; it offers my version of why it matters. *SPQR* takes its title from another famous Roman catchphrase, *Senatus PopulusQue Romanus*, 'The Senate and People of Rome'. It is driven by a personal curiosity about Roman history, by a conviction that a dialogue with ancient Rome is still well worth having and by the question of how a tiny and very unremarkable little village in central Italy became so dominant a power over so much territory in three continents.

This is a book about how Rome grew and sustained its position for so long, not about how it declined and fell, if indeed it ever did in the sense that Gibbon imagined. There are many ways that histories of Rome might construct a fitting conclusion; some have chosen the conversion of the emperor Constantine to Christianity on his deathbed in 337 CE or the sack of the city in 410 CE by Alaric and his Visigoths. Mine ends with a culminating moment in 212 CE, when the emperor Caracalla took the step of making every single free inhabitant of the Roman Empire a full Roman citizen, eroding the difference between conqueror and conquered and completing a process of expanding the rights and privileges of Roman citizenship that had started almost a thousand years earlier.

SPQR is not, however, a simple work of admiration. There is much in the classical world – both Roman and Greek – to engage our interest and demand our attention. Our world would be immeasurably the poorer if we did not continue to interact with theirs. But admiration is a different thing. Happily a child of my times, I bridle when I hear people talking of 'great' Roman conquerors, or even of Rome's 'great' empire. I have tried to learn to see things from the other side too.

In fact, SPQR confronts some of the myths and half-truths about Rome with which I, like many, grew up. The Romans did not start out with a grand plan of world conquest. Although eventually they did parade their empire in terms of some manifest destiny, the motivations that originally lay behind their military expansion through the Mediterranean world and beyond are still one of history's great puzzles. In acquiring their empire, the Romans did not brutally trample over innocent peoples who were minding their own business in peaceable harmony until the legions appeared on the horizon. Roman victory was undoubtedly vicious. Julius Caesar's conquest of Gaul has not unfairly been compared to genocide and was criticised by Romans at the time in those terms. But Rome expanded into a world not of communities living at peace with one another but of endemic violence, rival power bases backed up by military force (there was not really any alternative backing), and mini-empires. Most of Rome's enemies were as militaristic as the Romans; but, for reasons I shall try to explain, they did not win.

Rome was not simply the thuggish younger sibling of classical Greece, committed to engineering, military efficiency and absolutism, whereas the Greeks preferred intellectual inquiry, theatre and democracy. It suited some Romans to pretend that was the case, and it has suited many modern historians to present the classical world in terms of a simple dichotomy between two very different cultures. That is, as we shall see, misleading, on both sides. The Greek city-states were as keen on winning battles as the Romans were, and most had little to do with the brief Athenian democratic experiment. Far from being unthinking advocates of imperial might, several Roman writers were the most powerful critics of imperialism there have ever been. 'They create desolation and call it peace' is a slogan that has often summed up the consequences of military conquest. It was written in the second century CE by the Roman historian Tacitus, referring to Roman power in Britain.

The history of Rome is a big challenge. There is no single story of Rome, especially when the Roman world had expanded far outside Italy. The history of Rome is not the same as the history of Roman Britain or of Roman Africa. Most of my focus will be on the city of Rome and on Roman Italy, but I shall take care also to look in at Rome from the outside, from the point of view of those living in the wider territories of the empire, as soldiers, rebels or ambitious collaborators. And very different kinds of history have to be written for different periods. For the earliest history of Rome and when it was expanding in the fourth century BCE from small village to major player in the Italian peninsula, there are no accounts written by contemporary Romans at all. The story has to be a bold work of reconstruction, which must squeeze individual pieces of evidence – a single fragment of pottery, or a few letters inscribed on stone – as hard as it can. Only three centuries later the problem is quite the reverse: how to make sense of the masses of competing contemporary evidence that may threaten to swamp any clear narrative.

Roman history also demands a particular sort of imagination. In some ways, to explore ancient Rome from the twenty-first century is rather like walking on a tightrope, a very careful balancing act. If you look down on one side, everything seems reassuringly familiar: there are conversations going on that we almost join, about the nature of freedom or problems of sex; there are buildings and monuments we recognise and family life lived out in ways we understand, with all their troublesome adolescents; and there are jokes that we 'get'. On the other side, it seems completely alien territory. That means not just the slavery, the filth (there was hardly any such thing as refuse collection in ancient Rome), the human slaughter in the arena and the death from illnesses whose cure we now take for granted; but also the newborn babies thrown away on rubbish heaps, the child brides and the flamboyant eunuch priests.

This is a world we will begin to explore through one particular moment of Roman history, which the Romans never ceased to puzzle over and which modern writers, from historians to dramatists, have never ceased to debate. It offers the best introduction to some of the key characters of ancient Rome, to the richness of Romans' discussion of their own past and to the ways in which we continue to recapture and try to make sense of it – and to why the history of Rome, its Senate and its People still matter.

CHAPTER ONE

·

CICERO'S FINEST HOUR

SPQR: 63 BCE

OUR HISTORY OF ancient Rome begins in the middle of the first century BCE, more than 600 years after the city was founded. It begins with promises of revolution, with a terrorist conspiracy to destroy the city, with undercover operations and public harangues, with a battle fought between Romans and Romans, and with citizens (innocent or not) rounded up and summarily executed in the interests of homeland security. The year is 63 BCE. On the one side is Lucius Sergius Catilina ('Catiline' in English), a disgruntled, bankrupt aristo-crat and the architect of a plot, so it was believed, to assassinate Rome's elected officials and burn the place down – writing off all debts, of rich and poor alike, in the process. On the other side is Marcus Tullius Cicero (just 'Cicero' from now on), the famous orator, philosopher, priest, poet, politician, wit and raconteur, one of those marked out for assassination – and a man who never ceased to use his rhetorical talents to boast how he had uncovered Catiline's terrible plot and saved the state. This was his finest hour.

In 63 BCE the city of Rome was a vast metropolis of more than a million inhabitants, larger than any other in Europe before the nine-teenth century; and, although as yet it had no emperors, it ruled over an empire stretching from Spain to Syria, from the South of France to the Sahara. It was a sprawling mixture of luxury and filth, liberty and exploitation, civic pride and murderous civil war. In the chapters that follow we shall look much further back, to the very start of Roman time and to the early exploits, belligerent and otherwise, of the Roman people. We shall think about what lies behind some of those stories of early Rome that still strike a chord today, from 'Romulus and Remus' to 'The Rape of Lucretia'. And we shall be asking questions that historians have asked since antiquity itself. How, and why, did an ordinary little town in central Italy grow so much bigger than any other city in the ancient Mediterranean and come to control such a huge empire? What, if anything, was special about the Romans? But with the history of Rome it makes little sense to begin the story at the very beginning.

It is only in the first century BCE that we can start to explore Rome, close up and in vivid detail, through contemporary eyes. An extraordinary wealth of words survives from this period: from private letters to public speeches, from philosophy to poetry – epic and erotic, scholarly and straight from the street. Thanks to all this, we can still follow the day-to-day wheeling and dealing of Rome's political grandees. We can eavesdrop on their bargaining and their trade-offs and glimpse their back-stabbing, metaphorical and literal. We can even get a taste of their private lives: their marital tiffs, their cash-flow problems, their grief at the death of beloved children, or occasionally of their beloved slaves. There is no earlier period in the history of the West that it is possible to get to know quite so well or so intimately (we have nothing like such rich and varied evidence from classical Athens). It is not for more than a millennium, in the world of Renaissance Florence, that we find any other place that we can know in such detail again.

What is more, it was during the first century BCE that Roman writers themselves began systematically to study the earlier centuries of their city and their empire. Curiosity about Rome's past certainly goes back further than that: we can still read, for example, an analysis of the city's rise to power written by a Greek resident in the mid second century BCE. But it is only from the first century BCE that Roman scholars and critics began to pose many of the historical questions that we still pose even now. By a process that combined learned research with a good deal of constructive invention, they pieced together a version of early Rome that we still rely on today. We still see Roman history, at least in part, through first-century BCE eyes. Or, to put it another way, Roman *history*, as we know it, started here.

Sixty-three BCE is a significant year in that crucial century. It was a time of near disaster for the city. Over the 1,000 years that we will be exploring in this book, Rome faced danger and defeat many times. Around 390 BCE, for example, a posse of marauding Gauls occupied the city. In 218 BCE the Carthaginian warlord, Hannibal, famously crossed the Alps with his thirty-seven elephants and inflicted terrible losses on the Romans before they eventually managed to fight him off. Roman estimates of casualties at the Battle of Cannae in 216 BCE, up to 70,000 deaths in a single afternoon, make it as great a bloodbath as Gettysburg or the first day of the Somme, maybe even greater. And, almost equally fearsome in the Roman imagination, in the 70s BCE a scratch force of ex-gladiators and runaways, under the command of Spartacus, proved more than a match for some ill-trained legions. The Romans were never as invincible in battle as we tend to assume, or as they liked to make out. In 63 BCE, however, they faced the enemy within, a terrorist plot at the heart of the Roman establishment.

The story of this crisis can still be traced in intimate detail, day by day, occasionally hour by hour. We know precisely where much of it happened, and in a few places we can still look up to some of exactly the same monuments as dominated the scene in 63 BCE. We can follow the sting operations that gave Cicero his information on the plot and see how Catiline was forced out of the city to his makeshift army north of Rome and into a battle with the official Roman legions that cost him his life. We can also glimpse some of the arguments, controversies and wider questions that the crisis raised and still does. The tough

1. The heavy arches and columns of the *'Tabularium'*, built into Michelangelo's Palazzo above, is still a major landmark at one end of the Roman Forum. Constructed just a couple of decades before Cicero was consul in 63 BCE, it must then have seemed one of the most splendid recent architectural developments. Its function is less clear. It was obviously a public building of some kind, but not necessarily the 'Record Office' (*tabularium*) that is often assumed.

response by Cicero – including those summary executions – presented in stark form issues that trouble us even today. Is it legitimate to eliminate 'terrorists' outside the due processes of law? How far should civil rights be sacrificed in the interests of homeland security? The Romans never ceased to debate 'The Conspiracy of Catiline', as it came to be known. Was Catiline wholly evil, or was there something to be said in mitigation of what he did? At what price was revolution averted? The events of 63 BCE, and the catchphrases created then, have continued to resonate throughout Western history. Some of the exact words spoken in the tense debates that followed the discovery of the plot still find their place in our own political rhetoric and are still, as we shall see, paraded on the placards and banners, and even in the tweets, of modern political protest.

Whatever its rights and wrongs, 'The Conspiracy' takes us to the centre of Roman political life in the first century BCE, to its conventions, controversies and conflicts. In doing so, it allows us to glimpse in action the 'Senate' and the 'Roman People' – the two institutions whose names are embedded in my title, SPQR (*Senatus PopulusQue Romanus*). Individually, and sometimes in bitter opposition, these were the main sources of political authority in first-century BCE Rome. Together they formed a shorthand slogan for the legitimate power of the Roman state, a slogan that lasted throughout Roman history

2. SPQR is still plastered over the city of Rome, on everything from manhole covers to rubbish bins. It can be traced back to the lifetime of Cicero, making it one of the most enduring acronyms in history. It has predictably prompted parody. '*Sono Pazzi Questi Romani*' is an Italian favourite: 'These Romans are mad'.

and continues to be used in Italy in the twenty-first century CE. More widely still, the senate (minus the *PopulusQue Romanus*) has lent its name to modern legislative assemblies the world over, from the USA to Rwanda.

The cast of characters in the crisis includes some of the most famous figures in Roman history. Gaius Julius Caesar, then in his thirties, made a radical contribution to the debate on how to punish the conspirators. Marcus Licinius Crassus, the Roman plutocrat who notoriously remarked that you could count no one rich if he did not have the cash to raise his own private army, played some mysterious part behind the scenes. But centre stage, as Catiline's main adversary, we find the one person whom it is possible to get to know better than anyone else in the whole of the ancient world. Cicero's speeches, essays, letters, jokes and poetry still fill dozens of volumes of modern printed text. There is no one else in antiquity until Augustine – Christian saint, prolific theologian and avid self-scrutiniser – 450 years later, whose life is documented in public and private fully enough to be able to reconstruct a plausible biography in modern terms. And it is largely through Cicero's writing, his eyes and his prejudices that we see the Roman world of the first century BCE and much of the city's history up to his day. The year 63 BCE was the turning point of his career: for things were never quite so good for Cicero again. His career ended twenty years later, in failure. Still confident of his own importance, occasionally a name to conjure with but no longer in the front rank, he was murdered in the civil wars that followed the assassination of Julius Caesar in 44 BCE, his head and right hand pinned up in the centre of Rome for all to see – and to mangle and maim.

Cicero's grisly death presaged a yet bigger revolution in the first century BCE, which began with a form of popular political power, even if not a 'democracy' exactly, and ended with an autocrat established on the throne and the Roman Empire under one-man rule. Though Cicero may have 'saved the state' in 63 BCE, the truth is that the state in the form he knew was not to last much longer. There was another revolution on the horizon, which would be more successful than Catiline's. To the 'Senate and Roman People' was soon added the overweening figure of the 'emperor', embodied in a series of autocrats who were part of Western history, flattered and abused, obeyed and ignored, for centuries. But that is a story for later in *SPQR*. For now we shall put down our feet in one of the most memorable, meatiest and most revealing moments in the whole of Roman history.

Cicero versus Catiline

The conflict between Cicero and Catiline was partly a clash of political ideology and ambition, but it was also a clash between men of very different backgrounds. Both of them stood at, or very near, the top of Roman politics; but that is where the similarity ends. In fact, their contrasting careers offer a vivid illustration of just how varied political life in Rome of the first century BCE could be.

Catiline, the would-be revolutionary, had the more conventional, more privileged and apparently safer start in life, as in politics. He came from a distinguished old family that traced its lineage back centuries to the mythical founding fathers of Rome. His ancestor Sergestus was said to have fled from the East to Italy with Aeneas after the Trojan War, before the city of Rome even existed. Among his blue-blooded forebears, his great-grandfather was a hero of the war against Hannibal, with the extra claim to fame of being the first man known to have entered combat with a prosthetic hand – probably just a metal hook that replaced his right hand, lost in an earlier battle. Catiline himself had a successful early career and was elected to a series of junior political offices, but in 63 BCE he was close to bankruptcy. A string of crimes was attached to his name, from the murder of his first wife and his own son to sex with a virgin priestess. But whatever his expensive vices, his financial problems came partly from his repeated attempts to secure election as one of the two consuls, the most powerful political posts in the city.

Electioneering at Rome could be a costly business. By the first century BCE it required the kind of lavish generosity that is not always easy to distinguish from bribery. The stakes were high. The men who were successful in the elections had the chance to recoup their outlay, legally or illegally, with some of the perks of office. The failures – and, like military defeats, there were many more of those in Rome than is usually acknowledged – fell ever more deeply into debt.

That was Catiline's position after he had been beaten in the annual elections for the consulship in both 64 and 63 BCE. Although the usual story is that he had been leaning in that direction before, he now had little option but to resort to 'revolution' or 'direct action' or 'terrorism', whichever you choose to call it. Joining forces with other upper-class desperadoes in similar straits, he appealed to the support of the discontented poor within the city while mustering his makeshift army outside it. And there was no end to his rash promises of debt relief (one of the most despicable forms of radicalism in the eyes of the Roman landed classes) or to his bold threats to take out the leading politicians and to put the whole city to flames.

Or so Cicero, who was one of those who believed he had been earmarked for destruction, summed up his adversary's motives and aims. He was of a very different stock from Catiline. He came from a wealthy, landed background, as all high-level Roman politicians did. But his origins lay outside the capital, in the small town of Arpinum, about 70 miles from Rome, or at least a day's journey at the ancient speed of travel. Though they must have been major players locally, no one in his family before him had ever been prominent on the Roman political scene. With none of Catiline's advantages, Cicero relied on his native talents, on the high-level connections he assiduously cultivated – and on speaking his way to the top. That is to say, his main claim to fame was as a star advocate in the Roman courts; and the celebrity status and prominent supporters that this gave him meant that he was easily elected to each of the required series of junior offices in turn, just like Catiline. But in 64 BCE, where Catiline failed, Cicero succeeded in winning the race for the next year's consulship.

That crowning success had not been an entirely foregone conclusion. For all his celebrity, Cicero faced the disadvantage of being a 'new man', as the Romans called those without political ancestry, and at one stage he even seems to have considered making an electoral pact with Catiline, seedy reputation or not. But in the end, the influential voters swayed it. The Roman electoral system openly and unashamedly gave extra weight to the votes of the rich; and many of them must have concluded that Cicero was a better option than Catiline, whatever their snobbish disdain for his 'newness'. Some of his rivals called him just a 'lodger' at Rome, a 'part-time citizen', but he topped the poll. Catiline ended up in the unsuccessful third place. In second place, elected as the other consul, was Gaius Antonius Hybrida, uncle of a more famous Antonius ('Mark Antony'), whose reputation turned out to be not much better than Catiline's.

By the summer of 63 BCE, Cicero appears to have got wind of definite danger from Catiline, who was trying his luck as a candidate again. Using his authority as consul, Cicero postponed the next round of elections, and when he finally did let them go ahead, he turned up at the poll with an armed guard and wearing a military breastplate clearly visible under his toga. It was a histrionic display, and the combination of civilian and military kit was alarmingly incongruous, rather as if a modern politician were to enter the legislature in a business suit with a machine gun slung over his shoulder. But it worked. These scare tactics, combined with Catiline's vociferously populist programme, made sure that he was once more defeated. Claiming that he was a down-and-out standing up for other down-and-outs could hardly have endeared him to elite voters.

Soon after the elections, sometime in the early autumn, Cicero began to receive much clearer intelligence of a violent plot. For a long time he had been getting trickles of information through the girlfriend of one of Catiline's 'accomplices', a woman named Fulvia, who had more or less turned double agent. Now, thanks to a further piece of treachery from the other side, and via the wealthy Marcus Crassus as intermediary, he had a bundle of letters in his hands that directly incriminated Catiline and referred to the terrible bloodshed that was planned – information soon supplemented by definite reports of armed forces gathering north of the city in support of the insurrection. Finally, after he dodged an assassination attempt planned for 7 November, thanks to a tip-off from Fulvia, Cicero summoned the senate to meet the next day so that he could formally denounce Catiline and frighten him out of Rome.

The senators had already, in October, issued a decree urging (or allowing) Cicero as consul 'to make sure that the state should come to no harm', roughly the ancient equivalent of a modern 'emergency powers' or 'prevention of terrorism' act, and no less controversial. Now, on 8 November, they listened while Cicero went through the whole case against Catiline, in a blistering and well-informed attack. It was a marvellous mixture of fury, indignation, self-criticism and apparently solid fact. One minute he was reminding the assembled company of Catiline's notorious past; the next he was disingenuously regretting that he himself had not reacted to the danger speedily enough; the next he was pouring out precise details of the plot – in whose house the conspirators had gathered, on what dates, who was involved and what exactly their plans were. Catiline had turned up to face the denunciation in person. He asked the senators not to believe everything they were told and made some jibes about Cicero's modest background, compared with his own distinguished ancestors and their splendid achievements. But he must have realised that his position was hopeless. Overnight he left town.

In the senate

This encounter in front of the senate between Cicero and Catiline is the defining moment of the whole story: the two adversaries coming face to face in an institution that lay at the centre of Roman politics. But how should we picture it? The most famous modern attempt to bring before our eyes what happened on that 8 November is a painting by the nineteenth-century Italian artist Cesare Maccari (detail below and plate 1). It is an image that fits comfortably with many of our preconceptions of ancient Rome and its public life, grand, spacious, formal and elegant.

It is also an image with which Cicero would no doubt have been delighted. Catiline sits isolated, head bowed, as if no one wants to risk getting anywhere near him, still less to talk to him. Cicero, meanwhile, is the star of the scene, standing next to what seems to be a smoking brazier in front of an altar, addressing the attentive audience of

3. In Maccari's painting of the scene in the senate, Cicero is in full flood, apparently talking without the aid of notes. It nicely captures one of the defining aspirations of the Roman elite: to be a 'good man skilled in speaking' (*vir bonus dicendi peritus*).

toga-clad senators. Everyday Roman clothing – tunics, cloaks and even occasionally trousers – was much more varied and colourful than this. Togas, however, were the formal, national dress: Romans could define themselves as the *gens togata*, 'the race that wears the toga', while some contemporary outsiders occasionally laughed at this strange, cumbersome garment. And togas were white, with the addition of a purple border for anyone who held public office. In fact, the modern word 'candidate' derives from the Latin *candidatus*, which means 'whitened' and refers to the specially whitened togas that Romans wore during election campaigns, to impress the voters. In a world where status needed to be on show, the niceties of dress went even further: there was also a broad purple stripe on senators' tunics, worn beneath the toga, and a slightly narrower one if you were the next rank down in Roman society, an 'equestrian' or 'knight', and special shoes for both ranks.

Maccari has captured the senators' smart togas, even though he seems to have forgotten those significant borders. But in almost every other way the painting is no more than a seductive fantasy of the occasion and the setting. For a start, Cicero is presented as a white-haired elder statesman, Catiline as a moody young villain, when actually both were in their forties, and Catiline was the elder by a couple of years. Besides, this is far too sparsely attended a meeting; unless we are to imagine more of them somewhere offstage, there are barely fifty senators listening to the momentous speech.

In the middle of the first century BCE, the senate was a body of some 600 members; they were all men who had been previously elected to political office (and I mean *all men* – no woman ever held political office in ancient Rome). Anyone who had held the junior position of quaestor, twenty of them elected each year, went automatically into the senate with a seat for life. They met regularly, debating, advising the consuls and issuing decrees, which were, in practice, usually obeyed – though, as these did not have the force of law, there was always the awkward question of what would happen if a decree of the senate was flouted or simply ignored. No doubt attendance fluctuated, but this particular meeting must surely have been packed.

As for the setting, it looks Roman enough, but with that huge column stretching up out of sight and the lavish, brightly coloured marble lining the walls, it is far too grand for almost anything in Rome in this period. Our modern image of the ancient city as an extravaganza of gleaming marble on a vast scale is not entirely wrong. But that is a later development in the history of Rome, beginning with the advent of one-man rule under the emperors and with the first systematic exploitation of the marble quarries in Carrara in North Italy, more than thirty years after the crisis of Catiline.

The Rome of Cicero's day, with its million or so inhabitants, was still built largely of brick or local stone, a warren of winding streets and dark alleys. A visitor from Athens or Alexandria in Egypt, which did have many buildings in the style of Maccari's painting, would have found the place unimpressive, not to say squalid. It was such a breeding ground of disease that a later Roman doctor wrote that you didn't need to read textbooks to research malaria – it was all around you in the city of Rome. The rented market in slums provided grim accommodation for the poor but lucrative profits for unscrupulous landlords. Cicero himself had large amounts of money invested in low-grade property and once joked, more out of superiority than embarrassment, that even the rats had packed up and left one of his crumbling rental blocks.

A few of the richest Romans had begun to raise the eyebrows of onlookers with their plush private houses, fitted out with elaborate paintings, elegant Greek statues, fancy furniture (one-legged tables were a particular cause of envy and anxiety), even imported marble columns. There was also a scatter of public buildings designed on a grand scale, built in (or veneered with) marble, offering a glimpse of the lavish face of the city that was to come. But the location of the meeting on 8 November was nothing like that.

Cicero had summoned the senators to meet, as they often did, in a temple: on this occasion a modest, old building dedicated to the god Jupiter, near the Forum, at the heart of the city, constructed on the standard rectangular plan, not the semicircular structure of Maccari's fantasy – probably small and ill lit, with lamps and torches only partly compensating for a lack of windows. We have to imagine several hundred senators packed into a stuffy, cramped space, some sitting on makeshift chairs or benches, others standing, and jostling, no doubt, under some venerable, ancient statue of Jupiter. It was certainly a momentous occasion in Roman history, but equally certainly, as with many things in Rome, much less elegant in reality than we like to imagine.

Triumph – and humiliation

The scene that followed has not been re-created by admiring painters. Catiline left town to join his supporters who had scratched together an army outside Rome. Meanwhile, Cicero mounted a clever sting operation to expose the conspirators still left in the city. Ill-advisedly, as it turned out, they had tried to involve in the plot a deputation of men from Gaul who had come to Rome to complain about their exploitation at the hands of Roman provincial governors. For whatever reason – maybe nothing more profound than an instinct for backing the winner – these Gauls decided to work secretly with Cicero, and they were able to provide clinching evidence of names, places, plans and some more letters with incriminating information. Arrests followed, as well as the usual unconvincing excuses. When the house of one of the conspirators was found stuffed with weapons, the man protested his innocence by claiming that his hobby was weapon collecting.

On 5 December, Cicero summoned the senate again, to discuss what should be done with the men now in custody. This time the senators met in the temple of the goddess Concord, or Harmony, a sure sign that affairs of state were anything but harmonious. Julius Caesar made the daring suggestion that the captured conspirators should be imprisoned: either, according to one account, until they could be properly tried once the crisis was over or, according to another, for life. Custodial sentences were not the penalties of choice in the ancient world, prisons being little more than places where criminals were held before execution. Fines, exile and death made up the usual repertoire of Roman punishment. If Caesar really did advocate life imprisonment in 63 BCE, then it was probably the first time in Western history that this was mooted as an alternative to the death penalty, without success. Relying on the emergency powers decree, and on the vociferous support of many senators, Cicero had the men summarily executed, with not even a show trial. Triumphantly, he announced their deaths to the cheering crowd in a famous one-word euphemism: *vixere*, 'they have lived' – that is, 'they're dead'.

Within a few weeks, Roman legions defeated Catiline's army of discontents in North Italy. Catiline himself fell fighting bravely at the front of his men. The Roman commander, Cicero's fellow consul, Antonius Hybrida, claimed to have bad feet on the day of the final battle and handed over leadership to his number two, raising suspicions in some quarters about exactly where his sympathies lay. And he was not the only one whose motives were questioned. There have been all sorts of possibly wild, certainly inconclusive, speculation, going back to the ancient world, about which far more successful men might secretly have been backing Catiline. Was he really the agent of the devious Marcus Crassus? And what was Caesar's true position?

Catiline's defeat was nonetheless a notable victory for Cicero; and his supporters dubbed him *pater patriae*, or 'father of the fatherland', one of the most splendid and satisfying titles you could have in a highly patriarchal society, such as Rome. But his success soon turned sour. Already on his last day as consul, two of his political rivals prevented him from giving the usual valedictory address to a meeting of the Roman people: 'Those who have punished others without a hearing,' they insisted, 'ought not to have the right to be heard themselves.' A few years later, in 58 BCE, the Roman people voted, in general terms, to expel anyone who had put a citizen to death without trial. Cicero left Rome, just before another bill was passed specifically singling him out, by name, for exile.

So far in this story the *Populus(Que) Romanus* (the *PQR* in *SPQR*) has not played a particularly prominent role. The 'people' was a much larger and amorphous body than the senate, made up, in political terms, of all male Roman citizens; the women had no formal political rights. In 63 BCE that was around a million men spread across the capital and throughout Italy, as well as a few beyond. In practice, it usually comprised the few thousand or the few hundred who, on any particular occasion, chose to turn up to elections, votes or meetings in the city of Rome. Exactly how influential the people were has always – even in the ancient world – been one of the big controversies in Roman history; but two things are certain. At this period, they alone could elect the political officials of the Roman state; no matter how blue-blooded you were, you could only hold office as, say, consul if the Roman people elected you. And they alone, unlike the senate, could make law. In 58 BCE Cicero's enemies argued that, whatever authority he had claimed under the senate's prevention of terrorism decree, his executions of Catiline's followers had flouted the fundamental right of any Roman citizen to a proper trial. It was up to the people to exile him.

The sometime 'father of the fatherland' spent a miserable year in North Greece (his abject self-pity is not endearing), until the people voted to recall him. He was welcomed back to the cheers of his supporters, but his house in the city had been demolished and, as if to drive the political point home, a shrine to Libertas had been erected on its site. His career never fully recovered.

Writing it up

The reasons why we can tell this story in such detail are very simple: the Romans themselves wrote a great deal about it, and a lot of what they wrote has survived. Modern historians often lament how little we can know about some aspects of the ancient world. 'Just think of what we don't know about the lives of the poor,' they complain, 'or of the perspectives of women.' This is as anachronistic as it is deceptive. The writers of Roman literature *were* almost exclusively male; or, at least, very few works by women have come down to us (the autobiography of the emperor Nero's mother, Agrippina, must count as one of the saddest losses of classical literature). These men were also almost exclusively well off, even though some Roman poets did like to pretend, as poets still occasionally do, that they were starving in garrets. The complaints, however, miss a far more important point.

The single most extraordinary fact about the Roman world is that so much of what the Romans wrote has survived, over two millennia. We have their poetry, letters, essays, speeches and histories, to which I have already referred, but also novels, geographies, satires and reams and reams of technical writing on everything from water engineering to medicine and disease. The survival is largely due to the diligence of medieval monks who transcribed by hand, again and again, what they believed were the most important, or useful, works of classical literature, with a significant but often forgotten contribution from medieval Islamic scholars who translated into Arabic some of the philosophy and scientific material. And thanks to archaeologists who have excavated papyri from the sands and the rubbish dumps of Egypt, wooden writing tablets from Roman military bases in the north of England and eloquent tombstones from all over the empire, we have glimpses of the life and letters of some rather more ordinary inhabitants of the Roman world. We have notes sent home, shopping lists, account books and last messages inscribed on graves. Even if this is a small proportion of what once existed, we have access to more Roman literature – and more Roman writing in general – than any one person could now thoroughly master in the course of a lifetime.

So how is it, exactly, that we know of the conflict between Catiline and Cicero? The story has come down to us by various routes, and it is partly the variety that makes it so rich. There are brief accounts in the works of a number of ancient Roman historians, including an ancient biography of Cicero himself – all written a hundred years or more after the events. More important, and more revealing, is a long essay, stretching over some fifty pages of a standard English translation, which offers a detailed narrative, and analysis, of the *War against Catiline*, or *Bellum Catilinae*, to use what was almost certainly its ancient title. It was written only twenty years after the 'war', in the 40s BCE, by Gaius Sallustius Crispus, or 'Sallust', as he is now usually known. A 'new man' like Cicero and a friend and ally of Julius Caesar, he had a very mixed political reputation: his period as a Roman governor in North Africa was infamous, even by Roman standards, for corruption and extortion. But despite his not entirely savoury career, or maybe because of it, Sallust's essay is one of the sharpest pieces of political analysis to survive from the ancient world.

Sallust did not simply tell the unfolding story of the attempted uprising, its causes and its upshot. He used the figure of Catiline as an emblem of the wider failings of first-century BCE Rome. In Sallust's view, the moral fibre of Roman culture had been destroyed by the city's success and by the wealth, greed and lust for power that had followed its conquest of the Mediterranean and the crushing of all its serious rivals. The crucial moment came eighty-three years before the war against Catiline, when in 146 BCE Roman armies finally destroyed Carthage, Hannibal's home base on the north coast of Africa. After that, Sallust thought, no significant threats to Roman domination were left. Catiline may have had positive qualities, as Sallust accepted, from bravery in the front line of battle to extraordinary powers of endurance: 'his ability to withstand hunger, cold or sleep deprivation was incredible'. But he symbolised much of what was wrong with the Rome of his day.

Behind Sallust's essay lie other vivid documents, which ultimately go back to the hand of Cicero himself and give his version of what happened. Some of the letters he wrote to his closest friend, Titus Pomponius Atticus – a wealthy man who never entered formal politics but often pulled the strings from the sidelines – mention his initially friendly relations with Catiline. Mixed in with domestic news, about the birth of his son ('Let me tell you, I have become a father ...') and the arrival of new statues from Greece to decorate his house, Cicero explains in 65 BCE that he was contemplating defending Catiline in the courts, in the hope that they might later work together.

How such private letters ended up in the public domain is something of a mystery. Most likely, a member of Cicero's household made copies of them available after his death and they quickly circulated among curious readers, fans and enemies. Nothing was ever *published*, in quite our sense, in the ancient world. Almost a thousand letters in all survive, written both to and by the great man over the last twenty years or so of his life. Revealing his self-pity in exile ('All I can do is weep!') and his anguish on the death of his daughter after childbirth while covering topics from thieving agents, through society divorces, to the ambitions of Julius Caesar, they are some of the most intriguing documents we have from ancient Rome.

Equally intriguing a survival, and perhaps even more surprising, is part of a long poem that Cicero wrote to celebrate the achievements of his consulship; it is no longer complete, but it was famous, or infamous, enough that more than seventy lines of it are quoted by other ancient writers and by Cicero himself in later works. It includes one of the most notorious lines of Latin doggerel to have made it through the Dark Ages: '*O fortunatam natam me consule Romam*' – a jingle with something of the ring of 'Rome was sure a lucky state / Born in my great consulate'. And, in what has been seen as a major, if slightly hilarious, lapse of modesty, it seems to have featured an 'assembly of the gods' in which our superhuman consul discusses with the divine senate on Mount Olympus how he should handle Catiline's plot.

By the first century BCE, reputation and fame in Rome depended not just on word of mouth but also on publicity, sometimes elaborately, even awkwardly, orchestrated. We know that Cicero tried to persuade one of his historian friends, Lucius Lucceius, to write a celebratory account of his defeat of Catiline and its sequel ('I am extremely keen,' he said in a letter, 'that my name should be put in the limelight in your writing'); and he also hoped that a fashionable Greek poet, whose tricky immigration case he had defended in the Roman courts, would compose a worthy epic on this same subject. In the event, he had to write his own verse tribute – to himself. A few modern critics have tried, not very convincingly, to defend the literary quality of the work, and even of what has become its signature line ('*O fortunatam natam ...*'). Most Roman critics whose views on the topic survive satirised both the vanity of the enterprise and its language. Even one of Cicero's greatest admirers, a keen student of his oratorical techniques, regretted that 'he had gone quite so over the top'. Others gleefully ridiculed or parodied the poem.

But the most direct access that we have to the events of 63 BCE comes from the scripts of some of the speeches that Cicero gave at the time of the uprising. Two were delivered to public meetings of the Roman people, updating them on the progress of the investigations into Catiline's conspiracy and announcing victory over the dissidents. One was Cicero's contribution to the debate in the senate on 5 December which determined the appropriate penalty for those under arrest. And, most famous of all, there was the speech that he gave to the senate on 8 November, denouncing Catiline, in the words that we should imagine coming out of his mouth in Maccari's painting.

Cicero himself probably circulated copies of all these soon after they had been delivered, laboriously transcribed by a small army of slaves. And, unlike his efforts at poetry, they quickly became admired and much-quoted classics of Latin literature, and prime examples of great oratory to be learned and imitated by Roman schoolboys and would-be public speakers for the rest of antiquity. They were even read and studied by those who were not entirely fluent in Latin. That was certainly going on in Roman Egypt four hundred years later. The earliest copies of these speeches to survive have been found on papyrus dating to the fourth or fifth century CE, now just small scraps of what were originally much longer texts. They include the original Latin and a word-for-word translation into Greek. We must imagine a native Greek speaker in Egypt struggling a little, and needing some help, in getting to grips with Cicero's original language.

Many later learners have struggled too. This group of four speeches, *Against Catiline* (*In Catilinam*) or the *Catilinarians*, as they are now often known, went on to enter the educational and cultural traditions of the West. Copied and disseminated via the medieval monasteries, they were used to drill generations of pupils in the Latin language, and they were closely analysed as literary masterpieces by Renaissance intellectuals and rhetorical theorists. Even today, in mechanically printed editions, they keep their place in the syllabus for those who learn Latin, and they remain models of persuasive oratory, whose techniques underlie some of the most famous modern speeches, including those of Tony Blair and Barack Obama.

It did not take long for the opening words of Cicero's speech given on 8 November (the *First Catilinarian*) to become one of the best known and instantly recognisable quotes of the Roman world: '*Quo usque tandem abutere, Catilina, patientia nostra?*' ('How long, Catiline, will you go on abusing our patience?'); and it was closely followed, a few lines later in the written text, by the snappy, and still much repeated, slogan '*O tempora, o mores*' ('O what a world we live in!', or, literally, 'O the times, O the customs!'). In fact, the phrase '*Quo usque tandem ...'* must already have been firmly embedded in the Roman literary consciousness by the time that Sallust was writing his account of the 'war', just twenty years later. So firmly embedded was it that, in pointed or playful irony, Sallust could put it into Catiline's mouth. *'Quae quo usque tandem patiemini, o fortissimi viri?'* ('How long will you go on putting up with this, my braves?') is how Sallust's revolutionary stirs up his followers, reminding them of the injustices they were suffering at the hands of the elite. The words are purely imaginary. Ancient writers regularly scripted speeches for their protagonists, much as historians today like to ascribe feelings or motives to their characters. The joke here is that Catiline, Cicero's greatest enemy, is made to voice his antagonist's most famous slogan.

That is only one of the wry ironies and pointed, paradoxical 'misquotations' in the history of this distinctive phrase. It often lurked in Roman literature whenever revolutionary designs were at stake. Just a few years after Sallust, Titus Livius, or 'Livy', as he is better known, was writing his own history of Rome from its beginning, originally in 142 'books' – a vast project, even though an ancient book amounted to what fitted onto a roll of papyrus and is closer to the length of a modern chapter. What Livy had to say about Catiline has been lost. But when he wanted to capture the civil conflicts of hundreds of years earlier, in particular the 'conspiracy' of one Marcus Manlius, who in the fourth century BCE was supposed to have incited the Roman poor to rebellion against the oppressive rule of the elite, he went back to a version of the classic words. *'Quo usque tandem ignorabitis vires vestras?'* ('How long will you go on being ignorant of your strength?') he imagined Manlius asking his followers to get them to realise that, poor though they were, they had the manpower to succeed.

The point here is not merely about an echo of language. Nor is it just about the figure of Catiline as a byword for villainy, though he certainly plays that part often enough in Roman literature. His name came to be used as a nickname for unpopular emperors, and half a

century later Publius Vergilius Maro (or 'Virgil', as he is now usually known) gave him a cameo role in the *Aeneid*, where the villain
is pictured being tortured in the underworld, 'trembling at the face
of the Furies'. More important is the way that the conflict between
Catiline and Cicero became a powerful template for understanding
civil disobedience and insurrection throughout Roman history and
beyond. When Roman historians wrote about revolution, the image
of Catiline almost always lay somewhere behind their accounts, even
at the cost of some strange inversions of chronology. As his carefully
chosen words hint, Livy's Marcus Manlius, a nobleman turning to
doomed revolution, supported by an impoverished rabble, was largely
a projection of Catiline back into early Roman history.

The other side of the story

Might there not be another side to the story? The detailed evidence
we have from Cicero's pen, or point of view, means that his perspective will always be dominant. But it does not necessarily mean that it
is true in any simple sense, or that it is the only way of seeing things.
People have wondered for centuries quite how loaded an account
Cicero offers us, and have detected alternative views and interpretations just beneath the surface of his version of events. Sallust himself
hints as much. For, although his account is heavily based on Cicero's
writing, by transferring the famous *'Quo usque tandem'* from the
mouth of Cicero to that of Catiline, he may well have been reminding
his readers that the facts and their interpretations were, at the very
least, fluid.

One obvious question is whether the speech we know as the *First
Catilinarian* really is what Cicero said to the assembled senators in the
Temple of Jupiter on 8 November. It is hard to imagine that it was a
complete fabrication. How would he have got away with circulating

a version that bore no relationship to what he had said? But almost certainly it is not a word-for-word match. If he spoke from notes and the ancient equivalent of bullet points, then the text we have presumably lies somewhere between what he remembered saying and what he would have liked to have said. Even if he was reading from a fairly complete text, when he circulated the speech to friends, associates and those he wanted to impress, he would almost certainly have improved it somewhat, tidying up the loose ends and inserting a few more clever one-liners, which might have been missed out or slipped his mind on the day.

A lot hangs too on exactly when it was circulated and why. We know from one of his letters to Atticus that Cicero was arranging for the *First Catilinarian* to be copied in June 60 BCE, when he must have been well aware that the controversy over his execution of the 'conspirators' was not likely to go away. It would have been tempting and convenient for Cicero to use the written text of the speech in his own defence, even if that meant some strategic adjustments and insertions. In fact, the repeated references, in the version we have, to Catiline as if he were a foreign enemy (in Latin *hostis*) may well be one of the ways in which Cicero responded to his opponents: by referring to the conspirators as enemies of the state, he was implying that they did not deserve the protection of Roman law; they had lost their civic rights (including the right to trial). Of course, that may already have been a leitmotiv in the oral version of the speech given on 8 November. We simply do not know. But the term certainly took on far greater significance – and I strongly suspect was given far greater emphasis – in the permanent, written version.

These questions prompt us to look harder for different versions of the story. Never mind Cicero's perspective, is it possible to get any idea of how Catiline and his supporters would have seen it? The words and the views of Cicero now dominate the contemporary evidence for the mid first century BCE. But it is always worth trying to read his version, or any version of Roman history, 'against the grain', to prise apart the small chinks in the story using the snatches of other, independent, evidence that we have and to ask if other observers might have seen things differently. Were those whom Cicero described as monstrous villains really as villainous as he painted them? In this case, there is just about enough to raise some doubts about what was really going on.

Cicero casts Catiline as a desperado with terrible gambling debts, thanks entirely to his moral failings. But the situation cannot have been so simple. There was some sort of credit crunch in Rome in 63 BCE, and more economic and social problems than Cicero was prepared to acknowledge. Another achievement of his 'great consulate' was to scotch a proposal to distribute land in Italy to some of the poor in the city. To put it another way, if Catiline behaved like a desperado, he might have had a good reason, and the support of many ordinary people driven to desperate measures by similar distress.

How can we tell? It is harder to reconstruct economics than politics across 2,000 years, but we do get some unexpected glimpses. The evidence of the surviving coins of the period is particularly revealing, both of the conditions of the times and of the ability of modern historians and archaeologists to squeeze the material they have in ingenious ways. Roman coins can often be precisely dated, because at this period they were newly designed each year and 'signed' by the annual officials who were responsible for issuing them. They were minted using a series of individually hand-cut 'dies' (or stamps), whose minor differences in detail are still visible on the finished coins. We can calculate roughly how many coins an individual die could stamp (before it became too blunt to make a crisp image), and if we have a large enough sample of coins we can estimate roughly how many dies had been used altogether in minting a single issue. From that we can get a rough and ready idea of how many coins were produced each year: the more dies, the more coins, and vice versa.

4. This silver coin was minted in 63 BCE, its design showing one of the Roman people voting on a piece of legislation, casting a voting tablet into a jar for counting. The differences in detail between the two versions well illustrate the differences in the die stamps. The name of the official in charge of the mint that year, Longinus, is also stamped on the coin.

According to these calculations, the number of coins being minted in the late 60s BCE fell so sharply that there were fewer overall in circulation than there had been a few years before. The reasons for this we cannot reconstruct. Like most states before the eighteenth century or even later, Rome had no monetary policy as such, nor any financial institutions where that kind of policy could be developed. But the likely consequences are obvious. Whether he recklessly gambled away his fortune or not, Catiline – and many others – might have been short of cash; while those already in debt would have been faced with creditors, short of cash themselves, calling in their loans.

All this was in addition to the other long-standing factors that might have given the humble or the have-nots in Rome an incentive to protest or to join in with those promising radical change. There was the enormous disparity of wealth between rich and poor, the squalid living conditions for most of the population, and probably for much of the time, even if not starvation, then persistent hunger. Despite

Cicero's dismissive descriptions of Catiline's followers as reprobates, gangsters and the destitute, the logic of some of his own account, and of Sallust's, suggests otherwise. For they either state or imply that Catiline's support evaporated when it was reported that he intended to burn the city down. If so, we are not dealing with down-and-outs and complete no-hopers with nothing to lose – and everything to gain – from total conflagration. Much more likely, his supporters included the humble suffering poor, who still had some stake in the survival of the city.

Cicero, inevitably, had an interest in making the most of the danger that Catiline posed. Whatever his political success, he held a precarious position at the top of Roman society, among aristocratic families who claimed, like Catiline, a direct line back to the founders of the city, or even to the gods. Julius Caesar's family, for example, was proud to trace its lineage back to the goddess Venus; another, more curiously, claimed descent from the equally mythical Pasiphae, the wife of King Minos, whose extraordinary coupling with a bull produced the monstrous Minotaur. In order to secure his position in these circles, Cicero

5. This Roman tombstone of the fourth century CE illustrates one simple way of striking a coin. The blank coin is placed between two dies, resting on an anvil. The man on the left is giving this 'sandwich' a heavy blow with a hammer to imprint the design on the blank. As the tongs in the hands of the assistant on the right suggest, the blank has been heated to make the imprinting easier.

was no doubt looking to make a splash during his year as consul. An impressive military victory against a barbarian enemy would have been ideal, and what most Romans would have dreamt of. Rome was always a warrior state, and victory in war the surest route to glory. Cicero, however, was no soldier: he had come to prominence in the law courts, not by leading his army in battle against dangerous, or unfortunate, foreigners. He needed to 'save the state' in some other way.

Some Roman commentators noted that the crisis played very much to Cicero's advantage. One anonymous pamphlet, attacking Cicero's whole career and preserved because it was once believed, wrongly, to be from the pen of Sallust, states explicitly that he 'turned the troubles of the state to his own glory', going so far as to claim that his consulship was 'the cause of the conspiracy' rather than the solution. To put it bluntly, one basic question for us should be not *whether* Cicero exaggerated the dangers of the conspiracy, but *how far*.

The most determined modern sceptics have deemed the whole plot not much more than a figment of Cicero's imagination – in which case the man who claimed to be a 'weapons enthusiast' was exactly that, the incriminating letters were forgeries, the deputation of Gauls were a complete dupe of the consul and the rumoured assassination attempts were paranoid inventions. Such a radical view seems implausible. There was, after all, a hand-to-hand battle between Catiline's men and Roman legions, which can hardly be dismissed as a figment. It is much more likely that, whatever his original motives, Catiline – far-sighted radical or unprincipled terrorist – was partly driven to extreme measures by a consul spoiling for a fight and bent on his own glory. Cicero may even have convinced himself, whatever the evidence, that Catiline was a serious threat to the safety of Rome. That, as we know from many more recent examples, is how political paranoia and self-interest often work. We will never be quite sure. The 'conspiracy' will always be a prime example of the classic interpretative dilemma: were there really 'reds under the bed', or was the crisis, partly at least, a conservative invention? It should also act as a reminder that in Roman history, as elsewhere, we must always be alert to the other side of the story – which is part of the point of this *SPQR*.

Our Catiline?

The clash between Cicero and Catiline has offered a template for political conflict ever since. It can hardly be a coincidence that Maccari's painting of the events of 8 November was commissioned, along with other scenes of Roman history, for the room in the Palazzo Madama that had just become the home of the modern Italian senate; presumably a lesson was intended for the modern senators. And over the centuries the rights and wrongs of the 'conspiracy', the respective faults and virtues of Catiline and Cicero, and the conflicts between homeland security and civil liberties have been fiercely debated, and not only among historians.

Occasionally the story has been drastically rewritten. One medieval tradition in Tuscany has Catiline surviving the battle against the Roman legions and going on, as a local hero, to have a complicated romantic entanglement with a woman called Belisea. Another version gives him a son Uberto, and so makes him the ancestor of the Uberti dynasty in Florence. Even more imaginatively, Prosper de Crébillon's play *Catilina*, first performed in the mid eighteenth century, conjures up an affair between Catiline and Cicero's daughter, Tullia, complete with some steamy assignations in a Roman temple.

When the conspiracy has been replayed in fiction and on stage, it has been adjusted according to the political alignment of the author and the political climate of the times. Henrik Ibsen's first drama, written in the aftermath of the European revolutions of the 1840s, takes the events of 63 BCE as its theme. Here a revolutionary Catiline is pitted against the corruption of the world in which he lived, while Cicero, who could have imagined nothing worse, is almost entirely written out of the events, never appearing on stage and barely mentioned. For Ben Jonson, by contrast, writing in the aftermath of the Gunpowder Plot, Catiline was a sadistic anti-hero, whose victims were so numerous that, in Jonson's vivid imagination, a whole navy was required to ferry them across the River Styx to the Underworld. His Cicero is not particularly likeable either but instead a droning bore; indeed so boring that at the play's first performance, in 1611, many members of the audience walked out during his interminable denunciation of Catiline.

Jonson was being unfair to Cicero's powers of persuasive oratory – at least if the continuing use of his words, quoted and strategically adapted, is anything to go by. For his *First Catilinarian* speech, and

6. In 2012, Hungarian protesters against the Fidesz party's attempts to rewrite the constitution blazoned Cicero's famous phrase, in Latin. But it has not been reused only in political contexts. In a notorious intellectual spat, Camille Paglia substituted the name of French philosopher Michel Foucault for Catiline's: 'How long, O Foucault ... ?'

especially its famous first line ('How long, Catiline, will you go on abusing our patience?'), still lurks in twenty-first-century political rhetoric, is plastered on modern political banners and is fitted conveniently into the 140 characters of a tweet. All you need do is insert the name of your particular modern target. Indeed, a stream of tweets and other headlines posted over the time I was writing this book swapped the name 'Catilina' for, among others, those of the presidents of the United States, France and Syria, the mayor of Milan and the State of Israel: '*Quo usque tandem abutere, François Hollande, patientia nostra?*' Quite how many of those who now adopt the slogan could explain exactly where it comes from, or what the clash between Cicero and Catiline was all about, it is impossible to know. Some may be classicists with a political cause, but that is unlikely to be true of all these objectors and protesters. The use of the phrase points to something rather different from specialist classical expertise, and probably more important. It is a strong hint that, just under the surface of Western politics, the dimly remembered conflict between Cicero and Catiline still acts as a template for our own political struggles and arguments. Cicero's eloquence, even if only half understood, still informs the language of modern politics.

Cicero would be delighted. When he wrote to his friend Lucceius, asking the historian to commemorate the achievements of his consulship, he was hoping for eternal fame: 'the idea of being spoken about by posterity pushes me to some sort of hope for immortality,' he wrote with a touch of well-contrived diffidence. Lucceius, as we saw, did not oblige. He might have been put off by Cicero's blatant request that he 'neglect the rules of history' to write up the events rather more fulsomely than accurately. But in the end, it turned out that Cicero achieved more immortality for his achievements in 63 BCE than Lucceius could ever have given him, being quoted and requoted over 2,000 years.

We shall find many more of these political conflicts, disputed inter-pretations and sometimes uncomfortable echoes of our own times in the chapters that follow. But it is now the moment to turn back from the relatively firm ground of the first century BCE to Rome's deepest history. How did Cicero and his contemporaries reconstruct the early years of their city? Why were their origins important to them? What does it mean to ask 'Where did Rome begin?' How much can we, or could they, really know of earliest Rome?

CHAPTER TWO

·

IN THE BEGINNING

Cicero and Romulus

ACCORDING TO ONE Roman tradition, the Temple of Jupiter where Cicero harangued Catiline on 8 November 63 BCE had been established seven centuries earlier by Romulus, Rome's founding father. Romulus and the new citizens of his tiny community were fighting their neighbours, a people known as the Sabines, on the site that later became the Forum, the political centre of Cicero's Rome. Things were going badly for the Romans, and they had been driven to retreat. As a last attempt to snatch victory, Romulus prayed to the god Jupiter – not just to Jupiter, in fact, but to Jupiter *Stator*, 'Jupiter who *holds men firm*'. He would build a temple in thanks, Romulus promised the god, if only the Romans would resist the temptation to run for it, and stand their ground against the enemy. They did, and the Temple of Jupiter Stator was erected on that very spot, the first in a long series of shrines and temples in the city built to commemorate divine help in securing military victory for Rome.

That at least was the story told by Livy and several other Roman writers. Archaeologists have never managed firmly to identify any remains of this temple, which must in any case have been much re-built by Cicero's time, especially if its origins really did go back to the beginning of Rome. But there can be no doubt that, when he chose to summon the senate to meet there, Cicero knew exactly what he was doing. He had the precedent of Romulus in mind and was using the location to make a point. He wanted to keep the Romans steadfast (to 'hold them firm') in the face of their new enemy, Catiline. In fact, he said almost exactly that at the end of his speech, when – no doubt gesturing to the statue of the god – he appealed to Jupiter Stator and reminded his audience of the foundation of the temple:

> You, Jupiter, who were established by Romulus in the same year as the city itself, the god who, we rightly say, holds firm the city and the empire – you will keep this man and his gang away from your temple and the temples of the other gods, from the houses of the city and its walls, from the lives and fortunes of all the citizens of Rome ...

The implication that Cicero was casting himself as a new Romulus was not lost on the Romans of his day, and the connection could rebound: some people used it as another excuse to sneer at his small-town origins by calling him 'the Romulus of Arpinum'.

This was a classic Roman appeal to the founding fathers, to the stirring tales of early Rome and to the moment when the city came into being. Even now, the image of a wolf suckling the baby Romulus and his twin brother Remus signals the origins of Rome. The famous bronze statue of the scene is one of the most copied and instantly recognisable works of Roman art, illustrated on thousands of souvenir postcards, tea towels, ashtrays and fridge magnets, and plastered all over the modern city as the emblem of Roma football club.

Because this image is so familiar, it is easy to take the story of Romulus and Remus – or Remus and Romulus, to give them their usual Roman order – rather too much for granted and to forget that it is one of the oddest 'historical legends' of any city's foundation at any period, anywhere in the world. And myth or legend it certainly is, even though Romans assumed that it was, in broad terms, history. The wolf's nurturing of the twins is such a strange episode in a very peculiar tale that even ancient writers sometimes showed a healthy

7. Whatever the exact date of the wolf herself, the baby twins are certainly later additions, made in the fifteenth century explicitly to capture the founding myth. Copies are found all over the world, partly thanks to Benito Mussolini, who distributed them far and wide as a symbol of *Romanità*.

scepticism about the appearance of a conveniently lactating animal to suckle the pair of abandoned babies, right on cue. The rest of the narrative is an extraordinary mixture of puzzling details: not only the unusual idea of having two founders (Romulus *and* Remus) but also a series of decidedly unheroic elements, from murder, through rape and abduction, to the bulk of Rome's first citizens being criminals and runaways.

These unsavoury aspects have so struck some modern historians that they have suggested that the whole story must have been concocted as a form of anti-propaganda by Rome's enemies and victims, threatened by aggressive Roman expansion. That is an over-ingenious, not to say desperate, attempt to explain the oddities of the tale, and it misses the most important point. Wherever and whenever it originated, Roman writers never stopped telling, retelling and intensely debating the story of Romulus and Remus. There was more at stake in this than just the question of how the city first took shape. As they crammed into Romulus' old temple to listen to the new 'Romulus of Arpinum', those senators would have been well aware that the foundation story raised even bigger questions, of what it was to be Roman, of what special characteristics defined the Roman people – and, no less pressing, of what flaws and failings they had inherited from their ancestors.

To understand the ancient Romans, it is necessary to understand where they believed they came from and to think through the significance of the story of Romulus and Remus and of the main themes, subtleties and ambiguities in other foundation stories. For the twins were not the only candidates for being the first Romans. Throughout most of Roman history, the figure of the Trojan hero Aeneas, who fled to Italy to establish Rome as the new Troy, bulked large too. And no less important is to try to see what might lie behind these stories. 'Where did Rome begin?' is a question that has proved almost as seductive, and teasing, for modern scholars as for their ancient predecessors. Archaeology offers a sketch of earliest Rome very different from that of the Roman myths. It is a surprising one, often puzzling and controversial. Even the famous bronze wolf is keenly debated. Is it, as has usually been thought, one of the earliest works of Roman art to survive? Or is it, as a recent scientific analysis has suggested, really a masterpiece of the Middle Ages? In any case, excavations under the modern city over the past hundred years or so have uncovered a few traces from maybe as far back as 1000 BCE of the tiny village on the river Tiber that eventually became Cicero's Rome.

Murder

There is no single story of Romulus. There are scores of different, sometimes incompatible, versions of the tale. Cicero, a decade after his clash with Catiline, gave one account in his treatise *On the State*. Like many politicians since, he took refuge in political theory (and some rather pompous pontificating) when his own power was fading. Here, in the context of a much longer philosophical discussion on the nature of good government, he dealt with the history of the Roman 'constitution' from its beginning. But after a succinct start to the story – in which he awkwardly evaded the issue of whether Romulus really was the son of the god Mars while casting doubt on other fabulous elements of the tale – he got down to a serious discussion of the geographical advantages of the site that Romulus chose for his new settlement.

'How could Romulus,' Cicero writes, 'have exploited more brilliantly the advantages of being close to the sea while avoiding its disadvantages than by placing the town on the banks of a never-failing river that flows consistently into the sea, in a broad stream?' The Tiber, he explains, made it easy to import supplies from abroad and to export any local surplus; and the hills on which the city was built provided not only an ideal defence against enemy attack but also a healthy living environment in the midst of a 'pestilential region'. It was as if Romulus had known that his foundation would one day be the centre of a great empire. Cicero displays some good geographical sense here, and many others since have pointed to the strategic position of the site, which gave it an advantage over local rivals. But he patriotically draws a veil over the fact that throughout antiquity the 'never-failing river' also made Rome the regular victim of devastating floods and that, despite the hills, 'pestilence' (or malaria) was one of the biggest killers of the ancient city's inhabitants (it remained so until the end of the nineteenth century).

Cicero's is not the best-known version of the foundation story. The one that underlies most modern accounts goes back in its essentials to Livy. For a writer whose work is still so important to our understanding of early Rome, surprisingly little is known about 'Livy the man': he came from Patavium (Padua), in the north of Italy, began writing his compendium of Roman history in the 20s BCE and was on close enough terms with the Roman imperial family to have encouraged the future emperor Claudius to take up history writing. Inevitably, the story of Romulus and Remus features prominently in his first book, with rather less geography and rather more colourful narrative than Cicero gives it. Livy starts with the twins, then briskly follows the tale through to the later achievements of Romulus alone, as Rome's founder and first king.

The little boys, Livy explains, were born to a virgin priestess by the name of Rhea Silvia in the Italian town of Alba Longa, in the Alban Hills, just south of the later site of Rome. She had not taken this virginal office of her own free will but had been forced into it after an internecine struggle for power that saw her uncle Amulius take over as king of Alba Longa after ousting his brother, Numitor, her father. Amulius had then used the cover of the priesthood – an ostensible honour – to prevent the awkward appearance of any heirs and rivals from his brother's line. As it turned out, this precaution failed, for Rhea Silvia was soon pregnant. According to Livy, she claimed that she had been raped by the god Mars. Livy appears to be as doubtful about this as Cicero; Mars, he suggests, might have been a convenient pretence to cover an entirely human affair. But others wrote confidently about a disembodied phallus coming from the flames of the sacred fire that Rhea Silvia was supposed to be tending.

As soon as she gave birth, to twins, Amulius ordered his servants to throw the babies into the nearby river Tiber to drown. But they survived. For, as often happens in stories like this in many cultures, the men who had been given this unpleasant task did not (or could not bring themselves to) follow the instructions to the letter. Instead, they left the twins in a basket not directly in the river but – as it was in flood – next to the water that had burst its banks. Before the babies were washed away to their death, the famous nurturing wolf came to their rescue. Livy was one of those Roman sceptics who tried to rationalise this particularly implausible aspect of the tale. The Latin word for 'wolf' (*lupa*) was also used as a colloquial term for 'prostitute' (*lupanare* was one standard term for 'brothel'). Could it be that a local whore rather than a local wild beast had found and tended the twins?

Whatever the identity of the *lupa*, a kindly herdsman or shepherd soon found the boys and took them in. Was his wife the prostitute? Livy wondered. Romulus and Remus lived as part of his country family, unrecognised until years later, when – now young men – they were accidentally reunited with their grandfather, the deposed king Numitor. Once they had reinstated him as king of Alba Longa, they set out to establish their own city. But they soon quarrelled, with disastrous results. Livy suggests that the same rivalry and ambition that had marred the relationship of Numitor and Amulius trickled down the generations to Romulus and Remus.

The twins disagreed about where exactly to site their new foundation – in particular, which one of the several hills that later made up the city (there are, in fact, more than the famous seven) should form the centre of the first settlement. Romulus chose the hill known as the Palatine, where the emperors' grand residence later stood and which has given us our word 'palace'. In the quarrel that ensued, Remus, who had opted for the Aventine, insultingly jumped over the defences that Romulus was constructing around his preferred spot. There were various versions of what happened next. But the commonest (according to Livy) was that Romulus responded by killing his brother and so became the sole ruler of the place that took his name. As he struck the terrible, fratricidal blow, he shouted (in Livy's words): 'So perish anyone else who shall leap over my walls.' It was an appropriate slogan for a city which went on to portray itself as a belligerent state, but one whose wars were always responses to the aggression of others, always 'just'.

Rape

Remus was dead. And the city that he had helped to found consisted of just a handful of Romulus' friends and companions. It needed more citizens. So Romulus declared Rome an 'asylum' and encouraged the rabble and dispossessed of the rest of Italy to join him: runaway slaves, convicted criminals, exiles and refugees. This produced plenty of men. But in order to get women, so Livy's story goes, Romulus had to resort to a ruse – and to rape. He invited the neighbouring peoples, the Sabines and the Latins, from the area around Rome known as Latium, to come and enjoy a religious festival plus entertainments, families and all. In the middle of the proceedings, he gave a signal for his men to abduct the young women among the visitors and to carry them off as their wives.

Nicolas Poussin, famous for his re-creations of ancient Rome, captured the scene in the seventeenth century: Romulus stands on a dais calmly overseeing the violence that is going on below, against a background of monumental architecture still under construction. It is one image of the early city that the Romans of the first century BCE would have recognised. Though they sometimes pictured Romulus' Rome as one of sheep, mud huts and bog, they often also aggrandised the place as a splendid, preformed classical city. It is also a scene that has been reimagined in all kinds of different ways, and media, throughout history. The 1954 musical *Seven Brides for Seven Brothers* parodies it (in this case, the wives are abducted at an American barn raising). In 1962, as a direct response to the terror of the Cuban Missile Crisis, Pablo Picasso reworked Poussin's version in one of a series of paintings on the theme with a yet harsher violent edge (see plate 3).

Roman writers were forever debating this part of the story. One dramatist wrote a whole tragedy on the theme, which sadly does not survive beyond a single quotation. They puzzled over its details, wondering, for example, how many young women were taken. Livy does not commit himself, but estimates varied from just thirty to the spuriously precise and implausibly large figure of 683 – apparently the view of the African prince Juba, who was brought to Rome by Julius Caesar and spent many of his early years there studying all kinds of learned topics, from Roman history to Latin grammar. More than anything else, though, it was the apparent criminality and violence of the incident that preoccupied them. This occasion was, after all, the very first Roman marriage, and it was where Roman scholars looked when they wanted to explain puzzling features or phrases in traditional

8. This Roman silver coin, of 89 BCE, shows two of Rome's first citizens carrying off two of the Sabine women. The name of the man responsible for minting the coin, almost legible underneath the scene, was Lucius Titurius Sabinus – which presumably accounts for his choice of design. On the other side is the head of the Sabine king, Titus Tatius.

wedding ceremonies; the celebratory shout '*O Talassio*', for example, was said to come from the name of one of the young Romans at the event. Was the inevitable implication that their institution of marriage originated in rape? Where did the dividing line fall between abduction and rape? What did the occasion say, more generally, about the belligerence of Rome?

Livy defends the early Romans. He insists that they seized only unmarried women; this was the origin of marriage, not of adultery. And by stressing the idea that the Romans did not *choose* the women but took them at random, he argues that they were resorting to a necessary expedient for the future of their community, which was followed by loving talk and promises of affection from the men to their new brides. He also presents the Roman action as a response to the unreasonable behaviour of the city's neighbours. The Romans, he explains, had first done the correct thing, by asking the surrounding peoples for a treaty which would have given them the right to marry each other's daughters. Livy explicitly – and wildly anachronistically – refers here to the legal right of *conubium*, or 'intermarriage', which much later was a regular part of Rome's alliances with other states. The Romans turned to violence only when that request was unreasonably rebuffed. That is to say, this was another case of a 'just war'.

Others presented it differently. Some detected right at the origin of the city all the telltale signs of later Roman belligerence. The conflict, they argued, was unprovoked, and the fact that the Romans took only thirty women (if thirty it was) demonstrates that war, not marriage, was uppermost in their minds. Sallust gives a hint of this view. At one point in his *History of Rome* (a more general treatment than his *War against Catiline*, surviving only in scattered quotations in other authors), he imagines a letter – and it is only *imagined* – supposedly written by one of Rome's fiercest enemies. It complains about the predatory behaviour of the Romans throughout their history: 'From the very beginning they have possessed nothing except what they have stolen: their home, *their wives*, their lands, their empire.' Perhaps the only way out was to blame it all on the gods. What else could you expect, another Roman writer suggested, when Romulus' father was Mars, the god of war?

The poet 'Ovid' – Publius Ovidius Naso, to give him his Roman name – took a different line again. Roughly Livy's contemporary, he was as subversive as Livy was conventional – ending up banished in 8 CE, partly for the offence caused by his witty poem, *Love Lessons*, about how to pick up a partner. In this he turns Livy's story of the abduction on its head and presents the incident as a primitive model of flirtation: erotic, not expedient. Ovid's Romans start by trying to 'spot the girl they each fancy most' and go for her with 'lustful hands' once the signal is given. Soon they are whispering sweet nothings in the ears of their prey, whose obvious terror only enhances their sex appeal. Festivals and entertainments, as the poet wickedly reflects, have always been good places to find a girl, from the earliest days of Rome. Or to put it another way, what a great idea Romulus had for rewarding his loyal soldiers. 'I'll sign up,' Ovid jokes, 'if you give me that kind of pay.'

The girls' parents, so the usual story has it, certainly did not find the abduction either funny or flirtatious. They went to war with the Romans for the return of their daughters. The Romans easily defeated the Latins but not the Sabines, and the conflict dragged on. It was at this point that Romulus' men came under heavy attack in their new city and he was forced to call on Jupiter Stator to stop the Romans from simply running for their lives, as Cicero reminded his audience – without reminding them that the whole war was over stolen women. The hostilities were only halted in the end thanks to the women themselves, who were now content with their lot as Roman wives and mothers. They bravely entered the field of battle and begged their husbands on one side and fathers on the other to stop the fighting. 'We'll better die ourselves,' they explained, 'than live without either of you, as widows or as orphans.'

Their intervention worked. Not only was peace brought about, but Rome was said to have become a joint Roman–Sabine town, a single community, under the shared rule of Romulus and the Sabine king Titus Tatius. Shared, that is, until a few years later, when, in the kind of violent death that became one of the trademarks of Roman power politics, Tatius was murdered in a nearby town during a riot that was partly of his own making. Romulus became the sole ruler again, the first king of Rome, with a reign of more than thirty years.

Brother versus brother, outsiders versus insiders

Not far under the surface of these stories lie some of the most important themes of later Roman history, as well as some of the deepest Roman cultural anxieties. They have a lot to tell us about Roman values and preoccupations, or at least about the preoccupations of those Romans with time, money and freedom to spare; cultural anxieties are often a privilege of the rich. One theme, as we have just seen, was the nature of Roman marriage. Just how brutal was it destined to be, given its origins? Another, glimpsed already in the words of the Sabine women who were trying to reconcile their warring fathers and husbands, was civil war.

One of the big puzzles about this foundation legend is its claim that two founders were involved, Romulus and Remus. Modern historians have floated all kinds of solutions to explain the apparently redundant twin. Perhaps it points to some basic duality in Roman culture, between different classes of citizen or different ethnic groups. Or maybe it reflects the fact that later there were always two consuls in Rome. Or perhaps deeper mythic structures are involved, and Romulus and Remus are some version of the divine twins that are found in various corners of world mythology, from Germany to Vedic India, including in the biblical story of Cain and Abel. But whatever solution we choose (and most modern speculation has not been very convincing), an even bigger puzzle is that fact that one of the founding twins really was redundant – since Remus was killed by Romulus, or in other versions by one of his henchmen, on the very first day of the city.

For many Romans, who did not sanitise the story under the label of 'myth' or 'legend', this was the most unpalatable aspect of the foundation. It seems to have made Cicero so uncomfortable that, in his own account of Rome's origin in *On the State,* he does not mention it: Remus appears at the start, to be exposed with Romulus, but then just fades out of the tale. Another writer – the historian Dionysius of Halicarnassus, a resident of Rome in the first century BCE but usually called after his home town on the coast of modern Turkey – chose to depict Romulus as inconsolable at the death of Remus ('he lost the will to live'). Yet another, known to us only as Egnatius, had a bolder way of getting round the problem. The only thing recorded about this Egnatius is that he overturned the story of the murder entirely and asserted that Remus survived to a ripe old age, actually outliving his twin.

It was a desperate, and no doubt unconvincing, attempt to escape the bleak message of the story: that fratricide was hard-wired into Roman politics and that the dreadful bouts of civil conflict that repeatedly blighted Rome's history from the sixth century BCE on (the assassination of Julius Caesar in 44 BCE being only one example) were somehow predestined. For what city, founded on the murder of brother by brother, could ever escape the murder of citizen by citizen? The poet Quintus Horatius Flaccus ('Horace') was just one writer of many who answered that question in the obvious way. Writing around 30 BCE, in the aftermath of the decade of fighting that followed Caesar's death, he lamented: 'Bitter fate pursues the Romans, and the crime of a brother's murder, ever since the blood of blameless Remus was spilt onto the ground to be a curse on his descendants.' Civil war, we might say, was in the Roman genes.

To be sure, Romulus could be, and often was, paraded as a heroic founding father. His unease about the fate of Remus did not prevent Cicero from trying to take over Romulus' mantle in his clash with Catiline. And, despite the shadow of the murder, images of the suckling twins were found all over the ancient Roman world: from the capital itself – where there was once a statue group of them in the Forum and another on the Capitoline Hill – to the far-flung parts of the empire. In fact, when the people of the Greek island of Chios wanted to demonstrate their allegiance to Rome in the second century BCE, one of the things they decided to do was to erect a monument depicting, as they put it, 'the birth of Romulus, the founder of Rome, and his brother Remus'. The monument does not survive. But we know about it because the Chians recorded their decision on a marble plaque, which does. All the same, there remained a definite moral, and political, edginess to the character of Romulus.

Edgy in a different way was the idea of the asylum, and the welcome, that Romulus gave to all comers – foreigners, criminals and runaways – in finding citizens for his new town. There were positive

9. Romulus and Remus reached the furthest corners of the Roman Empire. This mosaic of the fourth century CE was found at Aldborough in the north of England. The wolf is an engagingly jolly creature. The twins, apparently floating perilously in mid air, seem as much an afterthought as the Renaissance additions in the Capitoline group.

aspects to this. In particular, it reflected Roman political culture's extraordinary openness and willingness to incorporate outsiders, which set it apart from every other ancient Western society that we know. No ancient Greek city was remotely as incorporating as this; Athens in particular rigidly restricted access to citizenship. This is not a tribute to any 'liberal' temperament of the Romans in the modern sense of the word. They conquered vast swathes of territory in Europe and beyond, sometimes with terrible brutality; and they were often xenophobic and dismissive of people they called 'barbarians'. Yet, in a process unique in any pre-industrial empire, the inhabitants of those conquered territories, 'provinces' as Romans called them, were gradually given full Roman citizenship, and the legal rights and protections that went with it. That culminated in 212 CE (where my *SPQR* ends), when the emperor Caracalla made every free inhabitant of the empire a Roman citizen.

Even before then, the elite of the provinces had entered the political hierarchy of the capital, in large numbers. The Roman senate gradually became what we might now describe as a decidedly multicultural body, and the full list of Roman emperors contains many whose origins lay outside Italy: Caracalla's father, Septimius Severus, was the first emperor from Roman territory in Africa; Trajan and Hadrian, who reigned half a century earlier, had come from the Roman province of Spain. When in 48 CE the emperor Claudius – whose avuncular image owes more to Robert Graves' novel *I, Claudius* than to real life – was arguing to a slightly reluctant senate that citizens from Gaul should be allowed to become senators, he spent some time reminding the meeting that Rome had been open to foreigners from the beginning. The text of his speech, including some of the heckling that apparently even an emperor had to endure, was inscribed on bronze and put on display in the province, in what is now the city of Lyon, where it still survives. Claudius, it seems, did not get the chance that Cicero had to make adjustments for publication.

There was a similar process with slavery. Roman slavery was in some respects as brutal as Roman methods of military conquest. But for many Roman slaves, particularly those working in urban domestic contexts rather than toiling in the fields or mines, it was not necessarily a life sentence. They were regularly given their freedom, or they bought it with cash they had managed to save up; and if their owner was a Roman citizen, then they also gained full Roman citizenship, with almost no disadvantages as against those who were freeborn. The contrast with classical Athens is again striking: there, very few slaves were freed, and those who were certainly did not gain Athenian citizenship in the process, but went into a form of stateless limbo. This practice of emancipation – or manumission, to follow the Latin term – was such a distinctive feature of Roman culture that outsiders at the time remarked upon it and saw it as a powerful factor in Rome's success. As one king of Macedon observed in the third century BCE, it was in this way that 'the Romans have enlarged their country'. The scale was so great that some historians reckon that, by the second century CE, the majority of the free citizen population of the city of Rome had slaves somewhere in their ancestry.

The story of Romulus' asylum clearly points to this openness, suggesting that the diverse make-up of Rome was a characteristic that went back to its origins. There were insiders who echoed the view of the king of Macedon that Romulus' policy of inclusiveness was an important part of the city's success; and for them the asylum was something to be proud of. But there were also dissenting voices that stressed a far less flattering side to the story. It was not only some of Rome's enemies who saw the irony of an empire that traced its descent back to the criminals and riff-raff of Italy. Some Romans did too. In the late first or early second century CE, the satiric poet 'Juvenal' – Decimus Junius Juvenalis – who loved to pour scorn on Roman pretensions, lambasted the snobbery that was another side of life at Rome, and he ridiculed those aristocrats who boasted of a family tree going back centuries. He ends one of his poems with a sideswipe at Rome's origins. What are all these pretensions based on, anyway? Rome was from its very beginning a city made up of slaves and runaways ('Whoever your earliest ancestor was, he was either a shepherd or something I'd rather not mention'). Cicero may have been making a similar point when he joked in a letter to his friend Atticus about the 'the crap' or 'the dregs' of Romulus. He was poking fun at one of his contemporaries, who, he said, addressed the senate as if he were living 'in the *Republic* of Plato', referring to the philosopher's ideal state – 'when in fact he is in the *faex* (crap) of Romulus.'

In short, Romans could always see themselves following in Romulus' footsteps, for better or worse. When Cicero gestured to Romulus in his speech against Catiline, it was more than a self-aggrandising appeal to Rome's founding father (though it was certainly that in part). It was also an appeal to a story that prompted all kinds of discussion and debate among his contemporaries about who the Romans really were, what Rome stood for and where its divisions lay.

History and myth

The footsteps of Romulus were imprinted on the Roman landscape. In Cicero's day, you could do more than visit Romulus' Temple of Jupiter Stator: you could enter the cave where the wolf was supposed to have cared for the baby twins, and you could see the tree, replanted in the Forum, at which the boys were said to have washed up from the river. You could even admire Romulus' own house, a small wood-and-thatch hut where the founder was supposed to have lived, on the Palatine Hill: a visible slice of primitive Rome in what had become a sprawling metropolis. This was, of course, a fabrication, as one visitor at the end of the first century BCE half hinted: 'they add nothing to it to make it more revered,' he explained, 'but if any part of it is damaged, by bad weather or old age, they make it good and restore it as far as possible to what it was before'. No certain archaeological traces of the hut have been found, unsurprisingly, given its flimsy construction. But it survived in some form, as a memorial to the city's origins, until at least the fourth century CE, when it was mentioned in a list of notable landmarks in Rome.

These physical 'remains' – temple, fig tree and carefully patched-up hut – were part and parcel of Romulus' status as an historical character. As we have seen, Roman writers were not gullible dupes, and they queried many details of the traditional stories even while retelling them (the role of the wolf, the divine ancestry and so forth). But they expressed no doubt that Romulus had once existed, that he had made crucial decisions that governed the future development of Rome, such as the selection of the city's site, and that he had more or less single-handedly invented some of its defining institutions. The senate itself, according to some accounts, was the creation of Romulus, as was the ceremony of 'triumph', the Roman victory parade that regularly followed the city's biggest (and bloodiest) successes in war. When, at the end of the first century BCE, a monumental list of all the Roman generals who had ever celebrated a triumph was inscribed on a series of marble panels in the Forum, Romulus headed the roster. 'Romulus, the king, son of Mars,' ran that first entry, 'year one, on 1 March, for a victory over the people of Caenina', commemorating his speedy defeat of one nearby Latin town whose young women had been stolen – and not admitting a glimmer of public scepticism about his divine parenthood.

Roman scholars worked hard to define Romulus' achievements and to reach an accurate chronology of the earliest phases of Rome. One of the liveliest controversies of Cicero's day was the question of when exactly the city was founded. Precisely how old was Rome? Learned minds ingeniously counted back in time from the Roman dates they did know to earlier dates they did not and tried to synchronise events in Rome with the chronology of Greek history. In particular they tried to match up their history with the regular four-year cycles of the Olympic Games, which apparently offered a fixed and authentic time frame – although, as is now recognised, this was itself partly the product of earlier ingenious speculation. It was a tricky and highly specialised debate. But gradually the different views coalesced around the middle of what we call the eighth century BCE, as scholarly opinion reached the conclusion that Greek and Roman history 'began' at roughly the same time. What became the canonical date, and one still quoted in many modern textbooks, partly goes back to a scholarly treatise, the *Book of Chronology*, by none other than Cicero's friend and correspondent Atticus. It does not survive, but it is supposed to have pinpointed Romulus' foundation of the city to the third year of the sixth cycle of Olympic Games; that is to say, 753 BCE. Other calculations narrowed this down further, to 21 April, the date on which modern Romans still, to this day, celebrate the birthday of their city, with some rather tacky parades and mock gladiatorial spectacles.

There is often a fuzzy boundary between myth and history (think of King Arthur or Pocahontas), and, as we shall see, Rome is one of those cultures where that boundary is particularly blurred. But despite all the historical acumen that Romans brought to bear on this story, there is every reason for us to see it, in our terms, as more or less pure myth. For a start, there was almost certainly no such thing as a founding moment of the city of Rome. Very few towns or cities are founded at a stroke, by a single individual. They are usually the product of gradual changes in population, in patterns of settlement, social organisation and sense of identity. Most 'foundations' are retrospective constructions, projecting back into the distant past a microcosm, or imagined primitive version, of the later city. The name 'Romulus' is itself a give-away. Although Romans usually assumed that he had lent his name to his newly established city, we are now fairly confident that the opposite was the case: 'Romulus' was an imaginative construction out of 'Roma'. 'Romulus' was merely the archetypal 'Mr Rome'.

Besides, the writers and scholars of the first century BCE who have bequeathed to us their version of Rome's origins had not much more direct evidence of the earliest phases of Rome's history than modern writers have, and in some ways perhaps less. There were no surviving documents or archives. The few early inscriptions on stone, valuable as they are, were not as early as Roman scholars often imagined, and, as we shall discover at the end of this chapter, they sometimes hopelessly misunderstood early Latin. True, they had access to a few earlier historical accounts that no longer survive. But the earliest of these were composed in about 200 BCE, and there was still a great chasm between that date and the city's origins, which could be bridged only with the help of a very mixed bag of stories, songs, popular dramatic performances and the shifting and sometimes self-contradictory amalgam that makes up oral tradition – constantly adjusted in the telling

10. Found in Etruscan territory this engraved mirror (the reflecting face was on the other side) appears to show some version of the suckling of Romulus and Remus by the wolf. If so, dating to the fourth century BCE, it would be one of the earliest pieces of evidence for the story. But some, perhaps over-sceptical, modern scholars have preferred to see here a scene from Etruscan myth, or a pair of infinitely more shadowy and mysterious Roman deities, the twin 'Lares Praestites'.

and retelling to changing circumstances and audiences. There are a few fleeting glimpses of the Romulus story back to the fourth century BCE, but then, unless we bring the bronze wolf back into the picture, the trail stops.

Of course, to put it another way, it is precisely because the story of Romulus is mythic rather than historical, in the narrow sense, that it encapsulates so sharply some of the central cultural questions of ancient Rome and is so important for understanding Roman history, in its wider definition. The Romans had not, as they assumed, simply inherited the priorities and concerns of their founder. Quite the reverse: over centuries of retelling and then rewriting the story, they themselves had constructed and reconstructed the founding figure of Romulus as a powerful symbol of their preferences, debates, ideologies and anxieties. It was not, in other words, to go back to Horace, that civil war was the curse and destiny of Rome from its birth; Rome had projected its obsessions with the apparently unending cycle of civil conflict back onto its founder.

There was always the possibility too of adjusting or reconfiguring the narrative, even when it had reached a relatively fixed literary form. We have already spotted, for example, how Cicero chose to draw a veil over the murder of Remus, and Egnatius to deny it entirely. But Livy's account of the death of Romulus gives a vivid glimpse of how the story of Rome's origins could be made to resonate directly with recent events. The king, he explains, had ruled for thirty years when suddenly in a violent storm he was covered by a cloud and disappeared. The sorrowing Romans soon concluded that he had been snatched from them to become a god – crossing the boundary between human and divine in a way that Rome's polytheistic religious system sometimes allowed (even if it seems faintly silly to us). But some people at the time, Livy concedes, told a different story: that the king had been assassinated, hacked to death by the senators. Livy did not entirely invent either of these parts of his plot: Cicero, for example, had earlier reported Romulus' apotheosis, albeit with a degree of scepticism; and an overambitious politician in the 60s BCE was once threatened with 'the fate of Romulus', and that, presumably, did not mean becoming a god. But writing just a few decades after the murder of Julius Caesar, who was both hacked to death by senators and then given the status of a god (ending up with his own temple in the Forum), Livy offers a particularly loaded and emphatic account. To miss the echoes of Caesar here would be to miss the point.

Aeneas and more

The story of Romulus and Remus is by turns intriguing, puzzling and hugely revealing of big Roman concerns, at least among the elite. And, to judge from the designs on coins or the themes of popular art, knowledge of the stories was widespread – even if hungry peasants did not spend much time worrying about the niceties of the Rape of the Sabines. But the extra complication, to be added to this already complex picture of the legend of Rome's origins, is that the story of Romulus and Remus was not the city's only foundation story. There were several others that existed side by side. These included minor variants on standard themes, as well as alternatives that seem to us frankly idiosyncratic. One Greek idea, for example, brought the re-nowned Odysseus and echoes of Homer's *Odyssey* into the story by suggesting that Rome's real founding father was a man called Romus, the result of Odysseus' affair with the witch Circe, whose magical island was sometimes imagined to lie just off the coast of Italy. This was a neat, although implausible, bit of cultural imperialism that gave Rome a Greek parentage.

The other legend that was equally firmly embedded in Roman history and literature is the story of the Trojan hero Aeneas, who escaped from the city of Troy after the mythical war between Greeks and Trojans that is the backdrop of Homer's *Iliad*. After leading his son by the hand and carrying his elderly father from the burning ruins, he eventually made his way to Italy, where his destiny was to refound his native city on Italian soil. He brought with him the traditions of his homeland and even some precious talismans rescued from the destruction.

There are as many puzzles, problems and ambiguities in this story as in the tale of Romulus, and unresolved questions about where,

11. A fourth-century CE mosaic, from the floor of a bath-suite at Low Ham Roman villa in the south of England, was decorated with a series of scenes from Virgil's *Aeneid*: Aeneas arriving in Carthage, Dido and Aeneas out hunting and here the passion of the Carthaginian queen and the Trojan hero rendered as succinctly as could be.

when and why it originated. These are made even more complicated, as well as enormously enriched, thanks to the *Aeneid*, Virgil's great twelve-book poem on the theme, written during the rule of the first Roman emperor, Augustus, and one of the most widely read works of literature ever. This has become *the* story of Aeneas. And it has bequeathed to the Western world some of its most powerful literary and artistic highlights, including the tragic love story of Aeneas and Dido, the queen of Carthage, where Aeneas washes ashore on his long journey from Troy (on the coast of modern Turkey) to Italy. When Aeneas resolves to follow his destiny and leave for Italy, abandoning Dido, she commits suicide by throwing herself on a burning pyre. 'Remember me, remember me', runs her haunting aria in Henry Purcell's seventeenth-century operatic version of the theme. The problem is that it is often hard to know which elements of the story we owe to Virgil (including, almost certainly, most of the encounter with Dido) and which are part of a more traditional tale.

There is no doubt that the figure of Aeneas as the founder of Rome featured in literature – and made its mark on the landscape – well before the first century BCE. There are passing references to him in that role in Greek writers of the fifth century BCE; and in the second century BCE, ambassadors from the Greek island of Delos appealing for an alliance with Rome seem to have taken care to remind the Romans, as part of their pitch, that Aeneas had stopped off at Delos on his journey west. In Italy, Dionysius of Halicarnassus was convinced that he had seen the tomb of Aeneas, or at least an ancient memorial to him, at the town of Lavinium, not far from Rome: 'well worth seeing,' he observed. There was also a popular story that among the precious objects kept in the temple of the goddess Vesta in the Roman Forum – where virgin priestesses, like Rhea Silvia of the Romulus legend, guarded a sacred flame that was supposed never to be extinguished – was the very statue of the goddess Pallas Athena that Aeneas had brought from Troy. Or so one Roman tale had it. There were various rival candidates for rescuing this famous image, and any number of cities all over the Greek world claimed to possess the real thing.

It goes without saying that the story of Aeneas is as much a myth as the story of Romulus. But Roman scholars puzzled over the relationship of these two foundation legends and expended enormous amounts of energy trying to bring them into historical alignment. Was Romulus the son, or maybe the grandson, of Aeneas? And if Romulus had founded Rome, how could Aeneas also have done so? The biggest difficulty was that there was an uncomfortable gap between the eighth-century BCE date that the Romans assigned to the origins of their city and the twelfth-century BCE date that they commonly gave to the fall of Troy (also taken as an historical event). By the first century BCE some sort of coherence was reached by constructing a complicated family tree, which linked Aeneas and Romulus, and at the 'right' dates: Aeneas became seen as the founder not of Rome but of Lavinium; his son Ascanius was said to have founded Alba Longa – the city from which Romulus and Remus were later cast out before they founded Rome; and a shadowy and, even by Roman standards, flagrantly fictional dynasty of Alban kings was constructed to bridge the gap between Ascanius and the magic date of 753 BCE. This is the version that Livy endorses.

The central claim of the story of Aeneas is one that echoes, or rather exaggerates, the underlying theme of Romulus' asylum. Where Romulus welcomed all comers to his new city, the story of Aeneas goes further, to claim that the 'Romans' really were originally 'foreigners'. It is a paradox of national identity, which stands in glaring contrast to the foundation myths of many ancient Greek cities, such as Athens, which saw their original population as springing miraculously from the very soil of their native land. And other variant accounts of Rome's origins repeatedly emphasise that foreignness. In fact, in one episode of the *Aeneid*, the hero visits the site of the future city of Rome and finds it already settled by primitive predecessors of the Romans. And who are they? They are a group of settlers under a certain King Evander, an exile from the land of Arcadia in the Greek Peloponnese. The message is clear: however far back you go, the inhabitants of Rome were always already from somewhere else.

That message is most neatly summed up in a strange etymology recorded by Dionysius, among others. Greek and Roman intellectuals were fascinated by word derivations, which they were convinced gave the key not just to the origin of the word but also to its essential meaning. They were sometimes correct in their analysis, and sometimes extravagantly wrong. Their mistakes are often revealing, as in this case. Dionysius, at an early point in his history, reflects on yet another group of even more primitive inhabitants of the site that became Rome: the Aborigines. The derivation of this word should have been blindingly obvious: these were the people who had been there 'from the beginning' (*ab origine*). Dionysius, to be fair, does raise that explanation as a possibility, but – like others – he gives equal, or more, weight to the hugely improbable notion that the word derived not from *origo* but from the Latin *errare* ('to wander') and had originally been spelled *Aberrigines*. These people were, in other words, he writes, 'vagabonds of no fixed abode'.

The idea that any serious ancient scholars could turn a blind eye to the obviously correct etymology that was staring them in the face in favour of a silly idea that derived *Aborigines* from 'to wander' via a tendentious alternative spelling is not a reflection of their obtuseness. It shows just how ingrained the idea was that 'Rome' had always been an ethnically fluid concept, that the 'Romans' had always been on the move.

Digging up early Rome

The many stories of Romulus and the other founders tell us a good deal about how the Romans saw their city, their values and their failings.

They show too how Roman scholars debated the past and studied their history. But they tell us nothing, or at most very little indeed, about what they claim to: that is, what earliest Rome was like, the processes by which it became an urban community and when. One fact is obvious. Rome was already a very old city when Cicero was consul in 63 BCE. But, if there is no surviving literature from the founding period and we cannot rely on the legends, how can we access any information about the origins of Rome? Is there any way of throwing light on the early years of the little town by the Tiber that grew into a world empire?

However hard we try, it is impossible to construct a coherent narrative that could replace the legends of Romulus or Aeneas. It is also very hard, despite many confident assertions to the contrary, to pin precise dates onto the earliest phases of Roman history. But we can begin to get a much better idea of the general context in which the city developed and enjoy a few surprisingly vivid (and some even more tantalisingly elusive) glimpses into that world.

One way of doing this is by turning away from the foundation stories and seeking out clues lurking in the Latin language or in later Roman institutions that might point back to earliest Rome. The key here is what is often simply, and wrongly, termed the 'conservatism' of Roman culture. Rome was no more conservative than nineteenth-century Britain. In both places, radical innovation thrived in dialogue with all kinds of ostensibly conservative traditions and rhetoric. Yet Roman culture *was* marked by a reluctance ever entirely to discard its past practices, tending instead to preserve all kinds of 'fossils' – in religious rituals or politics, or whatever – even when their original significance had been lost. As one modern writer has nicely put it, the Romans were rather like people who acquire all kinds of brand-new kitchen equipment but can't ever bear to throw away their old gadgets, which continue to clutter up the place even though they are never used. Scholars, both modern and ancient, have often suspected that some of these fossils, or old gadgets, may be important evidence for the conditions of earliest Rome.

One favourite example is a ritual that took place in the city in December each year, known as the Septimontium ('Seven hills'). What happened at this celebration is not at all clear, but one learned Roman noted that 'Septimontium' was the name of Rome before it became 'Rome', and another gave a list of the 'hills' (*montes*) involved in the festival: Palatium, Velia, Fagutal, Subura, Cermalus, Oppius, Caelius and Cispius (Map 2). The fact that there are eight names suggests that something has got confused somewhere along the line. But more to the point, the oddity of this list (Palatium and Cermalus are both parts of the hill generally known as the Palatine), combined with the idea that 'Septimontium' was the predecessor of 'Rome', has raised the possibility that these names might reflect the sites of separate villages that preceded the fully fledged town. And the absence of a couple of obvious hills from the list, Quirinal and Viminal, has tempted some historians to go even further. Roman writers regularly referred to both of those hills as *colles* rather than the more usual Latin *montes* (the meaning of the two words is more or less identical). Does that distinction point to two separate linguistic communities somewhere in Rome's early history? Could we possibly be dealing – to press the argument even further – with some version of the two groups reflected in the story of Romulus, the Sabines associated with the *colles*, the Romans with the *montes*?

Just possibly we could. There is little doubt that the Septimontium is related in some way to Rome's distant past. But in exactly what way, and quite how distant, is very hard to know. The arguments are no firmer than I have made them seem, probably even less so. Why, after all, should we trust that learned Roman's claim that Septimontium was the early name of the city? It was just as likely a desperate guess, to explain an archaic ceremony that baffled him almost as much as it does us. And the insistence on two communities seems suspiciously driven by a desire to rescue at least some part of the legend of Romulus for 'history'.

Much more tangible is the evidence of archaeology. Dig down deep in the city of Rome, below the visible ancient monuments, and a few traces of a much earlier, primitive settlement, or settlements, remain. Beneath the Forum itself lie the remains of an early cemetery, which caused tremendous excitement when they were first unearthed, at the start of the twentieth century. Some of the dead had been cremated, their ashes placed in simple urns alongside jugs and vases which originally contained food and drink (one man had been given little quantities of fish, mutton and pork – and possibly some porridge). Others were buried, sometimes in simple oak coffins made by splitting a trunk and hollowing it out. One girl, about two years old, had been put in her grave wearing a beaded dress and an ivory bracelet. Similar finds have been made in other places all over the ancient city. Far below one of the later grand houses on the Palatine Hill, for example, lay the ashes of a young man, interred with a miniature spear, maybe a symbol of how he had spent his life.

The dead and buried are often much more prominent than the living in the archaeological record. But cemeteries imply the existence of a community, and traces of that are presumably to be found in the groups of huts whose faint outlines have been detected under various parts of the later city, including on the Palatine. We have little idea of their character (beyond their construction in wood, clay and thatch), still less of the lifestyle they supported. But we can fill in some of the gaps if we look just outside Rome. One of the best preserved, and most carefully excavated, of these early structures was found at Fidenae, a few miles north of the city, in the 1980s. It is a rectangular building, some 6 by 5 metres, made of wood (oak and elm) and rammed earth – so-called *pisé de terre* construction, still in use up to the present day – with a rough and ready portico around it, formed by the overhanging roof. Inside was a central hearth, some large pottery storage jars (plus a smaller one, which seems to have been a container for potting clay) and traces of some fairly predictable foodstuffs (cereals and beans) and domestic animals (sheep, goats, cows and pigs). The most surprising discovery amid the debris was the remains of a cat, which died (perhaps it was tethered) in a savage fire that eventually destroyed the building. Its claim to fame now is as the earliest known domestic cat in Italy.

There are vivid glimpses of human and other life here, from the little girl laid out in her grave in her best dress to the poor 'mouser' whom no one let off his leash when the fire blazed. The question is what those glimpses add up to. The archaeological remains certainly demonstrate that there is a long and rich prehistory behind the ancient Rome we see, but quite how long is another matter.

Part of the problem is the conditions of excavation in the city itself. The site of Rome has been so intensively built on for centuries that we find these traces of early occupation only in spots that happen not to have been disturbed. The foundations dug in the first and second centuries CE for the vast marble temples in the Forum obliterated much of what then lay beneath the surface; the cellars of Renaissance

12. A typical cremation urn from the early cemeteries of Rome and the surrounding area. In the form of a simple hut, these houses for the dead are one of the best guides we have to the appearance of the accommodation for the living.

palazzi cut through even more in other parts of Rome. So we have only tiny snapshots, never the big picture. This is archaeology at its most difficult, and – although new fragments of evidence emerge all the time – its interpretation, and reinterpretation, is almost always contested and often controversial. For example, there is an ongoing debate about whether the small pieces of wattle and daub found in excavations in the Forum in the mid twentieth century indicate that there was an early hut settlement there too – or whether they were inadvertently introduced as part of the rubble used a few centuries later to provide a new raised surface for the area. It has to be said that, though fine for a cemetery, this would have been a rather damp and marshy place for a village.

Precise dating is even more contentious; hence my intentionally vague use of the word 'early' over the last few pages. It cannot be stressed enough that there is no certain independent date for any of the archaeological material from earliest Rome or the area round about, and that arguments still rage about the age of almost every major find. It has taken decades of work over the past century or so – using such diagnostics as wheel-made pottery (assumed to be later than handmade), the occasional presence in graves of Greek ceramics (whose dating is better, but still not perfectly, understood) and careful comparison from site to site – to produce a rough chronological scheme covering the period from around 1000 to 600 BCE.

On that basis, the earliest burials in the Forum would be around 1000 BCE, the huts on the Palatine around 750–700 BCE (excitingly close to 753 BCE, as many have observed). But even these dates are far from certain. Recent scientific methods – including 'radiocarbon dating', which calculates the age of any organic material by measuring the residual amount of its radioactive carbon isotope – have suggested that they are all too 'young', by as much as a hundred years. The hut at Fidenae, for example, was dated around the middle of the eighth century BCE according to traditional archaeological criteria, but that is pushed back towards the end of the ninth century BCE if we follow the radiocarbon. Currently, dates are in flux, even more than usual; if anything, Rome appears to be getting older.

What is certain is that by the sixth century BCE Rome was an urban community, with a centre and some public buildings. Before that, for the earliest phases, we have enough scattered finds from what is known as the Middle Bronze Age (between about 1700 and 1300 BCE) to suggest that some people were then living on the site, rather than just 'passing through'. Over the period in between, we can be fairly confident that larger villages grew up, probably (to judge from what ends up in the graves) with an increasingly wealthy group of elite families; and that at some point these coalesced into the single community whose urban character was clear by the sixth century BCE. We cannot know for sure when the inhabitants of those separate settlements first thought of themselves as a single town. And we have absolutely no idea when they first thought of, and referred to, that town as Rome.

Archaeology is not, however, just about dates and origins. The material dug up in the city, the area around it and even further afield has important things to tell us about the character of Rome's early settlement. First, it had extensive contacts with the outside world. I have already mentioned in passing the ivory bracelet of the little girl in the cemetery and the Greek pottery (made in Corinth or Athens) that turned up in Roman excavations. There are also signs of links with the north, in the form of a few jewels and decorations in imported amber; there is no clue of how these reached central Italy, but they certainly point to contact, direct or indirect, with the Baltic. Early Rome, from almost as far back as we can see it, was well connected, as Cicero hinted when he stressed its strategic location.

Second, there were similarities, and some important differences, between Rome and its neighbours. The Italian peninsula between about 1000 and 600 BCE was extremely mixed. There were many different

independent peoples, with many different cultural traditions, origins
and languages. The best documented are the Greek settlements in
the south, towns such as Cumae, Tarentum and Naples (Neapolis),
founded from the eighth century BCE on by immigrants from some
of the major cities in Greece – conventionally known as 'colonies'
but not 'colonial' in the modern sense of the word. To all intents and
purposes, much of the southern part of the peninsula, and Sicily, was
part of the Greek world, with a literate and artistic tradition linked
to match. It is no coincidence that some of the earliest specimens
of Greek writing to survive, maybe the very earliest, have actually
been discovered there. It is much harder to reconstruct the history
of any of the other inhabitants of the peninsula: from the Etruscans
to the north, through the Latins and Sabines on Rome's doorstep
to the south, to the Oscans, who formed the original population of
Pompeii, and Samnites beyond them. None of their literature, if they
had any, has survived, and for evidence of them we depend entirely
on archaeology, on texts inscribed on stone and bronze – sometimes
comprehensible, sometimes not – and on Roman accounts written
much later, often tinged with Roman supremacy; hence the standard
image of the Samnites as tough, barbaric, non-urbanised and dangerously primitive.

What archaeological finds do show, however, is that Rome in its
early days was very ordinary indeed. The development, from scattered
settlements into an urban community, that we can just about detect in
Rome seems to have happened at roughly the same period throughout
the neighbouring region to its south. And the material remains in the
cemeteries, local pottery and bronze brooches, as well as more exotic
imports, are fairly consistent there too. If anything, what has been
discovered in Rome is less impressive and less suggestive of wealth
than discoveries elsewhere. Nothing has emerged from the city to
compare with, for example, the finds from some extraordinary tombs
in nearby Praeneste – though that might just be bad luck or, as some

archaeologists have suspected, a case of some of the best finds from the nineteenth-century excavations in Rome having been stolen and directed straight to the antiquities market. One of the questions we shall have to address over the next couple of chapters is: when did Rome cease to be ordinary?

The missing link

The final question for this chapter, however, is whether the archaeological material must remain quite as separate from the mythic traditions of Romulus and Remus as I have presented them. Is it possible to link our investigations into the earliest history of Rome with the stories that the Romans themselves told, or with their elaborate speculations on the city's origins? Can we perhaps find a little more history in the myth?

This is a seductive temptation that has influenced a lot of modern work on early Rome by both historians and archaeologists. We have already spotted the attempt to make the story of the Septimontium reflect the dual nature of the city – Roman and Sabine – which the myth of Romulus emphasises. Recently the discovery of some early earthwork defences at the foot of the Palatine Hill has prompted all kinds of wild speculation that these were the very defences over which Remus jumped, to meet his death, on the city's foundation day. This is archaeological fantasy. There is no doubt that some early earthworks have been discovered, and that in itself is important – though how they relate to the early hut settlement on the top of the Palatine is puzzling. They are nothing whatsoever to do with the non-existent characters Romulus and Remus. And the attempts to 'massage' the dating of the structure, and its associated finds, to end up on 21 April 753 BCE (I am exaggerating only slightly) are special pleading.

There is just one location in the whole of the city Rome where it is possible to link the early material remains directly with the literary tradition. In so doing, we find not agreement and harmony between the two but a wide and intriguing gap. That location is at one end of the Forum, close to the slopes of the Capitoline Hill, a few minutes' walk from where Cicero attacked Catiline in the Temple of Jupiter Stator, and just next to the main platform (or *rostra*) from which speakers addressed the people. There, before the end of the first century BCE, in the pavement of the Forum was set a series of slabs in distinctively black stone forming a rectangle of roughly 4 by 3.5 metres, marked out with a low stone border.

At the turn of the nineteenth and twentieth centuries, the archaeologist Giacomo Boni – a celebrity at the time to rival Heinrich Schliemann, the discoverer of Troy, and with none of the dubious reputation for fraud – excavated below the black stone, where he found the remains of some much earlier structures. These included an altar, part of a large free-standing column and a short stone pillar that is covered in mostly unintelligible early Latin, probably one of the earliest texts in the language that we have. The place had been intentionally buried, and the fill included all kinds of extraordinary as well as everyday finds, from miniature cups, beads and knucklebones to some fine pieces of sixth-century BCE Athenian decorated pottery. The most obvious explanation, to judge from the finds, which seem to include religious dedications, is that this was an early shrine, possibly of the god Vulcan. It was covered over when the Forum was repaved sometime in the first century BCE – but to preserve the memory of the sacred site underneath, the distinctive black stone was laid above.

Later Roman writers were well aware of the black stone and had various ideas about what it signified. 'The black stone,' one wrote, 'marks an unlucky spot.' And they knew that there was something underneath it, going back centuries: not a religious shrine, as archaeologists are now fairly confident it was, but a monument connected with Romulus or his family. Several assumed it was the tomb of Romulus; others, perhaps worried that, if Romulus had become a god, he should not really have a tomb, thought it was the tomb of Faustulus, the foster father of Romulus and Remus; still others made it the tomb of one of Romulus' comrades, Hostilius, the grandfather of one of the later kings of Rome.

They also knew, whether because they had seen it before it was covered or from hearsay, that there was an inscription down there. Dionysius records two versions of what it was: the epitaph of Hostilius, 'documenting his bravery', or an inscription 'recording his deeds' put up after one of Romulus' victories. But it was certainly neither of those things. Nor was it, as Dionysius claims, 'written in Greek letters': it is bona fide early Latin. But it makes a marvellous example of both how much and how little Roman historians knew about the buried past – and how they so liked to

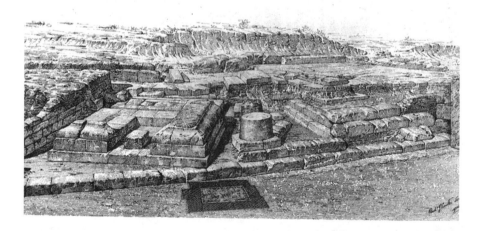

13. A diagram of the remains of the early shrine excavated by Giacomo Boni underneath the black stone in the Forum. On the left is an altar (a squared U-shape structure found elsewhere in Italy at this period). On the right stands what is left of the column, and just visible behind it is the inscribed pillar.

imagine the traces of Romulus still present on, or just below, the surface of their city.

What this text actually says – so far as we can make any sense of it – takes us into the next phase of Roman history and the series of almost equally mythical kings who were supposed to have followed Romulus.

CHAPTER THREE

·

THE KINGS OF ROME

Written on the stone

T HE INSCRIPTION DISCOVERED in 1899 under the black stone
in the Forum includes the word 'king', or in Latin *rex*: *RECEI*,
as it appears in the early form of the language used there. That single
word accounts for the inscription's fame and has changed the way the
history of early Rome has been understood ever since.

The text is in many respects extremely frustrating. It is incomplete,
the top third of the pillar not surviving. It is close to incomprehensible. The Latin is difficult enough anyway, but the missing section
makes it almost impossible to grasp the meaning fully. Even though

14. The early inscription on the
pillar excavated under the black
stone could easily be mistaken for
Greek, and indeed *was* by some later
ancient observers themselves. It is
in fact written in archaic Latin, in
letters very similar to Greek, and is
arranged in so-called *boustrophedon*
('ox-ploughing') style: that is,
the lines are read alternately
left to right, and right to left.

we can be certain that it does not mark the tomb of Romulus – or of anyone else – most interpretations amount to little more than brave attempts to string together into some vague sense the few individual words that are recognisable on the stone. One notable modern theory is that it was a warning not to let yoked animals drop excrement near the shrine – which would, apparently, have been a bad omen. It is also very hard to know how old it is. The only way to date the text is by comparing its language and script to the handful of other surviving

15. In this painting, 'The Oath of the Horatii' (1784), Jacques-Louis David depicts a legend from the reign of Tullus Hostilius, when Rome was at war with neighbouring Alba Longa. Two pairs of triplets, one on each side, agreed to fight it out themselves on behalf of their communities. Here David imagines the Roman Horatii taking their swords from their father. One of them returned home victorious, only to kill his sister (seen here weeping) who had been engaged to one of the enemy. It was a story, for the Romans no less than the eighteenth-century French, that both celebrated patriotism and questioned its cost.

examples of early Latin, for the most part equally uncertainly dated. Suggestions have ranged over 300 years, from around 700 to around 400 BCE. The current, fragile consensus is that it was inscribed in the second half of the sixth century BCE.

Despite all those unknowns, archaeologists instantly realised that the recognisable *RECEI* – in the dative case, meaning 'to or for the king' – supports what Roman writers themselves had claimed: that for two and a half centuries, up to the end of the sixth century BCE, the city of Rome had been under the control of 'kings'. Livy, among others, tells of a standard sequence of six monarchs following Romulus, each with a distinctive package of achievements attached to his name.

Their colourful stories – with a supporting cast of heroic Roman warriors, murderous rivals and scheming queens – take up the second half of the first book of Livy's *History*. After Romulus came Numa Pompilius, a peaceable character who invented most of the religious institutions of Rome; then Tullus Hostilius, a renowned warmonger; after him, Ancus Marcius, the founder of Rome's seaport at Ostia, 'Rivermouth'; then Tarquinius Priscus, or 'Tarquin the Elder', who developed the Roman Forum and the Circus Games; then Servius Tullius, a political reformer and the inventor of the Roman census; and finally, Tarquinius Superbus, 'Tarquin the Proud' or, perhaps better, 'the Arrogant'. It was the tyrannical behaviour of this second Tarquin, and of his family, that led to revolution, to the end of monarchy and to the establishing of 'liberty' and the 'free Republic of Rome'. He was a paranoid autocrat who ruthlessly eliminated his rivals, and a cruel exploiter of the Roman people, forcing them to labour on his fanatical building projects. But the awful breaking point came, as such breaking points did more than once in Roman history, with a rape – this time the rape of the virtuous Lucretia by one of king's sons.

Cautious scholars in the nineteenth century had been extremely doubtful about the historical value of these stories of the Roman kings. They argued that there was hardly any more firm evidence for these rulers than for the legendary Romulus: the whole tradition was based on garbled hearsay and misunderstood myth – not to mention the propagandist fantasies of many of the later leading families at Rome, who regularly manipulated or invented the 'history' of the early city to give their ancestors a glorious role in it. It was only a short step from this, and a step that many notable historians then took, to claim that the Roman 'regal period', as it is now often called, never existed; that those famous kings were figments of the Roman imagination; that the true history of early Rome was entirely lost to us.

RECEI in Boni's inscription successfully challenged that radical scepticism. No amount of special pleading (that, for example, *rex* here refers to a later religious official of the same name but not a king in the technical sense) could get round what now seemed undeniable: that Rome had once been some kind of monarchy. The discovery changed the nature of the debate on early Roman history, though, of course, it prompted other questions.

Even now, this inscription puts the idea of the Roman kings centre stage and raises the question of what kingship might mean in the context of a small, archaic community of a few thousand inhabitants living in wattle-and-daub huts on a group of hilltops near the river Tiber. The word 'king' almost certainly implies something much more formal, and grander, than we should be envisaging. But there were many different ways in which later Romans saw, or imagined, their early rulers. On the one hand, after the dramatic fall of Tarquinius Superbus, kings were an object of hatred for the rest of Roman history. To be accused of wanting to be *rex* was a political death sentence for any Roman; and no Roman emperor would ever countenance being called a king, even though some cynical observers wondered what the difference was. On the other hand, Roman writers traced many of their most significant political and religious institutions back to the regal period: if, in the legendary narrative, the city was conceived under Romulus, its gestation came under the kings, from Numa to the second Tarquin. Abominated as they were, kings were credited with creating Rome.

This regal period is caught in that intriguing territory that straddles the boundary dividing myth from history. These successor kings certainly appear more real than the founder. If nothing else, they have apparently real names, such as 'Numa Pompilius', unlike the fictional 'Romulus', or 'Mr Rome'. Yet throughout their stories we meet all kinds of flagrantly mythical elements. Some said that Servius Tullius, just like Romulus, was conceived from a phallus that emerged from a fire. It is almost always hard to identify what facts might be lurking in the fictional narrative that has come down to us. Merely to strip away the obviously fantastical elements and to assume that what is left represents an historical core is exactly the kind of simplistic approach that the nineteenth-century sceptics rightly resisted. Myth and history prove much more inextricably bound together than that. A full spectrum of possibilities and unknowables exists between the two extremes. Did someone called Ancus Marcius once exist but not do any of the things attributed to him? Were those things the work of some person or persons other than Ancus but of unknown name? And so on.

It is clear, however, that towards the end of the regal period – let's say the sixth century BCE, though precision dating remains as hard as ever – we begin to reach slightly firmer ground. As Boni's dramatic discoveries hint, it then becomes plausible, for the first time, to make some links between the stories the Romans told about their past, the archaeological traces in the ground and a historical narrative, in our sense of the term. What is more, we even get a glimpse of some of this history from the point of view of Rome's neighbours and enemies. Exploits of Servius Tullius almost certainly feature in a series of paintings discovered in a tomb in the Etruscan city of Vulci, 70 miles to the north of Rome. Dating from around the mid fourth century BCE, they are by several hundred years the earliest direct evidence for him that we have anywhere. Understanding the history of Rome at this period partly depends on exploiting for all they are worth the few such precious pieces of evidence we have; and we shall shortly be taking a closer look at this one.

Kings or chiefs?

The nineteenth-century sceptics had good reason to doubt the surviving Roman accounts of the regal period. There are all kinds of things about the kings that do not quite add up, most obviously their chronology. Even if we imagine unusually healthy lifespans, it is impossible to make seven kings, Romulus included, spread over the 250 years – from the mid eighth century to the late sixth century BCE – that Roman writers assigned to them. That would mean each of them reigned, on average, for more than three decades. No modern monarchy has ever equalled that consistent level of longevity.

The most economical solution to this problem is either to assume that the regal period was really much shorter than the Romans calculated or to propose that there were more kings than have come down in the record (there are, as we shall discover, a couple of potential candidates for these 'lost monarchs'). But it is also possible that the written tradition we have for this period is more fundamentally misleading than these simple solutions suggest and that, whatever the chronology, the character of Roman kingship was in reality radically different from what Livy and other Roman writers imply.

The biggest problem is that Rome's ancient historians tended systematically to modernise the regal period and to aggrandise its achievements, as if seeing them through some patriotic magnifying glass. According to their accounts, the early Romans already relied on such institutions as the senate and assemblies of the people, which were part of the political institutional furniture of the city half a millennium later; and in arranging the kingly succession (which was not hereditary) they followed complex legal procedures that involved the appointment of an *interrex* (a 'between king'), a popular vote for the new monarch and senatorial ratification. What is more, the power struggles and rivalries they imagine at those moments of transition would not have looked out of place in the court of the Roman emperor in the first century CE. In fact, Livy's account of the wheeling and dealing after the murder of Tarquinius Priscus – in which his scheming wife Tanaquil carefully concealed the death until she had firmly secured the throne for her favourite, Servius Tullius – is similar to the wheeling and dealing by Livia after the death of the emperor Augustus in 14 CE (p. 381). It is so similar that some critics have suspected that Livy, who was writing from the 20s BCE, could not possibly have completed this section of his *History* until after 14 CE and must have based his description on the events of that year.

Roman relations with neighbouring peoples are described on a similarly grand scale, complete with treaties, ambassadors and formal declarations of war. Their fighting too is presented as if it involved large-scale clashes between mighty Roman legions and equally mighty enemies: we read of the cavalry charging the opposing flanks, of the infantry being forced to yield, of the opposition driven to confusion ... and various other clichés (or truths) of ancient battle. Indeed, this kind of language seeps into modern accounts of the period, many of which also confidently refer to such things as the 'foreign policy' of Rome in the seventh and sixth centuries BCE.

At this point a reality check is required. However else we may choose to describe the urban community of the early Romans, it remains somewhere on the spectrum between tiny and small. Population size in what is effectively prehistory is notoriously difficult to estimate, but the best guess is that the 'original' population of Rome – at whatever moment it was when the aggregate of little settlements started thinking of itself as 'Rome' – amounted to at most a few thousand. By the time the last king was thrown out, towards the end of the sixth century BCE, according to standard modern calculations, we are probably dealing with something in the region of 20,000 to 30,000 inhabitants. This is only a best guess based on the size of the place, the amount of territory that Rome probably controlled at that point and what population we could reasonably expect it to support. But it is much more likely than the exaggerated totals that ancient authors give. Livy, for example, quotes the very first Roman historian, Quintus Fabius Pictor, who wrote around 200 BCE and claimed that towards the end of the regal period the number of adult male citizens was 80,000, making a total population of well over 200,000. This is a ludicrous figure for a new community in archaic Italy (it is not far short of the total population of the territories of Athens or Sparta at their height, in the mid fifth century BCE), and there is no archaeological evidence for a city of any such size at this time, although the number does at least have the virtue of matching the aggrandising views of early Rome found in all ancient writers.

It is, needless to say, impossible to know anything much about the institutions of this small, proto-urban settlement. But unless Rome was different from every other archaic township in the ancient Mediterranean (or early townships anywhere), it would have

16. This late sixth- or early fifth-century inscription discovered in 1977 about 40 miles south of Rome is one of the best pieces of evidence for private militia in the early city. It is a dedication to the god Mars (here, in the Latin of the time, the last word, 'MAMARTEI') by the 'SUODALES' of Publius Valerius (here, 'POPLIOSIO VALESIOSIO', on the first line) perhaps the same man as one of the semi-legendary consuls in the first year of the Republic (p. 129), Publius Valerius Publicola. His SUODALES (*sodales* in classical Latin) may be, politely, his 'companions'; more realistically, they may be his 'gang'.

been much less formally structured than the stories suggest. Complex procedures involving an *interrex*, popular voting and senatorial ratification are entirely implausible in this context; at best, they are a radical rewriting of early history in a much later idiom. Military activity is another good case in point. Here geography alone should give us pause. We need simply look at the location of these heroic battles: they were all fought within a radius of about 12 miles of the city of Rome. Despite the style in which they are recounted, as if they were mini-versions of Rome against Hannibal, they were probably something closer, in our terms, to cattle raids. They may not even have been 'Roman' engagements in the strict sense of the word at all. In most early communities, it took a long time before the various forms of private violence, from rough justice and vendetta to guerrilla warfare, came fully under public control. Conflict of all sorts was regularly in the hands of individuals with their own following, the ancient equivalents of what we might call private warlords; and there was a blurry distinction between what was conducted on behalf of the 'state' and what on behalf of some powerful leader. Almost certainly that was the case in early Rome.

So where does that leave the kings and the word *rex* on the inscription from the Forum? *Rex* can certainly mean 'king' in the modern sense – a sense we broadly share with the Romans of the first century BCE. They, like us, would have had in mind not just an image of autocratic power and its symbols but also a theoretical concept of monarchy as a form of government, to be contrasted with, for example, democracy or oligarchy. It is extremely unlikely that anything of this sort was in the minds of the men who centuries earlier carved the stone in the Forum. For them, *rex* would have signalled individual power and prominence, but in a much less structured, 'constitutional' way. When we are discussing the realities, rather than the myths, of this early period of Rome's history, it might be better to think in terms of chiefs or big men instead of kings, and to think of the 'chiefly' rather than the 'regal' period.

Foundation stories: religion, time and politics

For Roman writers, the kings who followed Romulus were part of the extended foundation process of the city of Rome. Like him, these rulers were assumed to be historical characters (even if more sceptical writers doubted some of the taller stories told about them); but again, it is clear that much of the tradition that has come down to us, far from reality, is a fascinating mythical projection of later Roman priorities and anxieties into the distant past. It is not hard to spot many of the same themes and concerns that we found in the story of Romulus. These successor kings, for example, were said to come from all kinds of different backgrounds: Numa, like Titus Tatius, was a Sabine; Tarquinius Priscus came from Etruria and was the son of a refugee from the Greek city of Corinth; Servius Tullius was, according to those who rejected the story of the miraculous phallus, the son of a slave or at least of a prisoner of war (such was the dispute over his parentage that of all the triumphing generals listed on the roster in the Forum, Servius is the only one whose father's name is omitted). Although we read of occasional Romans, usually the 'bad' ones in these stories, complaining that foreigners or the low-born are taking away their birthright, the overall message is unmistakeable: even at the very pinnacle of the Roman political order, 'Romans' could come from elsewhere; and those born low, even ex-slaves, could rise to the top.

Rome under the kings also continued to be torn apart by bitter civil war and family conflicts. Moments of succession proved particularly dangerous, and bloody. Of the seven kings, it was alleged that three were murdered; a divine lightning bolt struck another as punishment for a religious error; and Tarquinius Superbus was expelled. Only two died in their beds. It was the sons of Ancus Marcius, in resentment at being passed over for the throne, who hired the assassins of Tarquinius Priscus. Servius Tullius was murdered for similar reasons by Superbus, who was in league with his victim's own daughter. In a particularly gruesome twist, the daughter is supposed to have deliberately driven over the dead body with her carriage and brought her father's blood into her house on its wheels. This theme certainly picks up the idea that civil conflict was embedded in Roman politics, but it also points to another fault line in Roman political culture: that is, how power was transmitted from person to person or generation to generation. It is worth noting that more than half a millennium later, the first dynasty of new autocrats, the emperors from Augustus to Nero, had a similar, or even worse, record of brutal death, largely murder, or alleged murder, from within the family.

The regal period, however, did more than simply replay the issues that Romulus raised. To follow the logic of the story, by the end of Romulus' rule, Rome was still only half formed. Each of the successors made his own distinctive contribution, so ensuring that when the monarchy eventually fell, Rome was equipped with most of the characteristic institutions that made it Roman. Numa Pompilius and Servius Tullius were given the credit for the most significant of these. Servius Tullius is supposed to have devised the method of counting and rank-ordering the Roman people known as the census. This lay at the heart of ancient Rome's political process for centuries, enshrining in it a fundamental hierarchical principle: that the rich had by right more power than the poor. But before him, Numa is said to have established, more or less single-handedly, the structure of official Roman religion, and religious institutions that left their mark, and their names, well beyond the limits of this book. In fact, the official title of the Catholic popes even now – *pontifex*, or 'pontiff' – derives or was borrowed from the title of one of the priesthoods supposedly founded by Numa.

Looking back over their city's rise to dominance in the Mediterranean and beyond, later Romans attributed their extraordinary success not merely to military prowess. They had triumphed, they reasoned, because they had the gods on their side: their pious devotion to religion guaranteed their success. And, to reverse the axiom, any failure they encountered could be put down to some fault in their dealings with the gods: perhaps they had ignored bad omens, wrongly conducted a key ritual or run roughshod over religious rules. Their piety became a boast in their dealings with the outside world. At the beginning of the second century BCE, for example, when one Roman official wrote to the Greek town of Teos, on the western coast of modern Turkey, guaranteeing the Teans' political independence (in the short term, at least), he rammed that message home. We can still read his somewhat pompous words, inscribed on a block of marble that was displayed in the town: 'The fact that we Romans have, absolutely and consistently, judged reverence towards the gods as of first importance is proved by the favour we have received from them on this account. In addition, we are quite certain for many other reasons that our high respect for the divine has been evident to everybody.' Religion, in other words, underwrote Roman power.

There are a few glimpses of this in the story of Romulus. As well as dedicating the Temple of Jupiter Stator, he consulted the gods in deciding where exactly to found the new city: it was partly a disagreement about how to interpret the divine signs, observed in the flight of some birds, that led to the fatal quarrel between Romulus and Remus. But it was his successor, the peace-loving Numa, who was given the role of 'the founder of Roman religion'.

This did not make Numa a holy figure along the lines of Moses, the Buddha, Jesus or Muhammad. The traditional religion of Rome was significantly different from religion as we usually understand it now. So much modern religious vocabulary – including the word 'religion', as well as 'pontiff' – is borrowed from Latin that it tends to obscure some of the major differences between ancient Roman religion and our own. In Rome there was no doctrine as such, no holy book and hardly even what we would call a belief system. Romans *knew* the gods existed; they did not *believe in* them in the internalised sense familiar from most modern world religions. Nor was ancient Roman religion particularly concerned with personal salvation or morality. Instead it mainly focused on the performance of rituals that were intended to keep the relationship between Rome and the gods in good order, and so ensure Roman success and prosperity. The sacrifice of animals was a central element in most of these rituals, which otherwise were extraordinarily varied. Some were so outlandish that they undermine better than anything else the modern stereotype of the Romans as stuffy and sedate: at the festival of Lupercalia in February, for example, naked young men ran round the city whipping any women they met (this is the festival that the opening scene of Shakespeare's *Julius Caesar* re-creates). In general, it was a religion of doing, not believing.

In line with this, Numa's foundation had two different but related aspects. On the one hand, he established a series of priesthoods to perform or oversee major rituals, including, among an otherwise overwhelmingly male line-up, the Vestal Virgins, with their duty to

17. The head of a statue of a Vestal Virgin, from the second century CE, recognisable by her distinctive headdress. The Vestals were one of the very few groups of female priests of Roman public religion. They were also one of the very few full-time groups of religious officials, living 'on the job' in a house next to the temple of the goddess Vesta, with its sacred hearth, in the Forum. They were bound to chastity on pain of death.

keep the flame alight on the city's sacred hearth in the Forum. On the other hand, he devised a calendar of twelve months, which provided the framework for the annual roster of festivals, holy days and holidays. A crucial aspect of any organised community is its ability to structure time, and in Rome it was Numa who was given the credit for inventing that structure. What is more, notwithstanding all kinds of later innovations and refinements, the modern Western calendar remains a direct descendant of this early Roman version, as the names we give to our months show: every single one of them is Roman. Among all the things we fancy we have inherited from ancient Rome, from drains to place names, or the offices of the Catholic Church, the calendar is probably the most important and the most often overlooked. It is a surprising link between that early regal period and our world.

Whether or not anyone called Numa Pompilius ever existed is impossible to know; still less whether he did any of the things ascribed to him. Roman scholars discussed his career intensely, accepting some aspects of the tradition about him but firmly rejecting others. He could not possibly, for example, have been the pupil of the Greek philosopher Pythagoras, as one popular and tenacious story went; for, they argued, on any plausible chronology Pythagoras lived more than a century after Numa (or, as we now reckon, in the sixth rather than the seventh century BCE). But no matter how legendary or, at best, shadowy Numa was, one thing seems certain: some form of the calendar ascribed to him is the product of an early period in Rome's history.

In fact, the earliest written version of a Roman calendar that we have – although itself from no earlier than the first century BCE – points strongly in that direction. It is an extraordinary survival, found painted on a wall in the town of Antium (modern Anzio), some 35 miles south of Rome, and offers a vivid, if slightly perplexing, glimpse of how Romans of Cicero's time pictured their year. Nothing in early Rome would have been as complex as this. There are signs of all kinds of developments over the centuries, including some radical changes in the ordering of months and in the starting point of the year – for how else could November and December, meaning literally 'ninth month' and 'tenth month', respectively, have ended up in this calendar, and our own, as the eleventh and twelfth months in the sequence? But there are also hints of an ancient pedigree in this first-century BCE version.

Its system is basically one of twelve lunar months, with an extra month (the distant precursor of our extra day in a leap year) inserted from time to time to keep this calendar in proper alignment with the solar year. The biggest challenge facing primitive calendars everywhere is the fact that the two most obvious, natural systems of timekeeping are incompatible: that is to say, twelve lunar months, from new moon to new

18. The month of April from the earliest surviving Roman calendar, found painted on a wall in Antium, south of Rome. It is a highly coded document, laid out in twenty-nine days from top to bottom. In the left-hand column, a sequence of letters (A–H) designate a regular pattern of market days. In the second column more letter symbols (C, F, N etc.) define the public status of the day concerned (for example, C for *comitialis* indicates that an assembly might be held on that day). The words on the right mark the individual festivals, most being do to with agriculture in some form. The ROBIG(ALIA), for example, was concerned with protecting the growing crops from corn-blight, the VINAL(IA) with the new wine. Although this version dates only to the first century BCE, its basic principles are much older.

moon, add up to just over 354 days; and this cannot be made to match in any convenient way the 365¼ days of the solar year, which is the time it takes for the earth to make one complete circuit of the sun, from spring equinox to spring equinox, for instance. The wholesale insertion of an extra month every few years is just the kind of rough-and-ready method typical of early attempts to solve the problem.

No less revealing is the cycle of religious festivals that are recorded in the calendar. The nucleus of these may well have originated as far back as the regal period. Certainly the focus of many of them, so far as we can reconstruct it, is on the support of the gods for the seasonal concerns of animal husbandry and agriculture: sowing, harvesting, grape picking, storing and so forth – exactly the concerns that one would expect to weigh heavily in a small, archaic Mediterranean community. Whatever these festivals meant in the urban metropolis of the first century BCE, the majority of whose inhabitants would have had little to do with flocks, herds or harvesting, they probably do represent a snapshot of the priorities of the earliest Romans.

A different set of priorities is reflected in the political institutions attributed to Servius Tullius – sometimes now given the inappropriately grand title of 'the Servian Constitution', partly because they were so fundamental to the later working of Roman politics. He is supposed to have been the first to organise a census of the Roman citizens, formally enrolling them in the citizen body and classifying them in different ranks according to their wealth. But more than that, he linked this classification to two further institutions: the Roman army and the organisation of the people for voting and elections. The precise details are almost unfathomably complicated and have been debated since antiquity. Academic careers have been made and lost in the fruitless search for the exact arrangements supposedly put in place by Servius Tullius, and their subsequent history. But the basic outlines are clear enough. The army was to be made up of 193 'centuries', distinguished according to the type of equipment the soldiers used; this equipment was related to the census classification, on the principle of 'the richer you are, the more substantial and expensive equipment you can provide for yourself'. Starting at the top, there were eighty centuries of men from the richest, first class, who fought in a full kit of heavy bronze armour; below these came four more classes, wearing progressively lighter armour down to the fifth class, of thirty centuries, who fought with just slings and stones. In addition, above these there were an extra eighteen centuries of elite cavalry, plus some special groups of engineers and musicians, and at the very bottom of the pecking order a single century of the very poorest, who were entirely exempt from military service.

19. The Roman census. This detail of a late second-century BCE sculpture depicts the registration of citizens. On the left a seated official records the information on the wealth of the man standing in front of him. Though the exact procedure is not entirely clear, the connection with military organisation is indicated by the presence of the soldier on the right.

Servius Tullius is supposed to have used these same structures as the basis of one main voting assembly of the Roman people: the Centuriate Assembly (so called after the centuries), which in Cicero's day came together to elect senior officials, including the consuls, and to vote on laws and on decisions to go to war. Each century had just one block vote; and the consequence (or intention) was to hand to the centuries of the rich an overwhelming, built-in political advantage. If they stuck together, the eighty centuries of the richest, first class plus the eighteen centuries of elite cavalry could outvote all the other classes put together. To put it another way, the individual rich voter had far greater voting power than his poorer fellow citizens. This was because, despite their name – which looks as if it should mean that they comprised 100 (*centum*) men each – the centuries were in fact very different in size. The richest citizens were far fewer in number than the poor, but they were divided among eighty centuries, as against the twenty or thirty for the more populous lower classes, or the single century for the mass of the very poorest. Power was vested in the wealthy, both communally and individually.

In detail, this is not only terribly complicated but also anachronistic. Whereas some of the innovations attributed to Numa might not have been out of place, as we have seen, in early Rome, this is a flagrant projection into the past of much later Roman practices and institutions, complete with Servius Tullius as founding father. The complex system of property valuation entailed in the census is inconceivable in the early city; and the elaborate structures of the centuriate organisation in both army and assembly are totally out of scale with the citizen body of the regal period and with the likely character of its warfare (this isn't how you conduct a raid on the next-door village). Whatever changes in fighting or voting might have been instituted under some 'Servius Tullius', they could not have been anything like what Roman tradition claimed.

Yet by pushing all this back into the formative period of their city,

Roman writers were underlining the importance of some key institutions and key connections in Roman political culture, as they saw
it. In the census, they were highlighting the power of the state over
the individual citizen, as well as that characteristic commitment of
Roman officialdom to documenting, counting and classifying. They
were also pointing to a traditional connection between the political
and military roles of the citizen, to the fact that for many centuries
Roman citizens were also, by definition, Roman soldiers, and to one
of the treasured assumptions of many of the Roman elite: namely, that
wealth brought both political responsibility and political privilege.
Cicero reflects exactly that when he sums up Servius Tullius' political objectives in approving tones: 'He divided the people in this way
to ensure that voting power was under the control not of the rabble
but of the wealthy, and he saw to it that the greatest number did not
have the greatest power – a principle that we should always stand by
in politics.' In fact, this principle came to be vigorously contested in
the politics of Rome.

Etruscan kings?

Servius Tullius was one of the last three kings of Rome, sandwiched
between Tarquinius Priscus and Tarquinius Superbus. Roman scholars believed that they ruled over the city through the sixth century
BCE, until Superbus was finally deposed in (according to most accounts) 509 BCE. As we have just seen, parts of the narrative of this
period were no less mythologised than the story of Romulus. And
there are some chronological impossibilities – or, at least, the usual
implausible longevities – in the traditional tale. Even some ancient
writers were uncomfortable with the idea that there appeared to be
roughly 150 years between the birth of Priscus and the death of his
son Superbus, a problem they sometimes tried to solve by suggesting

that the second Tarquin was the grandson, not the son, of the first. Yet from this date on, it does become easier to align some aspects of what we read in Livy and other writers with what has been found in the ground. So, for example, traces of a temple (or temples) that appear to go back to the sixth century BCE have been uncovered in more or less the place where later Roman scholars claimed that Servius Tullius established two major shrines. This is still a long way from being able to say 'We have found the temples of Servius Tullius' (whatever exactly that would mean); but there is at least increasing convergence in the different strands of evidence.

For Romans, however, two things distinguished this group of kings from their predecessors. First was their particularly bloody story: Priscus was murdered by the sons of his predecessor; Servius Tullius was eased on to the throne in a palace coup masterminded by Tanaquil and was eventually murdered by Superbus. Second was their Etruscan connection. For the two Tarquins, this was a case of direct ancestry. Priscus is supposed to have migrated to Rome from the Etruscan town of Tarquinii, along with his Etruscan wife, Tanaquil, to seek his fortune – because he feared, so the story went, that his foreign blood, from his Greek father, would hold back his career in his home town. For Servius Tullius, it was more a case of being the favoured protégé of the Etruscan Priscus and Tanaquil. Cicero is unusual in insinuating, among all the other versions of this king's origins, that he was Priscus' illegitimate son.

The question that has often puzzled modern historians is how to explain this Etruscan connection. Why are these kings of Rome given an Etruscan pedigree? Was there really a period when Etruscan kings controlled the city?

So far we have focused on Rome's neighbours to the south, those that played a part in the foundation stories of Romulus and Aeneas: the Sabines, for example, or the little town of Alba Longa, founded by Aeneas' son and the place where Romulus and Remus were born. But

just to the north of Rome, stretching up into modern Tuscany, lay the
heartlands of the Etruscans, the richest and most powerful people in
Italy over the period when the first urban community of Rome was

20. Fragments of lifesize terracotta statues from the sixth-century BCE temple
often associated with Servius Tullius, depicting Minerva with her protégé
Hercules (recognisable from the lion skin around his shoulders). The Etruscans
were known for their expertise in terracotta statuary; here the influence of
Greek art is also clear – suggesting Rome's contacts with the wider world.

taking shape. The plural (*Etruscans*) is important. For these people did not form a single state but were a group of independent towns and cities which shared a language and distinctive artistic culture; the extent of their power varied over time, but at its widest, Etruscan settlements and recognisable Etruscan influence could be found as far south in Italy as Pompeii and beyond.

Modern visitors to the archaeological sites of Etruria have often been entranced by the romance of the place. The eerie cemeteries of the Etruscan towns, with their lavishly painted tombs, have captured the imaginations of generations of writers, artists and tourists, from D. H. Lawrence to the sculptor Alberto Giacometti. Indeed, Roman scholars of later periods too – after the Etruscan cities had one by one fallen to Rome – could see Etruria both as an intriguingly exotic subject of study and as the source of some of their own ceremonial,

21. One particular skill of the Etruscans was reading signs sent by the gods in the entrails of sacrificial animals. This bronze liver (second to third century BCE) was a guide to interpreting the organs of the victim. The liver is carefully mapped, with the gods concerned with each part clearly identified, to help make sense of the particular characteristics or blemishes that might be found there.

dress and religious practices. But certainly at the period of Rome's earliest history, these 'Etruscan places', to borrow Lawrence's title, were influential, rich and well connected in a way that far outstripped Rome. They had active trading links across the Mediterranean and beyond, as we can see in archaeological finds of amber, ivory and even an ostrich egg on one site, as well as in all the finely decorated classical Athenian pots that have come from Etruscan tombs – far more of these found in Etruria than in Greece itself. Underpinning this wealth and influence were natural mineral resources. There was so much bronzework in the Etruscan cities that even in 1546 enough was discovered at the site of Tarquinii alone to produce almost 3,000 kilos, once melted down, for decorating the church of St John Lateran in Rome. On a smaller but no less significant scale, recent analysis has shown that a piece of iron ore discovered on the island of Pithecusae (Ischia) in the Bay of Naples originally came from the Etruscan island of Elba; to fall back on a modernisation, it was presumably part of their 'export' trade.

Rome's position at Etruria's back door helped its rise to wealth and prominence. But was there something more sinister about those Etruscan kings? One suspicious view is that the story of the Etruscan connections of the two Tarquins and Servius Tullius covers up an invasion and takeover of Rome by Etruscans, probably on their way south, as they expanded into Campania. That is to say, the patriotic tradition at Rome rewrote this ignominious period of Roman history as if it revolved not around conquest but around the individual migration of Tarquinius Priscus and his subsequent rise to the kingship. The uncomfortable truth was that Rome had become an Etruscan possession.

This is a clever idea, but most unlikely. For a start, although there are clear traces of Etruscan art and other products in Rome and a handful of inscriptions written in the Etruscan language, there is nothing in the archaeological record to suggest a major takeover: close links between the two cultures, yes; conquest, no. But, perhaps more to the point, that model of 'state takeover' is inappropriate for the kind of relations we should be envisaging between these neighbouring communities, or at least it is not the only model. As I have already suggested, this was a world of big men and warlords: powerful individuals who were relatively mobile between the various towns of the region, sometimes in a friendly form of mobility, sometimes presumably not. Alongside them there must have been equally mobile members of their militia bands, traders, travelling craftsmen and migrants of any and every sort. Exactly who the Roman 'Fabius' was, whose name is inscribed on his tomb in the Etruscan town of Caere, it is impossible to know; nor can we be certain about the 'Titus Latinus' at Veii or the hybrid 'Rutilus Hippokrates' at Tarquinii, with his Latin first name and Greek second. But they give a clear indication that these places were relatively open communities.

It is, however, the story of Servius Tullius that provides the most vivid evidence of the warlords, the private militias and the different forms of migration, hostile and otherwise, that must have characterised this early society in Rome and its neighbours. It has almost nothing to do with the story of Servius Tullius, the Roman constitutional reformer and inventor of the census. Instead it seems to offer an Etruscan view – and it comes from the lips of the emperor Claudius, in his speech to the senate in 48 CE when he urged its members to allow leading men from Gaul to become senators. One of the arguments he used in support of his case was that even the early kings were a remarkably 'foreign lot'. When he reached Servius Tullius, things got even more interesting.

Claudius knew a good deal about Etruscan history. Among his many learned researches he had written a twenty-volume study of the Etruscans, in Greek, as well as compiling an Etruscan dictionary. On this occasion he could not resist explaining to the assembled senators, who might have begun to feel they were on the receiving end of a bit of a lecture, that outside Rome there was a different version of the story of Servius Tullius. This was not the story of a man who came to the throne thanks to the favour, or scheming, of his predecessor, Tarquinius Priscus, and Priscus' wife, Tanaquil. For Claudius, Servius Tullius was an armed adventurer:

> If we go along with the Etruscan version, he had once been the faithful follower of Caelius Vivenna and a comrade in his adventures; and later, when he had been driven out by a change of fortune, he left Etruria with all that remained of Caelius' militia and seized the Caelian Hill [in Rome], which then became called after his leader Caelius. When he had changed his own name (for his Etruscan name was Mastarna), he was given the name I have already mentioned [Servius Tullius] and took over the kingdom, to the very great advantage of the state.

The details that Claudius gives raise all kinds of puzzles. One is the name Mastarna. Is that a proper name or the Etruscan equivalent of the Latin *magister*, which in this context would mean something like 'boss'? And who is the Caelius Vivenna who is supposed to have given his name to the Caelian Hill in Rome? He and his brother Aulus Vivenna – usually said to have come from the Etruscan town of Vulci – crop up several times in ancient accounts of early Roman history, though in frustratingly incompatible, and typically mythic, ways: sometimes Caelius is a friend of Romulus'; sometimes this pair of Vivennas are dated to the time of the Tarquins; one late Roman writer imagined Aulus becoming the king of Rome himself (so was he then one of the city's lost rulers?); in Claudius' version it looks as if Caelius never made it to Rome at all. But what is clear here is the overall character of what Claudius is describing: rival militias, more or less itinerant warlords, personal loyalty, shifting identities – as different as you could imagine from the formal constitutional arrangements that most Roman writers attributed to Servius Tullius.

We get a similar impression from the set of paintings which once decorated a large tomb outside Vulci. Now known as the François Tomb (from the name of its nineteenth-century excavator – see plate 7), it must have been the crypt of a rich local family, to judge from its size, with ten subsidiary burial chambers opening off an entrance passage and central hall, and from the substantial quantity of gold found there. But for those interested in early Rome, it is the cycle of paintings in the central hallway – which probably date to the mid fourth century BCE – that make it so special. Prominently featured are scenes drawn from the wars of Greek mythology, largely the Trojan War. Balancing these are scenes of much more local fighting. Each character is carefully named, half of them also identified with the name of their home town, half of them not, presumably indicating that they are men from Vulci, so not needing further identification. They include the brothers Vivenna, Mastarna (the only other certain reference to him that survives) and a Gnaeus Tarquinius 'from Rome'.

No one has managed to work out exactly what is going on in these scenes, but it is not difficult to get the gist. There are five pairs of fighters involved. In four of these pairs, a local, Aulus Vivenna among them, is running his sword through an 'outsider'; the victims include Lares Papathnas from Volsinii and that Tarquinius from Rome. This man must surely be something to do with the kingly Tarquins, even though in the Roman literary tradition the first name of both those kings is Lucius, not Gnaeus. In the final pair, Mastarna is using his sword to cut through the ropes binding the wrists of Caelius Vivenna. One odd feature (and presumably a clue to the story) is that all but one of the victorious local men are naked, their enemies clothed. The most popular explanation is that the paintings depict some famous local escapade in which the Vivenna brothers and their friends were taken prisoner, stripped and bound by their enemies but managed to escape and turned their swords on their captors.

This is by far the earliest direct evidence to survive for any of the characters in the story of early Rome and their exploits. It also comes from outside, or at least the margins of, the mainstream Roman literary tradition. That does not, of course, necessarily make it true; the mythic tradition of Vulci may have been just as mythic as that of Rome. Nevertheless, what we see here gives a much more plausible vision of the warrior world of these early urban communities than do the aggrandising versions offered by Roman writers, and by some of their modern followers. It was a world of chiefdoms and warrior bands, not of organised armies and foreign policy.

Archaeology, tyranny – and rape

By the sixth century BCE, Rome was certainly a small urban community. It is often tricky to decide when a mere agglomeration of huts and houses becomes a town with a sense of itself as a community, with a shared identity and aspirations. But the idea of a structured Roman calendar, and with it a shared religious culture and rhythm of life, most likely goes back into the regal period. Archaeological traces too leave little doubt that by the sixth century BCE Rome had public buildings, temples and a 'town centre', which are clear indications of urban living, even if, in our terms, on a small scale. The chronology of these traces remains controversial: there is not a single piece of evidence on whose dating all archaeologists agree; and new discoveries are always altering the picture (though often not quite so significantly as their discoverers hope!). Nonetheless, it would now take a very determined, and blinkered, sceptic to deny the urban character of Rome at this period.

The remains in question are found in several places under the later city, but the clearest impression of this early town is found in the area of the Forum. By the sixth century BCE, its level had been artificially raised and some drainage work had been carried out, in both cases to protect the area from flooding; and at least one or two successive gravel surfaces had been laid, so that it could function as a shared central space for the community. The inscription with which we started this chapter was found at one end of the Forum, just beneath the slopes of the Capitoline Hill, in what had been an early shrine, with an outdoor altar. Whatever exactly the text means, it was certainly a public notice of some sort, which itself implies the framework of a structured community and recognised authority. At the other end of the Forum, excavations of the earliest levels under a cluster of later religious buildings, including those associated with the Vestal Virgins, have suggested that they go back to the sixth century BCE or even earlier. Not far from there, a few scant remains have been discovered of a series of substantial private houses of roughly the same date. The remains are *very* scant, but they do give a faint glimpse of some well-heeled big men living in style next to the civic centre.

It is hard to know how closely to match these archaeological remains to the literary tradition about the last kings of Rome. It is almost certainly going too far to suggest, as the excavators would like us to believe, that one of those sixth-century BCE houses near the Forum was actually the 'House of the Tarquins', supposing such a thing ever existed. But nor is it likely to be a complete coincidence that the Roman narratives of the last part of the regal period stress the building activities that the kings sponsored. Both of the Tarquins were supposed to have inaugurated the great Temple of Jupiter on the Capitoline Hill (later Roman writers found these two kings easy to confuse); and both were said to have built the Circus Maximus and to have commissioned shops and porticoes round the Forum. Servius Tullius, as well as having several temple foundations to his name, was often credited with surrounding the city with a defensive wall. This would be another key sign of a sense of shared community, although the surviving fortification now known as the Servian Wall is for the most part no earlier than the fourth century BCE.

The Italian phrase coined in the 1930s to describe this period, 'La

Grande Roma dei Tarquini' ('The Great Rome of the Tarquins'), may not be so misleading – though it depends a lot, of course, on exactly what is meant by 'Grande'. Rome was still, in absolute and relative terms, far from 'great'. But it was a larger and more urban community than it had been a hundred years earlier, having profited, no doubt, from its prime position for trading and its proximity to wealthy Etruria. So far as we can judge the town's extent in the middle of the sixth century BCE (part of that judgement inevitably comes down to guesswork), it was now substantially bigger than the Latin settlements to the south and at least as large as the largest Etruscan towns to the north, with a population of perhaps 20,000 to 30,000, although it had nowhere near the grandeur of some contemporary Greek settlements in Sicily and South Italy, and was significantly smaller. That is to say, Rome must have been a major player in the region, but it was not yet in any way extraordinary.

Not all the urban developments that Romans ascribed to the Tarquins were splendid in the obvious sense of the word. It was a characteristically Roman concern for the infrastructure of urban life that made later writers hail their achievements in constructing a drain: the *Cloaca Maxima,* or the 'Great(est) Drain'. Quite how much of what survives of this famous structure goes back to the sixth century BCE is far from clear: the substantial masonry sections that it is still possible to explore, and that still carry part of the overflow from the modern city and the detritus from modern bathrooms, are from several centuries later, and it now seems likely that the earliest attempts at some kind of drainage system go back earlier, to the seventh century BCE. But in the Roman imagination the *Cloaca* was always a wonder of Rome that was owed to its final kings: 'an amazing work and more than words can describe' enthused Dionysius, who presumably had in mind what was visible in his day, in the first century BCE. Yet it also had a darker side: it was not just a wonder but also a reminder of the cruel tyranny that for the Romans marked the end of the regal period. In a particularly lurid, and gloriously fantastical, account, Pliny the Elder (that is, Gaius Plinius Secundus, the extraordinary Roman polymath now best remembered as the one celebrity victim of the eruption of Vesuvius in 79 CE) describes how the people of the city were so exhausted by the construction work on the drain that many killed themselves. The king, in response, nailed the bodies of the suicides to crosses, in the hope that the shame of crucifixion would be a deterrent for others.

22. A surviving section of the underground *Cloaca Maxima*.
The original drain can have been nothing like as grand as this
later construction but this is the image that Roman writers
had when they wrote of Tarquin's building project. Some
Romans boasted of taking boats and rowing along it.

It was, however, not the exploitation of the labouring poor that was supposed finally to have brought the monarchy down, but sexual violence: the rape of Lucretia by one of the king's sons. This rape is almost certainly as mythic as the rape of the Sabines: assaults on women symbolically marking the beginning and the end of the regal period. What is more, the Roman writers who later told the story were probably influenced by Greek traditions, which often linked the culmination, and fall, of tyranny with sexual crimes. In sixth-century BCE Athens, for example, sexual advances by the ruler's younger brother towards another man's partner were said to have led to the overthrow of the Pisistratid dynasty. But mythic or not, for the rest of Roman time the rape of Lucretia marked a turning point in politics, and its morality was debated. The theme has been replayed and reimagined in Western culture almost ever since, from Botticelli, through Titian and Shakespeare, to Benjamin Britten; Lucretia even has her own small part in Judy Chicago's feminist installation *The Dinner Party*, among some 1,000 heroines of world history.

Livy tells a highly coloured tale of these last moments of the monarchy. It starts with a group of young Romans who were trying to find ways of passing the time while besieging the nearby town of Ardea. One evening, they were having a drunken competition about whose wife was best, when one of their number, Lucius Tarquinius Collatinus, suggested that they should simply ride back home (it was only a few miles away) and inspect the women; this would prove, he claimed, the superiority of his own Lucretia. Indeed it did: for while all the other wives were discovered partying in the absence of their menfolk, Lucretia was doing exactly what was expected of a virtuous Roman woman – working at her loom, among her maids. She then dutifully offered supper to her husband and his guests.

There was, however, a terrible sequel. For during that visit, we are told, Sextus Tarquinius conceived a fatal passion for Lucretia, and one evening shortly afterwards he rode back to her house. After being politely entertained again, he came to her room and demanded sex with her, at knifepoint. When the simple threat of death did not move her, Tarquinius exploited instead her fear of dishonour: he threatened to kill both her and a slave (visible in Titian's painting [see plate 4]) so that it would look as if she had been caught in the most disgraceful form of adultery. Faced with this, Lucretia acceded, but when Tarquinius had returned to Ardea, she sent for her husband and father, told them what had happened – and killed herself.

Lucretia's story remained an extraordinarily powerful image in Roman moral culture ever after. For many Romans, it represented a defining moment of female virtue. Lucretia voluntarily paid with her life for losing, as Livy put it, her *pudicitia* – her 'chastity', or better the 'fidelity', on the woman's part at least, that defined the relationship between Roman wife and husband. Yet other ancient writers found the story more difficult. There were poets and satirists who predictably

23. *Pudicitia*, as an important virtue in a woman, was stressed in many contexts. This silver coin of the emperor Hadrian, minted in the 120s CE, shows the personification of *Pudicitia* modestly sitting as a good Roman wife should. Around her, the words 'COS III' celebrate Hadrian holding the consulship for the third time, hinting at a connection between public male prestige and the proper behaviour of women.

questioned whether *pudicitia* was really what a man wanted in a wife. In one bawdy epigram, Marcus Valerius Martialis ('Martial' for short), who wrote a whole series of clever, sparky and rude verses at the end of the first century CE, jokes that his wife can be a Lucretia by day if she wants, so long as she is a whore by night. In another quip, he wonders whether Lucretias are ever quite what they seem; even the famous Lucretia, he fantasises, enjoyed risqué poems when her husband wasn't looking. More serious was the issue of Lucretia's culpability and the reasons for her suicide. To some Romans, it looked as if she was more concerned with her reputation than with real *pudicitia* – which surely resided in the guilt or innocence of her mind, not her body, and would not have been remotely affected by false allegations of sex with a slave. In the early fifth century CE, St Augustine, who was well versed in the pagan classics, wondered if Lucretia had been raped at all: for had she not, in the end, consented? It is not hard to detect here versions of some of our own arguments about rape and the issues of responsibility it raises.

At the same time, this was seen as a fundamentally political moment, for in the story it leads directly to the expulsion of the kings and the start of the free Republic. As soon as Lucretia stabbed herself, Lucius Junius Brutus – who had accompanied her husband to the scene – took the dagger from her body and, while her family was too distressed to speak, vowed to rid Rome of kings for ever. This was, of course, partly a retrospective prophecy, for the Brutus who in 44 BCE led the coup against Julius Caesar for his kingly ambitions claimed descent from this Brutus. After ensuring the support of the army and the people, who were appalled by the rape and fed up with labouring on the drain, Lucius Junius Brutus forced Tarquin and his sons into exile.

The Tarquins did not give up without a fight. According to Livy's implausibly action-packed account, Tarquinius Superbus made an abortive attempt to stage a counter-revolution in the city and, when that failed, joined forces with King Lars Porsenna of the Etruscan town of Clusium, who mounted a siege of Rome with the aim of restoring the monarchy – only to be defeated by the heroism of its newly liberated inhabitants. We read, for example, of the valiant Horatius Cocles, who single-handedly defended the bridge across the Tiber to block the advance of the Etruscan army (some said he lost his life in the process, others that he returned home to a hero's welcome); and

24. The three surviving columns, from a later rebuilding of the Temple of Castor and Pollux, still make their mark in the Roman Forum. The rest of the temple is largely destroyed but the sloping base of its steps, often used as a place for speakers to address the people, is still visible (bottom left). The little door is a reminder that the basements of temples were used for all sorts of different purposes. Excavations have shown that there was once a barber's shop/dentist in the basement of this one.

of the bravery of Cloelia, one of a group of young hostages taken by Porsenna, who daringly made her way back home by swimming across the river. Livy suggests that the Etruscans were eventually so impressed by the character of the Romans that they simply abandoned Tarquin. There were, however, less patriotic versions. Pliny the Elder was not the only ancient scholar to believe that Lars Porsenna became the king of Rome for a while; if so, he might have been another of those lost kings, and there might have been a very different end to the monarchy.

Deserted by Porsenna, as the standard story runs, Tarquin looked elsewhere for support. He was finally defeated in the 490s BCE (exact dates differ) together with some allies he had made in the nearby Latin towns, at the Battle of Lake Regillus, not far from Rome. It was a triumphant, and certainly partly mythic, moment in Roman history, for the gods Castor and Pollux were supposed to have been seen fighting on the Roman side and later watering their horses in the Roman Forum; a temple to them was erected there in gratitude for their help. Though many times rebuilt, this temple is still one of the landmarks of the Forum, a lasting Roman monument to getting rid of kings.

The birth of liberty

The end of the monarchy was also the birth of liberty and of the free Roman Republic. For the rest of Roman history, 'king', or *rex*, was a term of loathing in Roman politics, despite the fact that so many of Rome's defining institutions were supposed to have their origins in the regal period. There were any number of cases in the centuries that followed when the accusation that he was aiming at kingship brought a swift end to a man's political career. His royal name even proved disastrous for Lucretia's unfortunate widower, who, because he was a relation of the Tarquins, was shortly sent into exile. In foreign conflicts too, kings were the most desirable of enemies. Over the next few hundred years, there was always a particular frisson when a triumphal procession through the streets of the city paraded some enemy king in all his regal finery for the Roman populace to jeer and pelt. Needless to say, plenty of satire was also directed at those later Romans who happened to be landed with the surname (cognomen) 'King'.

The fall of the Tarquins – sometime, as the Romans had it, at the end of the sixth century BCE – amounted to a new start for Rome: the city began again, now as 'the Republic' (or in Latin *res publica*, meaning literally 'public thing' or 'public affairs') and with a whole series of new foundation myths. One powerful tradition, for example, insisted that the great Temple of Jupiter on the Capitoline Hill, a building that came to be a major symbol of Roman power and was later replicated in many Roman cities abroad, was dedicated in the very first year of the new regime. True, it had been vowed and, so it was often said, largely built under the kings, by Etruscan craftsmen; but the name of the formal dedicator blazoned across its façade was that of one of the leaders of the new Republic. And whatever the exact chronology of its construction, which is, to be honest, irrecoverable, it came to be seen as a building that shared its birth with the Republic and was a symbol of Republican history itself. Indeed, for centuries there was a Roman custom of each year hammering a nail into the temple's doorpost, not only marking the passing of Republican time but also physically linking that time to the temple's structure.

Even apparently natural features of Rome's cityscape were thought to have their origin in the Republic's first year. Many Romans knew, as well as modern geologists do, that the island in the middle of the river Tiber where it flows through Rome was in geological terms a relatively recent formation. But how, and when, did it emerge? Even now there is no definitive answer to that; but one Roman idea dated its origin to the very beginning of Republican rule, when the grain that had been growing on the private land of the Tarquins was thrown into the river. Because the water level was low, this piled up on the riverbed and gradually, as it collected silt and other refuse, formed an island. It is as if the shape of the city was born only with the removal of the monarchy.

Also born was a new form of government. As Tarquinius Superbus fled, the story goes, Brutus and, before his imminent exile, Lucretia's husband, Collatinus, straight away became the first consuls of Rome. These were to be the most important, defining officials of the new Republic. Taking over many of the duties of the kings, they presided over the city's politics at home and they led its soldiers in war; there was never any formal separation in Rome between such military and civilian roles. In that sense, despite being paraded as the antithesis of the kings, they represented the continuation of their power: one Greek theorist of Roman politics in the second century BCE saw the consuls as a 'monarchical' element in the Roman political system, and Livy insists that their insignia and badges of office were much the same as those of their kingly predecessors. But they embodied several key, and decidedly unmonarchical, principles of the new political regime. First, they were elected entirely by popular vote, not the half-and-half system of popular involvement that supposedly characterised the choice of king. Second, they held office for only a single year at a time, and one of their duties was to preside (as we saw Cicero doing in 63 BCE) over the election of their successors. Third, they held office together, as a pair. Two central tenets of Republican government were that office holding should always be temporary and that, except in emergencies when one man might need to take control for a short while, power should always be shared. As we shall see, through the centuries that followed these tenets were increasingly reiterated, and became increasingly difficult to uphold.

The consuls also gave their names to the year in which they held office. It goes without saying that the Romans could not have used the modern Western system of dating that I have been adopting in this book – and for the sake of clarity, readers will be relieved, will continue to use. 'The sixth century BCE' would have meant nothing to them. Occasionally they calculated dates 'from the foundation of the city', when they had reached some kind of agreement about when that was. But usually they referred to years by the names of the consuls in office. What we call, for example, 63 BCE was for them 'the consulship of Marcus Tullius Cicero and Gaius Antonius Hybrida'; and wine made 'when Opimius was consul' (121 BCE) was a particularly famous vintage. By Cicero's day, Romans had worked out a more or less complete list of consuls going back to the beginning of the Republic, and it was soon put on public display in the Forum along with the list of triumphing generals. It was largely this roster that enabled them to pinpoint the precise date of the end of the monarchy, as by definition it had to correlate with the date of the first consul.

The Republic, in other words, was not just a political system. It was a complex set of interrelationships between politics, time, geography and the Roman cityscape. Dates were directly correlated with the elected consuls; years were marked by the nails hammered into the temple whose dedication was traced back to the first year of the new regime; even the island in the Tiber was a product, quite literally, of the expulsion of the kings. Underpinning the whole thing was one single, overriding principle: namely, freedom, or *libertas*.

Fifth-century BCE Athens bequeathed the idea of democracy to the modern world, after the Athenian 'tyrants' were deposed and democratic institutions established at the end of the sixth century BCE – a chronological match with the expulsion of the Roman kings that was not lost on ancient observers, who were keen to present the history of the two places as if they ran in parallel. Republican Rome bequeathed the equally important idea of liberty. The first word of the second book of Livy's *History*, which begins the story of Rome after the monarchy, is 'free'; and the words 'free' and 'freedom' are together repeated eight times in the first few lines alone. The idea that the Republic was founded on *libertas* rings loudly throughout Roman literature, and it has echoed through radical movements in later centuries, in Europe and America. It is no coincidence that the slogan of the French Revolution – *Liberté, égalité, fraternité* – puts 'liberty' in pride of place; nor that George Washington spoke of restoring 'the sacred fire of liberty' to the West; nor that the drafters of the United States Constitution defended it under the pseudonym of 'Publius', taken from the name of Publius Valerius Publicola, another of the earliest consuls of the Republic. But how was Roman liberty to be defined?

That was a controversial question in Roman political culture for the next 800 years, through the Republic and into the one-man rule of the Roman Empire, when political debate often turned on how far *libertas* could ever be compatible with autocracy. Whose liberty was at stake? How was it most effectively defended? How could conflicting versions of the freedom of the Roman citizen be resolved? All, or most, Romans would have counted themselves as upholders of *libertas*, just as today most of us uphold 'democracy'. But there were repeated and intense conflicts over what that meant. We have already seen that, when Cicero was sent into exile, his house was demolished and a shrine of Libertas erected on its site. Not everyone would have approved. Cicero himself tells how during the performance of a play on the theme of Brutus, the first consul of the Republic, the crowd burst into applause at a line spoken by one of the characters: 'Tullius, who underpinned the citizens' liberty'. The play was actually referring to Servius Tullius and suggesting that liberty might have had a prehistory at Rome before the Republic, under a 'good king', but Marcus Tullius Cicero, to give him his full name, was convinced – maybe rightly – that the applause was for him.

Conflicts of this kind form one important theme in the chapters that follow. But before we explore the history of Rome in the first centuries of the Republic – the warfare at home, the victories for 'liberty' and the military victories over Rome's neighbours in Italy – we must look a little harder at the story of the birth of the Republic and the invention of the consulship. Predictably perhaps, it was not quite as smooth a process as the standard story, which I have given so far, makes it appear.

CHAPTER FOUR

·

ROME'S GREAT LEAP
FORWARD

*Two centuries of change: from the Tarquins to
Scipio Long-Beard*

How did the Republic really begin? Ancient Roman historians
were experts at turning historical chaos into a tidy narrative and
always keen to imagine that their familiar institutions went back much
further than they really did. For them the transition from monarchy to
Republic was as smooth as any revolution could be: the Tarquins fled;
the new form of government emerged fully formed; the consulship
was instantly established, providing the new order with its chronology from year one. In reality, the whole process must have been more
gradual than that story suggests, and messier. The 'Republic' was born
slowly, over a period of decades, if not centuries. It was reinvented
many times over.

Even the consuls did not go back to the beginning of the new
regime. Livy hints that the highest official in the state, and the one
whose job it was to bang the nail into the Temple of Jupiter each year,
was originally called the chief praetor, although the word 'praetor' was
later used for a junior official below the consuls. There are other early
titles recorded for those at the top of the political hierarchy, which only
complicate the picture. These include 'dictator', usually described as a
temporary position to cope with a military emergency, and without

the decidedly negative modern connotations of the word; and 'military tribunes with consular power', a mouthful aptly translated by one modern historian as 'colonels'.

There is still a big question mark over when exactly the defining office of the Republic was invented, or when and why some other office was renamed 'consul', or even when the fundamental Republican principle that power should always be shared was first defined. 'Chief praetor' smacks of hierarchy, not equality. But whatever the key date or dates, the list of consuls on which the chronology of the Republic was based – going back in an unbroken series to Lucius Junius Brutus and Lucius Tarquinius Collatinus in 509 BCE – was in its earliest parts the product of a good deal of adjustment, imaginative inference, clever guesswork and most likely outright invention. Livy conceded, looking back from the end of the first century BCE, that it was next to impossible to sort out with confidence the chronology of officeholders in this early period. It was, he wrote, simply too long ago.

There is also a question mark over how violent the fall of the monarchy was. The Romans envisaged a fairly bloodless regime change. Lucretia was the most prominent, tragic casualty, but, though warfare was to follow, Tarquin was allowed to escape unscathed. The archaeological evidence suggests that the process of change within the city was not quite so peaceful. At least, layers of burnt debris have been excavated in the Forum and elsewhere that are plausibly dated to around 500 BCE. They could be no more than the traces of an unfortunate series of accidental fires. They are enough to hint, however, that the overthrow of Tarquin might have been a bloody, rather than bloodless, coup, and that most of the internal violence was patriotically written out of the standard narrative.

The earliest known use of the word 'consul', in fact, dates from two hundred years later. It turns up in the first surviving example of those thousands upon thousands of loquacious Roman epitaphs carefully carved on tombs all over the empire, both extravagant and humble, which tell us so much about the lives of the deceased: the offices they held, the jobs they did, their aims, aspirations and anxieties. This one commemorates a man called Lucius Cornelius Scipio Barbatus (the last name means 'bearded', 'long-beard' or perhaps 'beardy') and was displayed on the front of his oversized sarcophagus, which once lay in the family tomb of the Scipios just outside Rome, as burials were not usually allowed within the city itself. Barbatus was consul in 298 BCE, died around 280 BCE and almost certainly founded this ostentatious mausoleum, an unashamed promotion of the power and prestige of his family, one of the most prominent in the Republic. His seems to have been the first of more than thirty burials in it, and his coffin-cum-memorial was placed in the most prominent position, opposite the door.

The epitaph was composed soon after his death. It is four lines long and must count as the earliest historical and biographical narrative to

25. The imposing sarcophagus of Barbatus dominated the large Tomb of the Scipios. The rough local stone (or tufa), and its simple, slightly rustic look, makes a strong contrast with the elaborately sculpted marble sarcophagi of the rich in later Roman centuries. Yet in the third century BCE this was the best and most sophisticated that money could buy.

survive from ancient Rome. Short as it is, it is one of the major turning points in our understanding of Roman history. For it provides hard, more or less contemporary information on Barbatus' career – quite different from the imaginative reconstructions, faint hints buried in the soil or modern deductions about 'what must have been' that surround the fall of the monarchy. It is eloquent on the ideology and world view of the Roman elite at this period: 'Cornelius Lucius Scipio Barbatus, offspring of his father Gnaeus, a brave man and wise, whose appearance was a match for his *virtus*. He was consul and censor and aedile among you. He took Taurasia and Cisauna from Samnium. He subdued the whole of Lucania and took hostages.'

Whoever wrote it – presumably one of his heirs – extracted what seemed to be the highlights of Barbatus' career. At home ('among you') he had been elected consul and censor, one of the two officials responsible for enrolling citizens and assessing their wealth; and he had held the more junior office of aedile, which by the first century BCE, and probably earlier, was largely concerned with the upkeep and supply of the city and with organising public shows and games. Further afield, the boasts were of his military successes in southern Italy, a couple of hundred miles from Rome: he had captured two towns from the Samnites, a people with whom the Romans were repeatedly in conflict during Barbatus' lifetime; and he had subdued the region of Lucania, taking hostages from the enemy, a standard Roman method of guaranteeing 'good behaviour'.

These exploits underline the importance of warfare in the public image of leading Romans, but they also point to the military expansion of Rome at the beginning of the third century BCE, now extending a long way from the city's back door. In a battle in 295 BCE in which Barbatus served three years after he was consul, Roman forces defeated an Italian army at Sentinum, not far from modern Ancona. This was the biggest and bloodiest battle fought in the peninsula up to that date and was so far from being of merely local concern that the news travelled widely and quickly, even by the rudimentary methods of ancient communication (messengers, word of mouth and on rare occasions a system of beacons). Sitting in his study on the Greek island of Samos, hundreds of miles away, the third-century BCE historian Duris decided that it was an event worth recording; a brief snatch of his account still survives.

Just as revealing are the other characteristics that the epitaph singles out for praise: Barbatus' bravery and wisdom and the fact that his outward appearance was equal to his *virtus*. That may mean 'virtue' in the modern sense, but it was often used more literally, to refer to the collection of qualities that defined a man (*vir*), virtue in Roman terms being the equivalent of 'manliness'. Either way, Barbatus was a man who displayed his qualities on his face. Although the popular image of the Roman man is hardly of someone much bothered with his appearance, in this open, competitive, 'face to face' society, the public figure was expected to look the part. As he walked through the Forum or stood up to address the people, his inner qualities were clearly revealed in how he looked. In Barbatus' case, unless he had simply inherited the name from his father, he sported a splendid beard, which may have been increasingly unusual at the time. One story has it that barbers first started to work in Rome in 300 BCE, and that for several centuries after that most Romans went clean-shaven.

Barbatus' Rome was very different from the Rome of the earliest Republic, two hundred years before, and it had ceased to be ordinary. Vast by the standards of the time, the city was home on a reasonable guess to something between 60,000 and 90,000 people. That put it roughly in the same bracket as a handful of the biggest urban centres in the Mediterranean world; Athens at this point had a population of considerably less than half that number, and never in its history had more than 40,000 in the city itself. What is more, Rome controlled directly a large swathe of land stretching from coast to coast, with a total population of well over half a million, and indirectly, by a series of agreements and alliances, much more – foreshadowing its later empire. It was a place whose organisation Cicero and his contemporaries, more than two centuries away, would have recognised. As well as the two annual consuls, there was a series of junior positions, including praetors and quaestors, beneath them (Romans usually called these officials 'magistrates', but their function was not principally legal). The senate, made up largely of those who had previously held public office, operated as a permanent council, and the hierarchical organisation of the citizens and the Centuriate Assembly, falsely attributed to King Servius Tullius and warmly approved by Cicero, underpinned the working of Roman politics.

There were other familiar aspects. These included an army organised in legions, the beginnings of an official system of coinage and signs of an infrastructure to match the city's size and influence. The first aqueduct to bring water into the growing conurbation was constructed in 312 BCE, a watercourse that ran mostly underground for some 10 miles from the nearby hills, not one of those extraordinary aerial constructions that we often now mean by 'aqueduct'. This was the brainchild of a contemporary of Barbatus, the energetic Appius Claudius Caecus, who in the same year also launched the first major Roman road, the Via Appia (the Appian Way, named after him), leading straight south from Rome to Capua. For most of its length its surface was, at best, gravel, not the impressive paving slabs we can still tread. But it was a useful route for Roman armies, a convenient means of more peaceful communication and in symbolic terms a stamp of Roman power and control over the Italian landscape. It was no coincidence that for his great family tomb Barbatus chose a prime position right beside it, at the city limits, for travellers going into and out of Rome to admire.

It was at some point during this crucial period between 500 BCE and 300 BCE, between the end of the Tarquins and the lifetime of Scipio 'Long-Beard', that many of Rome's characteristic institutions took shape. Romans not only defined the basic principles of Republican politics and liberties but also began to develop the structures, the assumptions and (to put it no more grandly) a 'way of doing things' that underpinned their later imperial expansion. This involved a revolutionary formulation of what it was to be Roman, which defined their ideas of citizenship for centuries, set Rome apart from every other classical city-state and eventually informed many modern views of the rights and responsibilities of the citizen. It was not for nothing that both Lord Palmerston and John F. Kennedy proudly broadcast the Latin phrase *Civis Romanus sum* ('I am a Roman citizen') as a slogan for their times. In short, Rome for the first time began to look 'Roman' as we understand it, and as they understood it. The big question is, how did that happen, when and why? And what evidence survives to help explain, or even describe, Rome's 'great leap forward'? The chronology remains murky, and it is absolutely impossible to reconstruct a reliable historical narrative. But it is possible to glimpse some fundamental changes both at home and in Rome's relations with the outside world.

Later Roman writers presented a clear and dramatic story of the fifth and fourth centuries BCE. On the one hand, they told of a series of violent social conflicts within Rome itself: between a hereditary group of 'patrician' families, who monopolised all political and religious power in the city, and the mass of the citizens, or 'plebeians', who were completely excluded. Gradually – in a vivid tale that involves strikes, mutinies and yet another (attempted) rape – the plebeians won the right or, as they would have put it, the *freedom* to share power on more or less equal terms with the patricians. On the other hand, they stressed a series of major victories in battle that brought most of the Italian peninsula under Roman control. These started in 396 BCE, when Rome's great local rival, the Etruscan town of Veii, fell after decades of warfare, and ended roughly a hundred years later, when victory against the Samnites made Rome by far the biggest power base in Italy, and caught the attention of Duris on Samos. Not that this was a story of unchallenged expansion. Soon after the defeat of Veii, in 390 BCE a posse of marauding 'Gauls' sacked Rome. Exactly who these people were is now impossible to know; Roman writers were not good at distinguishing between those whom it was convenient to lump together as 'barbarian tribes' from the north, nor much interested in analysing their motives. But according to Livy, the effects were so devastating that the city had to be refounded (yet again), under the leadership of Marcus Furius Camillus – war leader, dictator, 'colonel', sometime exile and another 'second Romulus'.

This narrative is based on firmer foundations than anything before. Admittedly, even in 300 BCE the earliest Roman literature was still decades away, and the later accounts looking back to this period contain plenty of myth, embellishment and fantasy. Camillus is probably not much less fictional than the first Romulus, and we have already seen how the words of Catiline were used to ventriloquise the speeches of an early Republican revolutionary, none of whose words could possibly have survived. Yet the end of this period stands on the brink of history and history writing as we know it, far beyond a simple four-line epitaph. That is to say, when the well-connected senator Fabius Pictor, who was born around 270 BCE, sat down to compose the first extended written account of Rome's past, he might well have remembered talking in his youth to people who had been eyewitnesses to events at the end of the fourth century BCE or who had talked to men of Barbatus' generation who were. Pictor's *History* does not survive beyond a few quotations in later writers, but it was famed in the ancient world. His name and a brief synopsis of his work have even been found painted on the walls of one of the few ancient libraries ever unearthed, in Taormina in Sicily, a combination of advertisement and library catalogue. Two thousand years later, we can read Livy, who had read Pictor, who had talked to people who remembered the world as it was around 300 BCE – a fragile chain of connection deep into antiquity.

Increasingly too, fragments of contemporary evidence survive, to set against the later Roman historical account or point to an alternative narrative. The career summary in Barbatus' epitaph is one of these. When Livy covers those years in his *History*, he writes of the Romans entering an alliance with, rather than subduing, Lucania, and he describes Barbatus fighting somewhere quite different, in northern Italy, and not very successfully at that. True, Barbatus' epitaph is likely to have magnified his achievements, and 'subdued' may have been how the Roman elite preferred to present an 'alliance'; but the inscription probably does help to correct Livy's later, slightly garbled, account. There are a number of other such fragments, including some striking paintings of about the same time, which depict scenes from the wars in which Barbatus fought. Among the most remarkable and revealing of all, however, are the eighty or so short clauses from the first written collection of Roman rules and regulations (or 'laws', to use the rather grand term that most ancient writers adopted), put together in the mid fifth century BCE and laboriously reassembled thanks to centuries of modern scholarly detective work. The collection is known as the Twelve Tables, from the twelve bronze tablets on which it was originally inscribed and displayed. It offers a window onto some of the concerns of those earliest Republican Romans, from worries about magic or assault to such tricky questions as whether it was allowed to bury a corpse with its gold teeth in place – an incidental insight into the skill of ancient dentistry that archaeology confirms.

So it is to the world of the Twelve Tables that we first turn, before going on to explore the radical changes, both internal and external, that followed. Reconstructing the history of this period is an intriguing and sometimes tantalising process, and part of the fun comes from wondering how some of the pieces of the incomplete jigsaw puzzle fit together and how to tell the difference between the fact and the fantasy. But there are enough pieces in place to be confident that the decisive change in Rome came in the fourth century BCE, in the generation of Barbatus and Appius Claudius Caecus and that of their immediate predecessors, and that what happened then, hard as it is to pin down in detail, established a pattern of Roman politics, at home and abroad, which lasted for centuries.

The world of the Twelve Tables

The Republican regime started with a whimper rather than a bang. There are all kinds of stirring tales told by Roman historians of the new political order, of warfare on a grand scale over the first few decades of the fifth century BCE and of larger than life heroes and villains, who have become the stuff of modern legend too. Lucius Quinctius Cincinnatus, for example, who more than two millennia later gave his name to the American city of Cincinnati, is supposed to have returned from semi-exile in the 450s BCE to become dictator and lead Roman armies to victory against their enemies before nobly retiring straight back to his farm without seeking further political glory. Gaius Marcius Coriolanus, by contrast, who inspired Shakespeare's *Coriolanus*, was

26. The farmer who saved the state. This twentieth-century statue from modern Cincinnati shows Cincinnatus returning the symbols of political office and going back to his plough. Many Roman stories presented him in this way as a no-nonsense patriot but there was another side to Cincinnatus, as a die-hard opponent of the rights of the plebeians and of the poor in the city.

reputedly a war hero turned traitor around 490 BCE, who joined
forces with a different enemy and would have invaded his home town
had not his mother and wife intervened to dissuade him. But the reality was quite different, and of much more modest dimensions.

Whatever the political organisation of the city when the Tarquins
were removed, archaeology makes it clear that for most of the fifth
century BCE, Rome was not thriving at all. A sixth-century BCE temple
that is sometimes linked to the name of Servius Tullius was one of
those buildings burned down in the fires around 500 BCE, and it was
not rebuilt for decades. And there was a definite decline in the imports
of Greek pottery at the same time, which is a good indicator of levels
of prosperity. Put simply, if the end of the regal period could reasonably be dubbed 'La Grande Roma dei Tarquini', the early years of the
Republic were far less grand. As for all the heroic warfare that bulks
so large in Roman accounts, it may have played a significant part in
the Roman imagination, but it was all very local, fought out within a
few miles' radius of the city. The likelihood is that this was traditional
raiding between neighbouring communities or guerrilla attacks, later
written up, anachronistically, as something more like formal military clashes. Much of it, no doubt, was still on a semi-private basis,
drummed up by independent warlords. That, at least, is what one
fabled incident in the early 470s BCE hints, when 306 Romans are said
to have perished in an ambush. They were all said to be from a single
family, the Fabii, plus their dependants, hangers-on and clients: more
a large gang than an army.

The Twelve Tables are the best antidote to those later heroising
narratives. The original bronze tablets no longer survive. But some
of their content has been preserved because later Romans looked on
this motley collection of regulations as the beginning of their distinguished tradition of law. What had been inscribed on bronze was
soon put into pamphlet form and was still being learned by heart,
so Cicero tells us, by schoolboys of the first century BCE. Long after

the rules had any practical force, they continued to be reissued and re-edited, and several ancient scholarly commentaries were compiled on the meaning of the individual clauses, their legal importance and language – to the irritation of some lawyers in the second century CE, who felt that their book-bound colleagues were rather too interested in the linguistic puzzles of old Roman precepts. None of this voluminous literature survives intact. But some of it is quoted or paraphrased in writing that does, and by scouring through this, including some of the remotest byways of Roman literature, scholars have tracked down the eighty or so clauses of those fifth-century BCE tables.

The whole process has been ferociously technical, and intricate debates still rage about the exact wording of the clauses, about how large and how representative a selection of the original they are and about how accurate the later Roman scholars were in their quotations. Some modernising has definitely gone on: the Latin looks archaic, but not quite archaic enough for the fifth century BCE, and on occasion the paraphrases have tried to bring the original sense into line with later procedures in Roman law. In some cases, even learned Roman lawyers misunderstood what they read in the Twelve Tables. The idea that a defaulting debtor who had several creditors could be put to death and his body divided between them, in appropriately sized pieces, according to the amount owed, looks like one such misunderstanding (or so many modern critics have hoped). All the same, these quotations offer the most direct route into mid-fifth-century BCE society, into its homes and families, worries and intellectual horizons.

It is a much simpler society, and its horizons much more restricted, than Livy's account ever implies. That is clear from the language and forms of expression as much as from the content. Although modern translations do their best to make it all sound fairly lucid, the original Latin wording is often far from that. In particular, the absence of nouns and differentiated pronouns can make it almost impossible to know who is doing what to whom. 'If he summons to law, he is to go. If he does not go, he is to call to witness, then is to seize him' presumably means, as it is usually translated, 'If *a plaintiff* summons *a defendant* to law, *the defendant* is to go. If he does not go, *the plaintiff* is to call *someone else* to witness, then is to seize *the defendant*.' But it does not exactly say that. All the signs are that whoever drafted this and many other clauses was still struggling to use written language to frame precise regulations, and that the conventions of logical argument and rational expression were very much in their infancy.

Yet the mere attempt to create a formal record of this sort was an important stage in what is now often called state formation. One of the key turning points in many early societies is the rudimentary, usually very partial, codification of law. In ancient Athens, for example, the work of Draco in the seventh century BCE, though now a byword for harshness ('draconian'), was notable as the first attempt there to put what had been oral rules into writing; a thousand years before that in Babylon, Hammurabi's code did something similar. The Twelve Tables are much on that pattern. They are a long way from being a comprehensive legal code and may well never have been intended as such. Unless the range of surviving quotations is very misleading, they included almost nothing on public, constitutional law. What they do imply is a commitment to agreed, shared and publicly acknowledged procedures for resolving disputes and some thought on dealing with practical and theoretical obstacles to that. What was to be done if the defendant was too elderly to come to meet the plaintiff? The plaintiff was to provide an animal to transport him. What was to happen if the guilty party was a child? The penalty in that case might be beating rather than hanging – a distinction that heralds our ideas of the age of criminal responsibility.

The themes of the regulations point to a world of multiple inequalities. There were slaves of various types, from defaulters on their loans who had fallen into some form of debt bondage to those fully enslaved, presumably (though this is only a guess) captured in raiding or war.

And their disadvantage was spelled out: the penalty for assault on a slave is set at half as much as for assault on a free man, whereas a slave could be punished with his life for an offence for which free citizens got off with not much more than a beating. But some slaves were eventually freed, as is clear from a reference to an ex-slave, or *libertus*.

There were hierarchies within the free citizen population too. One clause draws a distinction between patricians and plebeians, another between *assidui* (men of property) and *proletarii* (those without property – whose contribution to the city was the production of offspring, *proles*). Another refers to 'patrons' and 'clients' and to a relationship of dependency and mutual obligation between richer and poorer citizens that remained important throughout Roman history. The basic principle was that the client depended on his patron for protection and assistance, financial and otherwise, in return for a variety of services rendered, including votes in elections. Later Roman writing is full of rather high-flown rhetoric from the patron class on the virtues of the relationship, and miserable complaints from the side of the client about the humiliations they have to go through, all for a second-rate meal. In the Twelve Tables, the rule simply states: 'If a patron has done harm to his client, he is to be cursed' – whatever that meant.

For the most part, the Twelve Tables confront domestic problems, with a heavy focus on family life, troublesome neighbours, private property and death. They lay down procedures for the abandonment or killing of deformed babies (a practice common throughout antiquity, euphemistically known to modern scholars as 'exposure'), for inheritance and for the proper conduct of funerals. Particular clauses prohibit women from tearing their cheeks in mourning, funeral pyres being built too close to someone's house and the burial of gold – except dental gold – with the body. Criminal and accidental damage was another obvious concern. This was a world in which people worried about how to cope with their neighbour's tree overhanging their property (solution: it had to be cut back to a specified height) or with their neighbour's animals running amok (solution: the damage had to be made good or the animal surrendered). They worried about thieves breaking in at night, which was to be punished more harshly than daylight theft, about vandals destroying their crops or about stray weapons accidentally hitting the innocent. But, just in case this all sounds a bit too familiar, it was also a world in which people worried about magic. What should you do if some enemy bewitched your crops or cast a spell on you? Sadly, the remedy for this is lost.

To judge from the Twelve Tables, Rome in the mid fifth century BCE was an agricultural town, complex enough to recognise basic divisions between slave and free and between different ranks of citizen and sophisticated enough to have devised some formal civic procedures to deal consistently with disputes, to regulate social and family relations and to impose some basic rules on such human activities as the disposal of the dead. But there is no evidence that it was more than that. The strikingly tentative formulation of the regulations, in places awkward or even confusing, should call into question some of the references in Livy and other ancient writers to complicated laws and treaties at this period. And the absence, at least from the selection of clauses preserved, of any reference to a specific public official, apart from a Vestal Virgin (who as a priestess was to be free of her father's control), certainly does not suggest a dominant state apparatus. What is more, there is hardly any mention of the world outside Rome – beyond a couple of references to how particular rules applied to a *hostis* (a 'foreigner' or an 'enemy'; the same Latin word, significantly, can mean both) and one possible reference to sale into slavery 'in foreign country across the Tiber', as a punishment of last resort for debt. Maybe this collection had an intentionally internal rather than external focus. All the same, there is no hint in the Twelve Tables that this was a community putting a high priority on relations, whether of dominance, exploitation or friendship, beyond its locality.

It all seems a world away from the age of Cicero, and even from the age of Barbatus and Appius Claudius Caecus, a little over a hundred years later, with their parade of public offices, that new road striking south to Capua and the boast about hostages from Lucania (see plate 5). So what changed, and when?

The Conflict of the Orders

First, what happened in politics at home? The Twelve Tables were one of the outcomes of what is often now called the Conflict of the Orders (the Latin word *ordo* meaning, among other things, 'social rank'), which according to Roman writers dominated domestic politics in those crucial couple of hundred years after the end of the monarchy. This was the struggle by the plebeian citizens for full political rights and for parity with the elite, patrician citizens, who were generally loath to give up their hereditary monopoly of power. In Rome it was seen ever after as a heroic vindication of the political liberty of the ordinary citizen, and it has left its mark on the politics, and political vocabulary, of the modern world too. The word 'plebeian' remains an especially loaded term in our class conflicts; even in 2012, the allegation that a British Conservative politician had insulted a policeman by calling him a 'pleb' – short for 'plebeian' – led to his resignation from the government.

As the story of this conflict unfolds, it was only a few years after the Republic had been established, at the beginning of the fifth century BCE, that the plebeians began objecting to their exclusion from power and their exploitation by the patricians. Why fight in Rome's wars, they repeatedly asked, when all the profits of their service lined patrician pockets? How could they count themselves full citizens when they were subject to random and arbitrary punishment, even enslavement if they fell into debt? What right had the patricians to keep the plebeians as an underclass? Or, as Livy scripted the ironic words of one plebeian reformer, in terms uncannily reminiscent of twentieth-century opposition to apartheid, 'Why don't you pass a law to stop a plebeian from living next door to a patrician, or walking down the same street, or going to the same party, or standing side by side in the same Forum?'

In 494 BCE, plagued by problems of debt, the plebeians staged the first of several mass walkouts from the city, a combination of a mutiny and a strike, to try to force reform on the patricians. It worked. For it launched a long series of concessions which gradually eroded all the significant differences between patricians and plebeians and effectively rewrote the political power structure of the city. Two hundred years later there was little to patrician privilege beyond the right to hold a few ancient priesthoods and to wear a particular form of fancy footwear.

The first reform in 494 BCE was the appointment of official representatives, known as tribunes of the people (*tribuni plebis*), to defend the interests of the plebeians. Then a special assembly was established for plebeians only. This was organised, like the Centuriate Assembly, on a system of block voting, but the technical details were crucially different. It was not based on a hierarchy of wealth. Instead, the voting groups were defined geographically, with voters enrolled in tribes (*tribus*), or regional subdivisions of Roman territory, nothing to do with any ethnic grouping that the modern sense of 'tribe' might imply. Finally, after one last walkout, in a reform that Scipio Barbatus would have witnessed in 287 BCE, the decisions of this assembly were given the automatic binding force of law over all Roman citizens. A plebeian institution, in other words, was given the right to legislate over, and on behalf of, the state as a whole.

Between 494 and 287 BCE, amid yet more stirring rhetoric, strikes and threats of violence, all major offices and priesthoods were step by step opened up to plebeians and their second-class status was dismantled. One of the most famed plebeian victories came in 326 BCE,

28. One of the offices that always remained restricted to patricians was the 'flaminate' – ancient priesthoods of some of the major gods. A group of these priests are seen here on the first-century BCE Altar of Peace (see Fig. 65), recognisable by their strange headgear.

when the system of enslavement for debt was abolished, establishing the principle that the liberty of a Roman citizen was an inalienable right. An equally significant but more narrowly political milestone had been passed forty years earlier, in 367 BCE. After decades of dogged refusal and claims by hard-line patricians that 'it would be a crime against the gods to let a plebeian be consul,' it was decided to open one of the consulships to plebeians. From 342 BCE it was agreed that both consuls could be plebeian, if so elected.

By far the most dramatic events in the conflict surrounded the drafting of the Twelve Tables, in the mid fifth century BCE. The clauses that are preserved may be brief, allusive and even slightly dry, but, as the Romans told the story, they were compiled in an atmosphere involving a tragic, highly coloured mixture of deception, allegations of tyranny, attempted rape and murder. The story was that for several years, the plebeians had demanded that the city's 'laws' be made public and not be merely a secret resource of the patricians; and, as a concession, normal political offices were suspended in 451 BCE and ten men (*decemviri*) were appointed to collect, draft and publish them. In the first year, the *decemviri* successfully completed ten tables of laws, but the job was not finished. So for the following year another board was appointed, which proved to be of a very different, and far more conservative, character. This second board produced the remaining two tables, introducing a notorious clause banning marriage between patricians and plebeians. Although the initiative behind the drafting had originally been reformist, it turned into the most extreme attempt to keep the two groups utterly separate: 'the most inhuman law' Cicero called it, entirely against the spirit of Roman openness.

There was worse to come. This second board of *decemviri* – the Ten Tarquins, as they were sometimes known – started to ape the behaviour of tyrants, right down to sexual violence. In what was almost a replay of the rape of Lucretia, which had led to the foundation of the Republic, one of their number, the patrician Appius Claudius (a great-great-grandfather of the road builder) demanded sex with a young plebeian woman, the aptly named Virginia, unmarried but betrothed. Deception and corruption followed. Appius suborned one of his hangers-on to claim that she was his slave, who had been stolen by her so-called father. The judge in the case was Appius himself, who of course found in his accomplice's favour, and strode through the Forum to grab Virginia. In the arguments that followed, her father, Lucius Virginius, picked up a knife from a nearby butcher's stall and stabbed his daughter to death: 'I am making you free, my child, in the only way I can,' he shouted.

Virginia's story has always been even more unsettling than that of Lucretia. It not only combines domestic murder with the brutality of class conflict but inevitably raises the question of the price to be paid for chastity. What kind of model of fatherhood is this? Who was most at fault? Did high principles need to come at such a terrible cost? But once more, (attempted) rape turned out to be a catalyst of political change. The display of Virginia's body and a passionate speech that Virginius gave to the army led to riots, mutiny, the abolition of the tyrannical board of *decemviri* and, as Livy puts it, the recovery of liberty. Despite the taint of tyranny, the Twelve Tables remained. They were soon regarded as the honoured ancestor of Roman law, excluding the ban on intermarriage, which was quickly repealed.

This story of the Conflict of the Orders adds up to one of the most radical and coherent manifestos of popular power and liberty to survive from the ancient world – far more radical than anything to survive from classical democratic Athens, most of whose writers, when they had anything explicitly to say on the subject, were opposed to democracy and popular power. Taken together, the demands put into the mouths of the plebeians offered a systematic programme of political reform, based on different aspects of the freedom of the citizen, from freedom to participate in the government of the state and freedom to share in its rewards to freedom from exploitation and freedom of information. It is hardly surprising that working class movements in many countries in the nineteenth and early twentieth centuries found a memorable precedent, and some winning rhetoric, in the ancient story of how the concerted action of the Roman people wrung concessions from the hereditary patrician aristocracy and secured full political rights for the plebeians. Nor is it surprising that early trades unions could look to the plebeian walkouts as a model for a successful strike.

But just how accurate is the story that the Romans told of this conflict? And what light does it shed on Rome's 'great leap forward'? Here the pieces in the jigsaw puzzle become hard to fit together. But the outlines of a picture, and some probably crucial dates, do stand out.

Many aspects of the story as it has come down to us must be wrong, heavily modernised by later writers or, especially towards the beginning of the period of the conflict, still much more myth than history. Virginia is probably no less a fictional construct than Lucretia. There is an awkward mismatch between the surviving clauses of the Twelve Tables and the elaborate story of the *decemviri*. Why, if the compilation came directly out of the clashes between patricians and plebeians, is there just one reference to that distinction (in the marriage ban) in the clauses preserved? Much of the argument, and even more of the rhetoric, of the early plebeian reformers is almost certainly an imaginative reconstruction by writers of the first century BCE, drawing on the sophisticated debates of their own day rather than being a product of the world of the Twelve Tables – and it may well be better evidence for the popular political ideology of that later period than for the Conflict of the Orders. What is more, despite Roman certainty that the exclusion of plebeians from power in the state went back to the fall of the monarchy, there are hints that it developed only in the course of the fifth century BCE. The standard list of consuls, for example, however fictionalised it may be, includes in the early fifth century BCE plenty of recognisably plebeian names (including that of the first consul, Lucius Junius Brutus himself), which completely disappear in the second half of the century.

That said, there is no doubt that long periods of the fifth and fourth centuries BCE were fractured by social and political struggles between a privileged, hereditary minority and the rest. More than half a millennium later, the formal distinction between patrician and plebeian families still survived, as one of those 'fossils' I discussed earlier (p. 79), with a whiff of snobbery attached to it and not much more. It would be hard to explain why the distinction existed at all if the difference between the two groups had not once been a significant marker of political, social and economic power. There are also strong reasons to think that the year 367 BCE was a major turning point, even if not in quite the way Roman historians imagined it.

For them, this was the revolutionary moment when it was decided not only that the consulship should be open to plebeians but that one of the two consuls must always be a plebeian. If so, the law was flouted as soon as it was made, as on several occasions in the following years two patrician names are recorded as consuls. Livy noticed the problem and unconvincingly suggests that the plebeians were satisfied with getting the right to stand and not so bothered about being elected. Much more likely is that there was no obligatory plebeian consul but that this was the year when the consulship as the major annual office of state was established on a permanent basis, presumably open to both patricians and plebeians.

That would certainly fit with two other significant clues. First, even in the traditional Roman record, the entries for most of the years between the 420s and the 360s BCE name the mysterious 'colonels' as the chief officials of the state. That changes once and for all in 367 BCE, when consuls become the norm for the rest of Roman history. Second, it may well be that the senate was given its definitive form at this time. Roman writers tended to take it for granted that the origins of the senate went back to Romulus, as a council of 'old men' (*senes*), and that by the fifth century BCE it was already a fully fledged institution operating much as it did in 63 BCE. One highly technical entry in an ancient Roman dictionary implies a very different version, suggesting that it was only around the middle of the fourth century BCE that the senate was established as a permanent body with lifelong members rather than being just an ad hoc group of friends and advisors to whatever officials were in charge, with no continuity from one year, or even one day, to the next. If this is correct (and, of course, not all arcane pieces of technical information necessarily are), then it backs up the idea that the Roman political system took its characteristic form in the mid fourth century BCE. Whatever the precursors, whatever elements such as assemblies or the census, may long have been in place, Rome did not look distinctively 'Roman' for more than a century after 509 BCE.

That means that what we find outlined on Barbatus' tomb is not a traditional career of a traditional member of the Roman elite, though that is how he was later seen. Buried sometime in the early third century BCE, Barbatus was in fact a representative of the relatively new Republican order at home – and, as we shall now see, outside.

The outside world: Veii and Rome

The expansion of Roman power through Italy was dramatic. It is easy to be dazzled, or appalled, by Rome's later overseas empire, which eventually amounted to more than 2 million square miles, while taking for granted the idea that Italy was Roman. But the transformation of the small town by the Tiber in 509 BCE into a polity of more than 5,000 square miles in the 290s BCE, with effective control over at least half the Italian peninsula, and more to come, is almost as striking. How did that happen? And when?

Rome's relations with the outside world were entirely unremarkable, so far as we can tell, until around 400 BCE. Its trading relations with the wider Mediterranean had been no more than typical for an Italian town. Its direct interactions were mainly local, above all with the Latin communities to the south, which shared a common language, a sense of common ancestry and several common festivals and sacred sites with Rome. The most that can be said is that by the end of the sixth century BCE the Romans probably had some kind of control over some of the other Latins. Both Cicero and the historian Polybius (a shrewd Greek observer of Rome, who features prominently in the next chapter) claim to have seen documents, or 'treaties', from that period suggesting that Rome was then the leading player in this small, local Latin world. And, as we have seen, the story of the fifth century BCE suggests more or less annual bouts of fighting but on a limited scale, in whatever grandiose terms it was later lauded. Quite simply, if there had been serious casualties every year for decades, the little town of Rome would not have survived.

The moment of change came near the start of the fourth century BCE, with two events that play a leading, and hugely mythologised, role in all ancient accounts of Rome's expansion: the Roman destruction of the nearby town of Veii under the heroic Camillus in 396 BCE, and the destruction of Rome by Gauls in 390 BCE. What lay behind Rome's clash with Veii is completely unknown, but it was written up as if it were Italy's equivalent of the Trojan War: the ten-year siege that it took to capture the town, equalling the ten-year siege of Troy; and the victorious Romans eventually popping up inside the city from a tunnel under the Temple of Juno, as the equivalent of the Trojan Horse. The reality of the 'conquest' (which is probably too grand a term) must have been much more modest. This was not a clash of superpowers. Veii was a prosperous town, a little smaller than Rome, and just 10 miles away across the Tiber.

Yet the consequences of Roman victory were significant, even if not in the way suggested by Roman writers, who emphasised the enslavement of the population, with all their goods and chattels taken as spoils, and the total destruction of the town. Three hundred and fifty years later the poet Propertius conjured up a desolate picture of Veii in his day, as the home of no more than sheep and a few 'idle shepherds'. This is much more a moral lesson in the perils of defeat than an accurate description (Propertius may never have been to the place), for the archaeology of the site points to a very different truth. Although there may have been vicious looting, enslavement at the moment of Roman victory and an influx of new settlers, most of the local sanctuaries remained in operation as they had been before, the town remained occupied, even if on a smaller scale, and such evidence as we have of the countryside farms points to continuity rather than rupture.

The important change is of a different kind. Rome annexed Veii and its land, instantly increasing the size of Roman territory by about 60 per cent. Soon after, four new geographical tribes of Roman citizens were created, to include Veii, its indigenous inhabitants as well as new settlers. There are hints of other important developments at roughly the same time, possibly connected. Livy claims that it was in the run-up to the siege of Veii that Roman soldiers were first paid, from Roman taxes. Whether literally true or not (and whatever they were paid in, it was not yet coin), this may well be an indication of a move towards a more centralised organisation of Roman armies and the decline of private warfare.

Defeat soon followed victory. The story went that in 390 BCE a band of Gauls – possibly a tribe on the move looking for land or, more likely, a well-trained posse of mercenaries looking for work further south – routed a Roman army on the river Allia, not far from the city. The Romans apparently did little more than run away, and the Gauls marched on to take Rome. One apocryphal tale describes how a virtuous plebeian, the aptly named Marcus *Caedicius* ('disaster teller'), heard the voice of some unknown god warning him that Gauls were approaching, but his report was ignored because of his lowly status. It turned out to be a lesson for the patricians – learned the hard way – that the gods communicated with plebeians too.

Roman storytelling gave extravagant coverage to the capture of the city, with various acts of heroism mitigating the widespread destruction. Another poor man gave proof of plebeian piety when he threw his wife and children out of his cart and gave a lift to the Vestal Virgins, who were evacuating their sacred emblems and talismans to safety in the nearby town of Caere. Many elderly aristocrats decided simply to face the inevitable and sat patiently at home waiting for the Gauls, who for a moment mistook the old men for statues before massacring them. Meanwhile, Camillus, briefly in exile for the alleged embezzlement of spoils, returned just in time to stop the Romans from paying a large ransom to the Gauls, to dissuade his compatriots from simply abandoning the city and moving to Veii and to take charge of refounding the city. Or that at least is one version. A less honourable telling of the story has the Gauls triumphantly carrying off the ransom.

This is another case of Roman exaggeration. The various stories, which became commonplaces of Roman cultural memory, offered important patriotic lessons: in placing the claims of country above family, in bravery in the face of certain defeat, and in the dangers of measuring the worth of the city in terms of gold. The catastrophe became so much a part of the Roman popular imagination that some diehards were using it in 48 CE as an argument (or a desperate gambit) against the emperor Claudius' proposals to admit Gauls into

28. An early twentieth-century drawing (from an earlier photograph) of the remains of the Servian Wall near Rome's central train station. Sections of this fortification still greet travellers emerging from Roma Termini, though they are now rather bleakly enclosed behind railings.

the senate. There is, however, no archaeological evidence for the kind of massive destruction that later Romans imagined, unless those traces of burning now dated to around 500 BCE are in fact, as archaeologists once thought, the remains of a Gallic rampage a hundred years later.

The one clear surviving mark of the 'sack' on the Roman landscape is the vast defensive city wall, of which some impressive sections are still visible, constructed after the departure of the Gauls and built with some particularly durable stone that was one of the products of Rome's new territory around Veii. But there were powerful reasons why this defeat was a useful episode for Roman historians to stress. It set the scene for Roman anxieties about invaders from over the Alps, of whom Hannibal was the most dangerous, but not the only one. It helped to explain why so little hard information survived for early Rome (it had gone up in flames), and so it marked the start, in ancient terms, of 'modern history'. It answered the question of why in the later Republic the city of Rome, despite its world renown, was such an ill-planned rabbit warren: the Romans had had to rebuild hurriedly when the Gauls left. And it opened a new chapter in Rome's relations with the outside world.

The Romans versus Alexander the Great

What followed was a revolution in the size, scale, location and consequence of Roman conflict. True, the basic pattern of more or less annual warfare continued. Ancient writers thrilled to a long list of Roman battles fought in the fourth century BCE, celebrating, and no doubt exaggerating, heroic victories while lamenting a handful of shameful defeats and humiliating walkovers. The Battle of the Caudine Forks, in 321 BCE, at which the South Italian Samnites trounced the Romans, became almost as resonant as the Battle of the Allia or the sack of Rome seventy years earlier – even though it was not really a battle at all. The Romans were trapped in a narrow mountain gully, the Forks, with no water, and they simply surrendered.

Yet between the sack of Rome in 390 BCE and the Battle of Sentinum in 295 BCE, the manpower involved in these conflicts increased dramatically. Campaigns were fought further and further from Rome. Whereas Veii was 10 miles up the road, Sentinum was some two hundred miles away, across the Apennines. And the arrangements made between Rome and the defeated had far-reaching consequences for the future. The military impact of Rome by the end of the fourth century BCE was so great that Livy felt it worthwhile to compare Roman prowess with that of the world-conquering Alexander the Great, who between 334 and 323 BCE had led his Macedonian army on a spree of conquest from Greece to India. Livy wondered who would have won, the Romans or the Macedonians, if they had come head to head, a military conundrum that armchair generals still ponder.

There were two particularly significant conflicts in Italy in this period. First was the so-called Latin War, fought against Rome's Latin neighbours between 341 and 338 BCE. Shortly after followed the 'Samnite Wars', the occasion of Barbatus' victories. They were fought in phases between 343 and 290 BCE against a group of communities based in the mountainous parts of southern Italy: Samnites, who were much less rough and primitive than it suited the Romans to portray them but less urbanised than those in many other parts of the peninsula. Both of these 'wars' are rather artificial constructions, isolating two enemies and giving their names to the much more widespread, endemic fighting of the period, from a decidedly Romano-centric point of view (no Samnite ever fought a 'Samnite War'). That said, they do spotlight some important changes.

According to the usual story, the first was prompted by a revolt of the Latins against the dominant position of the Romans in the region. It remained a local conflict, but it was notable, even revolutionary, for the arrangements made afterwards between the Romans and the various Latin communities. For these gave Roman citizenship to vast numbers of the defeated, in numerous towns throughout central Italy, on a scale that went far beyond the precedent set at Veii. Whether this was a gesture of generosity, as many Roman writers interpreted it, or a mechanism of oppression, as it may well have seemed to those who found Roman citizenship imposed upon them, it was a crucial stage in the changing definition of what it meant to be 'Roman'. And it brought, as we shall soon see, enormous changes to the structure of Roman power.

Almost fifty years later, the decades of Samnite Wars ended, with more than half the peninsula under Rome's thumb in various ways, from treaties of 'friendship' to direct control. Roman writers presented these wars as if they were a struggle between two states for Italian supremacy. They were certainly not that, but the scale of the conflict was something new and set the stage for the future. At the Battle of Sentinum, the Romans faced a large group of enemies ('alliance' may be too formal a word for it): the Samnites themselves, as well as Etruscans and Gauls from the far north of the peninsula. The sheer number of combatants seems to have attracted the attention of Duris of Samos, who recorded a vast but implausible total of 100,000 Samnite and allied casualties. Roman writers saw this as a particularly heroic victory. It even became the theme of a jingoistic Roman tragedy two hundred years later, complete with a tragic chorus of Roman soldiers and featuring one of the Roman commanders who gave up his life to ensure his army's success. But they too debated, as modern scholars have continued to do, just how big this biggest of all battles was. Livy had no patience with estimates on the scale of Duris' or with even more inflated figures he came across in his researches. Whether his estimate of Roman forces at around 16,000 men (plus as many allies) is correct, it is impossible to know. One thing is certain, however: this was a different military world from the low-level skirmishes of the fifth century BCE.

It is a world we can still glimpse in an extraordinary discovery made in the 1870s in excavations at what would have been the edge of the ancient city of Rome: a tantalisingly small fragment of painting, from a tomb, probably dating to the early third century BCE. Originally much more extensive, covering a whole wall, it is arranged in a series of registers, one above the other, which are thought to feature scenes from these conflicts between Rome and the Samnites. If so, this is the first surviving painting in the West to show an identifiable, real-life military campaign – unless a rather generic scene of combat painted on a tomb in South Italy is actually, as some archaeologists have optimistically imagined, a proud depiction of the Samnite victory at the Caudine Forks (see plate 6).

The interpretation of the painting has been hugely controversial, and it is now sadly eroded, but the main outline is clear enough. The lowest register depicts hand-to-hand fighting, dominated by a man whose elaborate helmet extends into the scene above; higher up some imposing battlements still stand out. Each of the two best-preserved scenes shows a man in a short toga holding a spear. One of these, and possibly both, is named 'Q Fabius', plausibly the Quintus Fabius Maximus Rullianus who was commanding officer at Sentinum and who gave Barbatus his only known cameo role in the battle, instructing him to 'bring up the reserves from the rear'. Here he is shown – with a retinue of hangers-on behind him on a distinctly smaller scale – apparently in negotiation with 'Fannius', a warrior with no weapons, dressed in military kit including heavy leg guards and in one case a plumed helmet, who is extending his bare right hand. Is Fannius a Samnite, surrendering to a representative of 'the race that wears the toga' – here, already in the third century BCE, depicted as exactly that?

Seen in these simple, stylised images, the Romans may not look much of a match for Alexander the Great. But whether or not they would have been is precisely the issue Livy raises in the long digression in his *History* just after the description of the impressive Roman recovery from the humiliation at the Caudine Forks. It did not escape his notice that the Samnite Wars were taking place in Italy at the end of the fourth century BCE, which was more or less when the Macedonian king was on his devastating campaigns in the East. By Livy's day, Roman generals had long been keen to emulate Alexander. They had imitated his distinctive hairstyle, they had called themselves 'the Great' and both Julius Caesar and the first emperor, Augustus, had made a pilgrimage to Alexander's tomb in Egypt, Augustus – so it was said – accidentally breaking off the corpse's nose as he paid homage. So it is perhaps not surprising that Livy pondered a classic counterfactual question: who would have won if Alexander had turned his army westward and faced the Romans instead of the Persians?

Alexander, he concedes, was a great general, though not without his faults, drunkenness among others. But the Romans had the advantage of not depending on a single charismatic leader. They had depth in their command, supported by extraordinary military discipline. They also, he insisted, could call on far greater numbers of well-trained troops and – thanks to Roman alliances throughout Italy – summon reinforcements more or less at will. His answer, in short, was that, if given the chance, the Romans would have beaten Alexander.

Expansion, soldiers and citizens

In his roundabout way, Livy – who sometimes seems rather plodding in his analysis – offers a perceptive answer to the questions of what made the Roman armies at this period so good at winning and how it came about that Rome extended control so rapidly over so much of Italy. This is one of the few cases in which he looks beneath the surface of the narrative, to underlying social and structural factors, from the organisation of Roman command to Rome's resources of manpower.

It is worth pushing Livy's point a little further, to think harder about what was, in retrospect, the beginning of the Roman Empire.

Two things are clear and undermine a couple of misleading modern myths about Roman power and 'character'. First, the Romans were not by nature more belligerent than their neighbours and contemporaries, any more than they were naturally better at building roads and bridges. It is true that Roman culture placed an extraordinarily – for us, uncomfortably – high value on success in fighting. Prowess, bravery and deadly violence in battle were repeatedly celebrated, from the successful general parading through the streets and the cheering crowds in his triumphal procession to the rank-and-file soldiers showing off their battle scars in the middle of political debates in the hope of adding weight to their arguments. In the middle of the fourth century BCE the base of the main platform for speakers in the Forum was decorated with the bronze rams of enemy warships captured from the city of Antium during the Latin War, as if to symbolise the military foundation of Roman political power. The Latin word for 'rams', *rostra*, became the name of the platform and gave modern English its word 'rostrum'.

Yet it would be naïve to imagine that the other peoples in Italy were different. These were very disparate groups, much more varied – in language, culture and political organisation – than the shorthand 'Italians' implies. But to judge from the comparatively little we know about most of them, from the military equipment found in their graves or the occasional passing references in literature to their spoils, warfare and atrocities, they were just as committed to militarism as the Romans and probably just as greedy for profit. This was a world where violence was endemic, skirmishes with neighbours were annual events, plunder was a significant revenue stream for everyone and most disputes were resolved by force. The ambivalence of the Latin word *hostis* nicely captures the blurring of the boundary between 'the outsider' and 'the enemy'. So too does the standard Latin phrase for 'at home and abroad' – *domi militiaeque* – in which 'abroad' (*militiae*) is indistinguishable from 'on military campaign'. Most of the peoples in the peninsula no doubt shared that blurring. To be off one's home turf was always (potentially) to be at war.

Second, the Romans did not plan to conquer and control Italy. No Roman cabal in the fourth century BCE sat down with a map, plotting a land grab in the territorial way that we associate with imperialist nation-states in the nineteenth and twentieth centuries. For a start, simple as it sounds, they had no maps. What this implies for how they, or any other 'precartographic' people, conceived the world around them, or just over their horizons, is one of history's great mysteries. I have tended to write of the spread of Roman power through the *peninsula* of Italy, but no one knows how many – or, realistically, how few – Romans at this date thought of their homeland as part of a peninsula in the way we picture it. A rudimentary version of the idea is perhaps implied by references in literature of the second century BCE to the Adriatic as the Upper Sea and the Tyrrhenian as the Lower Sea, but notably this is on a different orientation from ours, east–west rather than north–south.

These Romans saw their expansion more in terms of changing relationships with other peoples than in terms of control of territory. Of course, Rome's growing power did dramatically transform the landscape of Italy. There was little that was more obviously transformative than a brand-new Roman road striking out across empty fields, or land being annexed and divided up among new settlers. It continues to be convenient to measure Roman power in Italy in terms of geographical area. Yet Roman dominion was primarily over people, not places. As Livy saw, the relations that the Romans formed with those people were the key to the dynamics of early Roman expansion.

There was one obligation that the Romans imposed on all those who came under their control: namely, to provide troops for the Roman armies. In fact, for most of those who were defeated by Rome and forced, or welcomed, into some form of 'alliance', the only long-term obligation seems to have been the provision and upkeep of soldiers. These peoples were not taken over by Rome in any other way; they had no Roman occupying forces or Roman-imposed government. Why this form of control was chosen is impossible to know. But it is unlikely that any particularly sophisticated, strategic calculation was involved. It was an imposition that conveniently demonstrated Roman dominance while requiring few Roman administrative structures or spare manpower to manage. The troops that the allies contributed were raised, equipped and in part commanded by the locals. Taxation in any other form would have been much more labour-intensive for the Romans; direct control of those they had defeated would have been even more so.

The results may well have been unintended, but they were ground-breaking. For this system of alliances became an effective mechanism for converting Rome's defeated enemies into part of its growing military machine; and at the same time it gave those allies a stake in the Roman enterprise, thanks to the booty and glory that were shared in the event of victory. Once the Romans' military success started, they managed to make it self-sustaining, in a way that no other ancient city had ever systematically done. For the single most significant factor behind victory at this period was not tactics, equipment, skill or motivation. It was how many men you could deploy. By the end of the fourth century BCE, the Romans had probably not far short of half a million troops available (compare the 50,000 or so soldiers under Alexander in his eastern campaigns, or perhaps 100,000 when the Persians invaded Greece in 481 BCE). This made them close to invincible in Italy: they might lose a battle, but not a war. Or as one Roman poet put it in the 130s BCE, 'The Roman people has often been defeated by force and overcome in many battles, but never in an actual war on which everything depends.'

There were, however, other far-reaching implications of the way the Romans defined their relations with other peoples in Italy. The 'allies', who were committed to no more than supplying manpower, were the most numerous, but they were only one of the categories concerned. To some communities over wide areas in central Italy, the Romans extended Roman citizenship. Sometimes this involved full citizen rights and privileges, including the right to vote or stand in Roman elections while also continuing to be a citizen of a local town. In other cases they offered a more limited form of rights that came to be known (self-explanatorily) as 'citizenship without the vote', or *civitas sine suffragio*. There were also people who lived on conquered territories in settlements known as colonies (*coloniae*). These had nothing to do with colonies in the modern sense of the word but were new (or expanded) towns usually made up of a mixture of locals and settlers from Rome. A few had full Roman citizenship status. Most had what was known as Latin rights. That was not citizenship as such but a package of rights believed to have been shared since time immemorial by the Latin towns, later formally defined as intermarriage with Romans, mutual rights to make contracts, free movement and so on. It was a halfway house between having full citizenship and being a foreigner, or *hostis*.

How this complicated mosaic of statuses had originated is again hard to know. Roman writers of the first century BCE, followed by modern legal scholars, tended to treat them as part of a highly technical, carefully calibrated system of civic rights and responsibilities. But that is almost certainly the product of later legal rationalisation. It is inconceivable that the men of the fourth century BCE sat down to debate the precise implications of *civitas sine suffragio* or the exact privileges that went with belonging to a 'Latin' colony. Much more likely, they were improvising their new relationships with different peoples in the outside world by using, and adjusting, their existing, rudimentary categories of citizenship and ethnicity.

The implications, however, were again revolutionary. In extending citizenship to people who had no direct territorial connections with the city of Rome, they broke the link, which most people in the classical world took for granted, between citizenship and a single city. In a systematic way that was then unparalleled, they made it possible not just to *become Roman* but also to be a citizen of two places at once: one's home town and Rome. And in creating new Latin colonies all over Italy, they redefined the word 'Latin' so that it was no longer an ethnic identity but a political status unrelated to race or geography. This set the stage for a model of citizenship and 'belonging' that had enormous significance for Roman ideas of government, political rights, ethnicity and 'nationhood'. This model was shortly extended overseas and eventually underpinned the Roman Empire.

Causes and explanations

There is no more vivid symbol of Rome's changed relationship to the outside world in the early fourth century BCE than the vast wall erected around the city in the years after the Gauls left, with a perimeter of 7 miles and in places as much as 4 metres thick. It was simultaneously a mammoth building project (more than 5 million man-hours of labour in the construction, according to one estimate) and a boastful symbol of Rome's prominence and place in the world. There is no doubt, as both ancient and modern historians agree, that it was around this time that Rome's military expansion outside its immediate neighbourhood began. Nor is there any doubt that the expansion, once started, was sustained more than anything by the resources of manpower that came with the alliances that followed its victories.

But what caused the change in the first place is a tricky question. What happened in the early fourth century BCE to start this new phase of Roman military activity? No ancient writer hazards an answer, beyond the implausible idea that the seed of world domination had somehow been planted. Maybe the invasion of the Gauls produced in the Romans a determination not to be caught out like that again, to take the offensive rather than being forced on to the defensive. Maybe it took only a couple of lucky victories in the endemic fighting of the region, followed by a couple of alliances and the extra manpower they brought, to ignite the process of expansion. Whatever the case, it seems likely that the dramatic changes in domestic politics had some part to play.

So far in exploring this period, I have largely kept the internal history of Rome separate from the story of its expansion. It makes for a clearer story, but it tends to obscure the impact of politics at home on relations further afield, and vice versa. By 367 BCE, the Conflict of the Orders had done something far more significant and wide-ranging than simply end political discrimination against the plebeians. It had effectively replaced a governing class defined by birth with one defined by wealth and achievement. That is partly the point of Barbatus' epitaph: patrician though the Scipio family was, what counts here are the offices he held, the personal qualities he displayed and the battles he won. No achievement was more demonstrable or more celebrated than victory in battle, and the desire for victory among the new elite was almost certainly an important factor in intensifying military activity and encouraging warfare.

Equally, it was power over increasingly far-flung peoples and the demands of a conquering army that drove many of the innovations that revolutionised life in Rome itself. One important example of this is coinage. From early in its history, the city had a standard system of determining monetary value by weight of metal; this is evident in the Twelve Tables, which assess penalties in units of bronze. But there was no coinage as such until the end of the fourth century BCE, when 'Roman' coins were first minted, in South Italy, probably to pay for warfare or road building there.

More generally, if we were to ask what transformed the relatively simple world of the Twelve Tables into the relatively complex world of the year 300 BCE, the most influential factor would surely be the sheer size of Rome's dominion and the organisational demands of fighting on a large scale. Simply the logistics of transport, supply and equipment entailed in mounting a campaign of 16,000 Romans (to use Livy's estimate), plus allies, would have demanded an infrastructure unthinkable in the mid fifth century BCE. Although I have tried to avoid such modernising terms as 'alliance' and 'treaty' when referring to Roman activity in the fifth century BCE, the network of Roman connections throughout the peninsula and the different definitions of Rome's relations with different communities by the end of the following century make those terms much less inappropriate. Roman military expansion drove Roman sophistication.

The family tomb of Scipio Barbatus now looks grandly archaic, and – with its coarse local stone, rather crudely carved decoration and slightly antiquated spelling (*consol* instead of *consul*, for example) – it might well have seemed quaintly old-fashioned to any Roman who entered it in the first century BCE. But in his day, Barbatus was part of a new generation who defined a new way of being Roman and a new place for Rome in the world. His descendants took that even further, and it is to them we now turn.

CHAPTER FIVE

·

A WIDER WORLD

The descendants of Barbatus

SCIPIO BARBATUS BUILT his tomb on a grand scale, and over the next 150 years around thirty of his descendants joined him there. The Scipio family included some of the most famous names of Roman history, as well as its fair share of also-rans and ne'er-do-wells. Eight of their epitaphs survive more or less complete, and several of those commemorate the kind of Romans usually hidden from history: the ones who did not quite make the grade or who died young, and the women. 'He who has been buried here was never surpassed in *virtus*. Just twenty years of age, he was entrusted to the tomb – in case you ask why no political office was entrusted to him,' the text on one sarcophagus of the middle of the second century BCE explains slightly defensively. Another has to fall back on the achievements of the young man's father ('his father crushed King Antiochus'). But others had more to boast of. The epitaph of Barbatus' son proclaims: 'He captured Corsica and the city of Aleria, and in gratitude dedicated a temple to the Gods of Storms.' A storm had nearly wrecked his fleet, and this was his thank offering to the appropriate gods for the happy outcome.

Other members of the family would have had even greater boasts. Publius Cornelius Scipio Africanus, a great-grandson of Barbatus, was the man who in 202 BCE secured the final defeat of Hannibal: he invaded the Carthaginian's home territory in North Africa and at the Battle of Zama, near Carthage, routed his army, with some help from Hannibal's elephants, who ran amok and trampled over their own side. Africanus' grave lay on his estate in South Italy and became something of a pilgrimage site for later Romans. But it is almost certain that among the memorials in the family tomb were once those of his brother Lucius Cornelius Scipio Asiaticus, the man 'who crushed King Antiochus' of Syria in 190 BCE; his cousin Gnaeus Cornelius Scipio Hispallus, a consul in 176 BCE; and his grandson Publius Cornelius Scipio Aemilianus. An adopted member of the family, Aemilianus invaded North Africa and finished Africanus' work: in 146 BCE he reduced the ancient city of Carthage to rubble and sold most of its surviving inhabitants into slavery.

The careers of these men point to a new world of Roman politics and expansion over the third and second centuries BCE. These are some of the key players, famous or infamous, in the series of military campaigns that gave the Roman Republic control over the whole Mediterranean and beyond. Their rather cumbersome names nicely sum up that new world. *Barbatus* presumably points to the bearer's appearance, and *Aemilianus* is a reference to the man's natural father, Lucius *Aemilius* Paullus, but *Africanus, Asiaticus* and *Hispallus* (from his father's service in Spain, *Hispania*) reflect the new horizons of Roman power. One reasonable way of translating 'Scipio *Africanus*' would be 'Scipio *hammer of Africa*'.

These were military men. But there was more to the Scipios than that. As anyone would have realised who spotted the statue of the Roman poet Quintus Ennius proudly displayed, alongside those of Africanus and Asiaticus, on the elegant façade of the family tomb, they were also in the thick of the Roman literary revolution, sponsors and patrons of the first generation of Roman literature. This was no coincidence. For the origin of literature at Rome was closely connected with Roman overseas expansion: 'The Muse imposed herself *in war-like fashion* on the fierce inhabitants of Rome,' as one second-century

BCE author described it. The beginning of empire and the beginning of literature were two sides of the same coin.

For centuries, Romans had used writing for various purposes: public notices, rules and regulations, claims of ownership scrawled on a pot. But it was increasing contact with the traditions of the Greek world, from the mid third century BCE, that was the catalyst to the production and preservation of literature as such. It was born in imitation of Greek predecessors, and in dialogue, competition and rivalry, at a moment that speaks for itself. In 241 BCE, just as Roman soldiers and sailors were finally winning Rome's first overseas war, in the predominantly Greek island of Sicily, somewhere back home a man called Livius Andronicus was busy adapting into Latin, from a Greek original, the first tragedy to be shown in Rome – which was staged the very next year, in 240 BCE.

The background and output of Livius Andronicus are typical of the cultural mix of this early writing and of its writers. He produced Latin versions not only of Greek tragedies but also of Homer's *Odyssey*; he had been enslaved as a prisoner of war, probably from the Greek city of Tarentum in South Italy, and later freed. A different mixture is seen in Fabius Pictor, the Roman senator who wrote the first history of Rome; Roman born and bred, he nevertheless composed his work in Greek, only later translated into Latin. The earliest literature actually to survive in any bulk, written around the turn of the third and second centuries BCE – the twenty-six comedies of Titus Maccius Plautus and Publius Terentius Afer ('Plautus' and 'Terence' from now on) – are carefully Romanised versions of Greek predecessors, featuring hapless love stories and farcical tales of mistaken identity often set in Athens but also sprinkled with gags about togas, public baths and triumphal parades. Terence, who lived in the early second century BCE, was reputed to be another ex-slave, originally from Carthage.

As the statue on the outside of the tomb suggests, Scipio Africanus was one of the sponsors of Ennius, most famous for his multivolume

29. A Roman plate of the third century BCE features an elephant carrying a fighting tower on her back with her calf behind. Whatever the dubious military advantage they gave, elephants soon became a powerful presence in the Roman popular imagination.

Latin epic poem on the history of Rome from the Trojan War until his own day, at the beginning of the second century BCE, and another South Italian, fluent in Latin, Greek and his native Oscan (a reminder of the linguistic variety of the peninsula). Aemilianus flaunted even stronger literary interests, in both Latin and Greek. He had such close connections with Terence that inventive Roman gossips wondered whether he had ghostwritten some of the plays. Wasn't the Latin just too elegant for someone of Terence's background? And Aemilianus was known to have the Greek literary classics on the tip of his tongue. As Carthage went up in flames in 146 BCE, one eyewitness spotted him shedding a tear and heard him quoting from memory an apposite line on the fall of Troy from Homer's *Iliad*. He was reflecting that one day the same fate might afflict Rome. Crocodile tears or not, they made their point.

That eyewitness was the closest of Aemilianus' literary friends and connections, a Greek historian, resident in Rome, by the name of Polybius. A shrewd observer of Roman politics at home and abroad, with a unique perspective on Rome from the inside and the outside, he hovers over much of the rest of this chapter – as the first writer to pose some of the big questions that we shall try to answer. Why and how did the Romans come to dominate so much of the Mediterranean in such a short time? What was distinctive about the Roman political system? Or as Polybius sternly put it: 'Who could be so indifferent or so idle that they did not want to find out *how*, and *under what kind of political organisation*, almost the whole of the inhabited world was conquered and fell under the sole power of the Romans in less than fifty-three years, something previously unparalleled?' Who indeed?

Conquest and consequences

Polybius' 'fifty-three years' covered the end of the third and the beginning of the second century BCE, but it was some sixty years earlier that the Romans first encountered an enemy from overseas. That was Pyrrhus, the ruler of a kingdom in northern Greece, who in 280 BCE sailed to Italy to support the town of Tarentum against the Romans. His self-deprecating joke – that his victories against Rome cost him so

30. This portrait of Pyrrhus made more than two hundred years after his death, found in a lavish villa just outside Herculaneum, is very likely to go back to an image made in his lifetime. There are several earlier 'portraits' of Romans, or their enemies, but none can be reliably tied to a historical individual. This is where we first see the real face of a character in the history of Rome.

many men that he could not afford another – lies behind the modern phrase 'Pyrrhic victory', meaning one that takes such a heavy toll that it is tantamount to defeat. The phrase is rather kind to the Romans' side of the story, for Pyrrhus was a serious match for them. Hannibal is supposed to have rated him the greatest military leader after Alexander the Great, and – according to a number of affectionate anecdotes – he was something of an engaging showman. He was the first to pull off the stunt of bringing elephants to Italy and on one occasion is supposed to have tried, unsuccessfully, to disconcert a visiting Roman by

31. The disastrous Roman expedition to North Africa in the First Punic War was given an heroic spin by the story of Marcus Atilius Regulus. After a Roman defeat there in 255 BCE, the Carthaginians released him to go home to negotiate a truce, on condition that he would return. In Rome, Regulus urged against any peace treaty, then – good as his Roman word – went back to Carthage to face death. This nineteenth-century painting re-creates his final departure from Rome, despite the pleas of his family.

revealing one of his beasts from behind a curtain. He is also the first character in the history of Rome to whom we can plausibly put a face.

From the invasion of Pyrrhus to 146 BCE – when Roman armies destroyed both Carthage, at the end of what was called the Third Punic War (from the Latin *Punicus*, or 'Carthaginian'), and, almost simultaneously, the wealthy Greek city of Corinth – there was more or less continuous warfare involving Rome and its enemies in the Italian peninsula and overseas. One ancient scholar isolated the year 'when Gaius Atilius and Titus Manlius were consuls' (235 BCE) as the only point in this period when hostilities were not taking place.

The most celebrated, and devastating, conflicts were the first two Punic Wars, against Carthage. The earlier lasted for more than twenty years (from 264 to 241 BCE), largely fought in Sicily and on the seas round about, except for one disastrous Roman excursion to the Carthaginian homeland, in North Africa. It ended with Sicily under Roman control – and after a few years Sardinia and Corsica too, though the epitaph of Barbatus' son rather exaggerates his achievements in 'capturing' the island. In one extraordinary recent find, some of the detritus of the final naval battle between Romans and Carthaginians has been dragged up from the bottom of the Mediterranean. Just off the Sicilian coast, close to where the two fleets are supposed to have met, underwater archaeologists exploring the area since 2004 have recovered several bronze rams from sunken warships (mostly Roman, but including one Carthaginian vessel), together with at least eight bronze helmets, one carrying a trace of some Punic graffiti, probably scratched by its drowned owner, and pottery amphorae that must have been carrying the ships' supplies (see plate 8).

On a very different geographical scale was the Second Punic War, which was fought between 218 and 201 BCE. It is now best remembered for the heroic failure of Hannibal, who crossed the Alps with his elephants (more of a propaganda coup than a practical military asset) and inflicted vast casualties on the Romans in Italy, most notoriously in 216 BCE at the Battle of Cannae in the south. Only after more than a decade of inconclusive warfare did Hannibal's home government – increasingly uneasy about the whole escapade and now with the invading army of Africanus to face – recall him to Carthage. But it was not merely an Italian and North African war. It had started with a clash between Romans and Carthaginians in Spain, hence the Roman fighting there through most of the second century BCE. And the possibility of support for Hannibal from Macedon pushed the Romans into a series of wars in northern Greece that ended with the defeat of the Macedonian king Perseus in 168 BCE by Aemilius Paullus, Scipio Aemilianus' natural father, and soon after with Roman control over the whole of what we call mainland Greece.

What is more, the Romans were also engaged in major conflicts with the Gauls in the far north of Italy in the 220s BCE. They made periodic interventions across the Adriatic too, partly to deal with so-called pirates (a catch-all term for 'enemies in ships') who were supported by the tribes and kingdoms on the opposite coast – or so it was said. And in 190 BCE, under the command of Scipio Asiaticus, they decisively defeated Antiochus 'the Great' of Syria. Not only was he busy modelling himself on Alexander the Great and extending his power base accordingly, but he had also given a home to Hannibal, now in exile from Carthage, who was reputed to be offering the king master classes in how to confront the Romans.

Military campaigning was a defining feature of Roman life, and Roman writers organised the history of this period, as I have just done, around its succession of wars, giving them the shorthand titles that have often stuck till the present day. When Sallust called his essay on Catiline's plot *The War against Catiline*, or *Bellum Catilinae*, he was reflecting, and maybe slightly parodying, the Roman tradition of seeing war as *the* structuring principle of history. It was a tradition that went back a long way. There is a surviving snatch of Ennius' epic poem on the history of Rome that refers explicitly to 'the Second Punic War', in which he had fought as a Roman ally; it was written even before the third had happened.

In practical terms the Romans directed enormous resources to warfare and, even as victors, paid a huge price in human life. Throughout this period, somewhere between 10 and 25 per cent of the Roman adult male population would have served in the legions each year, a greater proportion than in any other pre-industrial state and, on the higher estimate, comparable to the call-up rate in World War I. Twice as many legions fought at Cannae as had fought at Sentinum some eighty years earlier – which is a convenient indication of the increasing size of these conflicts and the ever more complex and demanding logistics of equipment, supply and animal transport. An army of the size the Romans and their allies fielded at Cannae would, for example, have needed around 100 tonnes of wheat alone, every day. The deals with the local communities that this implies, the marshalling of the hundreds of pack animals, who added to the demand by necessarily consuming part of what they carried, and the collection and distribution networks would have been inconceivable at the beginning of the century.

It is harder to put a figure on the casualties: there was no systematic tally of deaths on an ancient battlefield; and all numbers in ancient texts have to be treated with suspicion, victims of exaggeration, misunderstanding and over the years some terrible miscopying by medieval monks. Nevertheless, the combined total of the Roman casualty figures that Livy provides for all the battles that he records in the first thirty years of the second century BCE – so not including the massive losses sustained against Hannibal – comes to just over 55,000 dead. This is far too low. There was probably a patriotic tendency to downplay Roman losses; it is not clear whether allies as well as Roman citizens were included; there must have been some battles and skirmishes which do not feature in Livy's list; and those who subsequently died of their wounds must have been very many indeed (in most circumstances, ancient weapons were much better at wounding than killing outright; death followed later, by infection). But it gives a hint of the human cost of this warfare on the Roman side alone. The toll on the defeated is even harder to gauge but was presumably worse.

It is necessary, however, to see beyond this carnage, terrible as it was, to look harder at the reality and organisation of the fighting and to investigate the domestic politics that underpinned Roman expansion, as well as the Roman ambitions and wider geopolitics of the ancient Mediterranean that may have encouraged it. Polybius is the most important guide, but there is other vivid contemporary evidence – often documents inscribed on stone – that makes it possible to trace some of the interactions between the Romans and the outside world. Accounts still survive that capture at first hand the bewildering experiences in Rome of envoys from small Greek towns; and we can still read the texts of detailed treaties between the Romans and states abroad. The oldest fragment, from 212 BCE, is part of a much longer agreement between Rome and a group of Greek cities, and it sets out precise rules on how any war booty is to be divided between Rome and the others: basically, cities and houses to the Greeks, movable property to the Romans.

There were also important consequences for Rome itself of military success overseas. The literary revolution was only one part of it. By the mid second century BCE, the profits of warfare had made the Roman people by far the richest of any in their known world. Thousands upon thousands of captives became the slave labour that worked the Roman fields, mines and mills, that exploited resources on a much more intensive scale than ever before and fuelled Roman production and Roman economic growth. Bullion by the barrow load, taken (or stolen) from rich eastern cities and kingdoms, poured into the well-guarded basement of the Temple of Saturn in the Forum, which served as the state 'treasury'. And there was enough left over to line the pockets of the soldiers, from the grandest general to the rawest recruit.

There was plenty for Romans to celebrate. Some of the cash was ploughed into new civic amenities, from new harbour installations and vast warehouses on the Tiber to new temples lining the streets, commemorating the assistance of the gods in securing the victories that had brought all this wealth. And it is easy to imagine the widespread pleasure when in 167 BCE Rome became a tax-free state: the treasury was so overflowing – thanks, in particular, to the spoils from the recent victory over Macedon – that direct taxation of Roman citizens was suspended except in emergencies, although they remained liable to a range of other levies, such as customs dues or a special tax charged on freeing slaves.

Yet these changes were destabilising too. It was not just that some curmudgeonly Roman moralists worried about the dangerous effects of all this wealth and 'luxury' (as they put it). The expansion of Roman power raised big debates and paradoxes about Rome's place in the world, about what counted as 'Roman' when so much of the Mediterranean was under Roman control and about where the boundary between barbarism and civilisation now lay, and which side of that boundary Rome was on. When, for example, at the end of the third century BCE the Roman authorities welcomed the Great Mother goddess from the highlands of what is now Turkey and solemnly installed her in a temple on the Palatine, complete with her retinue of self-castrated, self-flagellating, long-haired priests – how Roman was that?

Winning, in other words, brought its own problems and paradoxes. But even the definition of 'winning' and 'losing' can be uncertain. Those uncertainties are sharply revealed in the story of the Battle of Cannae, in the second of the Punic Wars. It gives a glimpse of the strategy, the tactics and the real face of ancient combat, but for Polybius – and perhaps for Hannibal too – it raised the question of whether Rome's most notorious defeat was not in some ways the strongest indicator of its power.

Cannae and the elusive face of battle

In 216 BCE the authorities in Rome performed what Livy calls 'a very un-Roman ritual'. They buried alive in the city centre two pairs of human victims, Gauls and Greeks. It was the closest to human sacrifice that the Romans ever came, and Livy's embarrassment in telling the story is evident. Yet it was not the only time they did this: the same ritual had been carried out in 228 BCE in the face of a Gallic invasion from the north, and was again in 113 BCE, when another such invasion threatened. In 216 BCE the sacrifice was prompted by Hannibal's victory earlier that year at Cannae, two hundred miles away to the southeast, which had left vast numbers of Romans dead after a single afternoon's fighting (estimates vary from around 40,000 to 70,000 – in other words, something at the level of a hundred deaths a minute). There are all kinds of puzzles about this cruel ritual. Why this choice of nationalities? What relationship did it have to the similar burial alive of Vestal Virgins who were convicted of breaking their vow of chastity (which also happened in 216 BCE and 113 BCE)? It certainly points to the fear and panic that hit Rome after – to see it in his terms, for once – Hannibal's stunning victory.

The Battle of Cannae and the whole history of the Second Punic War have mesmerised generals, pundits and historians ever since. Probably no war has been refought so often in so many studies and lecture rooms or been scrutinised so intently by the military men of the modern world, from Napoleon Bonaparte to Field Marshal Montgomery and Norman Schwarzkopf. Its causes remain as clouded in speculation and second-guessing as they ever were. Retrospectively it became for the Romans another clash of superpowers, and the stuff of epic poetry. Virgil's *Aeneid* even gives it a mythic origin in Roman prehistory, when the Carthaginian queen Dido, abandoned by her lover Aeneas (on his way to found Rome), throws herself to her death onto a funeral pyre – cursing him and his whole race. In reality, it is hard to fathom either the Roman or the Carthaginian aims. Carthage, in its prime position on the North African coast, with impressive harbours and a grander cityscape than contemporary Rome, had wide trading interests in the western Mediterranean and might well have had reason to distrust the growing power of its Italian rival. Ancient and modern writers have pointed, in varying degrees, to Rome's provocation of Hannibal in Spain and Hannibal's grudge against Rome for its victory in the First Punic War. At the latest count, there are more than thirty versions of what really lay behind the conflict.

For many analysts, the strategic choices of the Romans and Carthaginians have been particularly intriguing, and revealing. On Hannibal's side, these go far beyond the favourite puzzles about what elephant route he might have taken across the Alps or whether his reported trick of breaking open Alpine rocks by pouring vinegar on them could ever have worked (probably not). The main issue has always been why on earth, after the stunning victory at Cannae, he did not go on to take the city of Rome while he had the chance but instead gave the Romans time to recover. Livy imagines one of Hannibal's officers, by the name of Maharbal, saying to him: 'You know how to win a victory, Hannibal; you don't know how to exploit it.' Montgomery is only one of the many later generals who have agreed with Maharbal. Hannibal was a brilliant soldier and dashing adventurer who had the final prize within his grasp, but for some unfathomable reason (loss of nerve or some flaw of character) he failed to take it. Hence his tragic glamour.

The eventual victory of the Romans highlights a much more down-to-earth clash of strategy and military style, between on the one hand Quintus Fabius Maximus Verrucosus Cunctator – the last three names, 'greatest, warty, delayer', being a characteristic Roman combination of boastfulness and realism – and on the other Scipio Africanus. Fabius took command after Cannae, avoided pitched battle with Hannibal and played a waiting game, combining guerrilla tactics with a scorched-earth policy, to wear down the enemy (hence 'de-layer'). For some observers, this canny strategy largely won the day. Despite his close association with Africanus, Ennius credited Fabius with ensuring Rome's survival: 'One man alone restored the state to us by delaying [*cunctando*],' he wrote. George Washington, the 'American Fabius', as he has sometimes been called, opted for similar tactics at the start of the American War of Independence, harassing rather than directly engaging the enemy, and even the British left-wing Fabian Society adopted his name and example – the message being, 'if you want the revolution to be successful, you must, like Fabius, bide your time'. But there have always been those who have thought Fabius a slowcoach or a ditherer rather than a clever strategist, in contrast to the much more dashing Scipio Africanus, who eventually took over the command and persuaded the senate to allow him to move the war into Africa and finish Hannibal off there. In describing that senate meeting, Livy scripts a largely imaginary debate between the cautious, elderly Fabius and Africanus, the energetic rising star. It polarises not only their different approaches to the war but also different ways of understanding Roman *virtus*. Did 'manliness' necessarily mean speed and vigour? Could it be heroic to be slow?

Retrospective generalship can be misleading, however, especially when it comes to re-creating what happened in any individual battle. Talk of tactics, and all the splendid military diagrams that usually ac-company it, offers a highly sanitised version of Roman warfare and suggests that we know more about the face of Roman battle than we do – even about such a momentous engagement as Cannae. It is true that there are lengthy accounts in Polybius (who may have consulted eyewitnesses), Livy and other historians, but these are incompatible in details, hard to follow and in places almost nonsensical. We do not even know where exactly the battle took place, and the different pro-posed sites are the result of trying to match up conflicting versions in ancient writers with the layout of the land, as it might have been then, not forgetting the changed course of the nearby river. What is more, despite the almost mystical modern admiration for Hannibal's battle plans at Cannae, which are still on the syllabus of military academies, they amounted to little more than a clever version of going round the back of the enemy. This was the one trick that ancient generals always tried if they could, for it offered the best chance of encircling the opposition and the only reliable way of killing or capturing them in large numbers.

Indeed, it is hard to see how more sophisticated tactics could have been deployed in an ancient battle with more than 100,000 men on the field. How the commanders could have issued effective instructions to their armies or how they could even have known what was going on in different areas of the fighting are almost complete mysteries. Add to that the polyglot forces, whether multinational mercenaries or non-Latin-speaking allies of the Romans, strange star turns (some of the Gauls apparently fought naked), cavalrymen trying to manoeuvre and fight without the benefit of stirrups (a later invention) and, in some engagements (though not at Cannae, as Hannibal's had all died by then), wounded elephants running wild and charging back into their own lines, and the picture is chaos. Aemilius Paullus may have had this in mind when he remarked: 'A man who knows how to conquer in battle also knows how to give a banquet and organise games.' He is usually taken to have been referring to the connection between military victory and spectacle; but he may have also been hinting that the talents of a successful general did not go far beyond basic organisational expertise.

Nevertheless, Cannae was indeed a crucial turning point in the Second Punic War, and in the longer history of Roman military expansion, precisely because the Romans lost so many men there and nearly ran out of cash. The basic bronze coin – the *as* – was reduced in weight over the course of the war, from almost 300 grams to just over 50. And Livy tells how in 214 BCE individual Romans were called upon to pay directly to man the fleet: a nice indication of the patriotism that surrounded the war effort, of the emptiness of the public treasury, but also of the cash that there still was in private hands, despite the crisis. Almost any other ancient state in that position would have been forced to surrender. Nothing underscores better the importance of Rome's enormous reserves of citizen and allied manpower than the single fact that it continued to fight the war. To judge from Hannibal's actions after Cannae, he perhaps saw this point too. It may not have been a loss of nerve that dissuaded him from marching on Rome. Realising that allied manpower sustained Rome's strength, he directed himself to the slow process of winning over the Italian allies – with some success, but never in sufficient numbers to undermine Roman durability.

That must also have been in Polybius' mind when he chose to insert into his *Histories* a long digression on the strength of the Roman political system, as it was at the time of Cannae. His overall aim was to explain why the Romans had conquered the world, and part of that explanation lay in the strength and stability of Rome's internal political structures. His account is the first more or less contemporary description of Roman political life to survive (Polybius was looking back fifty years or so but also mixing in observations of his own time); and at the same time it is the first attempt at a theoretical analysis of how Roman politics worked, one that sets the agenda even now.

Polybius on the politics of Rome

Polybius, who knew Rome as both an enemy and a friend, was uniquely well placed to reflect on the rise of the city and on its institutions. Born into the political aristocracy of a town in the Peloponnese, he was in his thirties in 168 BCE, when Aemilius Paullus defeated King Perseus, and he found himself one of 1,000 Greek detainees taken to Rome as part of the political purge, or precautionary measures, that followed.

Most of them were placed under a light-touch regime of house arrest and scattered among the towns of Italy. Polybius, who already had a reputation as a writer, was luckier. He quickly fell in with Aemilianus (they apparently met over the loan of some books) and his family and was allowed to stay in Rome, where he became the young man's de facto tutor and as close as 'father to son'. Snatches of Polybius' advice to Aemilianus were still being quoted, or misquoted, more than two hundred years later. 'Never come back from the Forum,' he is supposed to have urged, 'until you have made at least one new friend.'

The surviving hostages were released around 150 BCE. Only 300 were still alive, and one outspoken Roman is supposed to have complained about the senate wasting its time 'debating whether some elderly Greeks should be buried by undertakers here or in Greece'. But Polybius was soon back with his Roman associates, travelling with the army to Carthage and acting as an intermediary in the negotiations that followed the destruction of Corinth in 146 BCE. He

32. This image of Polybius was put up in the second century CE in a small town in Greece by a man who claimed to be one of the historian's descendants. His only 'portrait' to survive, it can hardly be a realistic likeness. In fact, it casts him in the guise of warriors from fifth century BCE classical Greece, 300 years before his time. To make things more complicated, the original sculpture has been lost and survives only as the plaster cast shown here.

was also still writing his *Histories*, which ended up spreading over forty books, mainly focusing on the years 220 to 167 BCE, with a brief flashback to the First Punic War and an epilogue to bring the story down to 146 BCE. Whoever was Polybius' main intended readership, Greek or Roman, his work became an important reference point for later Romans trying to understand their city's rise. It was certainly on Livy's desk when he was writing his *History*.

Predictably, modern historians have found it hard to know quite where to fix the boundary between Polybius the Roman hostage and critic of Roman rule and Polybius the Roman collaborator. He certainly sometimes performed a deft balancing act between his different loyalties, giving behind-the-scenes advice at one point to a distinguished Syrian hostage on how to slip away from his detention, while carefully insisting in his *Histories* that on the day of the great escape he himself was at home, 'ill in bed'. But whatever Polybius' political stance, he had the advantage of knowing both sides of the Roman story, and he had the opportunity to quiz some of the leading Roman players. He dissected Rome's internal organisation – which he insisted underpinned its success abroad – from a vantage point that combined a couple of decades of first-hand experience with all the sophistication of the Greek political theory in which he had been trained back home. His work is, in effect, one of the earliest surviving attempts at comparative political anthropology.

Not surprisingly, his account is a wonderful combination of acute observation, bafflement and occasionally desperate attempts to theorise Roman politics in his own terms. He scrutinised his Roman surroundings and his new Roman friends with care. He spotted, for example, the importance of religion, or 'fear of the gods', in controlling Roman behaviour, and he was impressed with the systematic efficiency of Roman organisation; hence his important – but now often skipped – discussion of military arrangements, with its teach-yourself rules on laying out an army camp, where the consul's tent should be pitched, how to plan a legionary baggage train, and the savage system of discipline. He was also sharp enough to see beneath the surface of various Roman customs and favourite pastimes to their underlying social significance. All those stories of Roman valour, heroism and self-sacrifice that he must have heard – told and retold around military campfires or at dinner tables – were not simply for amusement, he concluded. Their function was to encourage the young to imitate the gallant deeds of their ancestors; they were one aspect of the spirit of emulation, ambition and competition that he saw running right through Roman elite society.

Another aspect of this – one that he makes into an extended, if slightly ghoulish, case study – was to be found in the funerals of 'distinguished men'. Again, Polybius must have witnessed enough of these to draw out their deeper significance. The body, he explains, was carried into the Forum and placed on the *rostra*, normally propped up somehow in an upright position, so it was visible to a large audience. In the procession that followed, family members wore masks made in the likeness of the dead man's ancestors and dressed in the costume appropriate to the offices each had held (purple-bordered togas and so on), as if they were all present 'living and breathing'. The funeral address, delivered by a family member, started with the achievements of the corpse on the *rostra* but then went through the careers of all the other characters, who by this time were sitting on ivory, or at least ivory-veneered, chairs lined up next to the dead man. 'The most important upshot of this,' Polybius concludes, 'is that the younger generation is inspired to endure all suffering for the common good, in the hope of winning the glory that belongs to the brave.'

This is perhaps a rather rosy view of the competitive side of Roman culture. Unchecked competition eventually did more to destroy than to uphold the Republic. Even before that, it is a fair guess that for every young Roman inspired to live up to the achievements of his ancestors, there was another oppressed by the weight of tradition and expectation that fell upon him – as Polybius might have realised if he had chosen to reflect on all the stories in Roman culture about sons who killed their fathers. But it is a view nicely encapsulated in the words of another epitaph in the tomb of the Scipios, which it is tempting to think Polybius might have seen: 'I produced offspring. I sought to equal the deeds of my father. I won the praise of my ancestors so that they are glad that I was born to them. My career has ennobled my family line.'

At the heart of Polybius' argument, however, lay bigger questions. How could you characterise the Roman political system as a whole? How did it work? There was never a written Roman constitution, but Polybius saw in Rome a perfect example in practice of an old Greek philosophical ideal: the 'mixed constitution', which combined the best aspects of monarchy, aristocracy and democracy. The consuls – who had full military command, could summon assemblies of the people and could give orders to all other officials (except the plebeian tribunes) – represented the monarchical element. The senate, which by this date had charge of Rome's finances, responsibility for delegations to and from other cities and de facto oversight of law and security throughout Roman and allied territory, represented the aristocratic element. The people represented the democratic element. This was not democracy or 'the people' in the modern sense: there was no such thing as universal suffrage in the ancient world – women and slaves never had formal political rights anywhere. Polybius meant the group of male citizens as a whole. As in classical Athens, they – and they alone – elected the state officials, passed or rejected laws, made the final decision on going to war and acted as a judicial court for major offences.

The secret, Polybius suggested, lay in a delicate relationship of checks and balances between consuls, the senate and the people, so that neither monarchy nor aristocracy nor democracy ever entirely prevailed. The consuls, for example, might have had full, monarchical command on campaign, but they had to be elected by the people in the first place, and they depended on the senate for funding – and it was the senate which decided whether the successful general should be awarded a triumph at the end of his campaign, and a vote of the people was required to ratify any treaty that might be made. And so on. It was, Polybius argued, such balances across the political system that produced the internal stability on which Roman external success was built.

This is a clever piece of analysis, sensitive to the tiny differences and subtle nuances which distinguish one political system from another. To be sure, in some respects Polybius tries to shoehorn the political life that he witnessed at Rome into a Greek analytical model that does not entirely fit. Saddling his discussion with terms like 'democracy' is, for example, deeply misleading. 'Democracy' (*demokratia*) was rooted politically and linguistically in the Greek world. It was never a rallying cry at Rome, even in its limited ancient sense or even for the most radical of Roman popular politicians. In most of the conservative writing that survives, the word means something close to 'mob rule'. There is little point in asking how 'democratic' the politics of Republican Rome were: Romans fought for, and about, liberty, not democracy. Yet, in another way, by nudging his readers to keep sight of the people in their picture of Roman politics and to look beyond the power of the elected officials and the aristocratic senate, Polybius sparked an important debate that is still alive today. How influential was the popular voice in Roman Republican politics? Who controlled Rome? How should *we* characterise this Roman political system?

It is easy enough to paint a picture of Republican political processes as completely dominated by the wealthy minority. The upshot of the Conflict of the Orders was not popular revolution but the creation of a new governing class, comprising rich plebeians and patricians. The first qualification for most political offices was wealth on a substantial scale. No one could stand for election without passing a financial test that excluded most citizens; the exact amount needed to qualify is not known, but the implications are that it was set at the very top level of the census hierarchy, the so-called cavalry or equestrian rating. When the people came together to vote, the system of voting was stacked in favour of the wealthy. We have already seen how that worked in the Centuriate Assembly, which elected senior officials: if the rich centuries were united, they could determine the result without the poorer centuries even having the chance to vote. The other main assembly based on geographical 'tribal' divisions was more equitable in theory – but, as time went by, not necessarily so in practice. Of the thirty-five geographical divisions which were finally defined in 241 BCE (up to that point the number of tribes had increased as citizenship was extended through Italy), only four covered the city itself. The remaining thirty-one covered Rome's now far-flung rural territory. As votes could be cast only in person in the city, the influence of those who could afford the time and the transport to make the journey was overwhelming; the votes of the resident city population had an impact on only that tiny minority of urban tribes. Besides, strictly speaking, the assemblies were simply for voting, on a list of candidates or on a proposal put by a senior official. There was no general discussion; no proposals or even amendments could come from the floor; in the case of almost every piece of proposed legislation we know of, the people voted in favour of what was put before them. This was not popular power as we understand it.

Yet there was another side to it. As well as the formal prerogatives of the people that Polybius stresses, there are clear traces of a wider political culture in which the popular voice was a key element. The votes of the poor mattered and were eagerly canvassed. The rich were not usually united, and elections were competitive. Those holding, or seeking, political office set great store on persuading the people to vote for them or for their proposed laws and devoted enormous attention to honing the techniques of rhetoric that would allow them to do that. They ignored or humiliated the poor at their peril. One of the distinctive features of the Republican political scene were the semi-formal meetings (or *contiones*), often held immediately before the voting assemblies, in which rival officials tried to win over the people to their point of view (Cicero delivered his second and fourth speeches against Catiline, for example, at *contiones*). Quite how frequent or well attended they usually were, we do not know for sure. But there are several hints that they involved political passion, vociferous enthusiasm, and very loud noise. On one occasion, in the first century BCE, it was said that the shouting was so thunderous that a crow, which had the bad luck to be flying past, fell to the ground, stunned.

There are also all kinds of anecdotes about the importance and intensity of canvassing, and how the vote of the people could be won or lost. Polybius tells a curious story about the Syrian king Antiochus IV (*Epiphanes*, 'famous' or even 'manifest god'), the son of Antiochus the Great, who had been 'crushed' by Scipio Asiaticus. As a young man he had lived more than a decade as a hostage in Rome before being swapped for a younger relative, the one whom Polybius later advised on his escape plans. On his return to the East, he took with him a variety of Roman habits that he had picked up during his stay. These mostly came down to displaying a popular touch: talking with anyone he met, giving presents to ordinary people and making the rounds of craftsmen's shops. But most striking of all, he would dress up in a toga and go around the marketplace as if he were a candidate for election, shaking people by the hand and asking for their vote. This baffled the people in his showy capital city of Antioch, who were not used to this kind of thing from a monarch and nicknamed him *Epimanes* ('bonkers' or, to preserve the pun, 'fatuous'). But it is clear that one lesson that Antiochus had drawn from Rome was that the common people and their votes were important.

Equally revealing is an anecdote about another member of the Scipio family in the second century BCE, Publius Cornelius Scipio

Nasica. He was out canvassing one day in a bid to be elected to the office of aedile and was busy shaking the hands of voters (standard procedure, then as now) when he came across one whose hands were hardened by work in the fields. 'My goodness,' the young aristocrat joked, 'do you walk on them?' He was overheard, and the common people concluded that he had been taunting their poverty and their labour. The upshot, needless to say, was that he lost the election.

So what kind of political system was this? The balance between the different interests was certainly not as equitable as Polybius makes it seem. The poor could never rise to the top of Roman politics; the common people could never seize the political initiative; and it was axiomatic that the richer an individual citizen was, the more political weight he should have. But this form of disequilibrium is familiar in many modern so-called democracies: at Rome too the wealthy and privileged competed for political office and political power that could only be granted by popular election and by the favour of ordinary people who would never have the financial means to stand themselves. As young Scipio Nasica found to his cost, the success of the rich was a gift bestowed by the poor. The rich had to learn the lesson that they depended on the people as a whole.

An empire of obedience

Polybius was in no doubt that Rome's stable 'constitution' provided an important foundation for its success abroad. But he had experienced the sharp end of Roman warfare, and he also saw Rome as an aggressive power, with imperialist aims to take over the whole world. 'They made a daring bid,' he insists at the end of his account of the First Punic War, 'for universal domination and control – and they succeeded in their purpose.' Not everyone agreed. There were even some Greeks, he acknowledged, who suggested that Rome's conquests came about 'by chance or unintentionally'. Many Romans insisted that their overseas expansion resulted from a series of just wars, in the sense of wars undertaken with the necessary support of the gods, in self-defence or in the defence of allies, who had often solicited Rome's help. It was not aggression at all.

If Polybius had lived to see, less than a hundred years after his death, the larger-than-life-sized statues of Roman generals holding a globe in their hands, he would no doubt have felt vindicated. A vision of world mastery certainly lay behind many expressions of Roman power in the first century BCE and later ('an empire without limit', as Jupiter is made to prophesy in Virgil's *Aeneid*). But Polybius was wrong, as his own narrative of events clearly shows, to imagine that at this earlier period the Romans were driven by that kind of acquisitive imperialist ideology or some sense of manifest destiny. There was thirst for glory, desire for conquest, and sheer greed for the economic profits of victory at all levels of Roman society. It was not for nothing that the prospect of rich booty was dangled before the people when they were asked to vote on entering the First Punic War. But whatever fantasies might have been exchanged at the Scipios' parties, none of this adds up to a plan for world domination.

Much like the extension of Roman control within Italy, this expansion overseas in the third and second centuries BCE was more complicated than the familiar myth of the Roman legions marching in, conquering and taking over foreign territory. First, the Romans were not the only agents in the process. They did not invade a world of peace-loving peoples, who were just minding their own business until these voracious thugs came along. However cynical we might rightly be about Roman claims that they went to war only in response to requests for assistance from friends and allies (that has been the excuse for some of the most aggressive wars in history), part of the pressure for Rome to intervene did come from outside.

The world of the eastern Mediterranean, from Greece to modern

Turkey and beyond, was the context for most of Rome's military activity at this period. It was a world of political conflict, shifting alliances and continuous, brutal interstate violence, not unlike early Italy, but on a much vaster scale. This was the legacy of the smash-and-grab conquests of Alexander the Great, who died in 323 BCE, before he had to face what to do with those he had defeated. His successors formed rival dynasties, which became involved in a more or less unbroken series of wars and disputes with one another and with the smaller states and coalitions on their margins. Pyrrhus was one of these dynasts. Antiochus Epiphanes was another: after his detention at Rome and attempts at popular politics at home, he managed in his ten-year reign between 175 and 164 BCE to invade Egypt (twice), Cyprus, Judaea (also provoking the Maccabean Revolt), Parthia and Armenia.

The more powerful Rome was perceived to be, the more these warring parties looked on the Romans as useful allies in local power struggles and courted their influence. Representatives from the East repeatedly came to Rome in the hope of winning moral support or military intervention. That is a running theme in the historical accounts of the period: there are plenty of envoys reported, for example, in the run-up to Aemilius Paullus' campaign against Perseus, trying to persuade the Romans to do something about the ambitions of Macedon. But the most vivid picture of how this 'courting' worked in practice comes from Teos, a town on the western coast of modern Turkey. It is a mid-second-century BCE inscription recording the attempts made to draw the Romans into a minor dispute, about which nothing else is known, over some land rights between the city of Abdera in northern Greece and a local king, Kotys.

The text is a 'thank-you letter' carved on stone, addressed to the town of Teos by the people of Abdera. For the Teans had apparently agreed to send two men to Rome, almost lobbyists in a modern sense, to drum up Roman support for Abdera's case against the king. The Abderans describe exactly how this pair operated, right down to their regular house calls on key members of the senate. The delegates apparently worked so hard that 'they wore themselves out physically and mentally, and they met the leading Romans and won them over by paying obeisance to them every day'; and when some of the people they visited appeared to be on Kotys' side (for he had also sent envoys to Rome), 'they won their friendship by laying out the facts and paying daily calls at their atria', that is at the main central hall of their Roman houses.

The silence of our text on the outcome of these approaches hints that things did not go the Abderans' way. But the snapshot here of rival representatives not merely beating a path to the senate but pressing their case daily on individual senators gives an idea of just how actively and persistently Roman assistance could be sought. And the literally hundreds of statues of individual Romans – as 'saviours and benefactors' – put up in the cities of the Greek world show how that intervention, if successful, could be celebrated. We cannot now identify every piece of doublethink behind such words: there was no doubt as much fear and flattery involved as sincere gratitude. But they are a useful reminder that the simple shorthand 'Roman conquest' can obscure a wide range of perspectives, motivations and aspirations on every side of the encounter.

Besides, the Romans did not attempt to annex overseas territory systematically or to impose standard mechanisms of control. That partly explains why the process of expansion could be so quick: they were not establishing any infrastructure of government. They certainly extracted material rewards from those they defeated, but in different, ad hoc ways. They imposed vast cash indemnities on some states, a total of more than 600 tonnes of silver bullion in the first half of the second century BCE alone. Elsewhere they took over the ready-made regular taxation regimes set up by earlier rulers. Occasionally they devised new ways of raking off rich revenues. The Spanish silver mines, for example, once part of Hannibal's domain, were soon producing so much more ore that the environmental pollution from its processing can still be detected in datable samples extracted from deep in the Greenland ice cap. And Polybius, who visited Spain in the mid second century BCE, wrote of 40,000 miners, mostly slaves no doubt, working just one region of mining territory alone (not literally, perhaps: '40,000' was a common ancient shorthand for 'a very large number', like our 'millions'). The Romans' forms of political control were equally varied, ranging from hands-off treaties of 'friendship', through the taking of hostages as a guarantee of good behaviour, to the more or less permanent presence of Roman troops and Roman officials. What happened after Aemilius Paullus defeated King Perseus is just one example of how such a package of arrangements might look. Macedon was broken up into four independent, self-governing states; they paid tax to Rome, at half the rate that Perseus had levied it; and, in this case, the Macedonian mines were shut down, to prevent their resources from being used to build up a new power base in the region.

It *was* a coercive empire in the sense that the Romans took the profits and tried to ensure that they got their own way when they wanted, with the threat of force always in the background. It was not an empire of annexation in the sense that later Romans would understand it. There was no detailed legal framework of control, rules or regulations – or, for that matter, visionary aspirations. At this period, even the Latin word *imperium*, which by the end of the first century BCE could mean 'empire', in the sense of the whole area under direct Roman government, meant something much closer to 'the power to issue orders that are obeyed'. And *provincia* (or 'province'), which became the standard term for a carefully defined subdivision of empire under the control of a governor, was not a geographical term but meant a responsibility assigned to Roman officials. That could be, and often was, an assignment of military activity or administration in a particular place. From the later third century BCE, Sicily and Sardinia were regularly designated as *provinciae*, and from the early second century BCE two military *provinciae* in Spain were a standard fixture, though their boundaries were fluid. But it could equally well be a responsibility for, say, the Roman treasury – and, around the turn of the third and second centuries BCE, Plautus in his comedies uses the word *provincia* as a joke to refer to the duties of slaves. At this point, no Roman was sent out to be the 'governor of a province', as they later were.

What was at stake for the Romans was whether they could win in battle and then whether – by persuasion, bullying or force – they could impose their will where, when and if they chose. The style of this *imperium* is vividly summed up in the story of the last encounter between Antiochus Epiphanes and the Romans. The king was invading Egypt for the second time, and the Egyptians had asked the Romans for help. A Roman envoy, Gaius Popilius Laenas, was dispatched and met Antiochus outside Alexandria. After his long familiarity with the Romans, the king no doubt expected a rather civil meeting. Instead, Laenas handed him a decree of the senate instructing him to withdraw from Egypt immediately. When Antiochus asked for time to consult his advisors, Laenas picked up a stick and drew a circle in the dust around him. There was to be no stepping out of that circle before he had given his answer. Stunned, Antiochus meekly agreed to the senate's demands. This was an empire of obedience.

The impact of empire

It was also an empire of communication, mobility, misunderstanding and changing perspectives, as a closer look at that story of the delegation from Teos vividly reveals. It is easy enough to sympathise with the predicament of the underdog. The two men had sailed across half the Mediterranean on a journey that would have taken anything between two and five weeks, depending on the season of the year, the quality of the ship and whether they were prepared to sail after dark (night sailing could take a week off the journey but was fraught with added danger). When they arrived in Rome, they would have been faced with a city that was larger, but considerably less elegant, than some they had passed through on the journey. One unfortunate Greek ambassador at about the same time is known to have fallen into an open Roman sewer and broken his leg – and made the most of his convalescence by giving introductory lectures on literary theory to a curious audience.

Rome had strange, foreign customs too. Interestingly, whoever at Abdera composed the text on the stone did not even try to translate some distinctively Roman terms (such as *atria* and *patronus*, 'patron') but merely transcribed them in Greek script. When they did venture a translation, it could be decidedly odd. The envoys were said, for example, to have offered daily 'obeisance' to the Romans. The Greek word here, *proskynesis*, literally means 'bowing and scraping' or 'kissing the feet'. This presumably refers to the Roman practice of *salutatio*, which involved clients and dependants paying a morning call on their patrons but no kissing of feet at all – though maybe these foreign visitors saw the practice for the humiliation it was. We can only guess how they made contacts or put their case. Many wealthy Romans spoke some Greek, better than the Teans would have known Latin, but not always very well. Real Greeks were known to have made wicked fun of the terrible Roman accent.

Yet when this pair of Teans turned up in the city, some Romans may have felt unease too. For even if the attention and the recognition of Roman power was flattering, this was a new world, maybe almost as perplexing for them as for their visitors. What must it have felt like to be confronted with a stream of foreigners from as far away as it was possible to imagine, speaking too quickly in a language you only just understood, apparently extremely bothered about a small piece of land of which you knew nothing, and dangerously liable to bow down and kiss your feet? If, as Polybius put it, the Romans had conquered almost the whole of the known world in the fifty-three years up to 168 BCE, then over that same period Rome, and Roman culture, had been transformed too by those vastly expanded horizons.

This transformation involved movements of people, into and out of Rome, on a scale never before seen in the ancient world. When slaves from all over the Mediterranean poured into Italy and into Rome itself, it was certainly a story of exploitation; but it was also one of massive forced migration. The figures that ancient writers give for the captives taken by Romans in particular wars may well be exaggerations (100,000 in the First Punic War, for example, or 150,000 taken by Aemilius Paullus from just one part of Perseus' territory), and anyway many of them would not have been transported directly back to Rome but would have been sold to middlemen much closer to the point of capture. But it is a fair estimate that in the early second century BCE the numbers of new slaves arriving in the peninsula as a direct result of victories overseas averaged out at more than 8,000 per year, at a time when the total number of adult male Roman citizens, inside and outside the city, was in the order of 300,000. In due course, a significant proportion of these would have been freed and become new Roman citizens. The impact not only on the Roman economy but also on the cultural and ethnic diversity of the citizen body was enormous; the division between Romans and outsiders was increasingly blurred.

— At the same time, Romans poured overseas. There had been Roman travellers, traders and adventurers exploring the Mediterranean for centuries. 'Lucius son of Gaius', the mercenary who left his name on an inscription on Crete in the late third century BCE, cannot have been the first Roman to make his living in one of the world's oldest professions. But from the second century BCE, thousands of Romans were spending long periods outside the Italian peninsula. There were Roman traders swarming over the eastern Mediterranean, cashing in on the commercial opportunities that followed conquest, from the slave trade and the spice trade to more mundane army supply contracts. Antiochus Epiphanes even hired a Roman architect, Decimus Cossutius, for building works in Athens, and we can track this man's descendants and ex-slaves, still active in the construction business in Italy and the East decades later. But it was the soldiers, now serving for years on end overseas rather than just for the traditional summer campaign at Rome's back door, who made up the majority of ordinary Romans abroad. After the Second Punic War, there were regularly more than 30,000 Roman citizens in the army outside Italy, anywhere from Spain to the eastern Mediterranean.

This threw up a whole series of new dilemmas. In 171 BCE, for example, the senate was confronted with a deputation from Spain representing more than 4,000 men who were the sons of Roman soldiers and Spanish women. As there was no formal right of marriage between Romans and native Spaniards, these men were, in our terms, stateless. They cannot have been the only ones with this problem. When Aemilianus later came as a new broom to take over the army command in Spain, he is said to have thrown 2,000 'prostitutes' out of the Roman camp (I suspect that the women might have defined themselves rather differently). But in the case before the senate, the offspring concerned had the confidence to ask the Romans for a city to call their own, and presumably for some clarification about their legal position. They were settled in the town of Carteia on the southern tip of Spain, which – with the Romans' usual flair for improvisation – was given the status of a Latin colony and defined as 'a colony of ex-slaves'. How many hours of discussion it took the senators to decide that the bizarre combination of 'ex-slave' and 'Latin' offered the closest match available for the civic status of these technically illegitimate Roman soldiers' sons, we have no idea. But this certainly shows them grappling with the issues of what it was to be (partly) Roman outside Italy.

By the mid second century BCE, well over half the adult male citizens of Rome would have seen something of the world abroad, leaving an unknown number of children where they went. To put it another way, the Roman population had suddenly become by far the most travelled of any state ever in the ancient Mediterranean, with only Alexander the Great's Macedonians or the traders of Carthage as possible rivals. Even for those who never stepped abroad, there were new imaginative horizons, new glimpses of places overseas and new ways of understanding their place in the world.

The triumphal processions of victorious generals offered one of the most impressive windows onto the outside. When the Roman crowds lined the streets to welcome home their conquering armies, which paraded through the city with their profits and plunder on display, it was not only the astounding wealth that impressed them – though some of it would have astounded anyone at any period. When Aemilius Paullus returned in 167 BCE from his victory over King Perseus, it took three days to trundle all the loot through the city, including 250 truckloads of sculpture and painting alone, and so much silver coin that it needed 3,000 men to carry it, in 750 huge vessels. No wonder that Rome could afford to suspend all direct taxation. But it was also the dazzling display of foreign lands and customs that captured the popular imagination. Generals commissioned elaborate paintings and models to be carried in the procession, depicting famous battles and the towns they had captured, so that the people at home could see what their armies had been doing abroad. The heads of the crowd were turned by the defeated Eastern kings in their 'national dress' and exotic regalia, by such curiosities as the pair of globes made by the Greek scientist Archimedes, who was killed in the Second Punic War, and by the exotic animals that sometimes became the stars of the show. The first elephant to tread the streets of Rome appeared in the parade for the victory over Pyrrhus in 275 BCE. It was all a far cry, as one later writer observed, from 'the cattle of the Volsci and the flocks of the Sabines', which had been the only spoils a century or so earlier.

The comedies of Plautus and Terence offered a different kind of window, with some subtle and maybe unsettling reflections. It is true that the boy-gets-girl plots of almost all of these plays, adapted from Greek predecessors, are not now best known for their subtlety. The 'happy ending' to some of their rape stories can appal modern readers: 'Good news – the rapist was her fiancé all along', to summarise the dénouement of one. It is also clear that the original performances, in public celebrations of all kinds, from religious festivals to the 'after-party' of triumphs, were unruly, raucous occasions, attracting a wide cross section of the population of the city, including women and slaves. This is in sharp contrast to classical Athens, where the theatre audience, though larger than at Rome, was probably restricted to male citizens, unruly or not. Nonetheless, there was one thing that all these Roman plays demanded of those who came to watch: that they face the cultural complexity of the world in which they lived.

That was partly because the plays are set in Greece. The assumption was that the audience had some sense of places outside Italy, or at least some name recognition of them. The plots often turn on decidedly diverse themes. One comedy of Plautus brings a Carthaginian onto the stage, who babbles some possibly accurate, but still incomprehensible, Punic. Another features a couple of characters disguised as Persians – and to laugh at actors who are meant to be badly *disguised as* Persians is a much more knowing response than to laugh at actors who are simply meant to *be* Persians. But, with a sophistication that is startling at such an early stage in the history of Roman literature, Plautus exploits even further the hybrid character of his work, and of his world.

One of his favourite gags, which he repeats in the prologue to a number of plays, is some version of 'Demophilus wrote this, Plautus *barbarised* it', referring to his Latin ('barbaric') translation of a comedy by the Greek playwright Demophilus. This apparently throwaway line was, in fact, a clever challenge to the audience. For those of Greek origin, it no doubt gave the opportunity for a quiet snigger at the expense of the new, barbaric rulers of the world. For the others, it demanded the conceptual leap of imagining what they might look like from the outside. To enjoy the laugh, they had to understand, even if only as a joke, that to Greek eyes, Romans might appear to be barbarians.

The widening horizons of empire, in other words, disturbed the simple hierarchy of 'us over them', the 'civilised over the barbarous', which had underpinned classical Greek culture. Romans were certainly capable of scornfully dismissing conquered barbarians, of contrasting their own civilised, sophisticated selves with the crude, long-haired, woad-painted Gauls, or other supposedly inferior species. Indeed, they often did just that. But from this point on, there was always another strand of Roman writing, which reflected more subversively on the relative position of the Romans in the wider world and on how the balance of virtue was to be set between insiders and outsiders. When, three centuries later, the historian Tacitus insinuated that true 'Roman' virtue was to be found in the 'barbarians' of Scotland and not in Rome itself, he was developing a tradition of argument that went right back to these early days of empire, and of literature.

How to be Roman

The empire's new horizons also helped to create – or at least to define with much sharper edges and ideological significance – the image of the 'old-fashioned Roman'. That down-to-earth, no-nonsense, hardy, warts-and-all character plays his part in our stereotype of Roman culture even now. The chances are that he was largely a creation of this period too.

Some of the most outspoken voices of the third and second centuries BCE became famous for attacking the corrupting influence on traditional Roman behaviour and morals of foreign culture in general, and Greek culture in particular; their targets ranged from literature and philosophy to naked exercise, fancy food and depilation. In the forefront of the critics was Marcus Porcius Cato ('Cato the Elder'), a contemporary and rival of Scipio Africanus, whom Cato criticised for, among other things, cavorting in Greek gymnasia and theatres in Sicily. He is also supposed to have dubbed Socrates a 'terrible prattler', to have recommended a Roman medicinal regime of green vegetables, duck and pigeon (rather than anything to do with Greek doctors, who were liable to kill you) and to have warned that Roman power could be brought down by the passion for Greek literature. According to Polybius, Cato once remarked that one sign of the deterioration of the Republic was that pretty boys now cost more than fields, jars of pickled fish more than ploughmen. He was not alone in these views. In the middle of the second century BCE another prominent figure successfully argued that a Greek-style theatre being built in Rome should be demolished, as it was better and more character forming

33. Many Roman portraits in the second and first centuries BCE present their subjects as elderly, wrinkled and craggy. Now often known as the 'veristic' (or hyper-realistic) style, it is, in fact, a deeply 'idealising' form of representation, celebrating a particular version of how a Roman should look in contrast to the youthful perfection of so much Greek sculpture.

for Romans to watch plays standing up, as they had traditionally done, rather than sitting down in decadent Eastern fashion. In short, so these arguments went, what passed for Greek 'sophistication' was no more than insidious 'softness' (or *mollitia* in Roman jargon), which was bound to sap the strength of the Roman character.

Was this a simple conservative backlash against newfangled ideas being brought into Rome from outside, a bout of 'culture wars' between traditionalists and modernisers? In part, perhaps, it was. But it was also more complicated, and interesting, than that. For all his huffing and puffing, Cato had taught his son Greek, and his surviving writing – notably, a technical essay on farming and agricultural management, and substantial quotations from his speeches and from his history of Italy – shows that he was well practised in the Greek rhetorical tricks that he claimed to deplore. And some of the claims being made about 'Roman tradition' were little short of imaginative fantasy. There is no reason whatsoever to suppose that venerable old Romans had watched theatrical performances standing up. The evidence we have suggests quite the reverse.

The truth is that Cato's version of old-fashioned, no-nonsense Roman values was as much an invention of his own day as a defence of long-standing Roman traditions. Cultural identity is always a slippery notion, and we have no idea how early Romans thought about their particular character and what distinguished them from their neighbours. But the distinctive, hard-edged sense of tough Roman austerity – which later Romans eagerly projected back on to their founding fathers and which has remained a powerful vision of Romanness into the modern world – was the product of a powerful cultural clash, in this period of expansion abroad, over what it was to be Roman in this new, wider imperial world, and in the context of such an array of alternatives. To put it another way, 'Greeknesss' and 'Romanness' were as inseparably bound up as they were polar opposites.

That is exactly what we see, in a particularly vertiginous form, in the story Livy, among others, tells of how the Great Mother goddess was brought into Rome with tremendous fanfare from Asia Minor in 204 BCE, towards the end of the Second Punic War. This was a very Roman occasion. A book of Roman oracles that was supposed to go back to the reign of the Tarquins recommended that the goddess Cybele, as she was also known, be incorporated into the Roman pantheon. The

34. A second-century CE memorial to a priest of the Great Mother. His image is strikingly different from the standard toga-clad priests of Rome (Fig. 61), with his long hair, heavy jewellery, 'foreign' musical instruments, and the hints of self-flagellation in the whips and goads.

range of deities worshipped in Rome was proudly elastic, and the Great Mother was the patron deity of the Romans' ancestral home – Aeneas' Troy – and so, in a sense, belonged in Italy. They sent a senior deputation to collect the image of the goddess and transport her back, and they chose, as the oracle had insisted, 'the best man in the state' to receive her in Rome – who turned out to be another Scipio. He was accompanied in the welcoming party by a noble Roman woman, in some accounts a Vestal Virgin, and the image was taken from the ship and passed from the coast to the city, hand to hand, by a long line of other women. The goddess was temporarily lodged in the shrine of Victory until her own temple was built. It would be the first building in Rome, so far as we know, constructed using that most Roman of materials, and the one on which so many of the Romans' later architectural masterpieces relied: concrete.

Nothing could have pleased Cato more – except that not everything was quite as it seemed. The image of the goddess was not what the Romans could possibly have been expecting. It was a large black meteorite, not a conventional statue in human form. And the meteorite came accompanied by a retinue of priests. These were self-castrated eunuchs, with long hair, tambourines and a passion for self-flagellation. This was all about as un-Roman as you could imagine. And forever after it raised uncomfortable questions about 'the Roman' and 'the foreign', and where the boundary between them lay. If this was the kind of thing that came from Rome's ancestral home, what did that imply about what it was to be Roman?

CHAPTER SIX

·

NEW POLITICS

Destruction

THE LONG SIEGE, and final destruction, of Carthage in 146 BCE
was gruesome even by ancient standards, with atrocities reported
on both sides. The losers could be as spectacularly cruel as the victors.
On one occasion, the Carthaginians were supposed to have paraded
Roman prisoners on the city walls, flayed them alive and dismembered
them in full view of their comrades.

Carthage lay on the Mediterranean coast near modern Tunis and
was defended by a massive circuit of walls almost 20 miles in perimeter
(the walls of Rome constructed after the invasion of the Gauls were
well under half that length). It was only when Scipio Aemilianus had
cut the town off from the sea, and so from its access to supplies, that
after two years of siege operations the Romans managed to starve
the enemy into submission and storm the place. The one surviving
ancient description of these final moments includes plenty of lurid
exaggeration but also a shrewd sense of how difficult it must have
been to destroy a city as solidly built as Carthage – and a few probably
realistic glimpses of the carnage that went with defeat. In the assault,
the Roman soldiers fought their way up streets lined with multistorey
buildings; they jumped from rooftop to rooftop, throwing the occupants down on to the pavements and toppling and setting fire to the
structures as they went, until the debris they had made blocked their
path. The rubbish clearers followed, opening up a space for the next

wave of assault by blasting their way through the mixture of building material and human remains, in which it was said that the legs of the dying could be seen visibly writhing above the debris, their heads and bodies buried beneath. The bones that archaeologists have found in these layers of destruction, not to mention the thousands of deadly stone and clay sling bullets that have been unearthed, suggest that this description may not be as wide of the mark as we might hope.

There was the usual rush for plunder, and not just precious gold and silver. Aemilianus made sure that the famous agricultural ency-clopaedia by the Carthaginian Mago was rescued from the flames; back in Rome, the senate gave a committee of Roman linguists the unenviable task of translating into Latin its twenty-eight volumes on everything from how to preserve pomegranates to how to choose bullocks. There were mythical resonances too. Aemilianus' rueful quotation from Homer as he watched the destruction had its poign-ant side. But it was also a boast. Rome was now claiming its place in the cycle of great powers and great conflicts that started with the Trojan War. Carthage, meanwhile, was supposed to have ended as it had begun, with a man abandoning his lover in favour of Rome. One story told that, just as Virgil's hero Aeneas deserted Dido as the city was being built, so amid its destruction Hasdrubal, the Carthaginian commander, finally went over to the Romans, leaving his wife behind. She is supposed to have denounced him when, like Dido, she threw herself onto a funeral pyre.

Almost as devastating, a few months later, was the sack of Corinth, nearly 1,000 miles from Carthage, and the richest city in Greece. It had made a fortune from its prime trading position, with harbours on each side of the narrow strip of land separating the Peloponnese from the rest of Greece. Under the command of Lucius Mummius Achaicus, as he was later known from his victory over these 'Achaeans', the Roman legions took the place apart, looted its fabulous works of art, enslaved the people and set it ablaze. This was such a vast conflagration that the mixture of molten metal it produced was supposed to be the origin of a prized, and extremely expensive, material known as Corinthian bronze. Ancient experts did not believe a word of this particular story, but the image of the intense heat of the destruction melting first the precious bronze, then the silver and finally the gold, until they all streamed together, is a powerful one – and a vivid example of the close link in Roman imagination between art and conquest.

Mummius was a very different type from the Homer-loving Aemilianus, and he has gone down in history almost as a caricature of the uncultured Roman philistine. Polybius, who arrived at Corinth shortly after the Greek defeat, was shocked to see Roman soldiers using the backs of precious paintings as gaming boards, presumably with the nod of their commanding officer. And a joke was still circulating almost seven centuries later about how, when he was overseeing the shipment of the valuable antiques back home, Mummius told the captains that if any piece was damaged they would have to replace it with a new one. He was, in other words, so laughably boorish that he was unaware that a 'new-for-old deal' was inappropriate for such valuable antiques.

But this story was, like so many, double edged. At least one stern Roman commentator took a stance reminiscent of Cato in suggesting that it would have been better for Rome if more people had followed Mummius and kept their distance from Greek luxury. Perhaps a tradition of austerity ran in Mummius' family, for his great-great-grandson was the notoriously parsimonious and no-nonsense emperor Galba, who ruled for a few months in 68–69 CE after the downfall of the extravagant Nero. But whatever his views really were, Mummius disposed of the Corinthian spoils with care. Some were dedicated in temples in Greece, combining a show of piety with a subtle warning to the other Greeks. Many were put on display in Rome or presented to towns in Italy. Evidence for this is still emerging. In Pompeii in the precinct of the Temple of Apollo, just off the Forum, a statue plinth was cleaned in 2002, and under a later plaster coating was discovered an inscription in Oscan, the local language, proclaiming that whatever once stood on top of it had been a gift of 'L Mummis L kusul', or 'Lucius Mummius, son of Lucius, consul'. It must have been some choice object from Corinth.

Why, within the space of a few months, the Romans took such brutal measures against these two grand and famous cities has been debated ever since. After Africanus' victory at the Battle of Zama in 202 BCE, at the end of the war with Hannibal, Carthage had agreed to Rome's demands. Fifty years later, it had just paid off the last instalment of the vast cash indemnity the Romans had imposed. Was this final campaign of destruction simply an act of Roman vengeance, carried out on some trumped-up excuse? Or did the Romans have a legitimate fear of resurgent Carthaginian power, whether economic or military? Cato was the most vociferous enemy of Carthage, notoriously, tediously but ultimately persuasively ending every speech he made with the words 'Carthage must be destroyed' ('*Carthago delenda est*', in the still familiar Latin phrase). One of his stunts in the senate was letting a bunch of deliciously ripe Carthaginian figs drop from his toga. He then explained that they had come from a city only three days' journey away. This was a wilful underestimate of the distance between Carthage and Rome (just under five days would have been the quickest journey), but it was a powerful symbol of the dangerous proximity, and agricultural wealth, of a potential rival – and intended to provoke suspicion of the old enemy.

Corinth must have played a rather different role in Roman calculations. It had been one of several Greek cities to ignore some rather half-hearted and not very clear instructions that Rome had given in the 140s BCE trying to restrict alliances in the Greek world, and it had pursued its own agenda in regional politics. Worse still, the Corinthians had rudely sent packing a delegation of Roman envoys. No other place in Greece came in for the same treatment. Was Corinth being punished as an exemplary case for a public act of disobedience, even though it had been on a relatively trivial scale? Or was there a real suspicion that it could become an alternative power base in the eastern Mediterranean? Or, as Polybius insinuates at the end of his *Histories*, were the Romans starting to resort to extermination for its own sake?

Whatever motivations lay behind the violence of 146 BCE, the events of that year were soon seen as a turning point. In one way, they marked the acme of Roman military success. Rome had now annihilated its richest, oldest and most powerful rivals in the Mediterranean world. As Virgil presented it more than a hundred years later in the *Aeneid*, Mummius, by conquering Corinth, had at last avenged the defeat of Aeneas' Trojans by the Greeks in the Trojan War. But in another way, the events of 146 BCE were seen as the beginning of the collapse of the Republic and as the herald of a century of civil wars, mass murder and assassinations that led to the return of autocratic rule. Fear of the enemy, so this argument went, had been good for Rome; without any significant external threat, 'the path of virtue was abandoned for that of corruption'. Sallust was particularly eloquent on the theme. In his other surviving essay, on a war against the North African king Jugurtha at the end of the second century BCE, he reflects on the dire consequences of the destruction of Carthage: from the greed of all sections of Roman society ('every man for himself'), through the breakdown of consensus between rich and poor, to the concentration of power in the hands of a very few men. These all pointed to the end of the Republican system. Sallust was an acute observer of Roman power, but the collapse of the Republic was, as we shall see, not quite so easily explained.

The legacy of Romulus and Remus?

The period between 146 BCE and the assassination of Julius Caesar in 44 BCE, particularly its last thirty years, marked a high point of Roman literature, art and culture. The poet Catullus was writing what still ranks as some of the world's most memorable love poetry, addressed to a Roman senator's wife whose identity he, no doubt wisely, concealed under the pseudonym 'Lesbia'. Cicero was drafting the speeches that have been some of the touchstones of oratory ever since and was theorising principles of rhetoric, good government and even theology. Julius Caesar was composing an elegantly self-serving description of his campaigns in Gaul, one of the rare accounts by a general – or anyone else, for that matter – of his own military operations to survive from the ancient world. And the city of Rome was on the verge of transforming from an unplanned rabbit warren into the impressive capital that we now have in our minds. The first permanent stone theatre opened in 55 BCE, with a stage 95 metres wide, attached to a vast new complex of promenades, sculpture gardens and porticoes supported on marble columns (see Fig. 44). Now buried underground near the modern Campo de' Fiori, it once covered an area significantly larger than the later Colosseum.

Yet many Roman commentators focused on no such glittering achievements but on progressive political and moral decline. Roman armies still won very lucrative, and sometimes very bloody, victories abroad. In 61 BCE, Gnaeus Pompeius Magnus – 'Pompey the Great', as he styled himself, in imitation of Alexander – celebrated a triumph for his victory over King Mithradates VI of Pontus, who once occupied extensive territories around the Black Sea coast and had his eye on more. This was an even more spectacular occasion than the triumph of Aemilius Paullus a century before. The '75,100,000 drachmae of silver coin' carried in the procession was the equivalent of the entire annual tax revenue of the empire. It would have been enough to feed two million people for a year, and a good part of it went towards building that first, ostentatious, theatre. In the 50s BCE, the campaigns in Gaul, to the north, which were commanded and written up by Caesar, brought several million people under Roman control, not counting the million or so whom he is believed to have

35. A colossal statue, now in the Palazzo Spada in Rome, usually identified as a portrait of Pompey; the globe in the hand reflects a common symbol of Pompey as world conqueror. In the eighteenth and nineteenth centuries it was a particularly celebrated work and was even wrongly believed to be the very statue of Pompey at whose feet Julius Caesar was assassinated. Some blemishes on the marble were optimistically identified as the traces of Caesar's blood.

left dead in the process. Increasingly, however, Roman weapons were turned not against foreign enemies but against Romans themselves. Never mind any thoughts of Aeneas' Trojans; this was the legacy of Romulus and Remus, the fratricidal twins. The 'blood of innocent Remus', as Horace put it in the 30s BCE, was taking its revenge.

Looking back over the period, Roman historians regretted the gradual destruction of peaceful politics. Violence was increasingly taken for granted as a political tool. Traditional restraints and conventions broke down, one by one, until swords, clubs and rioting more or less replaced the ballot box. At the same time, to follow Sallust, a very few individuals of enormous power, wealth and military backing came to dominate the state – until Julius Caesar was officially made 'dictator for life' and then within weeks was assassinated in the name of liberty. When the story is stripped down to its barest and brutal essentials, it consists of a series of key moments and conflicts that led to the dissolution of the free state, a sequence of tipping points that marked the stages in the progressive degeneration of the political process, and a succession of atrocities that lingered in the Roman imagination for centuries.

The first was in 133 BCE, when Tiberius Sempronius Gracchus, a tribune of the people with radical plans to distribute land to the Roman poor, decided to seek a second year in office. To put a stop to this, an unofficial posse of senators and their hangers-on interrupted the elections, bludgeoned Gracchus and hundreds of his supporters to death and threw their bodies into the Tiber. Conveniently forgetting the violence that had accompanied the Conflict of the Orders, many Romans held this to be 'the first political dispute since the fall of the monarchy to be settled by bloodshed and the death of citizens'. There was soon another. Just over a decade later, Tiberius Gracchus' brother Gaius met the same fate. He had introduced an even more radical programme of reform, including a subsidised grain allowance for Roman citizens, and was successfully elected tribune for a second time. But in 121 BCE, when he was trying to prevent his legislation from being dismantled, he became the victim of another, more official, posse of senators. On this occasion the bodies of thousands of his supporters clogged the river. And it happened again in 100 BCE, when other reformers were battered to death in the senate house itself, the assailants using tiles from the building's roof as their weapons.

Three more sustained civil wars, or revolutionary uprisings (there is often a hazy boundary between them), followed in quick succession and in a sense added up to an on-and-off single conflict lasting more than twenty years. First, war was declared on Rome in 91 BCE by a coalition of Italian allies, or *socii* (hence the quaint, and deceptively harmonious, modern title of Social War). Within a couple of years the Romans more or less defeated the allies, and in the process gave most of them full Roman citizenship. Even so, the death toll – among men who had once served side by side in Rome's wars of expansion – was, according to one Roman estimate, around 300,000. Exaggerated as that figure may be, it still points to casualties on a scale not far from that of the war against Hannibal. Before the Social War was over, one of its commanders, Lucius Cornelius Sulla, a consul in 88 BCE, became the first Roman since the mythical Coriolanus to lead his army against the city of Rome. Sulla was forcing the hand of the senate to give him command in a war in the East, and when he returned from that victorious four years later, he marched on his home town once again and had himself appointed dictator. Before resigning in 79 BCE, he introduced a wholesale conservative reform programme and presided over a reign of terror and the first organised purge of political enemies in Roman history. In these 'proscriptions' (that is, 'notices', as they were known, in a chilling euphemism), the names of thousands of men, including about a third of all senators, were posted throughout Italy, a generous price on their heads for anyone cruel, greedy or desperate enough to kill them. Finally, the fallout from both these conflicts fuelled Spartacus' famous slave 'war', which began in 73 BCE and remains one of the most glamorised conflicts in the whole of Roman history. Brave as they were, this handful of breakaway slave-gladiators must have been reinforced by many of the disaffected Roman citizens in Italy; they could hardly otherwise have stood up to the legions for almost two years. This was a combination of slave rebellion and civil war.

By the 60s BCE, political order in Rome itself was repeatedly breaking down, replaced by street violence that became part of daily life. Catiline's 'conspiracy' was only one such incident among many. There were any number of occasions when rioting prevented elections from taking place, or when massive bribery was supposed to have swayed the decision of the electorate or of juries in the courts, or when murder was the weapon of choice against a political opponent. Publius Clodius Pulcher, the brother of Catullus' 'Lesbia' and the man who engineered Cicero's exile in 58 BCE, was later killed by a gang of paramilitary slaves owned by one of Cicero's friends in a seedy brawl in a city suburb ('the Battle of Bovillae', as it was grandly, and ironically, known). Where exactly the responsibility for his death lay was never clear, but he was given an impromptu cremation in the senate house, which burned down with him. By comparison, one controversial consul in 59 BCE got off lightly: he was merely pelted with excrement and spent the rest of his year of office barricaded at home.

Against this background, three men – Pompey, Julius Caesar and Marcus Licinius Crassus – made an informal deal to use their combined influence, connections and money to fix the political process in their own interests. This 'Gang of Three', or 'Three-Headed Monster', as one contemporary satirist put it, for the first time effectively took public decisions into private hands. Through a series of behind-the-scenes arrangements, bribes and threats, they ensured that consulships and military commands went where they chose and that key decisions went their way. This arrangement lasted for about a decade, starting around 60 BCE (private deals are hard to date precisely). But then, seeking to secure his personal position, Julius Caesar decided to follow the precedent of Sulla and take over Rome by force.

The essentials of what happened next are clear, even if the details are almost impenetrably complicated. Leaving Gaul in early 49 BCE,

Caesar famously crossed the river Rubicon, which formed the boundary of Italy, and marched towards Rome. Forty years had made a big difference. When Sulla turned his army on the city, all but one of his senior officers had refused to follow him. When Caesar did the same, all but one stayed with him. It was an apt symbol of how far scruples had eroded in such a short time. The civil war that followed, in which Caesar and Pompey, the one-time allies, were now the rival commanders, spread throughout the Mediterranean world. Rome's internal conflicts were no longer restricted to Italy. The decisive battle was fought in central Greece, and Pompey ended up murdered on the coast of Egypt, beheaded by some Egyptian double-dealers he had imagined were his allies.

This is a powerful story of political crisis and bloody disintegration, even told in its most skeletal form. Some of the underlying problems are obvious. The relatively small-scale political institutions of Rome, little changed since the fourth century BCE, were hardly up to governing the peninsula of Italy. They were even less capable of controlling and policing a vast empire. As we shall see, Rome relied more and more on the efforts and talents of individuals whose power, profits and rivalries threatened the very principles on which the Republic was based. And there was no backstop – not even a basic police force – to prevent political conflict from spilling over into murderous political violence in a huge metropolis of a million people by the mid first century BCE, where hunger, exploitation and gross disparities of wealth were additional catalysts to protests, riots and crime.

It is also a story that historians, both ancient and modern, tell with all the advantages and disadvantages of hindsight. Once the outcome is known, it is easy to present the period as a series of irrevocable and brutal steps in the direction of crisis or as a slow countdown to both the end of the free state and the return of one-man rule. But the last century of the Republic was more than a mere bloodbath. As the flowering of poetry, theory and art suggests, it was also a period when

Romans grappled with the issues that were undermining their political process and came up with some of their greatest inventions, including the radical principle that the state had some responsibility for ensuring that its citizens had enough to eat. For the first time, they confronted the question of how an empire should be administered and governed, rather than simply acquired, and devised elaborate codes of practice for Roman rule. In other words, this was also an extraordinary period of political analysis and innovation. Roman senators did not sit idly by as their political institutions lapsed into chaos, nor did they simply fan the flames of the crisis to their own short-term advantage (though there was certainly a bit of that). Many of them, from different ends of the political spectrum, tried to find some effective remedies. We should not allow *our* hindsight, *their* ultimate failure or the succession of civil wars and assassinations to blind us to their efforts, which are the main theme of this and the next chapter.

We shall look harder at some of the most famous conflicts and characters of the period to ask what exactly the Romans were arguing or fighting about. Some of the answers will take us back to the popular manifesto of liberty embedded in the accounts and reconstructions of the Conflict of the Orders. But there are new issues too, from the effect of the mass grant of full citizenship to the Italian allies to the question of how the profits of the empire should be shared. These themes are all inextricably intertwined: the success (or failure) of armies serving overseas had direct consequences on the home front; the political ambitions of men like Pompey and Caesar lay behind some of the wars of conquest; there was never any clear divide between the military and political roles of the Roman elite. Nevertheless, in the interests of a clear account of these crucial but complicated developments, Chapter 7 focuses on Rome abroad and on the rise of the overpowering dynasts, especially Pompey and Caesar, in the later part of the period. For now, we will concentrate mainly on questions to do with Rome and Italy and with the earlier part of the period, roughly – to put it in terms of some of the famous names that still dominate the narrative – from Tiberius Gracchus to Sulla and Spartacus.

Tiberius Gracchus

In 137 BCE Tiberius Gracchus – a grandson of Scipio Africanus, a brother-in-law of Aemilianus, and a war hero at the siege of Carthage, where he had been the first to scale the enemy wall – was travelling north from Rome to join the legions in Spain. As he rode through Etruria, he was shocked at the state of the countryside, for the land was being worked and the flocks tended by foreign slaves on industrial-scale estates; the small, peasant farmers, the traditional backbone of Italian agriculture, had disappeared. According to a pamphlet written by his younger brother Gaius, quoted in a much later biography, this was the moment when Tiberius first became committed to reform. As he later put it to the Roman people, many of the men who fought Rome's wars 'are called masters of the world but have not a patch of earth to call their own'. To him, that was not fair.

How far the smallholders really had disappeared from the land has puzzled modern historians much more than it did their ancient counterparts. It is not difficult to see how an agricultural revolution of that kind might have been a logical consequence of Roman warfare and expansion. During the war against Hannibal, at the end of the third century BCE, rival armies had tramped up and down the Italian peninsula for a couple of decades, with devastating effects on the farmland. The demands of service with the army overseas removed manpower from the agricultural workforce for years on end, leaving family farms without essential labour. Both of these factors could have made smallholders particularly vulnerable to failure, bankruptcy or buy-outs by the rich, who used the wealth they acquired from overseas conquest to build up vast land holdings, worked as agricultural ranches by the glut of slave labour. One modern historian echoed the sentiments of Tiberius when he grimly summed this up: whatever booty they came home with, many ordinary soldiers had been in effect 'fighting for their own displacement'. A good proportion of them would have drifted to Rome or other towns in search of a living, so swelling the urban underclass.

It is a plausible scenario. But there is not much hard evidence to back it up. Leaving aside the propagandist tone of Tiberius' eye-opening journey through Etruria (had he not travelled 40 miles north before?), there are few archaeological traces of the new-style ranches he reported and considerable evidence, on the contrary, for the wide-spread survival of small-scale farms. It is not even certain that either war damage or the absence of young unmarried men abroad would have had the devastating, long-term effect that is often imagined. Most agricultural land recovers quickly from that kind of trauma, and there would have been plenty of other family members to recruit to the workforce; and even if not, a few slave labourers would have been within the means of even relatively humble farmers. In fact, many historians now think that, if his motives were sincere, Tiberius seriously misread the situation.

Whatever the economic truth, however, he certainly saw the problem in terms of the displacement of the poor from farming land. So did the poor themselves, if the story of their graffiti campaign in Rome urging him to restore 'land to the poor' is true. And it was this problem that Tiberius determined to solve when he was elected a tribune of the people for 133 BCE. He straight away introduced a law to the Plebeian Assembly to reinstate smallholders by distributing plots of Roman 'public land' to the poor. This was part of the territory that Romans had seized in their takeover of Italy. In theory it was open to a wide range of users, but in practice rich Romans and rich Italians had grabbed much of it and turned it, to all intents and purposes, into their private property. Tiberius proposed to restrict their holdings to a maximum of 500 *iugera* (roughly 120 hectares) each, claiming that this was the old legal limit, and to parcel out the rest in small units to the dispossessed. It was a typical style of Roman reform, justifying radical action as a return to past practice.

The proposal prompted a series of increasingly bitter controversies. First, when one of his fellow tribunes, Marcus Octavius, repeatedly tried to veto it (some right of veto had been given to these 'people's representatives' centuries earlier), Tiberius rode roughshod over the objection and had the people vote his opponent out of office. This enabled the law to pass, and a board of three commissioners was established, a rather cosy group comprising Tiberius, his brother and his father-in-law, to oversee the reassigning of land. Next, when the senate, whose interests generally lay with the rich, refused to make anything more than a nugatory grant of cash to fund the operation (a blocking device well known in modern political disputes), Tiberius again turned to the people and persuaded them to vote to divert a recent state windfall to finance the commission.

By a convenient coincidence, King Attalus III of Pergamum had died in 133 BCE, and – combining a realistic assessment of Roman power in the eastern Mediterranean with a shrewd defence against assassination by rivals at home – he had made 'the Roman people' the heir to his property and large kingdom in what is now Turkey. This inheritance provided all the money needed for the commission's complex job of investigating, measuring and surveying, selecting new tenants, and setting them up with the basic tools of the farming trade. Finally, when Tiberius found himself increasingly attacked, and even accused of aiming at kingship (one nasty rumour hinted that he had been eyeing up the royal diadem and purple robes of Attalus), he decided to defend his position by standing for election as tribune again the following year; for as an officeholder he would be immune from prosecution. This was too much for some of his anxious opponents, and a posse of them, senators and assorted thugs, with improvised weapons and no official authority whatsoever, interrupted the elections.

Roman elections were time-consuming affairs. In the Plebeian Assembly, which chose the tribunes, the electorate came together in a single place, and the tribal groups voted in turn, each man – of many thousands – casting his vote individually, one after the other. Sometimes more than a day was needed to complete the process. In 133 BCE, the votes for the next year's tribunes were slowly being delivered on the Capitoline Hill when the posse invaded. A battle followed, in which Tiberius was bludgeoned to death with a chair leg. The man behind the lynch mob was his cousin Publius Cornelius Scipio Nasica Serapio, an ex-consul and the head of one of the main groups of Roman priests, the pontifices. He is said to have entered this deadly brawl having drawn his toga over his head, as Roman priests usually did when sacrificing animals to the gods. He was trying, presumably, to make the murder look like a religious act.

The death of Tiberius did not stop the work of redistributing the land. A replacement was found for him on the commission, and its activity over the next few years can still be traced in a series of boundary stones marking the intersections of the new property units, each one blazoning the names of the commissioners responsible. But there were

36. This Roman silver coin of the late second century BCE shows the procedures at the time for voting in the assemblies, by secret ballot. The man on the right is putting his voting tablet in the ballot box, from a raised plank, or 'bridge' (*pons*). On the left, another man is stepping up to the bridge, and taking his tablet from the assistant underneath. 'Nerva' written above the scene is the name of the man responsible for minting the coin.

more casualties too, on both sides. Some of the Gracchan supporters were put on trial in a special court established by the senate (on what charge is not clear), and at least one was put to death by being tied up in a sack with poisonous snakes – most likely an ingenious piece of invented tradition masquerading as a horrible, archaic Roman punishment. Scipio Nasica was quickly packed off on a convenient delegation to Pergamum, where he died the next year. Scipio Aemilianus, whose reaction to the news of the murder of Tiberius had been to quote another line of Homer, to the effect that he had brought it on himself, returned to Italy from fighting in Spain to take up the cause of those rich Italian allies who were being ejected from public land. He was found dead in his bed in 129 BCE, on the very morning when he was due to give a speech on their behalf. Unexplained deaths – and there were many of them – provoked Roman suspicion. In both these cases there were rumours of foul play. Some Romans, as they often did when no evidence was available, alleged malign female influence behind the scenes: the triumphant conqueror of Carthage, they claimed, had been the victim of a tawdry domestic murder by his wife and mother-in-law, who were determined that he should not undo the work of Tiberius Gracchus, their brother and son.

Why was Tiberius' land reform so bitterly contested? All kinds of self-interest were no doubt at work. Some observers at the time, and since, claimed that far from being genuinely concerned with the plight of the poor, Tiberius was driven by a grudge against the senate, which had humiliatingly refused to ratify a treaty he had negotiated when he was serving in Spain. Many of the wealthy must have resented losing land that they had long treated as part of their private estates, while those who were set to benefit from the distribution eagerly supported the reform. In fact, many flooded into the city from outlying areas of Roman territory specially to vote for it. But there was more to the conflict than that.

The clash in 133 BCE revealed dramatically different views of the power of the people. When Tiberius persuaded them to vote out of office the tribune who opposed him, his argument went along the lines of 'if the people's tribune no longer does what the people want, then he should be deposed'. That raised an issue still familiar in modern electoral systems. Are Members of Parliament, for example, to be seen as *delegates* of the voters, bound to follow the will of their electorate? Or are they *representatives*, elected to exercise their own judgement in the changing circumstances of government? This was the first time, so far as we know, that this question had been explicitly raised in Rome, and it was no more easily answered then than it is now. For some, Tiberius' actions vindicated the rights of the people; for others they undermined the rights of a properly elected official.

Similar dilemmas were at the bottom of the dispute over whether Tiberius should be re-elected as a tribune. Holding an office for two consecutive years, back to back, was not unprecedented, but some certainly thought it signalled a dangerous build-up of individual power and was another hint of monarchical ambitions. Others claimed that the Roman people had the right to elect whomsoever they wanted, no matter what the electoral conventions were. What is more, if Attalus had left his kingdom to 'the Roman people' (*populus Romanus*), was it not up to them, rather than the senate, to determine how the bequest was used? Should not the profits of empire benefit the poor as well as the rich?

Scipio Nasica, with his thugs, cudgels and chair legs, does not come across as an attractive character, and the surname Vespillo (or 'Undertaker') given to the senator who saw to the disposal of the bodies in the Tiber is an uncomfortable joke by any standards, ancient or modern. But their argument with Tiberius was a fundamental one, which framed Roman political debate for the rest of the Republic. Cicero, looking back from the middle of the next century, could present 133 BCE as a decisive year precisely because it opened up a major fault line in Roman politics and society that was not closed again during his lifetime: 'The death of Tiberius Gracchus,' he wrote, 'and even before that the whole rationale behind his tribunate, divided a united people into two distinct groups [*partes*].'

This is a rhetorical oversimplification. The idea that there had been a calm consensus at Rome between rich and poor until Tiberius Gracchus shattered it is at best a nostalgic fiction. It seems likely, from what is known of the political debates in the decade or so before 133 BCE (which is not much), that others had already asserted the rights of the people along much the same lines. In 139 BCE, for example, one radical tribune had introduced a law to ensure that Roman elections were conducted by secret ballot. There is little evidence to help flesh out the man behind this or to throw light on the opposition it must have aroused – though Cicero gives a hint when he says that 'everyone knows that the ballot law robbed the aristocrats of all their influence' and describes the proposer as 'a filthy nobody'. But it was a milestone reform and a fundamental guarantee of political freedom for all citizens, and one that was unknown in elections in the classical Greek world, democratic or not.

Nevertheless, it was the events of 133 BCE that crystallised the opposition between those who championed the rights, liberty and benefits of the people and those who, to put it in their own terms, thought it prudent for the state to be guided by the experience and wisdom of the 'best men' (*optimi*), who in practice were more or less synonymous with the rich. Cicero uses the word *partes* for these two groups (*populares* and *optimates*, as they were sometimes called), but they were not parties in the modern sense: they had no members, official leaders or agreed manifestos. They represented two sharply divergent views of the aims and methods of government, which were repeatedly to clash for almost a hundred years.

Gaius Gracchus

In one of the Roman world's most quoted jibes, the satirist Juvenal, writing at the end of the first century CE, turned his scorn on the 'mob of Remus', which – he claimed – wanted just two things: 'bread and circuses' (*panem et circenses*). As the currency of that phrase even now shows, it was a brilliant dismissal of the limited horizons of the urban rabble, presented here as if they were the descendants of the murdered twin: they cared for nothing but the chariot racing and food handouts with which the emperors had bribed, and effectively depoliticised, them. It was also a cynical misrepresentation of the Roman tradition of providing staple food for the people at state expense, which originated with Tiberius' younger brother Gaius Sempronius Gracchus, a tribune of the people in two consecutive years, 123 and 122 BCE.

Gaius did not introduce a 'corn dole'. To be precise, he successfully proposed a law to the Plebeian Assembly establishing that the state should sell a certain quantity of grain each month at a subsidised, fixed price to individual citizens in the city. Even so, the scale and ambition of this initiative were enormous. And Gaius seems to have planned the considerable infrastructure needed to support it: the public purchasing, distribution facilities and some form of identity checking (how otherwise did you restrict it to citizens?), as well as storage in new public warehouses built by the Tiber and rented lock-up space in others. How the whole operation was staffed and organised day to day is not known for certain. Public officials at Rome were given only the skeletal support of a few scribes, messengers and bodyguards. So, as with most of the state's responsibilities – right down to such tiny specialist jobs as repainting the face of the statue of the god Jupiter in his temple overlooking the city from the Capitoline Hill – much of the work of managing and distributing the grain was presumably in the hands of private contractors, who made money out of delivering public services.

Gaius' initiative came partly out of concern for the poor in the city.

In good years the crops of Sicily and Sardinia would have been more or less sufficient to feed a quarter of a million people – a reasonable, though slightly conservative, estimate for the population of Rome in the later second century BCE. But ancient Mediterranean harvests fluctuated dramatically, and prices sometimes went far beyond what many ordinary Romans – shopkeepers, craftsmen, day labourers – could afford. Even before Gaius, the state had sometimes taken pre-emptive measures to avoid famine in the city. One revealing inscription found in Thessaly in northern Greece records the visit of a Roman official in 129 BCE. He had come, cap in hand, 'because the situation in his country at the present time is one of dearth', and he went away with the promise of more than 3,000 tonnes of wheat and some very complicated transportation arrangements in place.

Charitable aims, however, were not the only thing in Gaius' mind, nor even the hard-headed logic, sometimes in evidence at Rome, that a hungry populace was a dangerous one. His plan also had an underlying political agenda about the sharing of the state's resources. That certainly is the point of a reported exchange between Gaius and one of his most implacable opponents, the wealthy ex-consul Lucius Calpurnius Piso Frugi (his last name, appropriately enough, means 'stingy'). After the law had been passed, Gaius spotted Frugi standing in line for his allocation of grain and asked him why he was there, since he so disapproved of the measure. 'I'm not keen, Gracchus,' he replied, 'on you getting the idea of sharing out my property man by man, but if that's what you're going to do, I'll take my cut.' He was presumably turning Gaius' rhetoric back on him. The debate was about who had a claim on the property of the state and where the boundary lay between private and public wealth.

The distribution of cheap grain was Gaius' most influential reform. Though it was amended and occasionally suspended over the decades that followed, its basic principle lasted for centuries: Rome was the only place in the ancient Mediterranean where the state took responsibility for the regular basic food supplies of its citizens. The Greek world, by contrast, had usually relied on occasional handouts in times of shortage, or sporadic displays of generosity on the part of the rich. But food distributions were only one of Gaius' many innovations.

Unlike all earlier Roman reformers, Gaius sponsored not just a single initiative but a dozen or so. He was the first politician in the city, leaving aside the mythical founding fathers, to have an extensive and coherent *programme*, with measures that covered such things as the right of appeal against the death penalty, the outlawing of bribery and a much more ambitious scheme of land distribution than Tiberius had ever proposed. This involved exporting surplus citizens en masse to 'colonies' not only in Italy but also, for the first time, overseas. Just a couple of decades after it had been razed and cursed, Carthage was earmarked as a new town to be resettled. But Roman memory was not so short, and this particular project was soon cancelled, even though some settlers had already emigrated there. It is impossible now to list all the legislation that Gaius proposed in just two years, still less to determine precisely what its terms and aims were. Apart from a substantial section of the text of a law governing the behaviour of Roman officials abroad and providing means of redress to those whom they abused (which we shall explore in the next chapter), the surviving evidence comes largely in the form of passing asides or much later reconstructions. But it is the range that is the key. To Gaius' opponents, that smacked dangerously of a bid for personal power. The programme overall certainly seems to have added up to a systematic attempt to reconfigure the relationship between the people and the senate.

That is how his Greek biographer, 'Plutarch' (in full, Lucius Mestrius Plutarchus), understood it more than two hundred years later when he singled out what must have been a flamboyant gesture by Gaius as he addressed his audiences in the Forum. Speakers before him had faced the senate house, with the audience squashed together in the small area known as the *comitium* just in front of it. Gaius flouted convention by strategically turning his back on the senate house when talking to the people, who now listened in the open piazza of the Forum. It was, Plutarch concedes, just a 'slight deviation' in practice, but it made a revolutionary point. Not only did it allow the participation of a much larger crowd; it signalled the freedom of the people from the controlling eye of the senate. Ancient writers, in fact, credit Gaius with a particularly sharp sense of the politics of place. Another story tells how, when there was to be a display of gladiators in the Forum (a favourite location before the Colosseum was built, two hundred years later), a number of high-ranking Romans put up temporary seating to

37. Angelica Kauffmann's painting of 'Cornelia, Mother of the Gracchi', with her young sons (1785). Cornelia is one of the few mothers in Rome credited with a powerful influence on her children's public career. She was reputed to dress less flashily than many women at the time. 'My children are my jewels' she used to say. Here Kauffmann imagines her presenting Tiberius and Gaius (on the left) to a female friend.

hire out for profit. During the night before the show, Gaius had it all dismantled, so that the ordinary people would have plenty of space to watch, without paying.

Unlike his elder brother, Gaius somehow succeeded in being elected tribune twice. But, in murky circumstances, he failed to be elected again for 121 BCE. In that year he resisted the efforts of the consul Lucius Opimius, a diehard who became something of a hero to the conservatives, to cancel much of his legislation. In the process he was killed, or he killed himself to forestall murder, by an armed gang under Opimius' command. The violence was not one-sided. It had broken out after one of the consul's attendants – apparently going to and fro with the innards from some animals that had just been sacrificed, which added a macabre touch to the scene – shouted some casual abuse at Gaius' supporters ('Let the decent guys pass, you tossers') and made an even ruder gesture. They turned on him and stabbed him to death with their writing styluses, a clear sign that they were not already armed, that they were a literate group, but that they were not merely innocent victims. In response, the senate passed a decree urging the consuls 'to make sure that the state should come to no harm', the same emergency powers act as was later passed during Cicero's clash with Catiline in 63 BCE. Opimius took the cue, gathered together an amateur militia of his supporters and put some 3,000 Gracchans to death, either on the spot or later in an impromptu court. It established a dubious and deadly precedent.

For this was the first occasion of several over the next hundred years when this decree was used to confront various crises, from civil disorder to alleged treason. It may have been devised as an attempt to put some kind of regulatory framework on the use of official force. Rome at this period had no police of any kind and hardly any resources for controlling violence beyond what individual powerful men could scratch together. The instruction 'to make sure that the state should come to no harm' could in theory have been intended to draw a line between the unauthorised actions of a Scipio Nasica and those sanctioned by the senate. In practice, it was a lynch mob's charter, a partisan excuse to suspend civil liberties and a legal fig leaf for premeditated violence against radical reformers. It is, for example, hard to believe that the 'Cretan archers' who joined Opimius' local supporters were on hand purely by chance. But the decree was always controversial and always liable to rebound, as Cicero discovered. Opimius was duly put on trial, and though he was acquitted, his reputation never entirely recovered. When he had the nerve, or naivety, to celebrate his suppression of the Gracchans by lavishly restoring the temple of the goddess Concord ('Harmony') in the Forum, some realist with a chisel summed up the whole murderous debacle by carving across the façade the words 'An act of senseless Discord produces a Temple of Concord'.

Citizens and allies at war

Shortly before Gaius' revolutionary reforms, in the mid 120s BCE a Roman consul was travelling through Italy with his wife and came to the small town of Teanum (modern Teano, about 100 miles south of Rome). The lady decided she wanted to use the baths there usually reserved for men, so the mayor had them prepared for her and the regular bathers thrown out. But she complained that the facilities were neither ready in time nor clean enough. 'So a stake was set up in the forum, and Teanum's mayor, the most distinguished man in the town, was taken and tied to it. His clothes were stripped off and he was beaten with sticks.'

This story has come down to us because it was told in a speech by Gaius Gracchus which was quoted verbatim by a literary scholar of the second century CE interested in analysing his oratorical style. It was a shocking example of Roman abuse of power, cited in support of yet another of Gaius' campaigns – to extend Roman citizenship

more widely in Italy. He was not the first to suggest this. His proposal
was part of a growing controversy about the status of Rome's allies
and the Latin communities in Italy. It ended with many of the allies
going to war on Rome in the Social War, one of the deadliest and most
puzzling conflicts in Roman history. The puzzle turns largely on what
the aims of the allies were. Did they resort to violence to force Rome
to grant them full Roman citizenship? Or were they trying to shake
themselves free of Rome? Did they want *in* or *out*?

The relations between Rome and the other Italians had developed
in different directions since the third century BCE. The allies had
certainly reaped handsome rewards from their joint campaigns with
Rome, in the form of the booty that came with victory and the commercial opportunities that followed. One family in the little town of
Fregellae, technically a Latin colony 60 miles south of Rome, was

38. The huge architectural developments in late second-century BCE Praeneste
were built into the later Renaissance palace, which still retains the basic shape
of the ancient sanctuary. The lower ramps and terracing are still clearly visible.

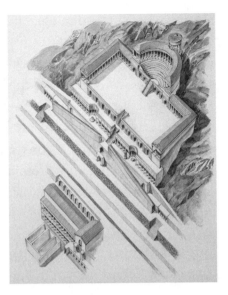

39. A reconstruction of the ancient sanctuary at Praeneste. From this it is clear that the semi-circular shape of the palace at the upper level reflects that of the underlying temple of the goddess Fortune. Interestingly, this was built more than half a century before Pompey's Theatre (Fig. 44), when there was nothing on this grand scale in Rome itself.

proud enough of these campaigns to decorate their house with terra-cotta friezes depicting the distant battles in which some of them had served. On a grander scale, the spectacular architectural development of many Italian towns provides concrete evidence of the allies' profit. At Praeneste, for example, just over 20 miles from Rome, a vast new sanctuary of the goddess Fortune was built, a masterpiece of display architecture – with a theatre, terracing, porticoes and colonnades – to rival anything anywhere else in the Mediterranean. It is hardly a coincidence that the names of several families from this town are found among those of the Roman and Italian traders on the Aegean island of Delos, one of the biggest commercial centres at the time, and a hub of the slave trade.

To outsiders in places such as Delos there was precious little difference between 'Romans' and 'Italians', and the terms were used more or less interchangeably to refer to both. Even in Italy the boundaries were becoming blurred or eroded. By the early second century BCE, all those who had been 'citizens without the vote' had gained the vote. At some point before the Social War, the Romans may have agreed that anyone who had held public office in a community with Latin status should be eligible for full Roman citizenship. In practice, a blind eye was often turned to Italians who simply claimed citizenship or got away with formally enrolling themselves at a Roman census.

Yet this kind of closer integration was only one side of it. Gaius' story of the Italian mayor is just one of a series of causes célèbres in which individual Romans, on a scale from tactless to cruel, were said to have hurt or humiliated prominent members of the allied communities. Another consul reputedly had a group of local dignitaries stripped and flogged because of some slip-up with his supply arrangements. True or not (and all of them come ultimately from uncorroborated attacks by Romans on other Romans), these anecdotes suggest an atmosphere of recrimination, bitterness and poisonous gossip, which was further fuelled by some high-handed actions on the part of the Roman state and a sense of political exclusion, and second-class status, on the part of leading allies. The senate began to take it for granted that it could lay down the law for the whole of Italy. Tiberius Gracchus' land reform, popular as it might have been to poor Romans, was a provocation to rich Italians whose 'public land' was removed, while excluding poor Italians from the distributions. The close personal relationships that some of the Italian elite had with leading Romans (how else did they enlist Scipio Aemilianus' help against Tiberius' land reform?) did not make up for the fact that they had no formal stake in Roman politics or decision-making.

In the 120s BCE, the 'Italian question' became increasingly divisive and provoked bouts of violent conflict. In 125 BCE the people of Fregellae attempted to break away from Rome but were crushed by a Roman army under the same Lucius Opimius who a few years later eliminated Gaius Gracchus. The remains of the friezes that had once proudly celebrated those joint campaigns were unearthed 2,000 years later from the wreckage of Fregellae's destruction. At the same time, in Rome, fears about outsiders flooding into the city were whipped up in a way familiar from many modern campaigns of xenophobia. One of Gaius' opponents, addressing a *contio*, or public meeting, conjured up visions of Romans being swamped. 'Once you have given citizenship to the Latins,' he urged his audience, 'I mean, do you think there will be any space for you, like there is now, in a *contio* or at games or festivals? Don't you realise they'll take over everything?' There were also occasionally formal attempts to repatriate immigrants or to prevent Italians from passing themselves off as full Roman citizens. It could prove dangerous to be too prominent a supporter of the Italian cause. In the autumn of 91 BCE the proposal of one Marcus Livius Drusus to extend citizen rights more widely in Italy ended with him being murdered at home, knifed as he was saying goodbye to a crowd of visitors.

That murder heralded full-blown war on a terrible scale. The tipping point came at the end of 91 BCE, when a Roman envoy insulted the people of Asculum in central Italy. They responded by killing him and all the other Romans in the town. This brutal piece of ethnic cleansing set the tone for what followed, which was not far short of civil war: 'It can be called a war against *socii*, to lessen the odium of it; the truth is it was a civil war, against citizens,' as one Roman historian later summed it up. And it involved fighting throughout much of the peninsula, including at Pompeii, where the marks of the battering by Roman artillery in 89 BCE can be seen even now on the city walls. The Romans invested enormous forces to defeat the Italians and won victory at the cost of heavy losses and considerable panic. After one consul was killed in battle, there was such grief in Rome when his body was brought back that the senate decreed that, in future, casualties should be buried where they fell, a decision that some modern states have also taken. But most of the conflict was over relatively quickly, within a couple of years. Peace was apparently hastened by one simple expedient: the Romans offered full citizenship to those Italians who had not taken up arms against Rome or were prepared to lay them down.

That certainly makes it look as if the aim of many allies in going to war had been to become fully Roman, ending their political exclusion and inferior status. That is how most ancient writers explain the conflict. 'They were seeking citizenship of the state whose power they were used to defending with their arms,' insists one, whose great-grandfather was an Italian who fought on the Roman side. And a favourite story of the successful transformation of Italians into Romans highlights the career of a man from the northern Italian region of Picenum: as a babe in arms he had been paraded among the prisoners in one of the triumphs celebrated at Rome for victories over the allies-turned-enemies; fifty years later, now a Roman general, he celebrated his own triumph for victory over the Parthians – the only man known to have been on both sides of a triumphal procession, a victim turned victor. But Roman writers may have been too ready to equate the outcome of the war with its aims or to give the Italians a goal that fitted more comfortably the later unity of Rome and Italy.

For the contemporary propaganda and organisation of the Italian side suggest that it was actually a breakaway movement, aiming at total independence from Rome. The allies seem to have gone some way towards establishing a rival state, under the name 'Italia', with a capital at a town renamed 'Italica' and even the word *Itali* ('Italians') stamped on their lead shots. They minted coins displaying a memorable image of a bull, the symbol of Italy, goring a wolf, the symbol of Rome. And one of the Italian leaders neatly turned the story of Romulus and Remus on its head by dubbing the Romans 'the wolves who have ravished Italian liberty'. That does not look like a plea for integration.

The easiest solution to the puzzle is to imagine that the allies were a loose coalition with many different aims, some determined to resist the Romans to the death, others much more prepared to make a deal. That is no doubt true. But there are more subtle considerations too, and hints that – like it or not – it was too late for Italian independence from Rome. The coinage certainly blazons some anti-Roman imagery.

But it was based entirely on the weight standards of Roman coinage, and many of the other designs were directly borrowed from Roman issues. It is as if the only cultural language with which the Italians could attack Rome was now a Roman one – a clear indication of just how far integration, or Roman domination of Italy, had already progressed.

Whatever the causes of the Social War, the effects of the legislation of 90 and 89 BCE that extended full citizenship to most of the peninsula were dramatic. Italy was now the closest thing to a nation state that the classical world ever knew, and the principle we glimpsed centuries earlier that 'Romans' could have dual citizenship and two civic identities, that of Rome and that of their home town, became the norm. If the figures reported by ancient writers are at all accurate, the number of Roman citizens increased at a stroke by about threefold, to something over a million. The potential impact of this, and the problems, were obvious. There was fierce debate, for example, on how to fit the new citizens into the voting tribes, including an unsuccessful

40. The most aggressively anti-Roman coin minted by the Italian allies in the Social War. The Roman wolf is entirely overpowered by the Italian bull, and beneath the design the name of the moneyer responsible is written in the Italian language of Oscan. The other side of the silver coin blazons the head of the god Bacchus and the name, also in Oscan, of one of the leading Italian generals.

proposal to restrict the influence of Italians in assemblies by enrolling them in a small number of extra tribes, which would always vote last. But the Romans never effectively adjusted their traditional political or administrative institutions to manage the new political landscape. There was never any system for registering votes outside Rome, so in practice only those Italians with the money and time to travel would have taken advantage of their new political clout. And the burden of formally enrolling that number of citizens seems to have almost defeated them, even though there was some attempt to devolve part of the work to local officials. A full census was carried out in 70 BCE (and it is from those figures that the estimate of 'something over a million' comes), but that was the last official enrolment until 28 BCE, at the beginning of the reign of the emperor Augustus. The gap is usually put down to political instability, but the size and difficulty of the task must surely have had something to do with it as well.

There is a vivid snapshot of some of the tricky problems that still lingered almost thirty years after the Social War in a speech that Cicero gave in 62 BCE in defence of the poet Archias – a man who had already celebrated in verse the achievements of a number of prominent Romans (sadly or not, none of it survives) and whom Cicero was hoping would turn out a suitable poem in praise of his victory over Catiline. Archias was born in Antioch in ancient Syria but claimed to be a Roman citizen, by the name of Aulus Licinius Archias, on the grounds that he had emigrated to Italy, had become a citizen of the town of Heraclea and so after the Social War had the right to Roman citizenship. This status was being contested in the courts. The defence ran into difficulties, however. There was no written proof that Archias was a citizen of Heraclea, because the town's record office had burned down in the Social War. There was little written proof of his Roman citizenship either, as he did not appear on any census list; he had, suspiciously we might think, been out of the country on the occasions of both the most recent censuses. So Cicero had to rely on some witnesses to vouch for him and on the private records of the praetor, now dead, who had first approved his claim.

What the jury made of it is unknown. Did they find the excuses for the missing documents rather thin? Or did they understand that this was exactly the kind of chapter of accidents, and identity loss, that often follows civil war? Either way, Cicero's defence is precious evidence for some of the controversies and administrative nightmares that must have lain just under the surface of the simple shorthand that 'citizenship was granted to the allies'. It was an extraordinarily bold move by the Romans, even if forced upon them; but there were probably many other Archiases caught up in the resulting legal tangles without the resources or influence to call on a Cicero to present their case.

Sulla and Spartacus

The Roman commander at the siege of Pompeii in 89 BCE, where the teenaged Cicero served as a very junior officer, was Lucius Cornelius Sulla *Felix*, meaning 'lucky' or, rather more imposingly, 'the favourite of the goddess Venus'. He faced well-organised opposition inside the town, to judge from a series of notices, uncovered beneath later plaster on the street façades, apparently giving instructions to the local militia on where to muster. The Pompeians seem to have held out for some time after Sulla had moved on to more important targets, but he made a big enough impact for some local graffiti artist to have scrawled his name on one of the towers of the town wall.

Sulla was to be a central and controversial figure in almost a decade of open warfare in and around the city of Rome and in a short and bloody period of one-man rule. Born into a patrician family that had fallen on hard times, he was elected consul for 88 BCE, aged about fifty. The conflicts started in that year when he invaded Rome, with troops he had been leading in the closing stages of the Social War, to reclaim the potentially glorious and lucrative command in the war against King Mithradates, which had been allocated to him and then suddenly transferred to a rival. They continued after he returned victorious to Italy in 83 BCE, when he fought for almost two years to take Rome back from the enemies who had gained control while he was away. During his absence, disagreements in the city had been fought out through violence, murder and guerrilla warfare. And rival generals had been sent out to take command against Mithradates, who were as much opposed to one another as they were to any foreign enemy; it was a situation that would have been faintly ludicrous had it not been so deadly.

Ancient writers paint a lurid, bloodthirsty and confusing picture of this whole period in the mid 80s BCE. Vicious fighting in the heart of the city marked both of Sulla's invasions of Rome. During the

41. A silver coin of Sulla, minted 84–83 BCE, boasting of the divine protection he enjoyed. On the one side is the head of Venus, with her son Cupid holding a palm – a symbol of victory – just visible to the right. On the other side, there are references to the military successes this protection brought: IMPER(ATOR) ITERUM records that he had twice (*iterum*) been publicly hailed as a mighty victor (*imperator*) by his troops; and among the symbols in the centre are two sets of armour that were used as trophies of victory.

second, the Temple of Jupiter on the Capitoline, the founding symbol of Republican Rome, burned down, and senators were not safe even in the senate house. Four of them – including an ancestor of the emperor Nero – were slaughtered as they sat there, at the hands of Sulla's enemies. Meanwhile, in the campaigns against Mithradates, one army commander was murdered by his second in command, who later killed himself after most of his troops deserted. The majority of the deserters decided to join forces with Sulla, though a couple of officers chose instead to throw in their lot with Mithradates, the enemy they were supposed to be fighting.

The grimmest anecdotes, however, surround the murderous proscriptions and the terror provoked by the clinically bureaucratic lists of those who were to be exterminated. Sulla's sadism was part of the story. Where his enemies a few years earlier had started the gory practice of pinning up the heads of their victims on the *rostra* in the Forum, Sulla was rumoured to have gone one worse, installing them as trophies in the atrium (or hall) of his house – a nasty parody of the Roman tradition of displaying the portrait heads of ancestors there. He also took the quotation of Greek literature to a new low when, presented with the head of a particularly young victim, he came up with a line from the comic dramatist Aristophanes to the effect that the boy was trying to run before he could walk. 'No one did me wrong whom I did not pay back in full' were among the words he penned for his tomb, a far cry from the epitaphs of the Scipios. But that was not all there was to it. Another part of the story was the eagerness of so many to join in the massacre, to settle old scores or simply to claim the financial rewards for the murders. Catiline was a notorious culprit, persuading Sulla to insert his personal enemies into the lists and, when his dirty work was done, washing the traces of human butchery off his hands in a sacred fountain.

How can we explain such violence? It is not enough to argue that it was less terrible than it is portrayed. That is true, up to a point.

Much of the narrative that has come down to us relies on partisan accounts by those keen to exaggerate the brutality of their enemies. The blackening of Catiline, for example, likely goes back to Cicero's propaganda. But only up to a point: Sulla's two invasions of Rome, the burning of the Temple of Jupiter, the warring legions and the proscription lists cannot simply be dismissed as the figments of a propaganda war. Nor is it enough to wonder what drove Sulla to do what he did. His motives have been debated ever since. Was he a brutal and calculating autocrat? Or was he making a last-ditch attempt to restore order in Rome? The point is that, whatever lay behind Sulla's actions (and that is as irrecoverable now as it ever was), the violence was much more widespread than could possibly be put down to the influence of one man.

The conflicts of this period were in many ways a continuation of the Social War: a civil war between former allies and friends developed into a civil war between citizens. What was eroded in the process was the fundamental distinction between Romans and foreign enemies, or *hostes*. Sulla in 88 BCE declared his rivals in the city *hostes*, the first time we know that the term was publicly used, as Cicero used it later, against a fellow Roman. As soon as he left the city, they promptly declared Sulla a *hostis* in return. This blurring of boundaries is captured in the military debacles in the eastern Mediterranean: old certainties were so radically overturned that soldiers deserting one Roman commander could apparently see both Sulla and King Mithradates as plausible options for their new allegiance; and one faction of Roman forces actually destroyed the city of Troy, Rome's ancestor. It was the mythical equivalent of patricide.

The Social War also ensured that there was plenty of military manpower readily available near Rome, soldiers with considerable practice in fighting their Italian kith and kin. The recent precedents for violence in the city, controversial and brutal as they were, had been relatively small scale and short term. But when fully armed legions replaced the kind of thugs who had murdered the supporters of the Gracchi, the city easily became the site of the full-scale and long-term warfare that defined the Sullan period. It was almost a return to the private armies of early Rome, as individual commanders, backed by different votes of the people or decrees of the senate, used their legions to pursue their own sectional struggles wherever it suited them.

Yet out of all this came an extraordinary, radically conservative attempt to rewrite Roman politics: wholesale change masquerading as an exercise in putting the clock back. Once re-established in the city in 82 BCE, Sulla engineered his own election as 'dictator for making laws and restoring order to the *res publica*'. The dictatorship was an old emergency office which gave sole power to an individual on a temporary basis to cope with a crisis, sometimes but not always military. The last person to hold the position had been appointed more than a century earlier, to conduct elections in 202 BCE, at the end of the Second Punic War, when both consuls were away from Rome. Sulla's dictatorship was different in two ways: first, there was no time limit placed on it; second, it entailed vast, unchecked powers to make or repeal any laws, with guaranteed immunity from prosecution. For three years that is exactly what he did, before resigning the office, retiring to his country house on the Bay of Naples and dying in his bed in 78 BCE. It was a surprisingly peaceful end, given his life's record, though several ancient writers were pleased to report how gruesome it was: his flesh was supposed to have dissolved into worms, which multiplied so quickly that they could not be removed. Sulla was the first dictator in the modern sense of the term. Julius Caesar would be the second. That particular version of political power is one of Rome's most corrosive legacies.

Sulla introduced a programme of reform on an even bigger scale than Gaius Gracchus. He cancelled some of the recent popular measures, including the subsidised corn ration. And he introduced a series of legal procedures and rules and regulations for office holding, many of which reasserted the central position of the senate as a state institution. He drafted in hundreds of members to double its size from about 300 to about 600 (there was never an absolutely fixed number), and he astutely changed the method of recruitment for the future to ensure that the new size would be maintained. Rather than senators being enrolled individually by the censors, from now on anyone who held the junior office of quaestor would automatically enter the senate, and at the same time the number of quaestors was increased from eight to twenty; this meant enough new recruits more or less to replace those who would have died each year. Sulla also insisted that political offices be held in a particular order and at a minimum age (no one could become quaestor, for example, before the age of thirty), and no office was to be held twice within ten years. This was an attempt to prevent exactly the build-up of personal power that he himself enjoyed.

These reforms were dressed up as a return to traditional Roman practice. In fact, many were nothing of the sort. There had been one or two previous attempts to regularise patterns of office holding, but by and large the earlier you go back in Rome's history, the more fluid any such rules become. There were also some unintended consequences. Increasing the number of quaestors solved one problem – senatorial recruitment – but in doing so created another. As the number of consuls remained just two, more and more men were being brought into the political race at the bottom who could never make it to the top position. To be sure, some did not want to, and some died before they reached the new minimum age, normally forty-two, for the consulship. But the system was almost guaranteed to intensify political competition and produce disgruntled failures, just like Catiline a couple of decades later.

One of Sulla's most notorious reforms offers a glimpse of his reasoning. Men holding the office of tribune of the people had introduced almost all the radical reforms since the Gracchi. So Sulla, who must have been aware of this, set out drastically to restrict the tribunes' powers. This was another office, like the dictatorship, that had been largely reinvented, probably in the decades before Sulla. It had been established in the fifth century BCE to represent the interests of the plebeians, but some of its rights and privileges made it a particularly attractive office for anyone looking for political power in much later periods. In particular, it carried the right to propose laws to the Plebeian Assembly as well as the right to interpose a veto on public business. This veto must have started in a very limited way. It is unthinkable that in the early days of the Conflict of the Orders the patricians would have allowed the plebeian representatives to block any decisions they chose. But by the time that Octavius repeatedly vetoed the laws of Tiberius Gracchus in 133 BCE, the principle must have been established, or asserted, that the tribune's right to intervene was almost unlimited.

Tribunes came in all political colours: both Octavius and the vigilante who killed Tiberius Gracchus with the chair leg were Tiberius' fellow tribunes. They were also at this period uniformly rich, and certainly not a voice of politics from the bottom. But the office retained its popular image. It was still open to plebeians only – though patricians who were keen enough could always get round the difficulty by being adopted into a plebeian family. And it was repeatedly used to introduce popular reforms. So Sulla shrewdly set about making it an unattractive office for anyone with political ambitions. He took away the tribunes' right to introduce legislation, curtailed their veto and made anyone who had held the tribunate ineligible for any future elected office – a guaranteed way of turning it into a dead end. The removal of these restrictions became the main rallying cry of the opposition to Sulla, and within ten years of his retirement all were repealed, paving the way for another generation of powerful and prominent tribunes. Even the emperors later boasted that they had 'the power of the tribunes' (*tribunicia potestas*), to suggest their concern for the ordinary people of Rome.

In retrospect, however, the tribunate seems something of a distraction. It was disagreement about the nature of political power that was dividing Roman politics, not the prerogatives of one particular office. Much more significant in the medium term, even if less visible and openly controversial, were some of Sulla's practical decisions on disbanding his long-serving legions. He settled many of the ex-soldiers in the towns of Italy that had fought against Rome in the Social War, and requisitioned nearby land to provide them with a livelihood. It must have seemed an easy way of punishing the rebels, but often both sides lost: some locals were dispossessed, while some of the veterans were better fighters than farmers and conspicuously failed to make a living off the land. In 63 BCE it was said that these ex-soldiers-turned-failed-smallholders swelled the ranks of Catiline's supporters. Even before then, the various victims of Sulla's settlements had a big part to play in what has become – thanks partly to Stanley Kubrick and Kirk Douglas – one of the best known of all ancient wars.

In 73 BCE, under the leadership of Spartacus, fifty or so slave gladiators, improvising weapons out of kitchen equipment, escaped from a gladiatorial training school at Capua in southern Italy and went on the run. They spent the next two years gathering support and withstanding several Roman armies until they were eventually crushed in 71 BCE, the survivors crucified in a grisly parade along the Appian Way.

It is hard now to see through the hype, both ancient and modern, to what was really going on. Roman writers, for whom slave uprisings were probably the most alarming sign of a world turned upside down, wildly exaggerate the number of supporters Spartacus attracted; estimates go as high as 120,000 insurgents. Modern accounts have often wanted to make Spartacus an ideological hero, even one who was fighting the very institution of slavery. That is next to impossible. Many slaves wanted freedom for themselves, but all the evidence from ancient Rome suggests that slavery as an institution was taken for granted, even by slaves. If they had a clearly formulated aim, the best guess is that Spartacus and his fellow escapees wanted to return to their various homes – in Spartacus' case probably Thrace in northern Greece; for others, Gaul. One thing is certain, though: they managed to hold out against Roman forces for an embarrassingly long time.

What explains that success? It was not simply that the Roman armies sent out against them were ill trained. Nor was it just that the gladiators had discipline and fighting skills developed in the arena and were powered by the desire for freedom. Almost certainly the rebel forces were stiffened with the discontented and the dispossessed among the free, citizen population of Italy, including some of Sulla's

42. This sketchy painting from Pompeii shows a man fighting on horseback – labelled, in the Oscan language, written from right to left, 'Spartaks', that is Spartacus. Cautious scholars are probably right to imagine that this is a scene of gladiatorial combat rather than of some engagement during the Spartacus rebellion. But even so, this may be the only surviving contemporary depiction of the famous slave gladiator.

ex-soldiers, who may well have felt more at home on military campaign, even against the legions in which they had once served, than on the farm. Seen in these terms, Spartacus' uprising was not only an ultimately tragic slave rebellion but also the final round in a series of civil wars that had started twenty years earlier with the massacre of Romans at Asculum that marked the beginning of the Social War.

Ordinary lives

The story of the political conflicts of this period tends to be the story of the clash of political principles and of widely divergent views about how Rome should be governed. It is a story of big ideas, and almost inevitably it becomes a story of big men, from Scipio Aemilianus to Sulla. For that is how the Roman writers, on whose accounts we now depend, told it, focusing on the heroes and anti-heroes, the larger-than-life personalities who appear to have determined the course of both war and politics. They also drew on material, now largely lost, that came from the pens of those men themselves: the speeches of Gaius Gracchus or – one of the saddest losses in the whole of classical literature – the shamelessly self-justificatory autobiography of Sulla, written in twenty-two volumes during his retirement, that later writers occasionally mentioned and consulted.

What is missing is the perspective of those outside this exclusive group: the view of the ordinary soldiers or voters, of the women or – with the exception of the many fictions about Spartacus – the slaves. The men who jumped from rooftop to rooftop in Carthage, the people who scrawled the graffiti urging Tiberius to land reform, the loose-tongued servant who insulted the supporters of Gaius, and the five wives of Sulla remain in the background or are at best bit-part players. Even when ordinary people do speak for themselves, their surviving words tend to be brief and non-committal: 'To Lucius Cornelius Sulla

Felix, dictator, son of Lucius, from his ex-slaves', as one inscription on
a stone pedestal runs; but who they were, what stood on top of the
pedestal and why they were dedicating it to him is anyone's guess. Just
as uncertain is how far the life of many men and women in the street
went on more or less as normal throughout most of this period while
those at the top fought it out with their legions. Or did the violence
and disintegration of civic order dog most of the population most of
the time?

Occasionally it is possible to see the effects of these conflicts trick-
ling down into ordinary, everyday life. Pompeii was one of those
little rebel towns that gained Roman citizenship after the Social War
but was soon forced to welcome a couple of thousand ex-soldiers,
who were given land that belonged to the locals. It was not a happy
mixture. Although far fewer than the original citizens, the veterans
soon made their presence aggressively felt. A couple of the richest
of them sponsored a vast new amphitheatre, though that may have
been as welcome an amenity to the original inhabitants as it was to
the Sullan thugs who were predictably keen on gladiatorial spectacle.
The record of office holding in the city for this period shows that the
new colonists somehow managed to exclude the old families of the
town. And in the 60s BCE, Cicero referred to long-running, chronic
disputes at Pompeii about, among other things, voting rights. The
knock-on effects of Sulla's siege were still being felt on the streets of
Pompeii decades later.

The most vivid testimony, however, to the risks and dilemmas for
the ordinary people caught up in these wars comes from a story about
the outbreak of the Social War at Asculum in 91 BCE. An eager audience, a mixture of Romans and locals, was enjoying some shows in the
town theatre when the drama moved offstage. The Roman part of the
crowd had not liked the anti-Roman stance of one comic performer
and attacked him so fiercely that they left the hapless actor dead. The
next comedian on the bill was a travelling player of Latin origin and

a great favourite with Roman audiences for his jokes and mimicry. Terrified that the other side of the audience would now turn on him, he had no option but to walk on to the stage where the other man had just been killed and to talk and joke his way out of trouble. 'I'm not a Roman either,' he said to the spectators. 'I travel throughout Italy searching for favours by making people laugh and giving pleasure. So spare the swallow, which the gods allow to nest safely in all your houses!' This touched them, and they sat back to watch the rest of the show. But it was only a brief comic interlude: soon after, all the Romans in the town were killed.

It is a poignant and revealing story, which captures the point of view of an ordinary stand-up comic facing an ordinary audience, which on this occasion was not just hostile but potentially murderous. And it is a powerful reminder of the very fine line throughout this period between normal civic life – going to the theatre, enjoying a comic turn or two – and deadly massacre. Sometimes the swallows were not spared.

CHAPTER SEVEN

·

FROM EMPIRE TO
EMPERORS

Cicero versus Verres

While the grim crosses were still lining the Appian Way in 70 BCE, the year after the final defeat of Spartacus' army, Cicero stood up in a Roman court to prosecute Gaius Verres on behalf of a number of wealthy Sicilians. His aim was to get them compensation for the thefts and depredations of Verres while he was the Roman governor of their island. The case launched Cicero's career, as he spectacularly defeated the established lawyers and orators lined up in Verres' defence. In fact, so spectacular was Cicero's success that after two weeks of what was set to be a long trial, Verres decided that the outcome was hopeless and, before the court reconvened after a holiday break, went into voluntary exile in Marseilles, with many of his ill-gotten gains. He lived on there till 43 BCE, when he was put to death in another pogrom of proscriptions that followed the assassination of Julius Caesar. The reason, ostensibly, was that he had refused to let Mark Antony have some of his precious Corinthian bronze.

The case over, and keen not to waste his hard work, Cicero circulated in written form what he had said at the opening of the trial, along with the remaining speeches that he would have given against Verres had it continued. The full text of these still survives, copied and recopied throughout the ancient world and the Middle Ages as a model of how to denounce an enemy. Several hundred pages in all, it is a litany of lurid examples of Verres' cruel exploitation of the inhabitants of Sicily, with flashbacks to earlier villainies before he reached the island in 73 BCE. It is the fullest account to survive of the crimes that Romans could commit abroad, under the cloak of their official status. For Cicero, the hallmark of Verres' behaviour, in Sicily and in his earlier overseas postings, was a grotesque combination of cruelty, greed and lust, whether for women, cash or works of art.

Cicero details, at enormous length, Verres' grooming of innocent virgins, his fiddling of the taxes, his profiteering from the corn supply, and his systematic thieving of some of the famous masterpieces of Sicily, interspersed with poignant tales of the victims. He lingers, for example, on the plight of one Heius, once the proud possessor of statues by some of the most renowned classical Greek sculptors, including Praxiteles and Polyclitus, heirlooms kept in a 'shrine' in his house. Other Romans had admired these, even borrowed them. Verres turned up and forced him to sell them for a ridiculously low price. Even worse, according to the culminating anecdote in this anthology of crime, was the fate of Publius Gavius, a Roman citizen living in Sicily. Verres had Gavius thrown into prison, tortured and crucified, on the specious grounds that he was a spy for Spartacus. Roman citizenship should have protected him from this degrading punishment. So, as he was flogged, the poor man repeatedly cried out, '*Civis Romanus sum*' ('I am a Roman citizen'), but to no avail. Presumably, when they chose to repeat this phrase, both Palmerston and Kennedy (see p. 137) must have forgotten that its most famous ancient use was as the unsuccessful plea of an innocent victim under a sentence of death imposed by a rogue Roman governor.

Judging a court case two thousand years old, when the arguments of only one side survive, and most of those written up later, is an impossible task. As prosecutors are almost bound to do, Cicero certainly exaggerated the wickedness of Verres, in a memorable but sometimes misleading combination of moral outrage, half-truths, self-promotion and jokes (in particular on the name 'Verres', which literally means 'hog' or perhaps 'snout in the trough'). And there are all kinds of cracks in his argument that any decent defence might well have exploited. Dreadful as the punishment of Gavius was, for example, no responsible Roman official on Sicily at that date could have failed to be on the lookout for agents of Spartacus; in fact, Spartacus was widely reported to be planning to cross to the island. Whatever Heius' regret at parting with his statues, and for such a low price, Cicero does concede that they were sold, not stolen (and anyway, were they really the original masterpieces they were cracked up to be?). Nevertheless, the defendant's hasty departure suggests that he was guilty enough of the charges laid before him to make a tactical retreat into a comfortable exile seem the sensible option.

This notorious case is just one of many controversies and dilemmas about Roman rule overseas that erupted during the last century of the Republic. By the 70s BCE, with vast territories under Roman sway as the result of two centuries of fighting, negotiation, aggression and good luck, the nature of Roman power and the Romans' assumptions about their relationship to the world they now dominated were changing. In the broadest terms, the rudimentary empire of obedience had at least partly transformed into an empire of annexation. *Provincia* had come to mean 'province' in the sense of a defined region under direct Roman control rather than just 'responsibility' or 'job', and the word *imperium* was now occasionally used in the sense of 'empire'. These shifts in terminology point to new concepts of Roman territory and a new framework of organisation, which raised new questions about what government abroad meant. How was a Roman governor expected to behave in the provinces? How was his job defined? What voice were the provincial populations to have, particularly in seeking redress against misrule? And what was to count as misrule? Issues of provincial government were brought into the very heart of domestic political debate. One precious piece of evidence for this is the text of the law under which Verres was prosecuted. It does not have the fame of Cicero's showy rhetoric, but it takes us behind the scenes to Roman attempts to devise a legal framework, and practical arrangements, for the rights of provincials.

Even more controversial, and central to the eventual collapse of Republican government, were questions of who could be trusted with the command, control and administration of the empire. Who was to govern the provinces, to collect the taxes, to command, or serve in, Rome's armies? Was the traditional governing class, with its principles of shared and short-term power, capable of handling the vast problems, administrative and military, that the empire now threw up? At the very end of the second century BCE, Gaius Marius, a 'new man', loudly blamed a string of Roman military defeats on the corruption of Rome's commanders, always open to a well-placed bribe. He went on to base a political career on his ability to score notable victories where they had disastrously failed, and to be elected consul no fewer than seven times, five in a row.

This was a pattern of repeated office holding that Sulla later banned, in his reforms of the late 80s BCE. But the underlying problem did not go away. The demands of defending, policing and sometimes extending the empire encouraged, or compelled, the Romans to hand over enormous financial and military resources to individual commanders for years on end, in a way that challenged the traditional structures of the state even more fundamentally than disputes at home between *optimates* and *populares* ever did. By the middle of the first century BCE, riding on the back of overseas conquest, Pompey the Great and Julius Caesar had become rivals for autocratic power: they commanded what were effectively their own private armies; they had flouted Republican principles even more comprehensively than Sulla or Marius; and they had opened up the prospect of one-man rule, which Caesar's assassination did not block.

In short, as the last part of this chapter reveals, the empire created the emperors – not the other way round.

Governors and governed

Verres is often seen as symptomatic of Roman rule abroad at this period, even allowing for gross exaggeration on Cicero's part: a particularly rotten apple maybe, but one of a generally poor crop. The traditional assumption that military victory should turn into booty for the conqueror or that the defeated should pay for their defeat (as Carthage had done when Rome demanded vast reparations after the Second Punic War) died hard. Individual governors found that a posting overseas could be an easy opportunity for recouping some of the expenses of getting elected to political office in Rome, not to mention for pleasure of all kinds, away from the watchful eyes of their peers in Rome.

In a rousing speech given on his return from a junior post in Sardinia, Gaius Gracchus had sharp words for his colleagues who went out there with 'amphorae full of wine and brought them home brimming with silver' – a clear criticism of their profiteering, as well as a hint of their dim view of the local grape. Roman rule was for the most part fairly hands off by the standards of more recent imperial regimes: the locals kept their own calendars, their own coinages, their own gods, their own varied systems of law and civic government. But wherever and whenever it was more direct, it seems to have fallen somewhere on the spectrum between ruthlessly exploitative at one end and negligent, under-resourced and inefficient at the other.

Cicero's experiences as governor of Cilicia in the late 50s BCE, described in vivid detail in his letters home, offer a glaring contrast to the depredations of Verres but still point to the messy reality of provincial government, with its endemic, chronic, low-level exploitation. Cilicia was a vast area of some 40,000 square miles in the wilds of what is now southern Turkey, with the island of Cyprus attached. Communications within the province were so unreliable that when Cicero first arrived he could not find out where his predecessor was, and three detachments of the two, under strength, underpaid and slightly mutinous, Roman legions stationed there seemed to have 'gone missing'. Were they perhaps with the previous governor? No one knew.

At this point, Cicero, who had no previous army experience except a short stint as a teenager in the Social War, seized the chance to grab a little military glory. After one successful skirmish against some of the more resistant locals in the mountains, he even preened himself for camping on the same spot as Alexander the Great almost 200 years earlier. 'A not inconsiderably better general than you or I,' he wrote to Atticus, either with wry irony or else stating the obvious. But most of the rest of his time was divided between hearing court cases that involved Roman citizens, adjudicating disputes between provincials, controlling the behaviour of his small staff, who seem to have specialised in insulting the local residents, and dealing with the demands of various friends and acquaintances.

One young colleague in Rome pestered him to have some panthers caught and dispatched back to the city – to star, and be slaughtered, in shows he was putting on there. Cicero was evasive, claiming that the animals were in short supply: they must have decided to emigrate to the neighbouring province to escape the traps, he quipped. Less of a joking matter was a problem over loans made by Marcus Junius Brutus. The man who six years later led Caesar's assassins was at this point up to his neck in usury, busy lending money to the people of Salamis, in Cyprus, at the illegal interest rate of 48 per cent. Cicero clearly sympathised with the Salaminians and withdrew the detachment of Roman soldiers that his predecessor had 'lent' to Brutus' agents to help them extract what they were owed; they were said to have besieged the council chamber in Salamis and starved to death five of the local councillors. But then, rather than offend the well-connected creditor, he proceeded to turn a blind eye to the whole issue. His main priority, anyway, was to quit the province and the job of governor as soon as he legitimately could ('the business bores me'). When his year was up, he walked out, leaving the vast region in the charge of one of his underlings, whom he admitted was 'only a boy, probably stupid, with no authority or self-control': so much for responsible government.

Yet that gloomy picture is only one side of the story of Roman provincial administration. Brutally as Roman demands must have fallen on many people in the provinces – and probably more brutally on the poor, whose plight almost all ancient writers ignore, than on the rich who came to Cicero's attention – exploitation was not unchecked. It is too easy to forget that the only reason the lurid details of Verres' misdeeds survive is that he was put on trial, and disgraced, for his treatment of the Sicilians. And Gaius Gracchus' reference to grasping Roman officials was intended to draw a contrast with his own upright behaviour in Sardinia, as the man who 'brought back empty the money belts [he] had taken out full of silver' and who never put his hands on a prostitute or a pretty slave boy. Corruption, money grabbing and sex tourism were matters of public criticism, accusations regularly levelled at political rivals and convenient weapons in character assassination. They were not, so far as we know, matters for public celebration or even smug boasting.

Many of the tales of misdeeds were part of a wider discussion that began towards the end of the second century BCE about what the rules and ethical principles for overseas government should be, or – to put it even more generally – about how Rome should relate to the outside world when foreigners became people to be governed as well as fought. This was a distinctive, and novel, Roman contribution to political theory in the ancient world. Cicero's earliest philosophical treatise, written in 59 BCE in the form of a letter to his brother, is largely concerned with honesty, integrity, impartiality and consistency in provincial rule. And a century before, in 149 BCE, a permanent criminal court had been established at Rome, with the main aim of giving foreigners compensation and the right of redress against extortion by their Roman rulers. No ancient Mediterranean empire had ever systematically tried to do this before. It may be a sign that corrupt government abroad started early. It also shows that there had long been a political will to tackle corruption. The law under which Verres was indicted, originally part of Gaius Gracchus' reform programme, shows what an enormous amount of care, precision and sophisticated legal thought had been devoted to this problem by the 120s BCE.

Eleven fragments of Gaius' compensation law, inscribed on bronze, were discovered around 1500 CE near Urbino in northern Italy. Two have since been lost and are known only from manuscript copies, but another was unearthed in the nineteenth century. Reassembled, in a jigsaw puzzle that has kept scholars occupied for half a millennium, they give us roughly half the text, which laid out the legal means for provincials to recover the value of what had been extorted from them by Roman officials, with damages on top. It is an extraordinary resource for understanding the practice and principles of Roman government, and an important reminder of the kind of information that, without such chance discoveries, easily slips through the net of the Roman historical tradition. For although Roman writers make passing allusion to this piece of legislation, they give no hint whatsoever that it was anything like what can be read here. The details have been preserved thanks only to the councillors of some Italian town in the late second century BCE, who decided to have the law inscribed on bronze for public display – and thanks to whoever stumbled across the fragments in the Renaissance and recognised their significance.

This is Roman law at its most careful and precise, demonstrating sophisticated skill in legal draughtsmanship almost without parallel anywhere in the classical world before this date, and a far cry from the pioneering but crude efforts of the Twelve Tables. The surviving

Latin text runs to about ten modern pages and goes through every aspect of the process of redress, from the question of who is allowed to bring a case ('any man of the Latin name or of foreign nations, or within the discretion, dominion, power or friendship of the Roman people') to the rewards and compensation that are to follow a successful prosecution (damages are set at double the loss incurred, and full Roman citizenship is offered to a successful prosecutor). In between, all kinds of problems are addressed. Assistance with the prosecution (a simple form of legal aid) is promised to those who needed it, as foreigners might well do. Provision is made for getting money out of men, like Verres, who bolted before the verdict was announced. There are also strict rules laid down governing conflict of interest: no one who belonged to the same 'club' as the defendant could serve as one of the fifty jurors assigned to each case. Even the precise method of voting is specified. Each juror must indicate his vote on a piece of boxwood of a particular size and drop it into an urn, with his fingers over the writing to conceal his decision – and with a bare arm, presumably to prevent any kind of fiddling going on under the folds of a toga.

How effectively this worked in practice is hard to know. Just over thirty prosecutions are recorded between the passage of the law in the 120s BCE and the case against Verres in 70 BCE, and almost half of those resulted in convictions. But these incomplete statistics are only part of the story. Realistically, even the promised assistance with a prosecution might not have encouraged victims to travel halfway across the Mediterranean to try to get redress, in an unfamiliar language and in the unfamiliar legal system of the ruling power. Besides, compensation was to be made only for financial loss, not for other forms of maltreatment (there was nothing for cruelty, abuse or rape, for example). Nonetheless, the law leaves no doubt that radical politicians such as Gaius were starting to be concerned with the wider world, and with the plight of the disadvantaged and disempowered not only among Roman citizens but also among the subjects of Rome's empire.

Senators under fire

There were, however, more than purely humanitarian issues behind this compensation law. In line with much of the rest of his programme in the 120s BCE, Gaius was also attempting to police the activities of senators. His reform had as much to do with the internal politics of Rome as with the suffering of provincials abroad. According to the regulations, it was only senators and their sons who were liable for prosecution under the law, even though many other Romans overseas were in a position to enrich themselves at the expense of the locals. And the juries who tried them were to be drawn exclusively and specifically from a class of those who were *not* senators, from the ranks of the Roman 'equestrians', or 'knights' (*equites*).

This was a technical but crucial distinction. The *equites* stood at the top of the Roman hierarchy of wealth, substantial property owners on a scale that set them apart from the vast majority of ordinary citizens, and they were often closely connected with senators, socially, culturally and by birth. They were a much larger group than the senators, many thousands by the end of the second century BCE, as against a few hundred senators. In fact, in strictly legal terms, senators were simply that subgroup of knights who had been elected to political office and so had entered the senate. But the interests of the two did not always coincide, and the equestrians were a far more diverse category. Among them were many wealthy men from the towns of Italy – their number increasing dramatically after the Social War – who would never have dreamt of standing for election at Rome, or men like Cicero's influential friend Atticus, who chose to stay on the sidelines of politics. There were also many who were involved in the kind of financial and commercial activities from which senators were formally debarred. Although there were, as usual, several ways to circumvent it, a law of the late third century BCE prohibited senators from owning large trading ships, defined as those that held more than 300 amphorae.

Some equestrians were involved in the potentially lucrative business of provincial taxation, thanks to another law of Gaius Gracchus. For it was he who first arranged that tax collecting in the new province of Asia should, like many other state responsibilities, be contracted out to private companies, often owned by equestrians. These contractors were known as *publicani* – 'public service providers' or 'publicans', as tax collectors are called in old translations of the New Testament, confusingly to modern readers. The system was simple, demanded little manpower on the part of the Roman state and provided a model for the tax arrangements in other provinces over the following decades (and was common in other early tax raising regimes). Periodic auctions of specific taxation rights in individual provinces took place at Rome. The company that bid the highest then collected the taxes, and anything it managed to rake in beyond the bid was its profit. To put it another way, the more the *publicani* could screw out of the provincials, the bigger their own take – and they were not liable to prosecution under Gaius' compensation law. Romans had always made money out of their conquests and their empire, but increasingly there were explicitly, and even organised, commercial interests at stake.

The compensation law drove a wedge between senators and *equites*. The original initiative combined the protection of Rome's subjects with the control of senatorial (mis)conduct. By specifying a wholly equestrian jury, it aimed to ensure that there was no collusion possible between a senatorial defendant and a jury of his friends, and – just to be on the safe side – equestrians with senators in their close family were also forbidden to participate in these trials. But the upshot was to bring senators and *equites* into conflict and sometimes to catch in the crossfire the very provincials whom the law had been passed to protect. It was often alleged, for example, that far from acting as impartial assessors of senatorial corruption, the equestrian jurors were such partisan supporters of the tax contractors that they would routinely return a guilty verdict on any innocent provincial governor who had tried to confront the contractors' depredations. One notorious case concerned a senator, convicted of extortion by a biased equestrian jury, who was so confident of his honourable record, reputation and popularity that he went into exile in the very province that was supposedly the scene of his crimes. There is a whiff of senatorial special pleading here. But even so, such stories point to a long-running controversy about who could be trusted to sit in judgement on Roman behaviour abroad: senators or *equites*? Over the decades following the passage of Gaius' law, reformers of different political persuasions reassigned the juries back and forth between the two groups.

This was still a live issue when Cicero prosecuted Verres in 70 BCE, and it gave that trial an extra political edge. Ten years earlier, Sulla, predictably, had handed over to senatorial jurors not only the compensation court but also a range of other criminal courts that had been established later to deal with such charges as treason, embezzlement and poisoning. By the time of the prosecution of Verres, the backlash against this was growing, and – in the written text at least – Cicero repeatedly urged the jury to convict the defendant partly to demonstrate that senators could be trusted with passing fair judgement on their peers. The plea came too late. Soon after the trial ended, new legislation, which set the pattern for the future, shared the juries between knights and senators. Verres' trial was the last occasion in this extortion court when a jury of senators tried a fellow senator: another of its claims to fame.

Rome for sale

The alleged corruption, incompetence and snobbish exclusivity of leading senators were important topics in wide political debates throughout the last century of the Republic. These were the central theme of Sallust's essay *The War against Jugurtha*, a devastating analysis of Rome's long failure to deal with the North African ruler who from about 118 BCE – by a combination of dynastic murder, intrigue and indiscriminate massacre – had begun to extend his control along the Mediterranean coast of Africa. The essay is a virulently partisan account, written some seventy years after the war, hugely moralising, highly dramatised and, in modern terms, a partly fictionalised reconstruction. It is a loaded assault on senatorial privilege, venality and disdain from the pen of a 'new man' in the senate.

Roman territory in North Africa in the late second century BCE was divided between the province of Africa (the area around the site of Carthage, directly administered in the new style by a Roman governor) and other regions that were still part of the old-style empire of obedience, including the nearby kingdom of Numidia. After one compliant Numidian king died in 118 BCE, there was a long power struggle between his nephew Jugurtha and a rival heir, which ended in 112 BCE with Jugurtha killing the rival, along with a large number of Roman and Italian traders who had the misfortune to be in the same town at the same time; they have usually been assumed to be entirely innocent victims, though Sallust's account hints that they may have been acting more like an armed militia. It was a lesson in the instability of that old style of control, which was always vulnerable to disobedience from those assumed to be obedient and to the inside knowledge that allies acquired through long contact with Rome. In Jugurtha's case, previous service with the army of Scipio Aemilianus in Spain, as the commander of an allied detachment of Numidian archers, gave him useful experience of Roman military tactics and useful connections on the Roman side.

For years, Roman responses to Jugurtha's activities ranged from cautious to ineffectual. The senate sent various deputations to Africa and tried in a rather desultory way to broker a deal between him and his rival. It was only after the massacre of the traders that Rome declared war, in 111 BCE, and dispatched an army, whose commander quickly stitched up a peace deal. Jugurtha was summoned to Rome but was promptly sent back home when it came to light that he had engineered the murder of a cousin in Italy for fear that he too might become a rival. Roman armies once again pursued him in Africa, with mixed success. By 107 BCE Jugurtha had been somewhat contained but was still on the loose.

This lamentable record in North Africa raised big questions. Was the senate capable of running the empire and of protecting Rome's interests overseas? If not, what kind of talent was required, and where could it be found? For several Roman observers, senatorial weakness for bribery was one major factor lying behind their failure: 'Rome's a city for sale and bound to fall as soon as it finds a buyer', as Jugurtha was supposed to have quipped when he left the city. The general incompetence of the governing class was another. For Sallust, that incompetence was a consequence of their narrow elitism and their refusal to recognise talent outside their own small group. The exclusion of the plebeians from political office had long ago been broken down, but two hundred years later – so this argument went – the new mixed aristocracy of patricians and plebeians had become in practice almost as exclusive. The same families monopolised the highest offices and the most prestigious commands, for generation after generation, and were not keen to let competent 'new men' in. The senate was dominated by the ancient equivalent of the old boy network.

Sallust's essay highlights the story of Gaius Marius, a 'new man' and experienced soldier who served in Africa in the war against Jugurtha as the second in command to one of those aristocrats, Quintus Caecilius Metellus. When Marius, who had reached the office of praetor, decided in 108 BCE to go back to Rome to stand for election to the consulship, with his eye on a big military command, he asked Metellus for support. Metellus' response, at least as Sallust scripted it, was a classic example of patronising snobbery. To become a praetor was quite good enough for a man of Marius' background, he sneered; let him not think of overreaching himself. Sallust sums it up even more sharply in his *War against Catiline*: 'Most of the aristocracy believed that the consulship had been almost polluted if some "new man" obtained it, however excellent he might be.' Marius was angry but not put off. He returned to the city to stand for the consulship. Once he had been elected, to the post he would hold for an unprecedented seven times, a vote in the popular assembly transferred the command against Jugurtha to him.

Sallust's account cannot be taken entirely at face value. Jugurtha may have been adept at slipping money into senatorial purses – it was a conviction in the Roman courts for accepting bribes on a delegation to Africa that finally forced Gaius Gracchus' murderer, Opimius, to retreat into exile. But Romans had a tendency to use bribery as a convenient excuse whenever war, elections or court verdicts did not go the way they hoped. Outright corruption of that kind was probably less common than they alleged. And, whatever the snobbery at the heart of the governing class, there was in practice more room for new, or newish, talent than Sallust's angry assertions allow. Surviving lists of names, which by this period are largely accurate, suggest that about 20 per cent of consuls in the late second century BCE came from families whose extended network of relations had not produced a consul in the previous fifty years, if ever.

Marius' career had an enormous impact on the rest of Republican history, in ways he can hardly have planned. First, when he returned to Africa to take command against Jugurtha, he enrolled in his army any citizen who was prepared to volunteer. Up to then, except in emergencies, Roman soldiers had officially been recruited only from families with some property. On that basis, recruitment problems had been evident for some time and may have lain behind Tiberius Gracchus' anxieties about the landless poor; for, if they had no land, they could not serve in the legions.

By enrolling all comers, Marius cut through that, but in the process he created a dependent, quasi-professional Roman army, which destabilised domestic politics for eighty years or so. These new-style legions increasingly relied on their commanders not only for a share of the booty but also for a settlement package, preferably of land, at the end of their military service, which would give them some guarantee of making a living in the future. The effects of this were felt in many ways. The conflicts in the small town of Pompeii after Sulla foisted his veterans on the place in 80 BCE were only one of many cases of local clashes, exploitation and resentment. Where the land for these soldiers was to come from, and at whose expense, became a perennial problem. But it was the relationship created between individual generals and their troops that had the most drastic consequences. In essence, the soldiers exchanged absolute loyalty to their commander for the promise of a retirement package – in a trade-off that at best bypassed the interests of the state and at worst turned the legions into a new style of private militia focused entirely on the interests of their general. When the soldiers of Sulla, and later of Julius Caesar, followed their leader and invaded the city of Rome, it was partly because of the relationship between legions and commanders forged by Marius.

Equally significant for the future was the role of the people in granting Marius his military commands. It was a vote of the assembly, proposed by a tribune and overturning the nomination of the senate, that put Marius in charge of the war against Jugurtha. This procedure had been used in one or two emergencies before. But in 108 BCE it came as a powerful assertion of the right of the people as a whole, rather than the senate, to decide who was to command Rome's armies. No sooner had Marius secured Roman victory in Africa and returned to Rome with Jugurtha in chains than another general was sacked by popular vote, after suffering a terrible defeat at the hands of German invaders from across the Alps. In an atmosphere of panic, which included a rare repetition of state-sponsored human sacrifice in Rome, his command too was assigned to Marius – who proceeded to justify the people's hopes and send the invaders packing.

Marius came to a sad end. He was already almost seventy years old when a tribune tried to use a vote of the popular assembly to transfer one last military command to him; this time it was without success. For this was 88 BCE, the command was against King Mithradates, and the rival commander was Sulla, who marched on Rome to prevent any such transfer (see pp. 241–2). While Sulla was away in the East, Marius died, a few weeks into his seventh consulship, to which he had been elected as an 'anti-Sullan' candidate. Some claimed that in his deathbed hallucinations, he acted as if he had won the command against Mithradates and issued instructions to his carers as if they were soldiers going to battle. It was a pitiful story of a deluded old man, but the principle of popular control of appointments abroad that he had championed was often reasserted over the following decades. Assemblies of the people repeatedly voted vast resources to those they were persuaded could best undertake the defence, or expansion, of Rome's empire. In effect, they voted autocrats into power, as the case of Pompey shows: Pompey the Great, as he called himself, but the Butcher to others.

Pompey the Great

Just four years after his prosecution of Verres, in 66 BCE Cicero addressed the Roman people in a public meeting on the security of the empire. Now a praetor, and with his eyes on the consulship, he was speaking in support of a proposal by a tribune to put Pompey in command of the long-running, on-and-off war against the same King Mithradates whom the Romans had been fighting, with mixed success, for more than twenty years. Pompey's powers were to include almost complete control over a large swathe of the eastern Mediterranean for

43. The head of Mithradates VI on one of his silver coins. The sweeping hair, tossed back, is reminiscent – no doubt intentionally – of the distinctive hairstyle of Alexander the Great. In Mithradates' conflict with Pompey 'the Great', two new, would-be Alexanders were fighting each other.

an unlimited period, with more than 40,000 troops at his disposal, and the right to make peace or war and to arrange treaties more or less independently.

Cicero may have been genuinely convinced that Mithradates was a real threat to Rome's security and that Pompey was the only man for the job. From the heartland of his kingdom on the Black Sea the king had certainly scored occasional terrifying victories over Roman interests across the eastern Mediterranean, including in 88 BCE a notorious, and highly mythologised, massacre of tens of thousands of Romans and Italians on a single day. Exploiting what must have been a widespread hatred of Roman presence and offering added incentives (any slave who murdered a Roman master was to be freed), he coordinated simultaneous attacks on Roman residents in towns on the west coast of what is now Turkey, from Pergamum in the north to Caunos, the 'fig capital' of the Aegean, in the south, killing – in highly inflated Roman estimates – somewhere between 80,000 and 150,000 men, women and children. If even nearly on that scale, this was a cold, calculating and genocidal massacre, but it is hard to resist the feeling that by the 60s BCE, after the campaigns of Sulla in the 80s BCE, Mithradates might have been disruptive rather than dangerous and that he had become a convenient enemy in Roman political circles: a bogeyman to justify potentially lucrative campaigns and a stick with which to beat one's rivals for their inactivity. Cicero also more or less admitted to having been leaned on by commercial interests in Rome, anxious about the effect of prolonged instability, real or imaginary, in the East on their private profits as much as on the finances of the state. The boundary between the two was carefully blurred.

In making the case for this special command, Cicero pointed to Pompey's lightning success the previous year in clearing the Mediterranean of pirates, also thanks to sweeping powers voted by a popular assembly. Pirates in the ancient world were both an endemic menace and a usefully unspecific figure of fear, not far different from the modern 'terrorist' – including anything from the navy of a rogue state to small-time human traffickers. Pompey got rid of them within three months (suggesting they may have been an easier target than they were painted) and followed up his success with a resettlement policy, unusually enlightened for either the ancient or the modern world. He gave the ex-pirates smallholdings at a safe distance from the coast, where they could make an honest livelihood. Even if some fared no better than Sulla's veterans, one of those who did take well to his new life makes a lyrical cameo appearance in Virgil's poem on farming, the *Georgics*, written in the late 30s BCE. The old man is living peacefully near Tarentum in southern Italy, now an expert on horticulture and beekeeping. His piracy days are long behind him; instead 'planting herbs scattered among the bushes and white lilies all around, vervain and slender poppies, in his spirit he equalled the riches of kings'.

Cicero's underlying argument, however, was that new problems called for new solutions. The danger Mithradates posed to Rome's commercial revenues, its taxation income and the lives of Romans based in the East demanded a change of approach. As the empire had expanded over the past two centuries, all kinds of adjustments had already been made in Rome's traditional system of office holding to cope with the demands of overseas government and to add to the available manpower. The number of praetors, for example, had increased to eight by the time of Sulla; and there was now a regular system by which elected officials went to provincial posts abroad for a year or two (as *proconsuls* or *propraetors*, '*in place of* consuls or praetors') after they had completed a year's duties in Rome. Yet these offices remained piecemeal and short term when what Rome needed in the face of an enemy such as Mithradates was the best general, with a lengthy command, over the whole of the area that might be affected by the war, with the money and soldiers to do the job, not hampered by the normal controls.

There was predictable opposition. Pompey was a radical and ambitious rule breaker who had already flouted most of the conventions of Roman politics that traditionalists were increasingly trying to insist on. The son of a 'new man', he had risen to military prominence by exploiting the disruption of the 80s BCE. When still in his twenties, he had put together three legions from among his clients and henchmen to fight on behalf of Sulla and was soon awarded a triumph for chasing down Sulla's rivals and assorted enemy princelings in Africa. It was then that he gained the nickname *adulescentulus carnifex*: 'kid butcher' rather than *enfant terrible*. He had held no elected office whatsoever when he was given, by the senate, a long-term command in Spain to deal with a Roman general who had 'gone native' with a large army, another hazard of a far-flung empire. Successful again, he ended up a consul for 70 BCE, at the age of just thirty-five and bypassing all the junior posts, flagrantly at odds with Sulla's recent rulings on office holding. So ignorant was he of what went on in the senate, which as consul he had to chair, that he resorted to asking a learned friend to write him a handbook of senatorial procedure.

A few hints of the objections made to this new command can be gleaned from Cicero's speech. His enormous emphasis, for example, on the immediate danger posed by Mithradates ('letters arrive every day telling how villages in our provinces are being burnt') strongly suggests that some people did claim at the time that it was being blown out of all proportion as an excuse to give vast new powers to Pompey. The objectors did not win the day, though they must have come to feel that their fears were not unfounded. Over the next four years, under the terms of his new command, Pompey set about redrawing the map of the eastern part of the Roman Empire, from the Black Sea in the north to Syria and Judaea in the south. In practice, he cannot have done this alone; he must have had the help of hundreds of friends, junior officers, slaves and advisors. But this particular rewriting of geography was always at the time ascribed to Pompey himself.

His power was partly the result of military operations. Mithradates was quickly driven out of Asia Minor, to his territories in the Crimea, where he was later ousted in a coup by one of his sons and killed himself; and there was a successful Roman siege of the fortress at Jerusalem, where two rivals were contesting the high priesthood and kingship. But more of this power came from a judicious mixture of diplomacy, bullying and well-placed displays of Roman force. Months of Pompey's time were devoted to turning the central part of Mithradates' kingdom into a directly governed Roman province, adjusting the boundaries of other provinces, founding dozens of new cities and ensuring that many of the local monarchs and dynasts had been downsized and made obedient in the old style.

In the triumph he celebrated in 61 BCE, after his return to Rome and on his forty-fifth birthday (no doubt a planned coincidence), Pompey is said to have worn a cloak that once belonged to Alexander the Great. Where on earth he had come across this fake, or piece of fancy dress, is impossible to know – and he did not deceive many shrewd Roman observers, who were no less sceptical about the authenticity of the fabric than we are. But it was presumably intended to match not only the name ('the Great') that he had borrowed from Alexander but also the ambitions of far-flung imperial conquest. Some

Romans were impressed, others decidedly dubious about the display. Pliny the Elder, writing just over a hundred years later, singled out for disapproval a portrait head of Pompey that the general himself had commissioned, made entirely of pearl: 'the defeat of austerity and the triumph of luxury'. But there was a bigger point. This celebration was the most powerful expression yet of the Roman Empire in territorial terms, and even of Roman ambition for world conquest. One of the trophies carried in the procession, probably in the shape of a large globe, had an inscription attached to it declaring that 'this is a trophy of the whole world'. And a list of Pompey's achievements displayed in a Roman temple included the telling if over-optimistic boast that he 'extended the frontiers of the empire to the limits of the earth'.

The first emperor

Pompey has a good claim to be called the first Roman emperor. True, he has usually gone down in history as the man who finally supported the cause of the Republic against the increasingly independent power of Caesar, and so as an opponent of imperial rule. But his treatment in the East and the honours showered upon him (or which he contrived) closely prefigured many of the defining elements of the Roman emperor's image and status. It was almost as if the forms and symbols of imperial rule that, a few decades later under Julius Caesar and even more his great-nephew, the emperor Augustus, became standard in Italy and Rome had their prototypes in Roman rule abroad.

Julius Caesar, for example, was the first living person whose head featured on a coin minted in Rome. Up to that point, Roman small change had paraded only images of long-dead heroes, and the innovation was a blatant sign of Caesar's personal power, followed by all later Roman rulers. But a decade earlier, communities in the East had produced coins showing Pompey's head. This honour went along with other extravagant compliments and even various forms of religious cult. A group of 'Pompey worshippers' (*Pompeiastae*) are known on the island of Delos. New cities took his name: Pompeiopolis, or 'Pompeytown'; Magnopolis, or 'City of the Great'. He was hailed as 'equal to a god', 'saviour' and even just 'god'. And at Mytilene on Lesbos a month in the calendar was renamed after him – just as, in Rome, months were later renamed after Julius Caesar and Augustus.

There were precedents for many of these accolades, individually. The kings who followed Alexander the Great, in territories from Macedon to Egypt, had often had their power expressed in more or less divine terms. Ancient polytheistic religions treated the boundary between gods and humans more flexibly and constructively than modern monotheisms. Earlier Roman commanders in the eastern Mediterranean had occasionally been honoured with religious festivals established in their names, and Cicero implies in a letter to Atticus from Cilicia that he had turned down the offer of a temple. Nonetheless, as a package, Pompey's honours were on a wholly new scale. It is hard to imagine how, after this kind of elevation in the East and after the independent power he had exercised in reorganising vast tracts of land, Pompey could have returned to Rome to become an ordinary senator, just one among many. On the surface, that is just what he did. There was no march on the city in the style of Sulla. But underneath there were hints of change back in Rome too.

Pompey's vast building scheme of theatre, gardens, porticoes and meeting rooms, all lined with famous works of sculpture, was a decidedly imperial innovation. It was far more extensive than the individual temples commonly erected by earlier generals in thanks for the help of the gods on the battlefield had ever been. Dedicated in 55 BCE, it was the first of a series of massive architectural developments that were a hallmark of later emperors, who tried to leave their stamp, in gleaming marble, on the Roman cityscape, and that form our image of ancient Rome today. There are also signs that even in Rome Pompey

44. A recent attempt to reconstruct the theatre that was the centrepiece of Pompey's building scheme, with its elaborate stage backdrop, and an auditorium that seated, according to one ancient estimate, 40,000 spectators, almost as many as the Colosseum. At the back of the auditorium was a small temple of Venus Victrix ('Giver of Victory'), pointing to the support of the gods for Pompey and to the military victory that financed the construction.

was presented, much like later emperors, in godlike terms. This was already a theme in Cicero's speech of 66 BCE which repeatedly refers to Pompey's talents as 'divine' or 'endowed by the gods', singling out his '*incredibilis ac divina virtus*' ('his unbelievable and godlike *virtus*'). Quite how literally to take the word *divina* is unclear, but in the Roman world it never became the completely dead metaphor that 'divine' often is now. At the very least, there was something a bit more than human about Pompey. That is strongly implied too by an honour voted to him on the proposal of two tribunes in 63 BCE, in anticipation of his return from the East: Pompey was to be allowed to wear the dress of a triumphing general whenever he attended the circus races.

This was much more significant than it may sound and certainly more than a matter of dress code. For the special costume traditionally worn by the successful general in his triumphal procession was identical to the costume worn by the statue of the god Jupiter in his temple on the Capitoline Hill. It was as if military victory allowed the general literally to step into a god's shoes, just for the day – which explains why the slave standing behind him in the chariot was supposed to have whispered in his ear, over and over again, 'Remember you're (just) a man.' To allow Pompey to dress up in triumphal regalia on other occasions was tantamount to giving him divine status outside that strictly defined ritual context. It must have seemed a risky step to take, for Pompey is said to have tried his new privilege only once – and that, as one Roman writer sharply observed some seventy years later, 'was once too often'.

How to balance individual achievement and celebrity with the notional equality of the elite and the principles of shared power had been a major dilemma throughout the Roman Republic. Many mythical stories of early Rome pose the problem of dashing heroes who step out of line to take on the enemy single-handedly. Did they deserve punishment for disobedience or honour for bringing victory to Rome? There were also historical figures before Pompey whose prominence had come into conflict with the traditional power structure of the state. Marius and Sulla are obvious examples. But more than a hundred years before them, despite, or because of, his series of tremendous victories, Scipio Africanus had spent the end of his life in virtual exile, after various attempts through the Roman courts to cut him down to size: hence his burial in southern Italy and not in the grand Scipio family tomb in Rome. There were even stories that he claimed divine inspiration and used to spend the night in the Temple of Jupiter to take advantage of his special relationship with the god. But by the middle of the first century BCE, the stakes were so much bigger, the size of Rome's operations and obligations so much greater and the resources of cash and manpower available so much larger that the rise of men such as Pompey was more or less unstoppable.

What eventually did stop Pompey was a rival, in the shape of Julius Caesar, a member of an old patrician family, with a political pro-gramme in the radical tradition of the Gracchi and eventually with ambitions that led directly to one-man rule. But first the two men were part of a notorious three-cornered alliance.

The Gang of Three

In 60 BCE, two years after he had returned to Rome, Pompey was frustrated that the senate had not yet formally ratified his eastern set-tlement, instead procrastinating by confirming it piece by piece, not en bloc. And, as any general then had to do, he was looking for land on which to settle his ex-soldiers. Marcus Licinius Crassus, who had finally led Roman troops to victory against Spartacus and was reput-edly the richest man in Rome, had recently taken up the case of a struggling company of state contractors. They had bid far too much for the tax rights of the province of Asia, and Crassus was trying to get them permission to renegotiate the price. Julius Caesar, the least experienced, and least wealthy, of the three, wanted to secure election to the consulship of 59 BCE and a major military command to follow, not merely the policing duties against brigands in Italy that the senate had in mind for him. Mutual support seemed the best way to achieve these various aims. So, in an entirely unofficial deal, they pooled re-sources, power, contacts and ambition to get what they wanted in the short term – and in the longer.

For many ancient observers this was another milestone on the road to the breakdown of Republican government. The poet Horace, looking back from the other side of that breakdown, was only one of those who singled out the year 60 BCE, when he referred, according to traditional Roman dating, to 'the civil war that began when Metellus was consul'. 'Cato the Younger' – the great grandson of 'the Elder' (p. 204) and one of Caesar's most uncompromising enemies – argued that the city was overturned not when Caesar and Pompey fell out but when they became friends. The idea that the political process had been fixed behind the scenes seemed in some ways worse than the open violence of the previous decades. Cicero captured the point nicely when he observed that in Pompey's notebook there was a list not only of past consuls but of future ones too.

It was not such a complete takeover as those comments imply. There were all kinds of strains, disagreements and rivalries between the three men, and if Pompey really did have a notebook with a list of the gang's choice of future consuls, the electoral process sometimes got the better of them and someone quite different, not at all to their liking, was voted in. Nonetheless, they did pull off their immediate goals. Caesar was duly elected consul for 59 BCE and, among a series of measures that strongly resembled the programmes of earlier, radical tribunes, sponsored legislation on behalf of the other two. He also secured a military command for himself in southern Gaul, to which a vast area on the other side of the Alps was soon added.

For much of the 50s BCE, the machinations of members of the gang continued to be a major force in Roman politics, even though Caesar made only periodic visits to Italy and Crassus never returned from the campaign he led in 55 BCE against the Parthian Empire, centred in what is now Iran, which in many ways replaced Mithradates in Roman fears. It is partly Crassus' early death that makes his role and importance within the trio difficult to assess. But the tragedy of his defeat and gory decapitation, and the humiliation of the capture of his army's ceremonial standards, resonated for years. The decisive Parthian victory came in 53 BCE at the Battle of Carrhae, on what is now the border between Turkey and Syria. Crassus' head was sent as a trophy to the Parthian king's residence, where it was instantly reused

45. A silver coin issued under Augustus celebrates the return by the Parthians of the Roman standards captured at the Battle of Carrhae. The Parthian who submissively offers back the standards is dressed in traditional Eastern trousers. The figure on the other side is, significantly, the goddess 'Honour'. In reality, it was more a negotiated deal than a military victory by the Romans.

as a prop, standing in for the head of the tragic Pentheus, decapitated by his mother, in a performance of Euripides' play *The Bacchae* (interestingly part of the Parthian repertoire). The standards remained a proud piece of Parthian booty until the emperor Augustus, by some adept diplomacy dressed up as a military achievement, brought them back to Rome in 19 BCE.

The controversies of this period in the mid first century BCE are documented in vivid microdetail, thanks largely to the letters of Cicero, sometimes written daily and full of unsubstantiated rumours, second-guessing, hints of plots, half-truths, gossip, unreliable speculation and foreboding. 'The political situation alarms me more each day' and 'There is a whiff of dictatorship in the air' are typical refrains, among more practical exchanges about loans and debts or triumphalist news of Caesar's daring, if very temporary, landing on Britain. They offer extraordinary evidence for politics as it happened that is unique in the classical world, and probably in any world before the fifteenth century CE. Yet they also tend to exaggerate the impression of confusion and political breakdown, or at least present a picture that is hard to compare with earlier periods. How disordered and cut-throat might the world of Scipio Africanus and Fabius Cunctator appear had their private letters and jottings survived rather than just the retrospective accounts of Livy and others? What is more, the overwhelming quantity of material from Cicero's pen can make it hard to see beyond his perspectives and prejudices.

The career of Publius Clodius Pulcher is a case in point. Clodius first crossed swords with Cicero in a scandal at the end of 62 BCE, after a man was discovered in what was supposed to be a solemn, all-female religious festival being led by Julius Caesar's wife. Some suspected that this was a lovers' tryst rather than a simple prank, and Caesar took the precaution of a speedy divorce, on the famous grounds that 'Caesar's wife must be above suspicion'. Many pointed the finger of blame at Clodius, who was put on trial, with Cicero appearing as a key witness for the prosecution. The upshot was an acquittal and lasting enmity between Clodius and Cicero – who predictably, but possibly wrongly, claimed that massive bribery had secured the verdict of not guilty.

Clodius' subsequent reputation for outright villainy has been almost entirely formed by Cicero's enmity. He has gone down in history as the mad patrician who not only arranged to be adopted into a plebeian family in order to stand for the tribunate but also put two fingers up to the whole process by choosing an adoptive father younger than himself. Once elected, in 58 BCE he engineered Cicero's exile for the tough line he had taken against Catiline's associates, introduced a series of laws that attacked the whole basis of Roman government, and terrorised the streets with his private militia. Rome was saved from this monster only when he was killed in 52 BCE after picking a fight with the slaves of one of Cicero's friends, at the so-called Battle of Bovillae. No alternative views of Clodius have survived. But almost certainly the other side of the story would have made him a radical reformer in the tradition of the Gracchi (one of his laws made the distribution of grain in the city entirely free), lynched by a reactionary thug and his hangers-on. Not even Cicero's efforts for the defence secured acquittal on the murder charge for his friend, who ended up a neighbour of Verres in exile in Marseilles.

The politics of the 50s BCE are a curious mixture of business as usual, perilous breakdown and ingenious, or desperate, attempts to adapt traditional political rules to meet new crises as they appeared. It is hard to know what to make of Cicero in the late 50s BCE, in the safety of his study, writing about the theory of Roman politics in ways that would have been familiar to Polybius while only a few hundred metres from his house on the Palatine there were increasingly frequent riots in the Forum and outbreaks of violence and arson, including the torching of the senate house for Clodius' funeral pyre. Perhaps this was his attempt to restore order, at least in his head. Others took more practical measures and devised some brave innovations. In 52 BCE, for example, after the murder of Clodius, Pompey was elected sole consul. Rather than resort to appointing a dictator to take charge of the growing crisis, with all the memories of Sulla's dictatorship, the senate decided to give to one man an office which by definition had always been shared between two. This time the gamble paid off. Within a few months Pompey had not only taken firm control of the city but also taken a colleague, albeit keeping it in the family: it was his new father-in-law.

More problematic were the tactics adopted by, or forced upon, Julius Caesar's fellow consul in 59 BCE, Marcus Calpurnius Bibulus, a staunch opponent of much of the legislation Caesar was introducing. Menaced by Caesar's supporters, showered with that all too familiar vehicle of Roman disaffection – excrement – and more or less confined to his house, he was unable to voice his opposition in any of the regular ways. So he stayed at home and sent out messages announcing that he was 'watching the heavens' for signs and omens. There was definite religious and political force behind this. The support of the gods underpinned Roman politics, and it was an essential axiom that no political decision could be taken until it was clear that there were no adverse omens. Yet 'watching the heavens' was never intended as a means of obstructing political action indefinitely, and those on Caesar's side claimed that Bibulus was illegitimately manipulating religious rules. The issue was never resolved. It was typical of the uncertainties of the period, and of the difficulties the Romans faced in making old rules solve new dilemmas, that for years the status of all the public business conducted in 59 BCE remained unclear. In the late 50s BCE Cicero was still wondering about the legality of Clodius' adoption and the settlement of Pompey's veterans. Had the legislation all been properly passed or not? Very different views were possible.

The most pressing political issue of the period, however, came not directly from Rome but from Caesar in Gaul. He had left Italy in 58 BCE on a five-year command, and this was rolled on for another five years in 56 BCE – with the warm support, in public at least, of Cicero, who pointed to the danger of Gallic enemies much as he had earlier pointed to the danger of Mithradates. Caesar's description of these campaigns in the seven volumes of his *Commentaries on the Gallic War*, an edited version of his official annual dispatches from the front line sent back to Rome, starts with its famous, clinical opener, *'Gallia est omnis divisa in partes tres'* ('The whole of Gaul is divided into three parts'). It ranks alongside Xenophon's description (the *Anabasis*, or *Going Up*) of his exploits with a Greek mercenary army, written in the fourth century BCE, as the only detailed eyewitness account of any ancient warfare to survive. It is not exactly a neutral document. Caesar had a shrewd eye for his public image, and the *Commentaries* is a carefully contrived justification of his conduct and parade of his military skills. But it is also an early example of what we might call imperial ethnography. Unlike Cicero, whose letters from Cilicia betray no interest whatsoever in the local surroundings, Caesar was deeply engaged with the foreign customs he witnessed, from the drinking habits of the Gauls, including the barbaric prohibition of wine among some tribes, to the religious rituals of the Druids. His is a wonderfully Roman vision of people whom he clearly did not entirely understand, but it still forms the basic reference point for modern discussions of the culture of pre-Roman northern Europe – an irony, given that it was a culture he was in the process of changing for ever.

Reading between the lines of the *Commentaries*, anyone will see that both genuine Roman anxieties about enemies in the north and Caesar's desire to outstrip in military glory any of his rivals drove the decade of warfare in Gaul. Caesar ended up bringing more territory under Roman control than Pompey had in the East and crossing over what Romans called 'the Ocean', the waterway that separated the known world from the great unknown, to set foot briefly on the remote and exotic island of Britain. It was a symbolic victory that resonated loudly back home, even earning a passing reference in a poem by Catullus, when he wrote about 'going to visit the memorials of "Caesar the Great": the Rhine in Gaul, the terrible sea and the faraway Britons'.

In doing this, Caesar laid the foundations for the political geography of modern Europe, as well as slaughtering up to a million people over the whole region. It would be wrong to imagine that the Gauls were peace-loving innocents brutally trampled by Caesar's forces. One Greek visitor in the early first century BCE had been shocked to find enemy heads casually pinned up at the entrance to Gallic houses, though he conceded that, after a while, one got used to the sight; and Gallic mercenaries had done good business in Italy until the power of Rome had closed their market. Yet the mass killing of those who stood in Caesar's way was more than even some Romans could take. Cato, driven partly no doubt by his enmity of Caesar and speaking from partisan as well as humanitarian motives, suggested that he should be handed over for trial to those tribes whose women and children he had put to death. Pliny the Elder, trying later to arrive at a headcount of Caesar's victims, seems strikingly modern in accusing him of 'a crime against humanity'.

The pressing question was what would happen when Caesar left Gaul and how after almost ten years there from 58 BCE, with the power and wealth he had accumulated, he was to be reintegrated into the ordinary mainstream of politics. As often, Romans debated this in highly legal terms. There were fierce and technical controversies about the precise date on which his military command was supposed to come to an end and whether he would then be allowed to move directly, without a break, into another consulship. For any period as a private citizen, out of office, would provide a window for a prosecution, among other things over the questionable legality of his acts in 59 BCE. On the one hand were those who, for whatever reasons, personal or principled, wanted to bring Caesar back down to size; on the other, Caesar and his supporters insisted that this treatment was humiliating, that his *dignitas* – a distinctively Roman combination of clout, prestige and right to respect – was being attacked. The underlying issue was brutally straightforward. Would Caesar, with more than 40,000 troops at his disposal only a few days from Italy, follow the example of Sulla or of Pompey?

Pompey himself cautiously remained on the sidelines almost up to the final breakdown and in the middle of 50 BCE was still trying to find Caesar a reasonably honourable exit strategy. In December of that year the senate voted by a majority of 370 to 22 that Caesar and Pompey should simultaneously give up their commands. Pompey was actually in Rome at the time, but since 55 BCE, thanks to another piece of ingenuity, he had been the governor of Spain, doing the job remotely, through deputies – an unprecedented arrangement that became a standard feature of the rule of the emperors. It is the clearest sign of the impotence of the senate at this point that, in response to this overwhelming vote, Pompey took no notice and Caesar, after a few more rounds of fruitless negotiation, marched into Italy.

Throwing the dice

Sometime around 10 January 49 BCE, Julius Caesar, with just one of his legions from Gaul, crossed the Rubicon, the river that marked the northern boundary of Italy. The exact date is not known, nor even the location of this most historically significant of rivers. It was more likely a small brook than the raging torrent of popular imagination, and – despite the efforts of ancient writers to embellish them with dramatic appearances of the gods, uncanny omens and prophetic dreams – the reality of the surroundings was probably mundane. For us, 'to cross the Rubicon' has come to mean 'to pass the point of no return'. It did not mean that to Caesar.

According to one of his companions on the journey – Gaius Asinius Pollio, historian, senator and founder of Rome's first public library

46. A portrait of Julius Caesar? Finding an authentic likeness of Caesar, apart from the tiny images on coins, has been one of the goals of modern archaeology. There are hundreds of 'portraits' made after his lifetime, but contemporary versions have been much more elusive. This portrait in the British Museum was once a favoured candidate, but is now suspected of being a fake.

– when he finally approached the Rubicon after some hesitation, Caesar quoted in Greek two words from the Athenian comic playwright Menander: literally, in a phrase borrowed from gambling, 'Let the dice be thrown.' Despite the usual English translation – 'The die is cast', which again appears to hint at the irrevocable step being taken – Caesar's Greek was much more an expression of uncertainty, a sense that everything now was in the lap of the gods. Let's throw the dice in the air and see where they will fall! Who knows what will happen next?

What did happen next was four years of civil war. Some of Caesar's supporters in Rome rushed to join him in northern Italy, while Pompey was pushed into the command of the 'anti-Caesarians' and decided to leave Italy and fight from his power base in the East. In 48 BCE his forces were defeated at the Battle of Pharsalus in northern Greece, and Pompey was murdered soon after, when he tried to take refuge in Egypt. But despite his famed speed (*celeritas* was one of his watchwords), Caesar still took three more years, until 45 BCE, to overcome his Roman adversaries in Africa and Spain, as well as to squash trouble from Pharnaces, the son and usurper of Mithradates. Between crossing the Rubicon and his death in March 44 BCE, Caesar made only fleeting visits to Rome; the longest was the five-month stretch from October 45 BCE. From the point of view of the city, he became a largely absent dictator.

In some ways, this civil war between Pompey and Caesar was as odd as the Social War. How many people it directly involved is impossible to say. The priority of many of the inhabitants of Italy, and of the empire, was probably to avoid getting inadvertently caught up in the struggles of rival armies and to keep clear of the crime wave that the war unleashed in Italy. Only occasionally do such ordinary people on the margins get even a small share of the limelight: the captain of a trading ship, Gaius Peticius, who kindly picked up a bedraggled Pompey from the Greek coast after the Battle

47. The family of the Peticius who rescued Pompey was active in trade in the eastern Mediterranean for centuries. This tombstone of one of his descendants, found in North Italy, features a loaded camel, which must have been a symbol – even a trademark – of his overseas business.

of Pharsalus is one; Soterides, a eunuch priest who inscribed on stone his worries about his male 'partner', who had sailed off with a party of local volunteers and been taken prisoner, is another. Of the partisans, on one side were the backers of Caesar, with his popular political programme and clear leanings towards one-man rule. Cicero assumed that this was where the sympathies and interests of the poor naturally lay. On the other side were a motley group of those who, for various reasons, did not like what Caesar was up to or the powers he seemed to be seeking. A few were probably as highly principled as they were unrealistic; as Cicero once said of Cato, 'he talks as if he were in the *Republic* of Plato, when in fact he is in the crap of Romulus'. But it was only later, in the romantic nostalgia under the early emperors, that they were reinvented en bloc as fully fledged freedom fighters and martyrs united in the struggle against autocracy. The irony was that Pompey, their figurehead, was no less an autocrat than Caesar. Whichever side won, as Cicero again observed, the result was set to be much the same: slavery for Rome. What came to be seen as a war between liberty and one-man rule was really a war to choose between rival emperors.

One major change, however, was that Roman civil war now involved almost all the known world. Whereas the wars between Sulla and his rivals had witnessed occasional incidents in the East, the war between the Caesarians and the Pompeians played out right across the Mediterranean, from Spain to Greece and Asia Minor. Famous names met their ends in far-flung places. Bibulus, Caesar's unfortunate colleague in 59 BCE, died at sea near Corfu as he was trying to blockade the Greek coast. The murderer of Clodius, Titus Annius Milo, left his exile to join a Pompeian uprising and fell in the toe of Italy, hit by a flying stone. Cato, once it was clear that Caesar was the inevitable victor, killed himself at the town of Utica on the coast of what is now Tunisia in the most gory way imaginable. According to his biographer, writing 150 years later, he stabbed himself with his sword but survived the gash. Despite attempts by friends and family to save him, he pushed away the doctor they had summoned and pulled out his own bowels through the still open wound.

Egypt had a significant supporting role too. It was there that Pompey, the man who had once ruled the Roman world, met his ignominious end in 48 BCE. He was expecting a warm welcome as he put to shore. In fact, he was decapitated by the henchmen of a local dynast, who calculated that disposing of the enemy leader would ingratiate him with Caesar. Reflecting on this moment, many Roman observers, Cicero included, agreed that it would have been far better for Pompey to have died a couple of years earlier, when he fell seriously ill in 50 BCE. As it was, 'his life lasted longer than his power'. The murder, however, proved a wrong move for its perpetrators. Caesar, who turned up a few days later, apparently wept as he was presented with Pompey's pickled head and shortly backed one of the rivals to the throne of Egypt. That rival was Queen Cleopatra VII, best known for her alliance, political and romantic, with Mark Antony in the next round of Roman civil wars. But at this point her interests lay with Caesar, with whom she had an open affair and – if her claims about paternity are to be believed – a child.

Back in Rome, Caesar's triumphal processions paraded spoils, animate and inanimate, from across the Roman world (see plate 9). His triumph of 46 BCE, celebrated during one of his brief visits to the city, displayed not only the Gallic rebel Vercingetorix but also Cleopatra's half-sister, who had been on the wrong side of the Egyptian power struggles; she was put on show next to a working model of the lighthouse of Alexandria. Caesar's victory over Mithradates' son Pharnaces, who had died in battle near the Black Sea, was commemorated in the same celebrations by a single placard on which was written one of the world's most famous slogans ever: 'Veni, vidi, vici' ('I came, I saw, I conquered', intended to capture the speed of Caesar's success). But there were alarming signs too, in the images of Caesar's Roman victims. Triumphal processions were supposed to celebrate victories over foreign enemies, not citizens of Rome. Caesar put on show shocking paintings of the dying moments of leading figures on the Pompeian side: from Cato disembowelling himself to Metellus Scipio throwing himself into the sea. The distaste of many people for this particular kind of triumphalism was registered in the tears of the crowds as these images were carried past. In retrospect, it was an uncanny foretaste of Caesar's bloody fate less than two years later.

The Ides of March

Julius Caesar was murdered on 15 March 44 BCE, the Ides on the Roman dating system. In parts of the Mediterranean world the civil war had by no means ended. Pompey's son Sextus still had a force of at least six legions in Spain and was continuing to fight for his father's cause. But Caesar was mustering a vast force of almost 100,000 soldiers for an attack on the Parthian Empire, a revenge for the ignominious defeat of Crassus at Carrhae and a useful opportunity for military glory against a foreign rather than a Roman enemy. It was just a few days before he was due to leave for the East, on 18 March, that a group of twenty or so disgruntled senators, supported actively or passively by a few dozen more, killed him.

Appropriately, the deed took place in a new senate house, which Pompey had built into his new theatre complex, in front of a statue of himself, which ended up splattered with Caesar's blood. Thanks in part to the reworking of the theme in Shakespeare's *Julius Caesar*, the murder of the Roman dictator in the name of *libertas* has been the template for last-ditch opposition to tyranny and for principled assassination ever since. It was no coincidence, for example, that John Wilkes Booth used 'Ides' as the code for the day on which he planned to kill Abraham Lincoln. But as a backwards glance through Roman history shows, this was the last in a series of murders of popular, radical but arguably too powerful politicians that started with the lynching of Tiberius Gracchus in 133 BCE. The question must be: what was Caesar trying to do and what made him so unacceptable to this group of senators that assassination seemed the only way out?

Despite his rare appearances in Rome, Caesar initiated a vast programme of reforms going beyond even the scale of Sulla's. One of them governs life even now. For – with some help from the specialist scientists he met in Alexandria – Caesar introduced into Rome what has become the modern Western system of timekeeping. The traditional Roman year was only 355 days long, and it had for centuries been the job of Roman priests to add in an extra month from time to time to keep the civic calendar in step with the natural seasons. For whatever reason – probably a combination of lack of expertise and lack of will – they had signally failed to get their calculations correct. The result was that the calendar year and the natural year were sometimes many weeks apart, with the Roman equivalent of harvest festivals falling when the crops were still growing and the climate in what was called April feeling more like February (which it was). The truth is that it is always dangerous in Republican history to assume that any given date is an accurate indication of the weather. Using Alexandrian know-how, Caesar corrected the error and, for the future, established a year with 365 days, with an extra day inserted at the end of February every four years. This was a far more significant outcome of his visit to Egypt than any dalliance with Cleopatra.

Other measures harked back to familiar themes from the previous hundred years. Caesar launched, for example, a large number of new overseas colonies to resettle the poor from the city of Rome, following up Gaius Gracchus' initiative with a successful foundation at Carthage. It was this, presumably, that allowed him to get away with reducing the number of recipients of free grain by about half, to 150,000 in all. He also extended Roman citizenship to those living in the far north of Italy, beyond the river Po, and at least proposed granting Latin status to the population of Sicily. But he had even more ambitious plans to overhaul Roman government, including attempts to regularise – even micromanage – all kinds of aspects of civic organisation, both in Rome and throughout Italy. These ranged from questions of who could hold office in local Italian communities (no gravediggers, pimps, actors or auctioneers unless they were retired) to issues of road maintenance (householders to be responsible for the footpath in front of their house) and traffic management (no heavy-goods vehicles in Rome during the daytime except for the purposes of temple building or repair, or for removing demolition rubble).

Caesar also became part of the calendar, as well as rewriting it. It may not have been until after his assassination that the month Quintilis was renamed Julius, our July, after him; Roman writers do not always make the chronology clear. But it was overweening honours of that sort, voted during his lifetime by a compliant senate, combined with his more or less official takeover of the democratic processes that provoked the deadly opposition. This went far beyond his head on the coinage. He was allowed to wear triumphal dress almost wherever he liked, including the triumphal laurel wreath, which he found convenient for disguising his bald patch. Temples and a priesthood in his honour seem to have been promised too, and his statue was placed in all the existing temples of Rome. His private house was even to be decorated with a triangular gable (or pediment), to give it the appearance of a temple, the home of a god.

Almost worse within the Roman context were the strong hints that he was aiming at becoming a king. On one famous but rather murky occasion, just a month before his assassination, his loyal lieutenant and one of the consuls of the year, Mark Antony, used the religious festival of the Lupercalia to offer Caesar a royal crown. It was obviously a carefully choreographed piece of propaganda, and it may have been designed as a test of public opinion. Would the watching crowd cheer when Caesar was offered the crown or not? If it did, would that be a cue to accept? Even at the time, Caesar's response and the overall message were disputed. Did he, as Cicero thought, ask Antony to send the crown to the Temple of Jupiter, the god who – Caesar insisted – was the only king of Rome? Or was it thrown to the audience and then put on a statue of Caesar? It was suspiciously unclear whether he was saying 'No, thank you' or 'Yes, please'.

Even if it was a 'No, thank you', his position as dictator, in various forms from 49 BCE, seemed pernicious to some. He was first appointed to the office for a short term, to conduct elections to the consulship for the next year, an entirely traditional procedure, except for the entirely untraditional fact that he oversaw the election of himself. In 48 BCE, after his victory at the Battle of Pharsalus, the senate again made him dictator for a year, and then in 46 BCE for ten years. Finally, by the start of 44 BCE he had become dictator for life: to the average observer, the difference between that and king must have been hard to discern. Under the terms of his dictatorship Caesar had the right directly to nominate some candidates for 'election', and he controlled the other elections behind the scenes more efficiently than Pompey had done with his notebook of future consuls' names. At the end of 45 BCE he caused a particular stir when the death of one of the sitting consuls was announced on the very last day of the year. Caesar instantly convened an assembly to elect one of his friends, Caius Caninius Rebilus, to the vacant post for just half a day. This prompted a flood of jokes from Cicero: Caninius was such an extraordinarily vigilant consul that 'he never once went to sleep in his whole term of office'; 'in the consulship of Caninius you may take it no one had breakfast'; 'Who were the consuls when Caninius was consul?' But Cicero was also outraged, as were many conservatives. For this was almost worse than fixing the elections; it was not taking the elected offices of the Roman Republic seriously.

What might now appear to be Caesar's best quality was, ironically, the one most flagrantly at odds with Republican tradition. He made much of his *clementia*, or mercy. He pardoned rather than punished his enemies, and he made a display of renouncing cruel retribution against fellow Romans, provided they gave up their opposition to him (Cato, Metellus Scipio and most Gauls were quite another matter, and

deserved all they got). Caesar had pardoned several of his future assassins, Brutus among them, after they had fought on the Pompeian
side in the civil war. In many ways, *clementia* was the political slogan
of Caesar's dictatorship. Yet it provoked as much opposition as gratitude, for the simple reason that, virtue though it may have been in
some respects, it was an entirely monarchical one. Only those with
the power to do otherwise can exercise mercy. *Clementia*, in other
words, was the antithesis of Republican *libertas*. Cato was said to have
killed himself to escape it.

So it was not just a case of simple ingratitude when Brutus and the
others turned on the man who had given them a second chance. It was
partly that. It was partly motivated by self-interest and disgruntlement,
driven by the assassins' sense of *dignitas*. But they were also defending
one view of liberty and one view of the importance of Republican

48. A silver coin issued by the 'liberators' of Rome the year after the
assassination of Caesar (43–42 BCE). One side celebrates the freedom
won: the *pileus*, worn by newly freed slaves, is flanked by the daggers
that did the deed, and underneath is the famous date EID MAR (the
'Ides of March', that is 15 March). On the other side, the head of Brutus
himself implies a rather different message. The portrayal of a living
person on a Roman coin was taken as a sign of autocratic power.

traditions going back, in Rome's mythology, to the moment when Brutus' distant ancestor was instrumental in expelling the Tarquins and became one of the first pair of consuls. In fact, the design of a silver coin later issued by the assassins underscores that very point, by featuring the distinctive hat – the *pileus*, or cap of liberty – that slaves wore when they were granted their freedom. The message was that the Roman people had been liberated.

Or had they? As we shall see, it turned out to be a very odd sort of freedom. If the assassination of Julius Caesar became a model for the effective removal of a tyrant, it was also a powerful reminder that getting rid of a *tyrant* did not necessarily dispose of *tyranny*. Despite all the slogans, the bravado and the high principles, what the assassins actually brought about, and what the people got, was a long civil war and the permanent establishment of one-man rule. But that is the story of Chapter 9. First we must turn to some of the equally important aspects of the history of Rome that lay behind the politics and the headlines.

CHAPTER EIGHT

·

THE HOME FRONT

Public and private

ONE SIDE OF the history of Rome is a history of politics, of war, of victory and defeat, of citizenship and of everything that went on in public between prominent men. I have outlined one dramatic version of that history, as Rome transformed from a small, unimpressive town next to the Tiber into first a local and eventually an international power base. Almost every aspect of that transformation was contested and sometimes literally fought over: the rights of the people against the senate, the questions of what liberty meant and how it was to be guaranteed, the control that was, or was not, to be exercised over conquered territory, the impact of empire, for good or bad, on traditional Roman politics and values. In the process, a version of citizenship was somehow invented that was new in the classical world. Greeks had occasionally shared citizenship, on an ad hoc basis, between two cities. But the idea that it was the norm, as the Romans insisted, to be a citizen of two places – to count two places as home – was fundamental to Roman success on the battlefield and elsewhere, and it has proved influential right up into the twenty-first century. This was a Roman revolution, and we are its heirs.

There are nevertheless some elusive sides to this story. It is only occasionally possible to discover the part in the grand narrative of Roman history up to the first century BCE that ordinary people, the women, the poor or the slaves played. We have found just a few cameo appearances: the frightened comedian on the stage at Asculum, the loud-mouthed servant who unwisely abused the supporters of Gaius Gracchus, the eunuch priest who worried about his friend in the civil war, even the poor cat trapped in the fire that destroyed the hut at Fidenae. There is much more evidence for all these groups in later periods, and they figure more prominently in the rest of this book. But what survives for the early centuries of Roman history tends to offer a one-sided picture of the priorities even of the elite Roman man. It is easy to get the impression that the main characters in the story were concerned with the big issues of Roman political power to the exclusion of anything else, as if the proud conquests, military prowess and election to political office that are blazoned on their tombstones were the be-all and end-all of their existence.

They were not. We have already glimpsed a few other aspects of their lives and interests, enjoying boy-meets-girl comedies on the stage, writing and learning poetry and listening to literary lectures given by visiting Greek ambassadors. It is not hard to imagine something of the day-to-day world of Polybius in Rome, as he pondered on the funerals he attended or shrewdly decided to claim sickness on the day a fellow hostage made his escape attempt. Nor is it hard to recapture something of the fun that the elder Cato must have had thinking up his stunt with the Carthaginian figs dropping out of his toga. But it is only in the first century BCE that we begin to have rich evidence for all the things that preoccupied the Roman elite beyond war and politics.

These range from curiosity about the language they spoke (one prolific scholar devoted twenty-five books to a history of Latin, its grammar and etymology) to intense scientific speculation on the origins of the universe and theological debate on the nature of the gods. The eloquent discussion of the folly of fearing death by Titus Lucretius Carus, in his philosophical poem *On the Nature of Things* (*De rerum natura*), is one of the highlights of classical literature and a beacon of good sense even now (those who do not exist cannot regret their non-existence, as part of the argument runs). But by far the most sustained insight into the interests, concerns, pleasures, fears and problems of one notable Roman comes from the thousand or so private letters to and from Cicero that were collected, edited and made public after his death in 43 BCE and have been read and studied ever since.

They contain, as we have seen, plenty of gossip from the highest echelons of Roman politics, and they throw rare light on the front line of provincial government as Cicero experienced it in Cilicia. But no less important, they reveal what else was claiming Cicero's attention while he was facing down Catiline, dealing with the Gang of Three, planning military strikes on troublesome locals or deciding where his loyalties lay in civil war. Alongside those political and military crises, at the same time he was worrying about money, dowries and marriages (his daughter's and his own), grieving at the death of those he loved, divorcing his wife, complaining about an upset stomach after an unusual menu at dinner, attempting to track down runaway slaves and trying to acquire some nice statues to decorate one of his many houses. For the first, and almost the only, time in Roman history these letters allow us to take a close look at what was going on behind one Roman front door.

This chapter follows up some of those themes in Cicero's letters. We will start with his experience of civil war and of the dictatorship of Julius Caesar – by turns messy and darkly funny, and about as far from the ringing public slogans of *libertas* and *clementia* as you could imagine – then move on to some fundamental questions that can get lost in all the political controversies, diplomatic negotiations and military campaigns. How long did Romans expect to live? At what age did people get married? What rights did women have? Where did the money come from to support the lavish lifestyles of the rich and privileged? And what about the slaves?

The other sides of civil war

In 49 BCE, after many weeks of indecision and despite his realistic sense that there was not much to choose between Caesar and Pompey, Cicero decided not to remain neutral in the civil war but to join the Pompeians and sail for their camp in northern Greece. Although not quite in the league of either of the protagonists, he was still a significant enough figure that neither side wanted him as a declared enemy. But some of his irritating habits made Cicero an unpopular member of Pompey's squad. His fellow fighters could not stand the way he went around the barracks with a scowl on his face while trying to relieve the tension by cracking feeble jokes. 'So why not employ him as guardian of your children, then?' he retorted when a decidedly inappropriate candidate was promoted to a command position on the grounds that he was 'mild mannered and sensible'. When the day of the Battle of Pharsalus came, Cicero used Polybius' tactic and was conveniently off sick. After the defeat, rather than move on from Greece to Africa with some of the hardliners, he returned directly to Italy to wait for an amnesty from Caesar.

Cicero's letters from this period, about 400 in all, reveal something of the tawdriness and the terror of civil war, as well as the disorganisation, the misunderstanding, the back-stabbing, the personal ambitions, even the bathos of this, or any, conflict and its aftermath. They offer a useful antidote to Caesar's artfully partisan *Commentaries on the Civil War*, written to match his *Commentaries on the Gallic War*, and to some of the high-flown rhetoric and big principles that the clash between Caesarians and Pompeians still evokes. Civil war had its seedy side too.

Part of Cicero's indecision in 49 BCE was caused not by political ambivalence but by almost farcical ambition. He had only just returned from Cilicia and was keen for the senate to award him a triumph to celebrate his successful skirmish in the province a year earlier, and the rules demanded that he neither enter the city nor dismiss his official staff until the decision on the award had been made. He was anxious about his family and uncertain whether his wife and daughter should remain in Rome. Could they be useful to him there? Would there be enough food for them? Would it give the wrong impression for them to stay in the city when other rich women were leaving? In any case, if he was to stand a chance of a triumph, he had little option but to spend a few months traipsing around outside Rome, increasingly inconvenienced and embarrassed by his detachment of official body-guards, who were still carrying the drooping laurel leaves that he had been awarded to celebrate his little victory. Eventually he accepted the inevitable: the senators had more pressing matters on their minds than his 'bauble', as he sometimes called it; he would give up any hope of a triumph and join Pompey.

Even when he returned from those inglorious few months on the front line, he still faced the personal ruptures, uncertainties and spill-over violence that were part and parcel, day-to-day, of the big story of civil war. There were quarrels with his brother, Quintus, who seemed to be trying to make his own peace with Caesar by bad-mouthing Cicero. There were suspicions about the killing in Greece of one of his friends, a prominent adversary of Caesar, who in an after-dinner fight had been fatally stabbed in the stomach and behind the ear. Was this just a personal quarrel about money, as Cicero suspected, for the killer was known to be short of cash? Or was Caesar somehow behind the death? Violence apart, even playing his cards right and maintaining good personal relations with the winning side could prove irksome.

It was never more irksome than when a couple of years later Cicero ended up entertaining Caesar to dinner in one of his seaside estates on the Bay of Naples, where many wealthy Romans from the city had luxury getaways. He gives a wry description of all the trouble it involved in a letter to his friend Atticus from the end of 45 BCE, which is also one of the most vivid pictures to survive of Caesar off duty (and a particularly favourite moment in Cicero's career for Gore

Vidal centuries later). Caesar was travelling with a battalion of no fewer than 2,000 soldiers as a guard and escort, which was an awful burden for even the most generous and tolerant host: 'a billeting rather than a visit', as Cicero puts it. And that was in addition to Caesar's large civilian following of slaves and ex-slaves. Cicero explains that he had three dining rooms laid up for visiting senior staff alone and made appropriate arrangements for those further down the social pecking order, while Caesar took a bath and had a massage before he reclined to dine, in the formal Roman fashion. He turned out to have a large appetite, partly because he had been following a course of emetics, which was a popular regime of detoxification among wealthy Romans involving regular vomiting; and he enjoyed urbane conversation more about literature than about 'anything serious' (see plate 14).

How his own slaves and staff coped with this invasion, Cicero does not stop to say, or perhaps did not notice, but he congratulated himself that the evening had passed off well, even though he did not relish a repeat: 'My guest was not the sort to whom you would say, "Please drop by again when you are next around". Once is enough.' The best one can observe is that entertaining a victorious Pompey would almost certainly have been just as much bother.

Cicero's letters also reveal that the trials of war and the demands of receiving a dictator were only one part of his troubles at the time. Between Caesar's crossing of the Rubicon and his assassination on the Ides of March, 44 BCE, Cicero's family and household fell apart. In those five years, he divorced Terentia, his wife of thirty years, and quickly remarried. He was aged sixty, his new bride, Publilia, was about fifteen years old and the relationship lasted only a few weeks before he sent her back to her mother. Meanwhile, his daughter Tullia was divorced from her third husband, Publius Cornelius Dolabella, an enthusiastic supporter of Caesar. Tullia was pregnant at the time of the divorce and died early in 45 BCE, shortly after giving birth to a son, who only briefly survived her. Her previous child by Dolabella had been born prematurely and had also died, just a couple of weeks old. Cicero was engulfed in grief, which did not help his relationship with his new bride, as he retreated to be alone on one of his more isolated estates and to plan how to commemorate his daughter; he was soon busy reflecting on how to give her some kind of divine status. As he put it, he wanted to ensure her 'apotheosis'.

Husbands and wives

Roman marriage was, in essence, a simple and private business. Unlike in the modern world, the state played little part in it. In most cases a man and a woman were assumed to be married if they claimed that they were married, and they ceased to be married if they (or if one of them) claimed they no longer were. That, plus a party or two to celebrate the union, was probably all there was to it for the majority of ordinary Roman citizens. For the wealthier, there were often more formal and more expensive wedding ceremonies, featuring a relatively familiar line-up for such a rite of passage: special clothes (brides traditionally wore yellow), songs and processions and the new wife being carried over the threshold of the marital home. Considerations of property bulked larger for the rich too, in particular a dowry that the father of the bride provided, to be returned in the event of divorce. One of Cicero's problems in the 40s BCE was that he had been forced to repay Terentia's dowry, while the cash-strapped Dolabella seems not to have repaid Tullia's, or at least not in full. Marriage to young Publilia would have held out the prospect of a substantial fortune to compensate.

The main purpose of marriage at Rome, as in all past cultures, was the production of legitimate children, who automatically inherited Roman citizen status if both parents were citizens or if they satisfied various conditions governing 'intermarriage' with outsiders. That is what lies at the heart of the story of the Sabine Women, which depicts the first marriage in the new city as a process of 'legitimate rape' for the purpose of procreation. The same message was paraded repeatedly on the tombstones of wives and mothers throughout Roman history.

One epitaph written sometime in the mid second century BCE, commemorating a certain Claudia, perfectly captures the traditional image: 'Here is the unlovely grave of a lovely woman,' it reads. '... She loved her husband with her heart. She bore two sons. One of these she leaves on earth, the other under the earth. She was graceful in her speech and elegant in her step. She kept the home. She made wool. That's what there is to say.' The proper role of the woman, in other words, was to be devoted to her husband, to produce the next generation, to be an adornment, to be a household manager and to contribute to the domestic economy, by spinning and weaving. Other commemorations single out for praise women who had remained

49. A Roman wall-painting depicts an idealised scene of an ancient wedding, mixing gods and humans. The veiled bride sits at the centre, on her new marital bed, being encouraged by the goddess Venus sitting with her. Against the bed leans a louche figure of the god Hymen, one of the deities supposed to protect marriage. On the far left, human figures make preparations for bathing the bride.

faithful wives to only one husband throughout their lives, and emphasise 'female' virtues of chastity and fidelity. Contrast the epitaphs of
Scipio Barbatus and his male descendants, where it is military action,
political office holding and prominence in public life that capture the
headlines.

To what extent this image of the Roman wife was, at any period,
more wishful thinking than an accurate reflection of social reality is impossible to know. There was undoubtedly a lot of vociferous nostalgia
in Rome for the tough old days, when wives were kept in their place.
'Egnatius Metellus took a cudgel and beat his wife to death because
she had drunk some wine,' insisted one first-century CE writer, with
apparent approval, referring to an entirely mythical incident in the
reign of Romulus. Even the emperor Augustus took advantage of the
traditional associations of wool working, in what was something like
the ancient equivalent of a photo opportunity, by having his wife Livia
pose at her loom in their front hall in full public view. But the chances
are that those tough old days were in part the product of the imagination of later moralists, as well as a useful theme for later Romans to
exploit in establishing their old-fashioned credentials.

No less problematic is the competing image, prominent in the
first century BCE, of a new style of liberated woman, who supposedly enjoyed a free social, sexual, often adulterous life, without much
constraint from husband, family or the law. Some of these characters
were conveniently dismissed as part of the demi-monde of actresses,
showgirls, escorts and prostitutes, including one celebrity ex-slave,
Volumnia Cytheris, who was said to have been the mistress at one
time or another of both Brutus and Mark Antony, so sleeping with
both Caesar's assassin and his greatest supporter. But many of them
were the wives or widows of high-ranking Roman senators.

The most notorious of all was Clodia, the sister of Cicero's great
enemy Clodius, the wife of a senator who died in 59 BCE, and the lover
of the poet Catullus, among a string of others. Terentia is rumoured

to have had her suspicions about even Cicero's relations with Clodius' sister. She was alternately attacked and admired as a promiscuous temptress, scheming manipulator, idolised goddess and borderline criminal. For Cicero she was 'the Medea of the Palatine', a clever coinage linking the passionate, child-murdering witch of Greek tragedy with Clodia's place of residence in Rome. Catullus gave her the soubriquet Lesbia in his poetry, not only as camouflage but in order to gesture back to the Greek poet Sappho, from the island of Lesbos: 'Let's live, my Lesbia, and let's love / And the mutterings of stern old men / Let's value them at a single penny ... / Give me a thousand kisses', as one poem starts.

Colourful as this material is, it cannot be taken at face value. Part of it is not much more than erotic fantasy. Part of it is a classic reflection of common patriarchal anxieties. Throughout history, some men have justified their domination of women by simultaneously relishing and deploring an image of the dangerous and transgressive female, whose largely imaginary crimes, sexual promiscuity (with the uncomfortable question marks this poses over any child's paternity) and irresponsible drunkenness demonstrate the need for tight male control. The story of Egnatius Metellus' uncompromising line with his tipsy wife and the rumours of Clodia's wild parties are two sides of the same ideological coin. Besides, in many cases the lurid descriptions of female criminality, power and excess are often not really about the women they purport to describe at all but vehicles for a debate about something quite different.

When Sallust focuses on a couple of women supposedly prominent in Catiline's conspiracy, he is using them as terrible symbols of the decadent immorality of the society that produced Catiline. 'Whether she was keener to squander her money or her reputation, it would have been hard to decide,' he jibes about one senator's wife, and the mother of one of Caesar's assassins, capturing what he saw as the spirit of the age. Cicero, for his part, used Clodia as a successful deflecting tactic in a tricky court case where he was defending one of his dodgier young friends, who was also one of Clodia's ex-lovers, on a charge of murder. It is from the speech he delivered then that the vast majority of the disreputable details of her behaviour come: from the serial adulteries to the wild beach-parties-turned-orgies. Cicero's aim was to shift the blame from his client by discrediting a jealous Clodia, making her a laughing stock, a bad influence on his client and the principal villain. It is hard to imagine that Clodia was an entirely celibate, stay-at-home wife and widow, but if she read Cicero's depiction of her in the comfort of her elegant Palatine home, whether she would have recognised herself is quite another matter.

It is clear, however, that Roman women in general had much greater independence than women in most parts of the classical Greek or Near Eastern world, limited as it must seem in modern terms. The contrast is particularly striking with classical Athens, where women of wealthy families were supposed to live secluded lives, out of the public eye, largely segregated from men and male social life (the poor, needless to say, did not have the cash or the space to enforce any such divisions). There were, to be sure, uncomfortable restrictions on women in Rome too: the emperor Augustus, for example, relegated them to the back rows of the theatres and gladiatorial arenas; the suites for women in public baths were usually markedly more cramped than those for men; and in practice male activities probably dominated the swankier areas of a Roman house. But women were not meant to be publicly invisible, and domestic life does not seem to have been formally divided into male and female spaces, with gendered no-go areas.

Women also regularly dined with men, and not only the sex workers, escorts and entertainers who provided the female company at classical Athenian parties. In fact, one of the early misdeeds of Verres turned on this difference between Greek and Roman dining practices. In the 80s BCE, when he was serving in Asia Minor, more than a decade before his stint in Sicily, Verres and some of his staff engineered an invitation to dinner with an unfortunate Greek, and after a considerable quantity of alcohol had been consumed they asked the host if his daughter could join them. When the man explained that respectable Greek women did not dine in male company, the Romans refused to believe him and set out to find her. A brawl followed in which one of Verres' bodyguards was killed and the host was drenched with boiling water; he was later executed for murder. Cicero paints the whole incident in extravagant terms, almost as a rerun of the rape of Lucretia. But it also involved a series of drunken misunderstandings about the conventions of female behaviour across the cultural boundaries of the empire.

Some of the legal rules that governed marriage and women's rights at this period reflect this relative freedom. There were, it is true, some hard lines claimed on paper. It may have been a nostalgic myth that once upon a time a man had the right to cudgel to death his wife for the 'crime' of drinking a glass of wine. But there is some evidence that the execution of a wife who was caught in adultery was technically within the husband's legal power. There is, however, not a single known example of this ever happening, and most evidence points in a different direction. A woman did not take her husband's name or fall entirely under his legal authority. After the death of her father, an adult woman could own property in her own right, buy and sell, inherit or make a will and free slaves – many of the rights that women in Britain did not gain till the 1870s.

The only restriction was the need for an appointed guardian (*tutor*) to approve whatever decision or transaction she made. Whether Cicero was being patronising or misogynistic or (as some critics generously think) having a joke when he put this rule down to women's natural 'weakness in judgement' is impossible to tell. But there is certainly no sign that for his wife it was much of a handicap: whether she was selling a row of houses to raise funds for Cicero in exile or raking in the rents from her estates, no *tutor* is ever mentioned. In fact, one of the reforms of Augustus towards the end of the first century BCE or early in the next was to allow freeborn citizen women who had borne three children to be released from the requirement to have a guardian; ex-slaves had to have four to qualify. It was a clever piece of radical traditionalism: it allowed women new freedoms, provided they fulfilled their traditional role.

Oddly, women had much less freedom when it came to the act of marriage itself. For a start, they had no real option whether to marry or not. The basic rule was that all freeborn women were to be married. There were no maiden aunts, and it was only special groups, such as the Vestal Virgins, who opted, or were compelled, to remain single. What is more, the freedom a woman enjoyed in the choice of husband could be very limited, certainly among the rich and powerful, whose marriages were regularly arranged to cement alliances, whether political, social or financial. But it would be naive to imagine that the daughter of a peasant farmer who wanted to do a deal with his neighbour, or the slave girl who was to be freed in order to marry her owner (a not uncommon occurrence), had much more say in the decision.

Marriage alliances underpinned some major developments in Roman politics in the late Republic. In 82 BCE, for example, Sulla attempted to secure Pompey's loyalty by 'giving' him his stepdaughter as a wife, although she was married to someone else at the time and pregnant by him; the gamble did not pay off, because the poor woman almost immediately died in childbirth. Twenty years later, Pompey sealed his agreement with Caesar in the Gang of Three by marrying Caesar's daughter, Julia. The stakes were not quite so high for Cicero and his daughter Tullia, but it is clear that family advancement and good connections were always in Cicero's mind, even if things did not necessarily go his way.

How to find a husband for Tullia was, he admitted, the thing that was worrying him most as he left Rome for the province of Cilicia in 51 BCE. After her two brief and childless marriages to men from distinguished families – one ending in the man's death, the other in divorce – a third match had to be arranged for her. On this occasion Cicero's letters offer a glimpse of the negotiations, as he canvassed a variety of suitable, and less suitable, candidates. One did not seem to be a serious proposition; another had nice manners; of another he reluctantly wrote, 'I doubt that our girl could be prevailed upon', acknowledging that Tullia had some say in the matter. But communications were a problem. As it took roughly three months for a letter to go from Cilicia to Rome and a reply to get back, it was hard for Cicero to keep control of the process, and he was more or less forced to leave the final decision to Terentia and Tullia. They picked none of his top choices but the recently divorced Dolabella instead, another man with unimpeachable aristocratic credentials and, by Roman accounts, an engaging rogue, inveterate seducer and unusually short. 'Who has tied my son-in-law to his sword?' is one of Cicero's best-remembered jokes.

Arranged marriages of this kind were not necessarily grey and emotionless unions. It was always said that Pompey and Julia were devoted to each other, that he was devastated when she died in childbirth in 54 BCE and that her death contributed to the political breakdown between Pompey and Caesar. The marriage, in other words, proved rather too successful for its intended purpose. And several of Cicero's earliest surviving letters to Terentia, whom he presumably married after some similar arrangement, are full of expressions of intense devotion and love, whatever emotions lay underneath: 'Light of my life, my heart's desire. To think that you, darling Terentia, are so tormented, when everyone used to go to you for help,' he wrote to her from exile in 58 BCE.

Equally, there are plenty of signs of marital squabbles, discontents and disappointments. Tullia soon found Dolabella more rogue than engaging, and within three years the pair were living apart. But the most persistently miserable marriage in Cicero's circle was that of his brother, Quintus, and Pomponia, the sister of Cicero's friend Atticus.

Predictably, and maybe unfairly, Cicero's letters throw most of the blame at the wife, but they also capture some of the arguments in uncannily modern terms. On one occasion, when Pomponia snapped, 'I feel like a stranger in my own house', in front of guests, Quintus came out with the classic complaint 'There, you see what I have to put up with every day!' After twenty-five years of this, they eventually divorced. Quintus is supposed to have remarked, 'Nothing is better than not having to share a bed.' Pomponia's reaction is unknown.

It is, however, Cicero's short-lived second marriage to Publilia, then in her early to mid teens, that sticks out from the all other stories. Cicero and Terentia had divorced, probably at the beginning of 46 BCE. Whatever the main reasons for the split – and Roman writers came out with plenty of unreliable speculation on the subject – the latest surviving letter from him to her, written in October 47 BCE, suggests that relations between the two had changed. Just a few curt lines to a wife he had not seen for two years (partly because he had been away with Pompey's forces in Greece), it amounts to a couple of instructions for his imminent arrival. 'If there is no basin in the bathhouse, have one installed' is the basic gist. Just over a year later, after considering other possibilities – including Pompey's daughter and a woman he deemed 'the ugliest I have ever seen' – Cicero married a girl at least forty-five years his junior. Was this usual?

A first marriage at around fourteen or fifteen was not remarkable for a Roman girl. Tullia was betrothed to her first husband when she was eleven and married by fifteen; when Cicero in 67 BCE refers to betrothing 'dear little Tullia to Gaius Calpurnius Piso', he means exactly that, *little*. Atticus was already considering future husbands when his daughter was just six. The elite might be expected to have arranged such alliances early. But there is plenty of evidence in the epitaphs of ordinary people for girls being married in their mid teens and occasionally as young as ten or eleven. Whether or not these marriages were consummated is an awkward and unanswerable question. By the same token, men seem generally to have married for the first time in their mid to late twenties, with a standard age gap in a first marriage of something like ten years, and some young brides would have found themselves married to an even older man on his second or third time around. Whatever the relative freedoms of Roman women, their subordination was surely grounded in that disequilibrium between an adult male and what we would call a child bride.

That said, the age gap of forty-five years caused puzzlement even at Rome. Why had Cicero done it? Was it just for the money? Or, as Terentia claimed, was it the silly infatuation of an old man? In fact, he faced some direct questions about why on earth, at his age, he was marrying a young virgin. On the day of the marriage he is supposed to have replied to one of these, 'Don't worry, she'll be a grown-up woman

50. A Roman tombstone for husband and wife (first century BCE). Both are ex-slaves: the husband on the left, Aurelius Hermia, is identified as a butcher from the Viminal hill in Rome; on the right, his wife, Aurelia Philematium, is described as 'chaste, modest and not gossiped about'. More disturbing for us is the timescale of their relationship. They had met when she was seven and, as the text says, 'he took her on his knee'.

[*mulier*] tomorrow'. The ancient critic who quoted this response thought that it was a brilliantly witty way of deflecting criticism and held it up for admiration. We are likely to put it somewhere on the spectrum between uncomfortably coarse and painfully bleak – one powerful marker of the distance between the Roman world and our own.

Birth, death and grief

Tragedy almost instantly overtook Cicero's new marriage. Tullia died soon after giving birth to Dolabella's son. Cicero appears to have been so incapacitated by grief that he retreated, without Publilia, to his property on the little island of Astura, off the coast south of Rome. His relationship with Tullia had always been very close – rather too intimate, according to the wild gossip of some of his enemies, indulging in the favourite Roman tactic of attacking an opponent through his sex life. It was certainly closer than that with her younger brother, Marcus, who among other minor failings never seems to have enjoyed the intellectual life, and philosophy lectures in Athens, to which his father had sent him. With Tullia's death, Cicero claimed, he had lost the one thing that kept him committed to life.

The production of children was a dangerous obligation. Childbirth was always the biggest killer of young adult women at Rome, from senators' wives to slaves. Thousands of such deaths are recorded, from high-profile casualties such as Tullia and Pompey's Julia to the ordinary women across the empire commemorated on tombstones by their grieving husbands and families. One man in North Africa remembered his wife, who 'lived for thirty-six years and forty days. It was her tenth delivery. On the third day she died.' Another, from what is now Croatia, put up a simple memorial to 'his fellow slave' (and probably his partner), who 'suffered agonies to give birth for four days, and did not give birth, and so she died'. To put this in a wider perspective, statistics available from more recent historical periods suggest that at least one in fifty women were likely to die in childbirth, with a higher chance if they were very young.

They were killed by many of the disasters of childbirth that modern Western medicine has almost prevented, from haemorrhage to obstruction or infection – though the lack of hospitals, where infections in early modern Europe easily passed from one woman to another, somewhat lessened that risk. Most women relied on the support of midwives. Beyond that, interventionist obstetrics probably only added to the danger. Caesarian sections, which despite the modern myth had no connection with Julius Caesar, were used simply to cut a live foetus out of a dead or dying woman. For cases where the baby was completely obstructed, some Roman doctors recommended inserting a knife into the mother and dismembering the foetus in the womb, a procedure which few women could possibly have come through safely.

Pregnancy and childbirth must have dominated most women's lives, including those whom Roman writers chose to present as carefree libertines. A few would have been most concerned about their inability to conceive at all or to carry through a pregnancy. Romans almost universally blamed the woman for a couple's failure to have children, and this was one standard reason for divorce. Modern speculation (no more than that) is that her second husband may have divorced Tullia, who did not deliver a live baby until her late twenties, on precisely those grounds. The majority of women, however, faced decades of pregnancies without any reliable way, except abstinence, of preventing them. There were some makeshift and dangerous methods of abortion. Prolonged breastfeeding might have delayed further pregnancies for those who did not, as many of the wealthy did, employ wet nurses. And a wide variety of contraceptive potions and devices were recommended, which ranged from completely useless (wearing the worms found in the head of a particular species of hairy spider) to borderline efficacious (inserting almost anything sticky into the vagina). But most of their contraceptive efforts were defeated by the fact that ancient science claimed that the days after a woman ceased menstruating were her most fertile, when the truth is exactly the opposite.

Those babies that were safely delivered had an even riskier time than their mothers. The ones that appeared weak or disabled would have been 'exposed', which may often have meant being thrown away on a local rubbish tip. Those that were unwanted met the same fate. There are hints that baby girls may generally have been less wanted than boys, partly because of the expense of their dowries, which would have been a significant element in the budget of relatively modest families too. One letter surviving on papyrus from Roman Egypt,

51. A Roman midwife from the port of Ostia is depicted at her work on a terracotta plaque from her tomb. The woman giving birth sits on a chair, the midwife sits in front of her for the delivery.

52. An ancient Roman vaginal speculum is uncannily like the modern version. But Roman ideas of the female body and its reproductive cycles were dramatically different from our own, from how conception happened to when and how it might be prevented (or encouraged).

written by a husband to his pregnant wife, instructs her to raise the child if it is a boy, but 'if it is a girl, discard it'. How often this happened, and what the exact sex ratio of the victims was, is a matter of guesswork, but it was often enough for rubbish tips to be thought of as a source of free slaves.

Those babies that were reared were still in danger. The best estimate – based largely on figures from comparable later populations – is that half the children born would have died by the age of ten, from all kinds of sickness and infection, including the common childhood diseases that are no longer fatal. What this means is that, although average life expectancy at birth was probably as low as the mid twenties, a child who survived to the age of ten could expect a lifespan not wildly at variance from our own. According to the same figures, a ten-year-old would on average have another forty years of life left, and a fifty-year-old could reckon on fifteen more. The elderly were not as rare as you might think in ancient Rome. But the high death rate among the very young also had implications for women's pregnancies and family size. Simply to maintain the existing population, each woman on average would have needed to bear five or six children. In practice, that rises to something closer to nine when other factors, such as sterility and widowhood, are taken into account. It was hardly a recipe for widespread women's liberation.

How did these patterns of birth and death affect the emotional life within the family? It has sometimes been argued that, simply because so many children did not survive, parents would have avoided deep emotional investment in them. One chilling image of the father in Roman literature and storytelling stresses his control over his children, not his affection, while dwelling on the terrible punishment he could exact for their disobedience, even to the point of execution. There is, however, almost no sign of this in practice. It is true that a newborn baby may not have been viewed as a person as such until after the decision whether or not to rear it had been taken and it had been formally accepted into the family; hence, to some extent, the apparently casual attitude to what we would call infanticide. But the thousands of touching epitaphs put up by parents to their young offspring suggest anything but lack of emotion. 'My little doll, my dear Mania, lies buried here. For just a few years was I able to give my love to her. Her father now weeps constantly for her', as the verses on one tombstone in North Africa run. Cicero too, in 45 BCE, for a time 'wept constantly' over the death of Tullia while documenting his grief and plans for her commemoration in a remarkable series of letters to Atticus.

No details are known about Tullia's death, except that it happened at Cicero's country house at Tusculum, outside Rome; and nothing at all is known of her funeral. Cicero almost immediately retreated alone to his hideaway on the island of Astura, where he read all the philosophy he could get his hands on about loss and consolation, and even wrote a treatise on bereavement to himself – before deciding, after a couple of months, that he should return to the house where she had died ('I'm going to conquer my feelings and go to the Tusculum house, else I'll never go back there'). By this stage he had already begun to channel his grief into her memorial, which was to be not a 'tomb' but a 'shrine' or a 'temple' (*fanum*, which in Latin has an exclusively religious meaning). His immediate concerns were with location, prominence and future upkeep, and he was soon planning to buy an estate in the suburbs, near what is now the Vatican, on which to site the building and was pre-ordering some columns.

He was aiming, he insisted, at Tullia's apotheosis. By this, he probably meant immortality in some general sense rather than any full-blown claim that she was to become a god, but it is nevertheless another instance of the fuzzy boundary that in the Roman world lay between mortals and immortals, and of the way in which divine powers and attributes were used to express the prominence and importance of individual human beings. There is a certain irony, however, in the fact that, while Cicero and his friends were increasingly anxious about the godlike honours being given to Caesar, Cicero was busy planning some kind of divine status for his dead daughter. But the project for the shrine in the end came to nothing, for the whole of the Vatican area became earmarked for a major piece of Caesar's urban redevelopment, and Cicero's chosen site was lost.

Money matters

The houses on Astura and at Tusculum were only two of some twenty properties that Cicero owned in Italy in 45 BCE. Some were elegant residential mansions. In Rome he had a large house on the lower slopes of the Palatine Hill, a couple of minutes' walk from the Forum, where many of the top-most drawer of the Roman elite, Clodia included, were his neighbours; his other houses were dotted throughout the peninsula, from Puteoli on the Bay of Naples, where he entertained Caesar to that rather crowded dinner party, to Formiae further north, where he had another seaside villa. Some were small rest houses or lodges strategically sited on roads between his far-flung larger properties, where he could stay overnight to avoid sleeping in seedy inns or lodging houses or imposing on friends. Some, including his family estates at Arpinum, were working farms, even if they had a luxury residence attached. Others were straightforward moneymaking rental properties, such as the low-grade building from which 'even the rats' had fled; two large, and even more lucrative, blocks to let in central Rome had been part of Terentia's dowry and in 45 BCE must recently have been returned on the divorce.

The total value of this property portfolio was something in the order of 13 million sesterces. In the eyes of ordinary Romans this was a vast holding, worth enough to keep more than 25,000 poor families alive for a year or to provide more than thirty men with the minimum wealth qualification for standing for political office. But it did not put Cicero into the bracket of the super-rich. In reflecting on the history of extravagance, Pliny the Elder states that in 53 BCE Clodius bought for almost 15 million sesterces the house of Marcus Aemilius Scaurus, one of Cicero's friends and a somewhat disreputable officer of Pompey's in Judaea in the 60s BCE. The remains of its basement have tentatively been identified, also on the Palatine slopes, near where the Arch of Titus still stands; they comprise about fifty small rooms and a bath, probably for slaves, and earlier generations of archaeologists confidently (and wrongly) identified them as a city-centre brothel. At yet another level up, the property of Crassus was worth 200 million sesterces; with that, he could indeed have paid for his own army (p. 26).

Despite some imaginative attempts, not a single one of Cicero's properties has been firmly identified on the ground. Yet it is possible to get some idea of what they were like from his accounts, including his plans for improvement, and from contemporary archaeological remains. The rich residences of the late Republican elite on the Palatine Hill are generally very poorly preserved, for the simple reason that over the first century CE the imperial palace that soon came to dominate the hill was built on top of them. Some of the most impressive traces from the earlier period are in the so-called House of the Griffins. These include several rooms of what must have been the ground floor of an impressive early first-century BCE house, still partly visible within the foundations of the palatial structures on top, complete with brightly painted walls and simple mosaic pavements. In overall plan and design, this and the other Palatine houses were probably not all that different from the much better preserved remains at Pompeii and Herculaneum.

The point about the residences of the Roman elite, whether of senators in Rome or of local bigwigs outside it, is that they were not private houses in modern terms; they did not (or not only) represent a place to escape from the public gaze. To be sure, there were some

53. Here the later foundations of the buildings above (on the right) have cut through what was once a splendid room of a Republican house, the 'House of the Griffins' on the Palatine. The house gets its name from the figures of griffins made in stucco; one is visible at the far end. The mosaic floor is a simple diamond decoration, the walls are painted with plain panels of colour, as if to imitate marble. Earlier generations of archaeologists speculated that this was the house of Catiline himself.

1. Maccari depicts an implausibly lavish senate house for Cicero's appearance on 8 November 63 BCE. It emphasises the isolation of Catiline (bottom right), from whom all the other senators keep a careful distance. That evening he left Rome to join his army.

2. Cicero's conflict with Catiline has been the source of modern humour. Thirty years before Maccari's tribute to Cicero, under the same title 'Cicero denounces Catiline', the scene was given a comic spin. Cicero is a parody of nineteenth-century political outrage, Catiline a gangster – and a few of the senators are already asleep.

3. In Nicolas Poussin's painting of the 'Rape of the Sabines' (1637–8), Romulus on the left calmly commands the scene from above. But Poussin makes clear the terrified and resistant women are being dragged off in what is little short of a violent battle. Pablo Picasso (1962) intensifies the horror of the story. The almost disintegrating bodies of the woman make a bitter contrast with the larger than life Roman warriors and their trampling horses.

4. Titian's version of 'Tarquin and Lucretia' (1571) confronts, rather than sanitises, the brutality of rape. Lucretia is presented as vulnerable, with tears in her eyes; Tarquin as a violent aggressor (with his jabbing knee and glinting dagger). Just emerging from the curtain in the background is the hand of the young slave whom Tarquin threatened to kill along with his victim, to make them look guilty of shameful adultery.

5. A glimpse into the world of Rome in the fourth century BCE – and a rare example of high quality artistic production at that period. These are the handles of the 'Ficoroni Cista', an elaborate bronze casket, so-called after its eighteenth-century collector. The inscription on the object records that it was made at Rome by Novios Plautios, and was given to her daughter by a woman called Dindia Macolnia.

6. This painting from an early third-century tomb at Rome offers a contemporary glimpse of the Samnite Wars. Fighting on the lowest register includes a figure (on the right) with a large plumed helmet. Above the apparent scenes of 'surrender' outside the battlement have sometimes been differently interpreted. Is perhaps the toga-clad 'Fabius' on the right giving some kind of military decoration to a Roman – not a Samnite – soldier on the left?

7. Scenes of fighting from the François Tomb at Vulci (mid fourth century BCE) hint at an Etruscan view of some of the characters in Roman history. Written labels identify the figure on the far left as 'Macstrna' or Mastarna who was, according to the emperor Claudius identical with Servius Tullius. On the far right 'Aule Vipenas' or Aulus Vivenna (perhaps a lost Roman king) dispatches an enemy.

8. Remnants of the First Punic War raised from the bottom of the sea off Sicily: here one of the rams of the warships. Several of these have writing stamped into the bronze. On the Roman rams we can read traces of officialdom: 'Lucius Quinctius the son of Gaius, the quaestor, approved this ram.' On the one surviving inscribed Carthaginian ram, we read: 'We pray to Baal that this ram will go into this enemy ship and make a big hole.' It is a clear contrast in national 'style'.

9. The most famous modern reconstruction of the Roman triumphal procession is by Andrea Mantegna, whose series of 'The Triumphs of Caesar' was painted for the Gonzaga family of Mantua in the late fifteenth century. This panel shows Caesar on his Renaissance-style triumphal chariot. Behind him stands the slave whose job was to whisper in the triumphant general's ear to remind him that he was, despite the glory, *just a man*.

10. The Column of Marcus Aurelius, the pair and rival of the more famous Column of Trajan, still stands almost forty metres high in central Rome. Spiralling all around it are scenes from the emperor's wars on the Danube that went on for most of his reign (161–180 CE). On the lowest level the bearded emperor is shown sacrificing. On the third level (above) a battle is waged around a German hut.

11. The emperor Caracalla's family. This painted wooden panel shows his father the emperor Septimius Severus with his mother Julia Domna behind. In front on the right is the young Caracalla; on the left the face of his brother, the murdered Geta, has been rubbed out.

12. A characteristic image of Livia, the wife of the first Augustus, sculpted in shiny – and expensive – black basalt from Egypt. Her hairstyle, with a roll of hair at the front and a bun at the back, was highly traditional, signalling old-fashioned Roman virtues.

13. One vivid trace of the luxury of the imperial court are the remains of the pleasure barges that the emperor Gaius had constructed on Lake Nemi, in the Alban Hills, between 37 and 41 CE. Though they were heavily damaged in World War II, some of the extravagant fitments and interior decoration still survive – like this bronze head of the snake-haired Medusa, which fitted over the end of one the wooden beams.

14. One image of Roman dining. This painting from Pompeii captures the hierarchies of a Roman party (note the small figure of a slave at the bottom left removing the guest's shoe) and the fantasies of excess (on the right another guest is already being sick). Although this particular occasion appears to be an all-male gathering, that was not the Roman norm.

15. The Bar of the Seven Sages at Ostia. Here the great thinker 'Solon ... of Athens' (his name is written in Greek on either side of him) watches the scene from his lavatory, while his advice on defecation appears above: 'To shit well (*ut bene cacaret*) Solon stroked his belly'.

16. A Roman slave collar. The tag offers a reward if the slave should have escaped: 'I have run away, catch me. Take me back to my master Zoninus and you will get a reward.' It is possible that some of these collars were intended for animal rather than human property. But the fact that we cannot now be certain of the difference between them tells its own story.

17. A gold bracelet found near Pompeii, inscribed 'Dominus suae ancillae' – 'From the master to his slave girl'. It may be a touching token of the man's affection and a hint at intimacy between the two. What the slave girl's attitude was to the present (and to the giver) we can only guess.

18. Three scenes from life in a laundry at Pompeii. At the top, workers are treading the cloth. In the centre, one man is brushing a piece of cloth, another carries a frame with an owl on top (a mascot of the laundry trade), while in the corner a customer waits with her maid. At the bottom, a woman on the left is collecting some article of clothing, and other garments hang on a line overhead.

19. A seal stone in carnelian commemorating the victory at Actium in 31 BCE. It shows Octavian in the guise of the god Neptune, carrying a trident and mounting a sea-chariot. The name of the engraver, or the owner, Popil(ius) Alb(anus) is written in Greek letters across the top.

20. The 'Great Cameo of France' dates to the reign of Tiberius and represents the imperial world order. Augustus, now a god, is reclining in heaven. In the middle register, Tiberius sits on the throne, flanked by his mother Livia. At the bottom, the conquered barbarians are in their place. It has been in France since the thirteenth century (hence the name), and was then misidentified as a biblical scene of Joseph at the Court of the Egyptian Pharaoh.

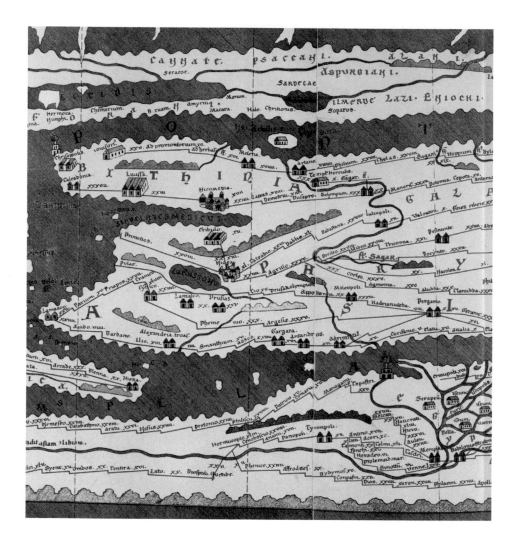

21. The 'Peutinger Table' (so called after one of its early owners) is a version of a map of the Roman empire made in the thirteenth century, but very likely based ultimately on the map displayed in first-century BCE Rome by Augustus and Agrippa. In our terms, it is more a route diagram than a map, almost seven metres long, showing the roads, rivers and towns of the empire. This section shows the Nile delta, with part of Crete to the left, and Asia Minor above.

hideaways, such as Cicero's retreat on Astura, and some parts of the house were more private than others. But in many ways domestic architecture was meant to contribute to the public image and reputation of the prominent Roman, and it was in his house that much public business was done. The great hall, or atrium, the first room a visitor normally entered after walking through the front door, was a key location. Usually double volume, open to the sky and designed to impress, with stuccoes, paintings, sculpture and impressive vistas off, it provided the backdrop to many encounters between the master of the house and a variety of subordinates, petitioners and clients – from ex-slaves needing help to that visiting delegation from Teos who went from atrium to atrium trying to kiss the Romans' feet (pp. 194–5, 197–9). Beyond that, on the standard plan, the house stretched back, with more entertaining rooms, dining areas, parlours-cum-bedrooms (*cubicula*) and covered walkways and gardens if there was space – the walls featuring decoration to match their function, from large display paintings to intimate panels and erotica. For visitors, the further they were welcomed into the less public parts of the house, the more honoured they were. Business with one's closest friends and colleagues might be done, as Romans put it, *in cubiculo*, that is, in one of those small, intimate rooms where one might sleep, though not exactly bedrooms in the modern sense. It is where, we might guess, the Gang of Three made their deals.

The house and its decoration contributed to the image of its owner. But impressive display had to be carefully calibrated against the possible taint of excessive luxury. Eyebrows were raised, for example, when Scaurus decided to use in the atrium of his Palatine house some of the 380 columns that he had bought to decorate a temporary theatre he had commissioned for public shows. They were made of Lucullan marble, a precious Greek stone known in Rome after the man who first imported it, Lucius Licinius Lucullus, Pompey's immediate predecessor in the war against Mithradates, and they were each over 11 metres high. Many Romans felt that Scaurus had made a serious mistake in adorning his house in a luxurious style more appropriate to fully public display. Sallust was not the only one to imagine that immoral extravagance somehow underlay many of Rome's problems.

On several occasions in his letters, Cicero can be found worrying about how to decorate his properties appropriately, how to project an image of himself as a man of taste, learning and Greek culture, and how to source the artworks that he needed in order to do that, not always successfully. A tricky problem he faced in 46 BCE reveals some of his slightly fussy concerns. One of his unofficial agents had acquired for him in Greece a small collection of statues that was both too expensive (he could have bought a new lodge, he explains, for the price) and quite unfit for the purposes he had in mind. For a start, there was a statue of the god of war Mars, when Cicero was supposed to be presenting himself as the great advocate of peace. Worse, there

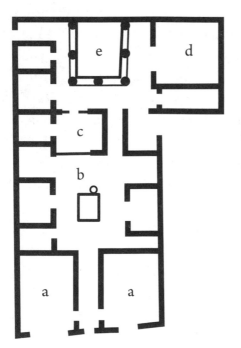

54. The plan of the 'House of the Tragic Poet' at Pompeii gives a good idea of the basic layout of a moderately wealthy Roman house, of the second and first centuries BCE. The narrow entrance runs between two shops (a) facing onto the street, and leads into the main hall, or atrium (b). The principal formal reception room (c) faced onto the atrium; beyond was a dining area (d) and a small colonnaded garden (e). The other small rooms, some upstairs, included the parlours-cum-bedrooms where the most favoured guests would be invited, for business as well as pleasure.

was a group of Bacchantes, the uninhibited, ecstatic, drunken followers of the god Bacchus, which could not possibly be used to decorate
a library as he wanted: you needed Muses for a library, he explained,
not Bacchantes.

Whether Cicero managed to sell these sculptures on, as he hoped,
or whether they ended up in a storeroom on one of his estates is not
recorded. But the story is a pointer to the way the domestic, as well as
the public, environment of Rome sucked in artworks, both antiques
and replicas, in a brisk trade with the Greek world. The material remains of that trade are now best documented by the cargoes that did
not make it, in a series of shipwrecks of Roman trading vessels that
divers have discovered on the bed of the Mediterranean. One of the
most stunning, probably to be dated sometime in the 60s BCE, to judge
from the coins it was carrying, sank between Crete and the southern
tip of the Peloponnese, near the island of Antikythera – hence its
modern name, 'the Antikythera wreck'. It was carrying bronze and
marble sculptures, including one exquisite miniature bronze figure
on a wind-up revolving base; luxury furniture; elegant bowls in glass
and mosaic; and most famous of all, the 'Antikythera Mechanism'.
This was an intricate bronze device with a clockwork mechanism,
apparently designed to predict the movements of the planets and
other astronomical events. Though rather a long way from the world's
first computer, as it has occasionally been dubbed, it must have been
destined for the library of some keen Roman scientist.

The relationship between leading late Republicans and their properties was in some ways, however, a curious one. Cicero and his friends
strongly identified with their houses. Beyond the carefully planned
arrangements of sculpture and artworks, the wax masks of their ancestors (*imagines*) that were worn in funeral processions were displayed
in the atria of aristocratic families, who sometimes had different sets
or copies for their different properties. On the atrium wall, a painted
family tree was one standard feature, and the spoils a man had taken

55. Some of the sculptures from the Antikythera wreck offer haunting images of partial decay. As in this once beautiful specimen, some parts of their marble flesh have corroded, other parts have been preserved in pristine condition – depending on where they lay in the sea and whether they were protected by the sand on the sea bed.

in battle, the ultimate mark of Roman achievement, might also be pinned up there for admiration. Conversely, if the political tide turned, the house could become almost a surrogate for aggression against its owner, or an additional target. When Cicero went into exile in 58 BCE, not only did Clodius and his gangs destroy his property on the Palatine, but considerable damage was done to his properties at Formiae and Tusculum too. And he was not the first who was said to have suffered this kind of punishment. Towards the mythical beginning of a long line of such cases, a radical called Spurius Maelius in the mid fifth century BCE was executed and his house pulled down when – in a classic conservative Roman inference – his generosity to the poor raised suspicions that he was aiming at tyranny.

Yet in another way, the connection between family and house was surprisingly loose. Quite unlike, for example, the British aristocracy, whose traditions put great store by the continuity of ownership of their country houses, the Roman elite were always buying, selling and moving. It is true that Cicero hung on to some family property in Arpinum, but he bought his Palatine house only in 62 BCE, from Crassus, who may have owned it as an investment opportunity rather than as a residence; and before that the house of Livius Drusus, where he was assassinated in 91 BCE, had stood on the site. Cicero's estate at Tusculum had passed from Sulla to a deeply conservative senator, Quintus Lutatius Catulus, and finally to a rich ex-slave, known to us only as Vettius, in the twenty-five years before Cicero bought it in the early 60s BCE. Presumably any masks in the atrium were packed up on the occasion of a sale and moved to the new property. But strangely it was the custom that the spoils of victory stayed with the house and did not move with the family of the man who had won them. In one of Cicero's later attacks on Mark Antony, he complains that Antony was living and drunkenly carousing in a house that had once belonged to Pompey, with rams from captured ships, probably seized in the campaign against the pirates, still adorning the entranceway.

This pattern of property transfer raises several basic questions. The sums involved were very large. In 62 BCE Cicero had to hand over 3.5 million sesterces for his new house on the Palatine, and there is almost no information about how this kind of payment was organised in practice. It is unlikely that Cicero's slaves simply wheeled truckloads of cash through the streets under armed guard. The whole transaction points instead either to the use of gold bullion, which would at least have required fewer trucks, or more likely to some system of paper finance or bonds, and so to a relatively sophisticated banking and credit system underpinning the Roman economy, for which only fleeting evidence now survives.

Even more basically, where did all the money come from in the first place? Just after buying the Palatine house, Cicero joked in a letter to his friend Publius Sestius that he was so up to his ears in debt 'that I'd be keen to join a conspiracy if there was one that would have me' – a wry allusion to the Catilinarian conspiracy of the previous year. Loans certainly must have been part of it, but most of them had to be repaid, sometimes sooner rather than later; Cicero was, for example, keen to pay off a large loan of almost a million sesterces to Julius Caesar before the outbreak of civil war made it embarrassing. So what were the sources of Cicero's income? How had he moved from a reasonably affluent local background to being one of the rich, even if far from the richest, at Rome? Some hints in the letters help to sketch out part of the picture.

First a negative. There is no sign that Cicero had any major trading or commercial interests. Strictly speaking, senators were banned from overseas trade, and the wealth of the political elite at Rome was always officially defined by, and rooted in, land. Nonetheless, some senatorial families profited from commercial ventures indirectly, whether through non-senatorial relations or by using their ex-slaves as front men. The family of the same Publius Sestius, the senator with whom Cicero joked about his debt, is one of the best examples of this. Thousands of wine amphorae of the early to mid first century BCE stamped 'SES' or 'SEST' have been discovered across the Mediterranean from Spain to Athens, with a particular concentration in southern Gaul, including some 1,700 in a shipwreck off Marseilles. These are the clear traces of a large commercial export business associated with some members of the Sestius family, who are known to have had estates near the northern Italian town of Cosa, where another concentration of the same kind of amphorae with the same stamp has been found. Whoever was formally in charge of the business, the profits surely seeped through to the senatorial Sestii too. But there are no hints that Cicero had any involvement in anything like that, apart from a few snobbish and inaccurate slurs made by his enemies that his father had been in the laundry business.

Some of Cicero's money came, quite traditionally, from rents and from the products of his agricultural land, boosted by the property that was part of Terentia's dowry. But he had two other main sources of substantial funds. The first was inheritances from outside his immediate family. In 44 BCE he claimed to have received in all a vast 20 million sesterces by that route. It is impossible now to identify all of the benefactors. But many of these legacies must have been paybacks from those he had helped in various ways, ex-slaves who had made their own fortunes or satisfied clients whom he had represented in court. Roman lawyers were expressly forbidden to receive fees for their service, and it is often rightly said that what Cicero gained by pleading in high-profile cases was public prominence. Yet often there

56. The site of the wreck off Marseilles was explored in the 1950s by a team of divers working with Jacques Cousteau. This is just part of the cargo of amphorae from Italy that the ship was carrying.

were financial returns in some indirect form too. Publius Sulla, the nephew of the dictator, can hardly have been unusual in rewarding Cicero for a successful defence in court. He lent 2 million sesterces towards the purchase of the Palatine house, and repayment seems not to have been demanded.

The other source was Cicero's province. While boasting, maybe correctly, that he had never broken the law in extorting money from the provincials, he still left Cilicia in 50 BCE with more than 2 million sesterces in local currency in his luggage. How exactly it was acquired is not certain: a combination perhaps of Cicero's meanness with his expense allowance and the profits from his minor victory, including selling off the captives into slavery afterwards. Rather than transport this money back to Italy, he deposited it on his way home with a company of *publicani* in Ephesus, apparently envisaging some form of cashless transfer of funds. But the civil war soon derailed whatever long-term plans he had for it. In early 48 BCE Pompey's war fund needed all the cash it could get, and Cicero agreed to lend this 2 million sesterces to him, which presumably went some way towards making up for his irritating behaviour in the camp. There is no suggestion that he ever got the money back. This profit of a war against a foreign enemy had ended up, as many others did, bankrolling a war of Roman against Roman.

Human property

There were also human beings among Cicero's property. In the letters, he mentions in all just over twenty slaves: a group of six or seven message boys, a few secretaries, clerks and 'readers' (who read books or documents aloud for the convenience of their master), as well as an attendant, a workman, a cook, a manservant and an accountant or two. In practice, his household must have been much bigger than this.

The servicing of twenty properties suggests an absolute minimum staff of 200, even if some were just small lodges and others were moth-balled for months on end: there were gardens to be tended, repairs to be carried out, furnaces to be stoked, security to be arranged, not to mention fields to be tilled on the working farms. It says a lot about the invisibility of slaves to the master that Cicero pays no attention to the vast majority of them. Most of those he does mention in his letters are, like the message boys and secretaries, concerned with the production and delivery of the letters themselves.

At a very rough guess there might have been between 1.5 and 2 million slaves in Italy in the middle of the first century BCE, making up perhaps 20 per cent of the total population. They shared the single defining characteristic of being human property in someone else's ownership. But that apart, they were just as varied in background and style of life as free citizens. There was no such thing as a typical slave. Some in Cicero's possession would have been enslaved abroad after defeat in war. Some would have been the product of a ruthless trade that made its profit by trafficking people from the margins of the empire. Others would have been 'rescued' from a rubbish tip or born as slaves, in-house, to slave women. Increasingly over the next centuries, as the scale of the wars of Roman conquest diminished, it was this 'home breeding' that became the major source of supply, so consigning slave women to much the same regime of childbearing as their free counterparts. More generally, slaves' conditions of life and work varied from cruel and cramped to borderline luxury. The fifty poky slave cubicles under the grand house of Scaurus were not the worst a slave would fear. Some, in larger industrial or agricultural op-erations, would have been more or less kept in captivity. Many would have been beaten. In fact, that vulnerability to corporal punishment was one of the things that made a slave a slave; Whipping Boy was one of their common nicknames. Yet there were also a few, a small minority who bulk largest in the surviving evidence, whose day-to-day lifestyle might have seemed enviable to the poor, free and hungry Roman citizen. By their standards, the slave aides of wealthy men in luxurious mansions, their private doctors or literary advisors, usually educated slaves of Greek origin, lived cosseted lives.

The attitudes of the free population to their slaves and to slavery as an institution were equally varied and ambivalent. For the owners, disdain and sadism sat side by side with a degree of fear and anxiety about their dependence and vulnerability, which numerous popular sayings and anecdotes capture. 'All slaves are enemies' was one piece of Roman wisdom. And in the reign of the emperor Nero, when someone had the bright idea to make slaves wear uniforms, it was rejected on the grounds that this would make clear to the slave population just how numerous they were. Yet any attempt to draw clear and consistent lines between slaves and free or to define the inferiority of slaves (were they things rather than people, some ancient theorists rather desperately wondered) was necessarily thwarted by social practice. Slaves and free in many contexts worked closely together. In the ordinary workshop, slaves might be friends and confidants as well as human chattel. And they were part of the Roman family; the Latin word *familia* always included the non-free and the free members of the household (see plates 16, 17).

For many, slavery was in any case only a temporary status, which added to the conceptual confusion. The Roman habit of freeing so many slaves may have been driven by all kinds of coldly practical considerations: it was certainly cheaper, for example, to give slaves their freedom than to keep them in their unproductive old age. But this was one crucial aspect of the widespread image of Rome as an open culture, and it made the Roman citizen body the most ethnically diverse that there ever was before the modern world – and it was a further cause for cultural anxiety. Were Romans freeing too many slaves? they asked. Were they freeing them for the wrong reasons? And what was the consequence of that for any idea of Romanness?

In most cases when Cicero notices his slaves more than in passing, it is because something has gone wrong, and his reactions reveal
some of these ambivalences and tensions in a day-to-day setting. In 46
BCE he wrote to one of his friends, then the governor of the province
of Illyricum, on the eastern coast of the Adriatic. He had a problem.
His librarian, a slave by the name of Dionysius, had been pilfering his
books and then, fearing that he would be exposed, had scarpered. It
turned out that Dionysius had been spotted in Illyricum (perhaps near
his original home), where he had apparently claimed that Cicero had
given him his freedom. 'It's not a big thing,' Cicero admitted, 'but it's
a weight on my mind.' He was asking that his friend keep an eye out,
to no avail, it seems. A year later he heard from the next governor that
'your runaway' had gone to ground among a local people, the Vardaei,
but nothing was ever heard of him again, even though Cicero fanta-
sised about seeing him brought back to Rome and led as a captive in
a triumphal procession.

He had had the same kind of trouble with an ex-slave a few years
earlier, another librarian, he explains in a letter to Atticus. This
Chrysippus – with his wonderfully learned Greek name, best known
from a third-century BCE philosopher – had been given the job of accompanying Cicero's son, Marcus, then in his mid teens, and Marcus'
slightly older cousin back to Rome from Cilicia. At some point on the
journey Chrysippus abandoned the young men. Never mind all his
minor pilferings, Cicero exploded, it was simply absconding that he
could not stand, as ex-slaves even after being granted their freedom
were still supposed to have obligations to their ex-master. Cicero's
reaction was to use a legal technicality to cancel Chrysippus' freedom
and re-enslave him. Too little, too late, of course: Chrysippus was
already off.

It is hard to judge the accuracy of Cicero's version of these stories.
How easy was it to sell on stolen books in Rome? Had Dionysius used
them to finance his escape? Did Cicero believe he still had them with

him (there was probably even less of a market among the Vardaei)? Or was the theft more a product of Cicero's paranoia and obsession with his library? Whatever the truth, these stories offer a useful antidote to the 'Spartacus model' of slave discontent and resistance. Very few slaves came head to head with Roman authority, still less with the Roman legions. Most resisted their master like this pair did, by just running away, going to ground and, if challenged, saying to their questioner, who almost certainly knew no better, that they had been freed anyway. On Cicero's side, this offers the image of a man for whom his slave household really could be the enemy within, even if that mostly came down to light fingers, and for whom the difference between those slaves he had freed and those he had not was narrower than many modern historians want to make it. It should be no surprise that, although *libertus* (freedman) is the standard Latin term for an ex-slave, on numerous occasions the word *servus* (slave) is used for both.

The one big exception to this picture is found in Cicero's relationship with his slave secretary Tiro, the man who in the medieval imagination was credited with the invention of a well-known form of shorthand. Tiro's origins are entirely unknown, unless the far-fetched Roman gossip was right to suspect that Cicero was so fond of him, he could only have been Cicero's natural son. He was freed with much celebration in 54 or 53 BCE, to become a Roman citizen under the name of Marcus Tullius Tiro. The relationship of Tiro with the whole Cicero family has often been seen as the 'acceptable face' of Roman slavery.

Many of the family's letters to him (no replies survive) brim with affection, chat and often concern about his health. 'Your health makes us terribly worried,' Quintus Cicero wrote, typically, in 49 BCE, '... and it's an enormous worry that you are going to be away from us for so long ... but really don't commit yourself to a long journey unless you are good and strong'. And the occasion of Tiro's grant of freedom was marked by joyous congratulation, and self-congratulation. Quintus again, writing to his brother from Gaul, where he was serving with

Julius Caesar, captures something of the significance of the change of status: 'I am really pleased with what you have done about Tiro and that you decided that his status was below what he deserved and that you would rather have him as a friend than a slave. I jumped for joy when I read your letter. Thank you.' Tiro appears almost to play the role of a surrogate son around whom the sometimes dysfunctional family could happily unite. But even so, there is a lingering ambivalence, and Tiro's servitude was never wholly forgotten. Years after his grant of freedom, Quintus wrote to Tiro to complain that, once again, no letter had arrived from him. 'I've given you a good thrashing, or at least a silent ticking off in my head', as Quintus puts it. A harmless bit of banter? A bad joke? Or a clear hint that in Quintus' imagination Tiro would always remain someone you could think of thrashing?

Towards a new history – of emperors

Tiro long outlived his master. Cicero, as we shall see, came to a gory end in December 43 BCE, as did his brother, Quintus. Tiro lived on, so it was said, until 4 BCE, when he died at the age of ninety-nine. He had spent the intervening years fostering and controlling Cicero's memory, helping to edit the correspondence and speeches and writing his biography, which – although it has not survived – became a standard source of information for later Roman historians. He even issued a large collection of his jokes. One of Cicero's later admirers suggested that his reputation for wit might have been better had Tiro only been a little more selective.

Tiro also lived to see a new permanent regime of one-man rule, emperors firmly installed on the throne of Rome and the old Republic an increasingly distant memory. This new regime is the theme of the last four chapters of SPQR, which explore the period of just over 250 years from the assassination of Caesar in 44 BCE to the early third century CE – more specifically, to the particular turning point in 212 CE when the emperor Caracalla gave Roman citizenship to every free inhabitant of the empire. It is a very different story from that of the first 700 or so years we have explored so far.

Roman history in this later period is in some ways much more familiar than anything earlier. It was during these centuries that most of those famous ancient landmarks still standing in the city of Rome were constructed: from the Colosseum, erected as a place of popular entertainment in the 70s CE, to the Pantheon ('Temple of All Gods'), built fifty years later, under the emperor Hadrian, and the only ancient temple that we can still walk into in more or less its original state – it was saved by its conversion into a Christian church without wholesale rebuilding. Even in the Roman Forum, the centre of the old city, where the big political battles of the Roman Republic took place, most of what we now see above ground was built under the emperors, not in the age of the Gracchi, or Sulla, or Cicero.

Overall there is much more evidence for the world of the first two centuries CE, even if no other individual ever stands out in quite such vivid detail as Cicero. That is not to do with the survival of vast new quantities of literature, poetry or history, though there are certainly volumes of that, and of increasingly varied types. We still have gossipy biographies of individual emperors; cynical satires, from the pens of Juvenal and others, pouring scorn on Roman prejudices; and extravagantly inventive novels, including the notorious *Satyricon*, written by Gaius Petronius Arbiter, a one-time friend and later victim of the emperor Nero and filmed 2,000 years later by Federico Fellini. This is a bawdy story of a group of rogues travelling round southern Italy, featuring orgies, cheap lodging houses with beds crawling with bugs, and a memorable portrait – and parody – of a rich and vulgar ex-slave, Trimalchio, who almost gave his name to a much later classic novel; the working title of F. Scott Fitzgerald's *The Great Gatsby* was *Trimalchio at West Egg*.

The dramatic change is rather in documents inscribed on stone. We have already analysed a few of these from centuries earlier, whether the tombstone of Scipio Barbatus or the semi-comprehensible inscription mentioning the 'king' (*rex*) dug up in the Forum. But in those early periods they were relatively few in number. From the first century CE, for reasons that no one has ever really fathomed, there was an explosion of writing on stone and bronze. In particular, thousands and thousands of epitaphs survive from right across the empire, commemorating relatively ordinary people or at least those with enough spare cash to commission some permanent memorial for themselves, however humble. They sometimes refer to little more than the occupation of the dead ('pearl seller', 'fishmonger', 'midwife' or 'baker'), sometimes to a whole life story. One peculiarly loquacious stone commemorates a woman with white skin, lovely eyes and small nipples who was the centre of a *ménage à trois* that split up after her death. There are also thousands of short biographies of leading citizens carved into the plinths of their statues all over the Roman world, and letters from emperors or decrees of the senate proudly displayed in far-flung communities of the empire. If the job of the historian of early Rome is to squeeze every single piece of surviving evidence for all it can tell us, by the first century CE the question is how to select the pieces of evidence that tell us the most.

An even bigger difference, however, in reconstructing this part of the story of Rome is that we must now largely do without the luxury, or constraint, of chronology. That is partly because of the geographical spread of the Roman world. There is no single narrative that links, in any useful or revealing way, the story of Roman Britain with the story of Roman Africa. There are numerous microstories and different histories of different regions which do not necessarily fit together and which, retold one by one, would make a decidedly unilluminating book. But it is also because, after the establishment of one-man rule at the end of the first century BCE, for more than two hundred years there is no significant history of change at Rome. Autocracy represented, in a sense, an end of history. Of course there were all kind of events, battles, assassinations, political stand-offs, new initiatives and inventions; and the participants would have had all kinds of exciting stories to tell and disputes to argue. But unlike the story of the development of the Republic and the growth of imperial power, which revolutionised almost every aspect of the world of Rome, there was no fundamental change in the structure of Roman politics, empire or society between the end of the first century BCE and the end of the second century CE.

So we shall start by looking in the next chapter at how, after the assassination of Julius Caesar, the emperor Augustus managed to establish one-man rule as a permanent fixture – perhaps the most important revolution in the story of Rome – and then explore the structures, problems and tensions that both underpinned and undermined that system for the next two centuries. The varied cast of characters will include dissident senators, the drunken clients of Roman bars and persecuted (and, for the Romans, troublesome) Christians. The big question is: how can we best understand the world of the Roman Empire under an emperor?

CHAPTER NINE

·

THE TRANSFORMATIONS
OF AUGUSTUS

Caesar's heir

CICERO MAY WELL have been sitting in the senate on the Ides of March 44 BCE when Caesar was assassinated, an eyewitness to a messy and almost bungled murder. A gang of twenty or so senators crowded round Caesar on the pretext of handing him a petition. One backbencher gave the cue for the attack by kneeling at the dictator's feet and pulling on his toga. The assassins were not very accurate in their aim, or perhaps they were terrified into clumsiness. One of the first strikes with the dagger missed entirely and gave Caesar the chance to fight back with the only weapon he had to hand – his sharp pen. According to the earliest account to survive, by Nicolaus of Damascus, a Greek historian from Syria writing fifty years later but likely drawing on eyewitness descriptions, several assassins were caught in 'friendly fire': Gaius Cassius Longinus lunged at Caesar but ended up gashing Brutus; another blow missed its target and landed in a comrade's thigh.

As he fell, Caesar cried out in Greek to Brutus, 'You too, child', which was either a threat ('I'll get you, boy!') or a poignant regret for the disloyalty of a young friend ('You too, my child?'), or even, as some suspicious contemporaries imagined, a final revelation that Brutus was, in fact, his victim's natural son and that this was not merely assassination but patricide. The famous Latin phrase '*Et tu, Brute?*' ('You too, Brutus?') is an invention of Shakespeare's.

The watching senators took to their heels; if Cicero was there, he was presumably no braver than the rest. But any quick escape was blocked by a crowd of thousands who were at that moment pouring out of the Theatre of Pompey next door, after a gladiatorial show. When these people got wind of what had happened, they too wanted to make for the safety of home as quickly as they could, despite Brutus' trying to assure them that there was no need to worry and that it was good news, not bad. The confusion only got worse when Marcus Aemilius Lepidus, one of Caesar's close colleagues, left the Forum to muster some soldiers stationed just outside the city, almost bumping into a group of assassins coming from the other direction to announce their victorious deed, closely followed in turn by three slaves carrying Caesar's body on a litter back to his house. It was an awkward job with only three of them, and reports were that the dictator's wounded arms dangled gruesomely over the sides.

That evening Cicero met Brutus and some of his fellow 'Liberators' on the Capitoline Hill, where they had installed themselves. He had not been part of the plot, but some said that Brutus had called out Cicero's name as he plunged his knife into Caesar – and in any case, as an elder statesman, he was likely to be a useful figurehead to have on board in the aftermath. Cicero's advice was clear: they should summon the senate to meet on the Capitoline straight away. But they dithered and left the initiative to Caesar's followers, who soon exploited the popular mood, which was certainly not behind the killers, despite Cicero's later fantasies that most ordinary Romans in the end believed that the tyrant had to go. The majority still preferred the reforms of Caesar – the support for the poor, the overseas settlements and the occasional cash handouts – to fine-sounding ideas of liberty, which might amount to not much more than an alibi for elite self-interest and the continued exploitation of the underclass, as those at the sharp end of Brutus' exactions in Cyprus could well have observed.

A few days later, Antony staged a startling funeral for Caesar, including a wax model suspended above the corpse, intended to make it easier for the audience to see all the wounds he had received, and where. A riot broke out, ending with the body being given an impromptu cremation in the Forum, the fuel partly provided by wooden benches from the nearby law courts, partly by the clothes that the musicians tore off themselves and threw into the flames, and partly by the jewels and their children's junior togas that women heaped on top.

There were, at least to start with, no reprisals. Brutus and Cassius thought it safer to leave the city after the demonstrations at the funeral, but they were not deprived of their political offices (both were praetors). Brutus was even allowed, as praetor, to sponsor a festival *in absentia*, but the Caesarians quickly replaced the play he had intended to present – on the first Brutus and the expulsion of the Tarquins – by one on a less topical theme from Greek mythology. Following a proposal by Cicero, the senate had earlier agreed that all Caesar's decisions should be ratified, in return for an amnesty for the assassins. It may well have been a fragile truce, but for the moment further violence had been avoided.

That changed when Caesar's appointed heir arrived in Rome, in April 44 BCE, from the other side of the Adriatic, where he had been involved in the preparations for an invasion of Parthia. Whatever the rumours and allegations, and whatever the status of the little boy whom Cleopatra had pointedly named Caesarion, Caesar had recognised no legitimate children. So he had taken the unusual step of adopting his great-nephew in his will, making him his son and the main beneficiary of his fortune. Gaius Octavius was then only eighteen years old and soon started capitalising on the famous name that came with his adoption by calling himself Gaius Julius Caesar – though to his enemies, as to most modern writers wanting to avoid confusion, he was known as Octavianus, or Octavian (that is, the 'ex-Octavius'). It was not a name he ever used himself. Why Caesar favoured this young man will always be a mystery, but Octavian certainly had an interest in ensuring that the murderers of the man who was now officially his father did not get off scot-free, and that no one among his many possible rivals, principally Mark Antony, should step into the dead dictator's shoes. Caesar was Octavian's passport to power, and after a compliant senate formally decided in January 42 BCE that Caesar had become a god, Octavian was soon trumpeting his new title and status: 'son of a god'. More than a decade of civil war followed.

Octavian – or Augustus, as he was officially known after 27 BCE (a made-up title meaning something close to 'Revered One') – dominated Roman political life for more than fifty years, until his death in 14 CE. Going far beyond the precedents set by Pompey and by Caesar, he was the first Roman emperor to last the course and the longest-serving ruler in the whole of Roman history, outstripping even the mythical Numa and Servius Tullius. As Augustus, he transformed the structures of Roman politics and the army, the government of the empire, the appearance of the city of Rome and the underlying sense of what Roman power, culture and identity were all about.

In the process of taking and holding power, Augustus also transformed himself, in a staggering shift from brutal warlord and insurgent to responsible elder statesman, signalled by his astute change of name. His early record as Octavian was a mixture of sadism, scandal and illegality. He fought his way into Roman politics in 44 BCE, using a private army and tactics that were not far short of a coup. He went on to be jointly responsible for a ghastly pogrom on the model of Sulla's proscriptions and, if Roman tradition is to be believed, to have plenty of blood, literally, on his hands. One lurid tale claims that he personally tore out the eyes of a senior official whom he suspected of plotting against him. Only a little less shocking to Roman sensibilities was the story of how he casually impersonated the god Apollo at a lavish banquet and fancy-dress party, held while the rest of the population was close to starving because of the deprivations of civil war. How he left all this behind to become the founding father of a new regime and, in the eyes of many, the model emperor and the benchmark against which his successors were often judged was a question that many observant Romans came to ask. And historians have puzzled and disagreed ever since, both about his radical transformation and about the nature of the regime he established and the basis of his power and authority. How did he do it?

The face of civil war

[handwritten margin notes: Octavian / Antony / Lepidus]

By the end of 43 BCE, in little more than eighteen months after Octavian's arrival in Italy, the politics of Rome had been turned upside down. Brutus and Cassius had been allocated provinces in the East and left Italy. Octavian and Antony had come to blows in a series of military engagements in northern Italy and then patched things up again by forming with Lepidus a 'triumvirate for establishing government'. This was a formal, five-year agreement that gave each of the three men (*triumviri*) power equal to consuls, their pick of what provinces they wanted and control over elections. Rome was in the control of a junta.

And Cicero was dead. He had made the mistake of speaking out too powerfully against Antony, and in the new round of mass murder that was the triumvirate's main achievement, his name featured among those of hundreds of other senators and knights on the dreaded lists. A special hit squad was sent for him in December 43 BCE, and they cut off his head as he was being carried in a litter away from one of his country properties in a hopeless attempt to go to ground (hopeless partly because one of the family's ex-slaves had leaked his whereabouts). It was another symbolic finale to the Roman Republic, and discussed for centuries afterwards. In fact, Cicero's last moments were endlessly replayed in Rome's oratorical training schools, where the question of whether he should have begged Antony for mercy or (even trickier) have offered to destroy all his writing in return for his life was a favourite debating topic on the curriculum. In reality, the sequel was more sordid. His head and right hand were sent to Rome and pinned up on the *rostra* in the Forum. Antony's wife Fulvia, who had once been married to Cicero's other great enemy Clodius, came to view the trophy. The story was that, in her gloating, she took the head down, spat on it and pulled out and pierced the tongue over and over with the pins she had removed from her hair.

Any fragile truce was now forgotten. In October 42 BCE, the united forces of the triumvirate defeated Brutus and Cassius near the town of Philippi in the far north of Greece (the focus of much of Shakespeare's *Julius Caesar*), and the victorious allies then began even more systematically to turn on one another. In fact, when Octavian returned from Philippi to Italy to oversee a massive programme of land confiscation, aimed at providing settlement packages for thousands of dangerously dissatisfied retiring soldiers, he soon found himself facing the armed opposition of Fulvia and Mark Antony's brother Lucius Antonius. They had taken up the cause of the landowners who had been dispossessed, and even managed to gain control of the city of Rome, albeit briefly. Octavian soon had them under siege in the town of Perusia (modern Perugia). Starvation forced their surrender early in 40 BCE, but the stage had been set for more than a decade of further war, interspersed with brief truces, between the different parties who claimed to represent Caesar's legacy.

It is often hard to make much coherent sense of the shifting coalitions and changing aims of the various players in the different rounds of this conflict. It remains anyone's guess what combination of indecision, political realignment and self-interest caused Cicero's one-time son-in-law Dolabella to change sides twice within a few months

– before taking a command against the Liberators in the East, tricking, torturing and executing the unfortunate governor of Asia en route, and meeting his own death in 43 BCE as he tried unsuccessfully to confront Cassius in Syria. 'Will anyone ever have the talent to put this all in writing so that it seems like fact, not fiction?' one later Roman author asked, clearly expecting the answer *no*. Yet confusing as the roles of many of the leading characters are, this conflict offers more evidence than any before in Roman history of what this kind of war meant for the rest of the population of Italy, soldier and civilian – including the real or scripted voices of some of the innocent victims.

The poor peasants who lost their land in the confiscations of the triumvirate are a focus of the poet Virgil's first major work, the *Eclogues* ('Selections'). Though he was later one of the 'poet laureates' of the Augustan regime, in the late 40s and early 30s BCE he shone the spotlight on the fallout of civil war in the once idyllic and innocent lives of the shepherds and herdsmen of rural Italy, with Octavian a powerful and sometimes menacing figure in the background. As they sing of life and loves in their pastoral world, some of his rustic characters turn out to be the disgruntled victims of expropriation. 'Some godless and ungrateful soldier will take over my carefully tended fields,' one complains. 'See where civil strife has brought us poor citizens.'

Other writers concentrated on the human side of the proscriptions in a series of stories about clever hiding places, pitiful suicides, and the brave loyalty or cruel treachery of friends, family and slaves. One ingenious wife saved her husband by bundling him into a laundry bag; another pushed hers into a sewer, where the foul smell successfully deterred would-be murderers. One pair of brothers apparently took refuge in a large oven until their slaves discovered them and killed one of them instantly (a revenge for his cruelty, we are meant to assume), while the other escaped – only to have his death leap into the Tiber foiled by some kindly fishermen, who mistook his jump for an accidental fall and hauled him out. There is almost certainly some embellishment, and added heroism, in these literary accounts. But they are not so different from the description of the conduct of one loyal wife, as it is plainly inscribed on her epitaph. This explains how she went in person to Lepidus to beg for her husband's life and came away, having been roughly handled, 'black and blue, as if she were a slave', as the text puts it – an indication not only of the woman's bravery but also of the almost automatic connection between slavery and corporal punishment.

There is some hint of what the rank-and-file soldiers might have been thinking too. In and around the modern town of Perugia, dozens of small sling bullets have been unearthed, deadly lead projectiles that

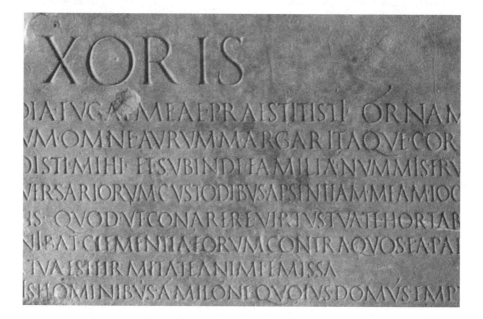

57. One fragment of the epitaph of the loyal wife. Sadly the names of the couple concerned are missing, but it is clear that he was a prominent senator. 'XORIS' on the first line is what remains of 'UXORIS' – 'wife'. In this section the wife's assistance during the husband's flight is recounted; the second line, for example, refers to the AURUM MARGARITAQUE ('the gold and the pearls') that she sent to provide funds for him.

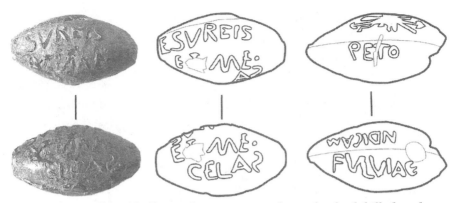

58. The small lead bullets, a few centimetres long, that both killed, and took a message to, the enemy. 'Esureis et me celas' ('You're famished and pretending not to be') has prompted other translations, including some explicitly erotic ones ('You're hungering for me ...'). On the right, the first known example of *landica*, here upside down.

'You're famished and pretending not to be', reads one message lobbed into the city, where starvation eventually led to surrender. Several others carry brutally obscene messages aimed at predictable parts of the anatomy of their different targets, male and female: 'Lucius Antonius, you baldy, and you too, Fulvia, open your arsehole'; 'I'm going for Madam Octavius' arsehole'; or 'I'm going for Fulvia's clitoris' (*landica*, the earliest attested use of the term in Latin). The unsettling overlap of military and sexual violence, plus the standard Roman pot-shot at a receding hairline, is probably typical of the ribaldry found on the legionary front line: part bravado, part aggression, part misogyny, part ill-concealed fear.

Lucius Antonius and Fulvia admitted defeat in early 40 BCE. How far she had been in joint military command is doubtful; for one of the easiest ways for the other side to attack Lucius, as they later attacked his brother, was to pretend that he was sharing command with a mere woman. In any case, Fulvia returned to Mark Antony in Greece and almost immediately died. For a while, the triumvirate was patched up, and as a pledge for the future, the widowed Antony married Octavian's sister, Octavia. It was, however, an empty pledge, as by this date Antony was already in the partnership that would come to define him; he was more or less living with Queen Cleopatra of Egypt, and she had just given birth to his twins. In any case, the coalition of three was soon reduced to two, when Lepidus, who had always been a junior player, was squeezed out in 36 BCE. When the final showdown came in 31 BCE, there was no doubt about the question at stake. Who was going to rule the Roman world? Was it to be Octavian or Antony – with Cleopatra at his side?

Cleopatra had been in Rome when Caesar was assassinated, lodging at one of the dictator's villas on the outskirts of the city. It was the best that Roman money could buy, though probably not a patch on the luxurious surroundings of her home in Alexandria. After the Ides of March 44 BCE, she quickly packed up and returned home ('The queen's exit does not worry me,' Cicero wrote to Atticus in a transparent understatement). But she kept her finger in Roman politics for obvious and pressing reasons: she still needed outside support to shore up her position as the ruler of Egypt, and she had plenty of cash and other resources to give to anyone prepared to offer it. She first fell in with Dolabella, Cicero's one-time son-in-law, but after his death turned to Mark Antony. Their relationship has forever been written up in erotic terms, whether hopeless infatuation on Antony's part or one of the greatest love stories in the history of the West. Passion may have been one element of it. But their partnership was underpinned by something more prosaic: military, political and financial needs.

In 40 BCE Octavian and Antony had effectively carved up the Mediterranean world between themselves, leaving just a small patch for Lepidus. So for much of the 30s BCE, Octavian operated in the West, dealing with any of his Roman enemies who remained at large – including the son of Pompey the Great, the main surviving link to the civil wars of the early 40s BCE – and conquering new territories across the Adriatic. Meanwhile, in the East, Antony mounted rather more high-profile campaigns, against Parthia and Armenia, but with very mixed success, despite the resources of Cleopatra.

Reports reaching Rome hyped the luxury of the couple's life in Alexandria. Fantastic stories circulated about their decadent banquets, and their notorious bet on who could stage the most expensive dinner party of all. One deeply disapproving Roman account records that Cleopatra won by providing a spread worth 10 million sesterces (almost as much as Cicero's grandest house), including the cost of a fabulous pearl which – in an act of conspicuous and entirely pointless consumption – she dissolved in vinegar and drank. Equally worrying for Roman traditionalists was the sense that Antony was beginning to treat Alexandria as if it were Rome, even to the point of celebrating the distinctively Roman ceremony of triumph there, after some minor victory in Armenia. 'For the sake of Cleopatra he bestowed on the Egyptians the honourable and solemn ceremonies of his own country', as one ancient writer reported the objections.

Octavian exploited these fears in a dramatic intervention in 32 BCE. Antony had divorced Octavia earlier in the year, and Octavian responded by getting his hands on Antony's will and reading out particularly incriminating selections from it to the senate. These revealed that Antony recognised young Caesarion as Julius Caesar's son, that he was planning to leave large amounts of money to the children he had had with Cleopatra and that he wanted to be buried in Alexandria by Cleopatra's side, even if he died in Rome. The rumour on the Roman streets was that his long-term plans were to abandon the city of Romulus and transfer the capital wholesale to Egypt.

It was against this background that open war broke out. At the start of the conflict in 31 BCE, the good money would probably have been on a victory for Antony: he had considerably more troops and more cash at his disposal. But Antony and Cleopatra lost the first battle at sea, near Actium (the name just means 'promontory') in northern Greece, and they never regained the initiative. For one of the world's decisive military engagements, which drew a final line under the Roman Republic, the Battle of Actium, in September 31 BCE, was a rather low-key, slightly tawdry affair – though perhaps more decisive military engagements are low-key and tawdry than we tend to imagine. Octavian's easy victory was owed to his second in command, Marcus Agrippa, who managed to cut off their opponents' supplies; to a handful of well-informed deserters who disclosed the enemy plans; and to Antony and Cleopatra themselves, who simply disappeared. As soon as Octavian's forces seemed to be getting the upper hand, they beat a hasty retreat from Greece to Egypt with a small detachment of ships, abandoning the rest of their soldiers and sailors, who understandably did not bother to go on fighting much longer.

The next year, Octavian sailed to Alexandria to finish the job. In what has often been written up as a kind of tragic farce, Antony stabbed himself when he thought that Cleopatra was already dead, though he lived just long enough to discover that she was not. A week or so later she too is said to have killed herself, with the bite from a snake smuggled into her quarters in a basket of fruit. According to the official version, her motive was to deprive Octavian of her presence in his triumphal procession: 'I will not be triumphed over,' she is supposed to have muttered over and over again. But it may not be so simple, or as Shakespearean, as that. Suicide by snake bite is a hard feat to pull off, and anyway the most reliably deadly snakes would be far too hefty to conceal in even a regal fruit basket. Although Octavian publicly regretted that he had lost the prize specimen for his triumph, he may privately have thought that the queen was less trouble dead than alive. At the very least – as several modern historians have suspected – he may have facilitated her death. He certainly took no chances with Caesarion, given his supposed paternity. Now aged sixteen, he was killed.

What was displayed in Octavian's triumph in the summer of 29 BCE was a full-scale replica of the queen at the moment of her death, and even in this form she caught the attention of the crowd. 'It was as if,' one later historian wrote, 'she was there with the other prisoners'. The procession was a carefully choreographed affair which took place over three days, ostensibly to celebrate Octavian's victories across the Adriatic in Illyricum and against Cleopatra at Actium and in Egypt. There was no explicit mention of Antony or any other enemy of the civil wars and none of the gruesome images of Roman death that Julius Caesar had ill-advisedly paraded in his celebrations fifteen years earlier. Yet there could have been no real doubt about who had really been defeated, or about what the consequences of Octavian's success would be. This was as much a coronation ritual as a victory parade.

Losers and winners

There is more to this story of the war between Octavian and Antony than meets the eye. What survives is the self-confident, self-justifying version written by the winners, Octavian and his friends. But the feasibility of suicide by snake bite is only one aspect of the history of this period that should raise suspicions. There is also a question mark over quite how extravagantly immoral, or anti-Roman, the lifestyle of Cleopatra and Antony really was. The accounts that have come down to us are not complete invention. One of the sources of Plutarch's biography of Mark Antony, written 150 years after Antony's death and full of some of the most lurid anecdotes of his life of luxury, was a descendant of a man who worked in Cleopatra's kitchens – and may well have preserved a view of the culinary style of her court from below stairs. But it is absolutely clear that, both at the time and even more so in retrospect, Augustus (as he was soon known) exploited the idea of a clash between his own deep-rooted, Roman, Western traditions and the 'oriental' excess that Antony and Cleopatra represented. In the war of words, and in later justifications of Augustus' rise to power, it became a struggle between the virtues of Rome and the dangers and decadence of the East.

The luxury of Cleopatra's court was wildly exaggerated, and relatively innocent occasions in Alexandria were twisted out of all recognition. However Antony chose to celebrate his Armenian victory in Alexandria, for example, there is no evidence except Roman criticisms to suggest that it was anything resembling a Roman triumph (the scant descriptions that survive suggest that it was more likely based on some ritual of the god Dionysus). And those incriminating quotations from Antony's will would certainly have been a prejudicial selection, even if not outright invention.

The Battle of Actium too played a key role in later representations. It was made out to be a much more impressive encounter than it really was, and built up to be the founding moment of the Augustan regime, which is still usually said to have begun in 31 BCE; one later historian went so far as to suggest that 'the second of September', the exact date of the encounter, is one of the few Roman dates worth remembering. A new town called Nicopolis ('Victoryville') was built near the battle site, as well as a vast monument overlooking the sea, decorated with rams from the captured ships and a frieze depicting the triumphal procession of 29 BCE. Rome was also filled with reminders of it, on everything from monumental sculpture to precious cameos (see plate 19), and many ordinary soldiers who had fought on the winning side proudly gave themselves the extra name Actiacus, or 'Actium-man'. What is more, in the Roman imagination the battle was almost instantly turned into a clash between solid, disciplined Roman troops and wild hordes of orientals. Despite the fact that Antony had the staunch support of several hundred senators, all the emphasis was on the exotic rabble, with – as Virgil put it – 'their barbarian wealth and weird weapons', and Cleopatra issuing commands by shaking an Egyptian rattle.

Cleopatra was a crucial element in this whole picture. Whether or not she, like Fulvia, really played the leading part in the military command, as ancient writers claimed, is debatable. But she was a useful target. By focusing on her rather than on Antony, Octavian could present the war as one fought against a foreign rather than a Roman enemy – and led by a commander not only dangerous, regal and seductive but also unnatural, in Roman terms, in undertaking the male responsibilities of warfare and command. Antony might even seem to be her victim, enticed from the proper path of Roman duty by a foreign queen. When Virgil in his *Aeneid*, written just a few years after Octavian's victory, imagines Queen Dido 'burning with love' in her African kingdom of Carthage and attempting to seduce Aeneas from his destiny of founding Rome, there is more than a faint echo of Cleopatra.

59. One fragment of the newly discovered victory monument at the site of the Battle of Actium shows Octavian's triumphal chariot at his procession of 29 BCE. Two children, seen beneath Octavian's arm, share the ride. They are most likely his own daughter Julia and Drusus, the son of his wife, Livia, by an earlier marriage, or possibly the children of Cleopatra and Mark Antony.

M·BILLIENVS·M·F
ROM·ACTIACVS
LEGIONE·XI·PROE
LIO·NAVALI·FACTO
IN·COLONIAM·DE
DVCTVS·AB·ORDI
[...]E·CVRIO·ALLE[...]
[...]O·ERV[...]

60. The tombstone of Marcus Billienus who served in the eleventh legion ('*legione XI*') in the Battle of Actium and took the name Actiacus ('Actium-man') to celebrate his own part in the victory. Although the bottom of the stone is missing, what does survive, combined with the find-spot, suggests that he ended up a local councillor (*decurio*) in a settlement of veterans in North Italy.

So is it possible to reconstruct an alternative version of the story? In detail, it is not. The problem is that in this case the victor's perspective is so dominating that it is easier to be suspicious of the standard line than to replace it. There are, however, a few hints of different perspectives. It is not difficult to see what the image of Octavian would have been if Antony had won at Actium: a sadistic young thug with a dangerous tendency to self-aggrandisement. In fact, some of the worst anecdotes about his youth may go back to Antony's negative propaganda, including the story of the fancy-dress banquet where Octavian impersonated the god Apollo; his biographer Gaius Suetonius Tranquillus (just 'Suetonius' from now on) explicitly states that this combination of sacrilege and extravagance was one of the accusations that Antony levelled at him.

Some people at the time were fatalistic, or realistic, enough to think that it would not make much difference whichever of them won. A curious anecdote about some talking ravens amusingly sums up that idea. Octavian, so the story goes, was returning to Rome after the Battle of Actium when he was met by an ordinary working man who had trained a pet raven to say, 'Greetings, Caesar, our victorious commander'. He was so impressed with the trick that he gave the man a substantial cash reward. But it turned out that the trainer had a partner, who was not given his share of the money and to make his point went to Octavian and suggested that the man should be asked to produce his other raven. The pair of chancers had been sensibly hedging their bets. When this second bird was brought out, it squeaked, 'Greetings, Antony, our victorious commander'. Happily, Octavian saw the funny side and simply insisted that the first man share the reward with his partner.

Part of the point of this story was to demonstrate Octavian's human touch and his generous attitude towards a couple of harmless tricksters. But there was a political message too. The pair of identikit birds, with their almost identikit slogans, is meant to hint that there was much less to choose between Octavian and his rival than the usual partisan story suggests. The victory of one rather than the other required no more adjustment than swapping one talking bird for another.

The riddle of Augustus

It is impossible even to guess how Antony would have ruled the Roman world if he had ever had the chance. But there is little doubt that whoever emerged as the victor after the long civil wars, the outcome was going to be not a return to Rome's traditional pattern of power sharing but some form of autocracy. By 43 BCE even Brutus the Liberator was striking coins featuring his own head, which was a fair indication of the direction in which he was moving (Fig. 48). It was not so clear what form that one-man rule would take or how it could be made to succeed. Octavian almost certainly did not return to Italy from Egypt with an autocratic master plan ready to apply. But through a long series of practical experiments, improvisations, false starts, a few failures and, very soon, a new name intended to consign the bloody associations of 'Octavian' to the past, he eventually devised a template for how to be a Roman emperor which lasted in most of its significant details for the next 200 years or so, and in broad terms much longer. Some of his innovations are still taken for granted as part and parcel of our mechanisms of political power.

For the founding father of all Roman emperors, however, it has always proved difficult to pin him down. In fact, the new name 'Augustus', which he adopted soon after his return from Egypt (and which I shall use from now on), captures the slipperiness very nicely. It is a word that evoked ideas of authority (*auctoritas*) and proper religious observance, echoing the title of one of the main groups of Roman priests, called the *augures*. It sounded impressive and had none of the unfortunate, fratricidal or regal associations of 'Romulus', another potential name which he is said to have rejected. No one had ever been called it before, although it had occasionally been used as a rather high-flown adjective meaning something more or less like 'holy'. All later emperors took over 'Augustus' as part of their title. But the truth is, it did not really *mean* anything. 'Revered One' gets it about right.

Even at the time of his funeral, people were debating exactly what Augustus' regime had been based on. Was it a moderate version of autocracy, founded on respect for the citizen, the rule of law and patronage of the arts? Or was it not far short of a blood-stained tyranny, under a ruthless leader who had not changed much since the years of civil war and with a series of high-profile victims executed either for plotting against him or for getting into bed with Julia, his daughter?

Whether people liked or loathed him, he was in many ways a puzzling and contradictory revolutionary. He was one of the most radical innovators Rome ever saw. He exercised such influence over elections that the popular democratic process withered: the large new building completed in 26 BCE to house the assemblies was soon more often used for gladiatorial shows than voting, and one of the first acts of his successor was to transfer what remained of the elections to the senate, leaving the people out entirely. He controlled the Roman army by directly hiring and firing the legionary commanders and by making himself the overall governor of all the provinces in which there was a military presence. He attempted to micromanage the behaviour of citizens in an entirely new and intrusive way, from regulating the sex life of the upper classes, who were to suffer political penalties if they did not produce enough children, to stipulating what people should wear in the Forum – togas only, no tunics, trousers or nice warm cloaks. And, unlike anyone before, he directed the traditional mechanisms of Roman literary patronage towards a concerted, centrally sponsored campaign. Cicero had been eager to find poets to celebrate his various successes. Augustus to all intents and purposes had writers such as Virgil and Horace on his payroll, and the work they produced offers a memorable and eloquent image of a new golden age for Rome and its empire, with Augustus centre stage. 'I have given them empire without limit' (*imperium sine fine*), Jupiter prophesies for the Romans in Virgil's *Aeneid*, national epic, instant classic and a book which landed straight on the school curriculum in Augustan Rome. It still remains (just) on the modern Western curriculum 2,000 years later.

Yet Augustus appears to have abolished nothing. The governing class remained the same (this was no revolution in the strict sense of the word), the privileges of the senate were in many ways enhanced, not removed, and the old offices of state, consulships and praetorships and so on, continued to be coveted and filled. Much of the legislation that is usually ascribed to Augustus was formally introduced, or at least fronted, by those regular officials. It was a standing joke that the pair of consuls who proposed one of 'his' laws promoting marriage were both bachelors. Most of his formal powers were officially voted to him by the senate and cast almost entirely in a traditional Republican format, his continued use of the title 'son of a god' being the only important exception. And he lived in no grand palace but in the sort of house on the Palatine Hill where you would expect to find a senator, and where his wife Livia could occasionally be spotted working her wool. The word that Romans most often used to describe his position was *princeps*, meaning 'first citizen' rather than 'emperor', as we choose to call him, and one of his most famous watchwords was *civilitas* – 'we're all citizens together'.

Even where he seems most visible, Augustus turns out to be elusive; and that was presumably part of his secret. One of his most significant and lasting innovations was to flood the Roman world with his

61. Two different images of Augustus. On the left, he appears in his role as priest, his toga pulled over his head, as was customary when offering a sacrifice. On the right, he is shown as a heroic, semi-divine warrior. At his feet is a small image of Cupid, reminding those who saw it of the emperor's descent through Aeneas from the goddess Venus herself.

portrait: heads stamped on the small change in people's pockets, life-size or larger statues in marble and bronze standing in public squares and temples, miniatures embossed or engraved on rings, gems and dining room silverware. This was on a vastly bigger scale than anything of the sort before. There is no earlier Roman for whom more than a handful of possible portraits are known, and most of those are uncertainly identified anyway (the temptation to give a name to otherwise anonymous heads, or to find a face for Cicero and Brutus and so on, often proving irresistible, despite the lack of evidence). Even for Julius Caesar, apart from coins, there are only a couple of very doubtful candidates for a portrait that was made during his lifetime. By contrast, about 250 statues, not to mention images on jewels and gems, found right across Roman territories and beyond, from Spain to Turkey and Sudan, show Augustus in many different guises, from heroic conqueror to pious priest.

These all have such similar facial features that standard models must have been sent out from Rome, in a coordinated attempt to spread the emperor's image to his subjects. They all adopt an idealising, youthful style that echoes the classical art of fifth-century BCE Athens and makes a glaring and loaded contrast with the craggy, elderly, wrinkled, exaggerated 'realism' that is characteristic of the portraits of the Roman elite in the earlier part of the first century BCE (Fig. 33). They were all intended to bring a far-flung population, most of whom would never see the man himself, face to face with their ruler. And yet they almost certainly look nothing like the real Augustus at all. Not only do they fail to match up with the one surviving written description of his features, which – trustworthy or not – prefers to stress his unkempt hair, his bad teeth and the platform shoes which, like many autocrats since, he used to disguise his short stature; they also look almost exactly the same throughout his life, so that at the age of seventy-plus he was still being portrayed as a perfect young man. This was at best an official image – to put it less flatteringly, a mask of power – and the gap between this and the flesh-and-blood emperor, the man behind the mask, has always been, for most people, impossible to bridge.

Unsurprisingly, several well-informed ancient observers decided that the enigma of Augustus was the whole point. Nearly 400 years later, in the mid fourth century CE, the emperor Julian wrote a clever skit on his predecessors, imagining them all turning up together for a grand party with the gods. They troop in, matching what had by then become their caricatures. Julius Caesar is so power crazy that he seems likely to unseat the king of the gods and party host; Tiberius looks terribly moody; Nero cannot bear to be parted from his lyre. Augustus enters like a chameleon who is impossible to sum up, a tricky old reptile continually changing colour, from yellow to red to black, one minute gloomy and sombre, the next parading all the charms of the goddess of love. The divine hosts have no option but to hand him over to a philosopher to make him wise and moderate.

Earlier writers hinted that Augustus relished this kind of tease. Why else did he choose for the design of his signet ring, with which he authenticated his correspondence – the ancient equivalent of a signature – the image of the most famous riddling creature in the whole of Greco-Roman mythology: the sphinx? Roman dissidents, who have been followed by a number of modern historians, pushed the point further, accusing the Augustan regime of being based on hypocrisy and pretence and of abusing traditional Republican forms and language to provide a cloak and disguise for a fairly hard-line tyranny.

There is certainly something in this. Hypocrisy is a common weapon of power. And on many occasions it may have suited Augustus to be just as Julian painted him, enigmatic, slippery and evasive, and to say one thing while meaning another. But that can hardly have been everything. There must have been firmer footings under the new regime than a series of riddles, doublespeak and pretence. So what were those footings? How did Augustus get away with it? That is the problem.

It is almost impossible to see behind the scenes of the Augustan regime, despite all the evidence we appear to have. This is one of the best-documented periods of Roman history. There are volumes of contemporary poetry, mostly singing the emperor's praises, though not always. Ovid's hilarious spoof on how to pick up a partner, which still survives under the title *Ars Amatoria* (*Love Lessons*), was sufficiently at odds with Augustus' moral programme that it was one reason for the poet ending up in exile on the Black Sea; his relationship with Julia may have been another. And any number of later historians and antiquarians found Augustus an interesting subject, whether they were reflecting on his imperial style or collecting his jokes and bons mots. The repartee with the raven trainers is only one example from a mini-anthology of his banter, which also includes some nice fatherly ribaldry on his daughter's habit of pulling out her grey hairs ('Tell me, would you rather be grey or bald ... ?'). Another memorable survival is the chatty, episodic biography written by Suetonius about 100 years after the emperor's death: it is the source of remarks about his teeth and hair, as well as many more reliable and unreliable snapshots and snippets, right down to his occasional poor spelling, his terror of thunderstorms and his habit of wearing four tunics and a vest under his toga in the winter.

Among all this, however, there is almost no good evidence, and certainly none of it contemporary, about the nuts and bolts, disputes and decision-making that underpinned the new politics of Rome. The few private letters of Augustus that Suetonius excerpts were chosen for what they say about his luck on the gambling table or his lunch menu ('a bit of bread and some dates in my carriage') rather than about any political strategy. Roman historians complained about almost exactly the same issue as the modern historian faces: when they tried to write the history of this period, they found that so much of importance had happened in private, rather than publicly in the senate house or Forum as before, that it was hard to know exactly what had taken place, let alone how to explain it.

What does survive, however, is the text of Augustus' curriculum vitae, a document that he wrote at the end of his life, summing up his achievements (*Res Gestae*, as the surviving version is usually titled in Latin – or 'What I Did'). It is a self-serving, partisan and often rose-tinted piece of work, which carefully glosses or entirely ignores the murderous illegalities of his early career. It is also a unique account, in roughly ten pages of modern text, of what the old reptile wanted posterity to know about his many years as *princeps*, how he defined the role and how he claimed to have changed Rome. It is worth attending to his sometimes surprising words before trying to look behind them.

What I did

A rare piece of archaeological good fortune has preserved this version of Augustus' life story. In his will he asked that it be inscribed on two bronze pillars at the entrance to his vast family tomb, as a permanent record of what he had done and something not far short of a job de-scription for his successors. The original pillars have long since been melted down, probably into some form of medieval ballistics, but the text was copied on stone in other parts of the empire, to memorial-ise his rule outside Rome too. Fragments of four of these copies have been discovered, including an almost complete version from Ankyra (modern Ankara).

This version had been inscribed on the walls of a temple in honour of 'Rome and Augustus', both in the original Latin and in a Greek translation, for the benefit of the largely Greek-speaking inhabitants of the area – and was preserved because the temple was turned into a Christian church in the sixth century CE and then later into part of a mosque. There are all kinds of stories of heroic efforts expended from the mid sixteenth century onwards in deciphering and copying the emperor's words at often perilous heights, until Kemal Atatürk, as the president of Turkey, proudly had the whole inscription uncovered and preserved in the 1930s to mark the 2,000th anniversary of Augustus' birth. But the simple fact that the best text of the emperor's words survives thousands of miles, and in the ancient world more than a month's journey, away from Rome sums up a lot about the imperial regime and its public face.

The *Res Gestae* is a rich source of detail about Augustus' career and the Roman world of his day. It starts with a delicately euphemistic description of his rise to power, which entirely omits any mention of the pogrom ('I liberated the state oppressed by the power of a faction' is how he refers to his clash with either Antony or Brutus and Cassius). It goes on to refer briefly to such things as his splendid

62. The Mausoleum of Augustus in Rome, outside which the bronze pillars bearing his account of his achievements once stood. It was on a scale quite out of proportion to even the richest tombs of the Republican aristocracy and stood in Rome throughout most of Augustus' long reign. Its early completion was partly a precautionary measure (there were numerous scares over Augustus' health) and partly an aggressive assertion of the emperor's power, of his dynastic aspirations and of his commitment to be buried in Rome.

63. The Temple of Rome and Augustus in Ankara, from where the most complete text of the *Res Gestae* comes (the minaret of the later mosque, partly built into it, is visible just behind). The Latin text was inscribed on both sides of the main entrance, the Greek over one of the outside walls. Neither version survives complete, the missing portions of Latin can be completed from the Greek and vice versa.

triumphal processions ('nine kings or children of kings' walked as captives before his chariot, he boasts, with typically Roman delight in captured royalty) and his emergency management of the Roman corn supply when famine loomed. For some modern historians the most important sentences are the couple that report the results of his censuses of Roman citizens, recording a total head count of 4,063,000 in 28 BCE, rising to 4,937,000 in 14 CE. These are the most reliable data we have for the size of the ancient Roman citizen body at any time, largely because, inscribed on stone, they are prone to none of the errors that careless manuscript copiers can easily introduce. Even so, there is still a fierce dispute about whether the figures include men only or women and children too – whether, in other words, the

Roman citizen population all told was around 5 million, allowing for some under-registration, or something over 12 million.

None of this, however, was Augustus' main theme. And many other likely topics find no place at all. There is nothing about his family, apart from one reference to honours paid to two of his adopted children who died young. There is nothing about his programme of moral legislation or his attempts to increase the birth rate, though the census figures may have been intended to demonstrate success on that score – probably erroneously, as it is much more likely that the creation of new citizens and more efficient counting lay behind most of the rise in numbers, rather than imperial finger wagging at the upper class for not producing enough babies. There is little more than allusive references to any individual piece of legislation or political reform. Instead, roughly two-thirds of the text is devoted to just three main subjects: Augustus' victories and conquests, his benefactions to the Roman people, and his buildings.

More than two pages of the modern text of the *Res Gestae* catalogue the territories he added to the empire, the foreign rulers he made subject to Rome and the embassies and suppliants who flocked to recognise the emperor's power. 'I extended the territory of all the provinces of the Roman people, which had neighbours not obedient to our rule,' he announces, with slight exaggeration, before moving on to itemise at what can now seem tedious length his imperial successes and military victories all over the world: Egypt made a Roman possession; the Parthians forced to return the Roman military standards lost in 53 BCE; a Roman army reaching the city of Meroe south of the Sahara and a fleet entering the North Sea; delegations arriving from as far afield as India, not to mention a mixed bag of renegade kings begging for mercy, with names gratifyingly exotic to a Latin ear – 'Artavasdes king of the Medes, Artaxares of the Adiabenians, Dumnobellaunus and Tincomarus of the Britons'. And that is only a small slice of it.

There is something entirely traditional about this. Military success had been one foundation of political power as far back in Roman history as it is possible to go. Augustus outstripped all possible rivals on this score, bringing more territory under Roman rule than anyone else before or after. Yet this was a new kind of imperialism too. The heading of the inscribed text, the closest thing it has to an original title, reads: 'This is how he made the world subject to the power of the people of Rome'. Pompey, more than half a century earlier, had just hinted at that kind of ambition. Augustus explicitly turned global conquest – and a 'joined-up' territorial view of an empire centred on Rome, rather than the old mosaic of obedient states – into a rationale for his rule. How all this would have come across to the provincial audience in Ankyra is impossible to know. But it is an idea reflected in other monuments that Augustus sponsored in the city of Rome, most famously in the world 'map' that he and his colleague Marcus Agrippa commissioned and put on public display. No trace of this survives, and the best guess is that it was something closer to an annotated plan of Roman roads than a realistic geography in our terms (see plate 21). But whatever its exact appearance, it fitted Augustus' vision of empire. As Pliny later put it, in his encyclopaedia, the map's purpose was to make 'the world [*orbis*] something for the city [*urbs*] to see', or to display the world as Roman territory under the emperor's rule.

Augustus' generosity to the ordinary people at home claims as much space in the *Res Gestae* as his conquests abroad. He was wealthy on a new scale. The combination of his inheritance from Caesar, the riches of Egypt that he seized after the defeat of Antony and Cleopatra and the occasional blurring of the boundary between state funds and his own meant that he could outbid anyone as a popular benefactor. Here he carefully lists his regular distributions of cash: the dates, the precise amounts he gave per head (often the equivalent of several months' pay for an ordinary worker) and the number of beneficiaries; 'these handouts of mine never reached fewer than 250,000 men,' he insists. He also catalogues other kinds of gifts and sponsorship. These were above all gladiatorial shows, 'athletic spectacles', wild beast hunts with animals specially imported from Africa (a later writer refers to 420 leopards on a single occasion) and one mock naval battle that became legendary. This was a huge triumph of engineering and ingenuity, for it was staged, as Augustus proudly explains, on an artificial lake, more than 500 metres by 350, specially constructed 'on the other side of the Tiber' (in modern Trastevere), and it featured 30 large warships plus even more smaller boats and 3,000 fighting men in addition to the rowers. On his own reckoning the Roman people could have counted on roughly one major entertainment at the emperor's expense each year. It was hardly the daily bloodbath of popular pleasure that the modern movie image of ancient Rome suggests, but it still involved a vast outlay of time, logistics and cash, as well as human and animal lives.

The message is clear. It was an axiom of the Augustan regime that the emperor paraded his generosity to the ordinary people of the city of Rome and that they in turn were to look to him as their patron, protector and benefactor. He made the same point when he took (or, technically, was given) 'the power of a tribune' for life. He was linking himself to the tradition of popular politicians, going back at least to the Gracchi, who stood up for the rights and welfare of the Roman in the street.

The final theme is his building. One part of this was a massive programme of restorations, of everything from roads and aqueducts to the Temple of Jupiter on the Capitoline, the founding monument of the Republic. With tremendous bravura, Augustus claims to have restored eighty-two temples of the gods in a single year – a number, not far short of all the temples in the city, that is clearly intended to underline his zealous piety, although it also suggests that the practical work done on each was not substantial. But like many tyrants, monarchs and dictators before and since, he also set about constructing what was in effect a new Rome and literally building himself into power. The *Res Gestae* itemises a wholesale redevelopment of the city centre, which exploited for the first time the marble quarries of northern Italy and the most lustrous, colourful and expensive stones that the empire had to offer. It turned the ramshackle old town into something that looked like an imperial capital. There was a huge new Forum to rival, if not overshadow, the old one, a new senate house, a theatre (still standing as the Theatre of Marcellus), porticoes, public halls (or basilicas) and walkways, as well as more than a dozen new temples, including one in honour of his father Julius Caesar. When Augustus said, as Suetonius quotes him, 'I found the city built of brick and left it built of marble,' this is what he meant. The *Res Gestae*

64. An imaginative reconstruction of Augustus' new Forum, which survives only in small sections (best now viewed from Mussolini's road, the Via dei Fori Imperiali, which overlies most of the Forum's piazza). Though certainly unreliable in detail, the drawing gives a good sense of the elaborate and highly planned character of this new development, in contrast to the rather ramshackle image of the old Republican Forum.

provides a gazetteer of his transformation of Rome's urban landscape.

It also amounts to a clear blueprint for one-man rule. Augustus' power, as he formulates it, is signalled by military conquest, by his role of protector and benefactor of the people in Rome and by construction and reconstruction on a vast scale; and it was underpinned by massive reserves of cash, combined with the display of respect for the ancient traditions of Rome. It was against this blueprint that every emperor for the next 200 years was judged. Even the most unmilitary types could use conquest to assert their right to rule, as the elderly Claudius did in 43 CE when he made as much as he possibly could out of 'his' victory, won entirely by his subordinates, over the island of Britain. And there was an ongoing competition among succeeding rulers about who could parade himself as the most generous to the Roman population or who could write his own story most noticeably into the fabric of the city. The emperor Trajan's soaring column, documenting his conquests across the river Danube in the early second century CE – and ingeniously securing maximum impact for minimum floor area – was one obvious winner. Hadrian's Pantheon was another. Finished in the 120s CE, the concrete span of its dome remained the widest in the world until 1958 (when it was beaten by the Centre of New Industries and Technologies building in Paris), and twelve of the original columns in its portico were each 12 metres high, carved from a single block of grey granite and specially transported 2,500 miles from the Egyptian desert. Ultimately this all went back to Augustus.

Power politics

The *Res Gestae* was always intended as a record of success, a retrospective parade of achievement that would also set a pattern for the future. It steers clear of any sign of difficulty, conflict or contest, except in briefly dismissing the long-dead adversaries of the civil war. And with its insistent series of first-person verbs ('I paid', 'I built', 'I gave') and matching pronouns (there are almost 100 'me's and 'mine's), it is more egocentric than any Roman public document before, composed in the style of an autocrat who appears to take his personal power for granted. That is, however, only one side of the Augustan story, seen from its successful end after more than forty years in power. It looked very different when he returned to Italy in 29 BCE, still as Octavian, with the example of Julius Caesar looming large. Caesar was his main access to power and legitimacy, as well as to that title 'son of a god', but he was also a warning of the fate that might lie in store. To be the son of an assassinated dictator was a mixed blessing. The big question in those early days was simple: how was he going to devise a form of rule that would win hearts and minds, defuse the opposition not wholly extinguished by the end of the war and allow him to stay alive?

Part of the answer came down to the language of power. For obvious Roman reasons, he did not call himself king. He made an elaborate show of rejecting the title 'dictator' too, distancing himself from Caesar's example. The story that a crowd of protesters once barricaded the senators in the senate house and threatened to burn it down over their heads if they did not make Augustus a dictator only added extra lustre to this refusal. Instead he chose to frame all his powers in terms of regular Republican office holding. To begin with, that meant being repeatedly elected consul, eleven times in all between 43 and 23 BCE, and on two isolated occasions later. Then, from the mid 20s BCE, he arranged to be granted a series of formal powers that were modelled on those of traditional Roman political offices but not the offices themselves: he took 'the power of a tribune' but did not hold the tribunate, and 'the rights of a consul' without holding the consulship.

This was a long way from the realities of traditional Republican practice, especially when he piled up multiple titles and offices together: the power of a tribune on top of the rights of a consul at the same time was unheard of; so too was his holding of not just one but all the major Roman priesthoods together. Whatever the later allegations of hypocrisy, he can hardly have been using these comfortable, old-fashioned titles to pretend that this was a return to the politics of the past. Romans were not, by and large, so unobservant that they would have failed to spot the autocracy lurking behind the fig leaf of 'the rights of a consul'. The point was that Augustus was cleverly adapting the traditional idioms to serve a new politics, justifying and making comprehensible a new axis of power by systematically reconfiguring an old language.

His rule was also presented as inevitable, as part of the natural and historical order: in short, as part of *how things were*. In 8 BCE the senate decided (who knows with what nudging?) that the month Sextilis, next to Julius Caesar's July, should be renamed August – and so Augustus became part of the regular passage of time, as he remains. Only the year before, the governor of the province of Asia had been thinking on similar lines when he persuaded the locals to align their calendar with the life cycle of the emperor and to begin their civic year on Augustus' birthday. The 23rd of September, the governor urged (in words still preserved in an inscription), might 'justly be considered equal to the beginning of all things ... for [Augustus] has given a different appearance to the whole world, a world which would have met its ruin if ... he had not been born'. In Rome, the language used might have been less overblown, but even there, myth and religion could usefully underpin Augustus' position. His claim to descend directly from Aeneas helped to portray the emperor as a fulfilment of Roman destiny, as the ordained refounder of Rome.

That is certainly one element in Virgil's epic story of Aeneas, with its clear echoes between the emperor and the legendary founding hero. But it is also seen vividly in the sculptural programme of Augustus' new Forum. This featured prominent statues of both Aeneas and Romulus and one of Augustus standing in a triumphal chariot in the centre of the piazza. The surrounding porticoes and arcades were lined with dozens of other statues, depicting 'the famous men of the Republic', each with a short text summing up his claim to fame: from Camillus and several Scipios to Marius and Sulla. The clear message was that the whole course of Roman history led up to Augustus, who now took centre stage. The story of the Republic had not been obliterated; it had been turned into a harmless backdrop to Augustan power, whose roots were found in the very origin of Rome. Or to put it another way, Augustus took over where the previous politics of Rome had collapsed. It was widely known that he was born in 63 BCE, the year of Catiline's conspiracy. Suetonius even claims that his father was held up by the birth and so was late for one of Cicero's big performances in the senate on the subject. No senatorial meeting was held on 23 September, so far as is known. But whether the story was an invention or not, the point was to present the same day as both the end of Republican politics, demonstrated in the corruption of Catiline, and the beginning of the life of the emperor.

There was, however, some much more ruthless realpolitik involved than this. Art, religion, myth, symbol and language, from the poetry of Virgil to the sculptural extravaganza of the new Forum, played an important part in grounding the new regime. But Augustus also took some down-to-earth steps to secure his position, by ensuring that the army was loyal to him and to no one else, by cutting off potential opponents from their support networks among the soldiers and the ordinary people and by transforming the senate from an aristocracy of competing dynasts, and possible rivals, into an aristocracy of service and honour. A classic 'poacher turned gamekeeper', Augustus set out to make sure that no one could easily follow the example of his own youth: that is, raise a private army and take over the state.

He took a monopoly on military force, but his regime was nothing like a modern military dictatorship. In our terms, Rome and Italy at this period were remarkably soldier free. Almost all the 300,000 Roman troops were stationed a safe distance away, near the boundaries of the Roman world and in areas of active campaigning, with only a very few troops, including the famous security forces known as the Praetorian Guard, based in Rome, which was otherwise a demilitarised zone. But Augustus became something no Roman had been before: the commander-in-chief of all the armed forces, who appointed their major officers, decided where and against whom the soldiers should fight, and claimed all victories as by definition his own, whoever had commanded on the ground.

He also secured his position by severing the links of dependence and personal loyalty between armies and their individual commanders, largely thanks to a simple, practical process of pension reform. This must count among the most significant innovations of his whole rule. He established uniform terms and conditions of army employment, fixing a standard term of service of sixteen years (soon raised to twenty) for legionaries and guaranteeing them on retirement a cash settlement at public expense amounting to about twelve times their annual pay or an equivalent in land. That ended once and for all the soldiers' reliance on their generals to provide for their retirement, which over the last century of the Republic had repeatedly led to the soldiers' private loyalty to their commander trumping their loyalty to Rome. In other words, after hundreds of years of a semi-public, semi-private militia, Augustus fully nationalised the Roman legions and removed them from politics. Although the Praetorian Guard continued to be a problematic political force, simply because of its proximity to the centre of power in Rome, only during two brief periods of civil war over the next two centuries, in the years 68 to 69 CE and again in 193 CE, were legions stationed outside the city instrumental in putting their candidates on the Roman throne.

This reform was one of the most expensive things Augustus ever did, and it was close to unaffordable. Unless he made a gross error in his arithmetic, the cost alone is an indication of the high priority he gave it. On a rough reckoning using the known military salary figures, the annual bill for regular pay combined with retirement packages for the whole army would now have come to about 450 million sesterces. That was, on an even rougher reckoning, the equivalent of more than half the total annual tax revenue of the empire. There are clear signs that, even with the huge reserves of state and emperor combined, it was hard to find the money. That is certainly the implication of the complaints of mutinous soldiers on the German frontier just after Augustus' death, who objected to being kept in service for much longer than the regulation twenty years or to being given a piece of worthless bog as a land settlement in lieu of a decent farm. Then as now, the easiest tactic for a government trying to reduce the pension bill was to raise the pension age.

At home there was a similar logic behind the gradual decline and eventual end of popular elections. This was not mainly an assault on what was left of Roman democracy, even if that was one inevitable consequence. More important, it was a clever way of inserting a wedge between the emperor's potential rivals and any large-scale popular or factional support in the city. Free elections had provided the glue of mutual dependence between prominent politicians and the people as a whole. As soon as ambitious individuals came to rely on the nod of the emperor rather than on the popular vote for public office and other sorts of preferment, they no longer had to attract the support of the people en masse, they were no longer compelled to build up a popular following and they had no institutional framework within which to do so. The intention was, as the *Res Gestae* more or less declares, that Augustus should monopolise the support of the people, edging the senators safely out of the picture.

Yet for all his autocratic power, Augustus still needed the senate. No sole ruler ever really rules alone. The Roman Empire had a light administrative footprint compared with the bureaucracy of all modern states and some ancient ones too. Even so, someone had to command the legions, govern the provinces, run the corn and water supplies and generally act as the deputy for an emperor who could not do every-thing. As is often the case in regime change, the new guard is more or less forced to rely on a carefully reformed version of the old guard, or – as we have seen in recent history – anarchy can result.

In broad terms, Augustus bought senatorial acquiescence and senat-orial service at the price of granting them honours, respect and in some cases new powers. Many of the old uncertainties were resolved, usually in the senate's favour. Senatorial decrees had previously been advisory only and in the last resort could be ignored or flouted, which was exactly what Caesar and Pompey did in 50 BCE when the senate instructed them both to disarm. These decrees were now given the force of law and gradually, along with the pronouncements of the em-peror, became the main form of Roman legislation. The split that Gaius Gracchus had opened up in the 120s BCE between senators and knights was made complete. The two groups were formally separated, and a new wealth qualification of a million sesterces, as against 400,000 for the knights, was now applied to a 'senatorial class'. Senatorial status was also made hereditary over three generations. That meant a senator's son and grandson could keep all the perks of being a senator without ever taking public office. Those perks increased too, as did the prohi-bitions that were intended to mark senatorial superiority: guaranteed front-row seats at all public shows on the one hand, an absolute ban on performing as an actor on the other.

In return, the senate became something much closer to an arm of administration in the service of the emperor. Augustus' introduction of a senatorial retirement age is just one hint of that. Senators also lost some of their most important and traditional marks of glory and status. For centuries, the acme of Roman ambition, the dream of every commander, even of the awkwardly unmilitary Cicero, had been to celebrate a triumph, parading through the streets with his spoils, prisoners and jubilant troops, dressed up as the god Jupiter. When on 27 March 19 BCE Lucius Cornelius Balbus, a one-time henchman of Julius Caesar, celebrated some victories he had scored on behalf of the new Augustan regime against some powerful Berber people on the edge of the Sahara, it was the last triumphal procession that an ordinary senatorial general was ever to have. Henceforth the ceremony was restricted entirely to emperors and their close family. It was not in the interests of the autocracy to share the fame and prominence that a triumph brought, and this was another glaring sign that the old Republic was finished.

It was also another case where a radical change of practice was made to seem somehow inevitable. As part of his celebration of the past – *as the past* – Augustus commissioned the register of all the triumphing generals, from Romulus to Balbus, displayed in the Roman Forum (p. 128). Much of it still survives, dug up in small fragments of a marble jigsaw puzzle that was first put together, it is said, by Michelangelo in the sixteenth century to decorate the new Palazzo dei Conservatori that he redesigned for the Capitoline Hill. It was laid out on four panels, and thanks to careful calculation on the part of the inscribers, the triumph of Balbus is recorded at the very bottom of the final panel, with no blank space underneath, leaving no room for more names. More than design symmetry was at stake here. The message was that the institution had not been interrupted in midstream. It had come to its natural end. There was no room for more.

Problems and successions

Things did not all go Augustus' way. Even through the generally celebratory ancient gloss on his rule, it is possible to glimpse what a much more troubled account might look like. In 9 CE, five years before his death, there was a terrible military disaster in Germany at the hands of local rebels and freedom fighters, which destroyed most of three legions. It did not stop the pacification of Germany from being a proud boast in the *Res Gestae*, but the severity of this defeat is supposed to have prompted Augustus to call a halt to projects for world conquest. At home there was more overt opposition to his rule than appears at first sight: there was offensive literature which ended up being burnt and conspiracies which he probably survived as much by luck as by anything else. Suetonius lists a number of dissidents and plotters, but as always with failed coups it is hard to tell what was driving them, between politics and personal grudges. It is never in the interests of the intended victim to give them a fair press.

In one case it seems likely that the changed political role of the elite and Augustus' control of elections was a major factor behind the discontent. The story of Marcus Egnatius Rufus, as it has come down to us, is predictably muddled in detail, but the bare bones are clear enough. Egnatius, first of all, challenged Augustus by making independent benefactions to the people. In particular, when he held the office of aedile in 22 BCE he used his own cash to set up a rudimentary city fire brigade. Augustus disapproved but decided to trump Egnatius by making 600 of his own slaves available for firefighting. A few years later, while Augustus was abroad, Egnatius attempted to stand for the consulship without the emperor's approval and at an illegally early age. This cannot have been an organised plot against the emperor: he was not in Rome to be disposed of anyway, which might have been why Egnatius thought he could get away with his stand. But when his candidacy was refused, there were popular riots. He was executed, on the decision of the senate, presumably with the absent emperor's agreement.

How many of his fellow senators sympathised with Egnatius Rufus is a matter of guesswork. We know nothing of his background and can only infer what his aims and motives were. Some modern historians have wanted to make him a kind of people's champion on the model of Clodius and other tribunes in the late Republic. But it looks much more likely that he was protesting against the erosion of senatorial independence and asserting the rights of the senators to their traditional links with the Roman people.

Beyond front-line politics, there were certainly subversive views of the symbolic world that Augustus was busy sponsoring, and his new image of Rome. The poet Ovid, a victim of the ruthless side of the Augustan regime, gives clear hints of how the mutterings on the street might have gone. Writing from his unhappy exile on the shores of the Black Sea, in a series of poems titled *Miseries* (*Tristia*) – often more barbed than sad – he took a witty potshot at the decoration of the temple dominating Augustus' new Forum, which featured statues of the gods Mars and Venus. As the father of Romulus and mother of Aeneas, these were the two founding deities of Rome. They were also the two most famous divine adulterers of classical mythology. As far back as Homer the story had been told of how Venus' cuckolded husband, Vulcan, the god of manufacture, had caught the pair embarrassingly *in flagrante*, cleverly trapping them in a metal net he specially constructed for the purpose. Hardly the appropriate symbol for the emperor's new, moral Rome, where adultery was a crime, the exiled poet insinuated. Some of the elaborate displays of *civilitas* may have backfired too. If it is really true that each time Augustus entered or left the senate he acknowledged every senator in turn by name, the whole palaver – allowing ten seconds per man and a fairly full house – would have taken about an hour and a half on entry and exit. For some it must have seemed a display of power rather than citizenly equality.

Even Virgil's *Aeneid*, the epic poem sponsored by the emperor himself, prompts troubling questions. The figure of Aeneas, Augustus' mythical ancestor and clearly intended to be some reflection of him, is a decidedly unstraightforward hero. Modern readers are probably much more disturbed than their ancient counterparts were by the way Aeneas abandons the unfortunate Dido and causes her terrible suicide on the pyre: the message is that mere passion should not deflect the pursuit of patriotic duty, and the dangerous image of Cleopatra behind the queen of Carthage underlines the point. But the final scene of the poem, in which Aeneas, now established in Italy, allows his rage to triumph as he brutally kills an enemy who has surrendered, has always been an unsettling conclusion. Such ambivalences have, of course, made the *Aeneid* a more powerful work of literature than thousands of lines of jingoistic praise would have been. But they continue to raise questions about Virgil's relationship with his patron and the Augustan regime. What went through Augustus' head when he first read, or listened to, those last lines? That was not for Virgil to tell. He died in 19 BCE, before, it was said, he had completed the final revision of his poem.

Augustus' bigger problem, however, was how to find a successor. It is clear that he intended to pass his power on. His enormous tomb in Rome, already completed in 28 BCE, was a powerful sign that he, unlike Antony, would be buried in Italian soil and that there would be a dynasty to follow him. He also built up the idea of an imperial family, including his wife Livia. One-man rule often brings women into greater prominence, not because they necessarily have any formal power but because, when one person takes key decisions of state in private, anyone with close access to that person is perceived as influential too. The woman who can whisper in her husband's ear wields more power de facto, or rather is often alleged to, than the colleague who can only send official requests and memos. On one occasion, Augustus acknowledged in a letter to the Greek city of Samos that Livia had been putting in a good word for it behind the scenes. But he seems more actively to have promoted her role beyond this, as a linchpin of his dynastic ambitions.

Livia had an official image in Roman sculpture, just as Augustus did (see plate 12). And she was granted a series of special legal privileges, including front-row seats at the theatre, financial independence and, from the civil war years, the right of *sacrosanctitas* ('inviolability'), modelled on the privilege of a tribune. *Sacrosanctitas* had originated in the Republic and had been intended to protect the people's representatives from attack. What in practice it protected Livia from is not so clear, but the important novelty is that it was explicitly based on the rights of a male public official. This was edging her into the official limelight more than any woman had been edged before. One poem, addressed to her on the death of her son Drusus in 9 BCE, even calls her *Romana princeps*. It was the female equivalent of a term regularly applied to Augustus, *Romanus princeps*, or 'first citizen of Rome', and meant something close to 'first lady'. An extravagant piece of hyperbole composed by a flatterer maybe, and certainly not a sign of growing emancipation of women in general, but it points to the public importance of the emperor's wife within a would-be imperial dynasty.

The trouble was that the couple had no children. Augustus had a single daughter, Julia, from an earlier marriage, and Livia already had Drusus and was pregnant with another son, Tiberius, when they married in 37 BCE. Whatever their later respectability, the start to their relationship had a scandalous tinge, branded by Antony as a disgraceful bit of philandering. In retaliation, presumably, for all the vicious rumours spread about his immoralities, he used to claim that the pair would meet at her husband's parties, go off to a convenient bedroom halfway through dinner and return looking tousled. But scandalous or respectable, the marriage produced no offspring: with Augustus, according to Suetonius, Livia had had just one premature stillbirth.

So the emperor went to great lengths to secure heirs who could be presented, in the circumstances, as legitimate successors. Julia, as his natural daughter, was the favourite instrument in his plans. She was married off first to her cousin Marcellus, who died when she was only sixteen; then to her father's friend and colleague Marcus Agrippa, more than twenty years her senior; then, in what must have looked the perfect arrangement, to Livia's son Tiberius. If an existing partner stood in the way of any of these matches, Augustus insisted on divorce. Only rarely does any hint survive of the personal cost of it all. Tiberius was reportedly devastated to be forced to part from his wife Vipsania Agrippina, the daughter of Agrippa by an earlier marriage, in order to marry Julia, who was now Agrippa's widow – a characteristic bit of dynastic confusion. On one occasion after their divorce Tiberius is said to have caught sight of Vipsania by chance, and it brought tears to his eyes; his minders made sure that he never saw her again. As for Julia, it may be that this series of arranged marriages had something to do with her notoriously rebellious sex life. One lurid story has it that she hosted wild parties on the *rostra* in the Forum; by a satisfying, or horrible, symmetry it was the very place from which her father had advocated his curbs on adultery. True or not, her affairs were one of the factors (alleged treason was another) that led to her being packed

65. Detail of a processional frieze from the Altar of Peace (*Ara Pacis*) in Rome commissioned in 13 BCE. This frieze featured the extended imperial family, including here on the left Agrippa. The woman behind him may be his then wife Julia, but she is more often identified as Livia.

off in 2 BCE to exile on an island about half a mile square and never returning to Rome.

The end result of all this dynastic planning is that the family tree of what is now called the Julio-Claudian dynasty (Julius being Augustus' family name, Claudius that of Livia's first husband) became so bafflingly complicated that is impossible to diagram clearly on paper, let alone recall in any detail. But even so, the desired heirs either did not appear or, if they did, died too soon. The marriage of Tiberius and Julia produced only one child, who did not survive childhood. Augustus adopted two sons of her marriage to Agrippa as a way of marking them out as heirs (while further confusing the family tree). They were carefully portrayed around the Roman world looking the spitting image of their adoptive father; but one died of an illness in 2 CE aged just nineteen, the other in 4 CE after being wounded on campaign in the East and before his marriage (to another relative) had produced a child. In the end, despite all his efforts, Augustus was back where he could have started all along, with Livia's son Tiberius, who became the next emperor in 14 CE. Pliny the Elder could not resist pointing out one other irony of this. Tiberius Claudius Nero, the new emperor's father, had been on Antony's side in the civil war, and his family had been among those besieged at Perusia. Augustus died, Pliny quipped, 'with the son of his enemy as his heir'.

Augustus is dead. Long live Augustus!

Augustus died on 19 August 14 CE, shortly before his seventy-sixth birthday, at one of his houses in southern Italy. According to Suetonius, he had been holidaying on the island of Capri, playing learned games with his guests – insisting, for example, that all the Roman guests should dress as Greeks and speak Greek, while all the Greek guests should act as Romans. The end was all very low-key. By the time he returned to the mainland, his stomach was giving him trouble, and eventually it forced him to his bed, where, somewhat surprisingly, given the fate of so many of his contemporaries, he died. There were rumours later that Livia had had a hand in his end, with some poisoned figs, to ease Tiberius' accession to power, just as some had said she had hastened the end of other family members for fear that they would spoil Tiberius' chances of the throne. But it was another case of unexplained deaths in the Roman world – as the majority were outside battle, childbirth and accident – attracting that sort of gossip whether there was any foundation for it or not. And poisoning was always supposed to be the woman's weapon of choice. It required no physical strength, only cunning, and was a frightful inversion of her traditional role of nurturer.

Others believed, more plausibly, that Livia played a major part in smoothing the transition from Augustus to Tiberius. As soon as her husband's death looked imminent, she sent for her son, who was about five days' journey away across the Adriatic. Meanwhile she kept issuing optimistic bulletins about Augustus' health until Tiberius arrived and the death could be announced; when the old man really died was always a matter of dispute. But whether it was before or after his heir's arrival, the accession proved fairly seamless. The body was carried more than 100 miles to Rome from where he died at Nola, on the shoulders of the leading men of the towns along the route. There was no coronation ceremony; whatever use Augustus had made of his triumph in 29 BCE, there was no specific Roman ritual to mark imperial accession. But Tiberius was already effectively in control as the new emperor when he arranged a meeting of the senate to make public Augustus' will, bequests and other instructions for the future and to discuss the funeral arrangements.

There are a few hints that the organisers were anxious about possible trouble. Why else did they have the ceremony and the funeral route guarded by troops? But all passed off peacefully, and in a way

66. This is a *simplified* version of the family and descendants of Augustus and Livia; emperors are marked in bold type. The complexities of adoption and multiple marriages, combined with any number of characters with the same name, make it close to baffling; but baffling complexity was part of the point of dynasty.

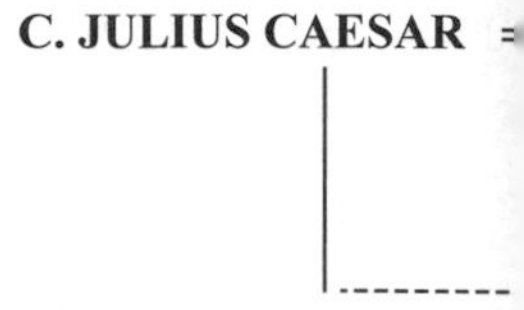

C. JULIUS CAESAR =

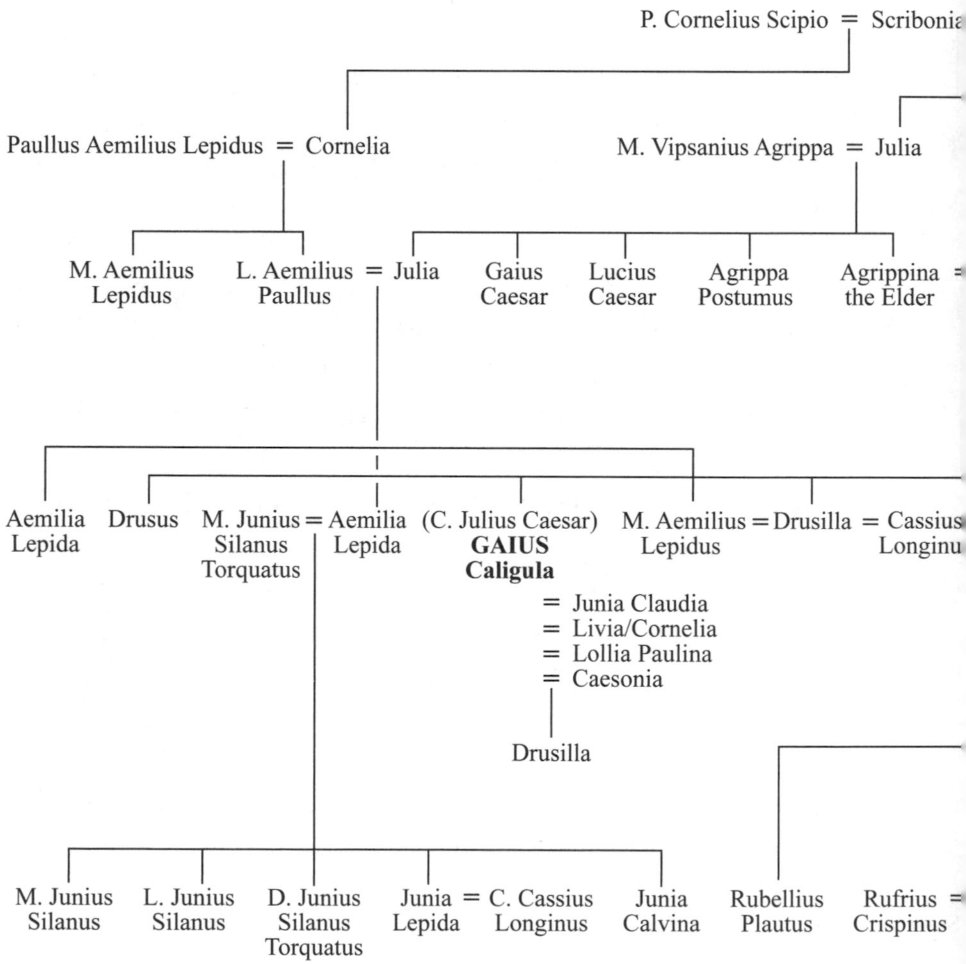

P. Cornelius Scipio = Scribonia

Paullus Aemilius Lepidus = Cornelia

M. Vipsanius Agrippa = Julia

M. Aemilius Lepidus

L. Aemilius Paullus = Julia

Gaius Caesar

Lucius Caesar

Agrippa Postumus

Agrippina the Elder =

Aemilia Lepida

Drusus

M. Junius Silanus Torquatus = Aemilia Lepida

(C. Julius Caesar) **GAIUS Caligula**
= Junia Claudia
= Livia/Cornelia
= Lollia Paulina
= Caesonia

M. Aemilius Lepidus = Drusilla = Cassius Longinus

Drusilla

M. Junius Silanus

L. Junius Silanus

D. Junius Silanus Torquatus

Junia Lepida = C. Cassius Longinus

Junia Calvina

Rubellius Plautus

Rufrius Crispinus =

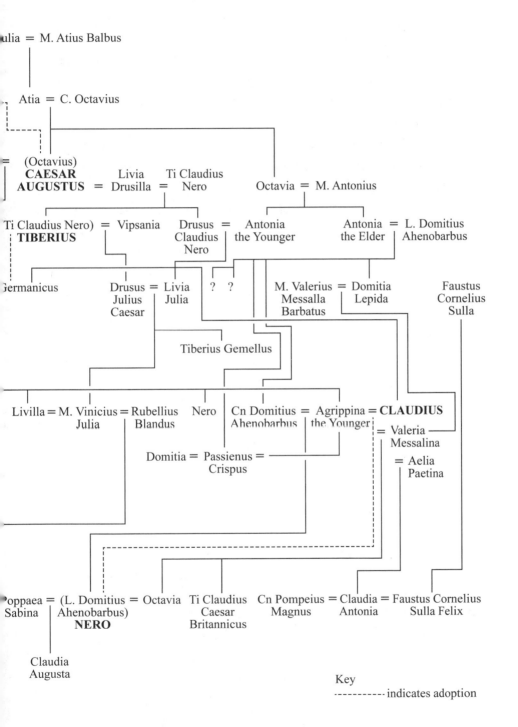

ulia = M. Atius Balbus

Atia = C. Octavius

= (Octavius)
CAESAR   Livia   Ti Claudius
AUGUSTUS = Drusilla = Nero   Octavia = M. Antonius

Ti Claudius Nero) = Vipsania   Drusus = Antonia   Antonia = L. Domitius
  TIBERIUS   Claudius the Younger   the Elder Ahenobarbus
                             Nero

Germanicus   Drusus = Livia   ? ?   M. Valerius = Domitia   Faustus
                  Julius   Julia   Messalla   Lepida   Cornelius
                  Caesar   Barbatus   Sulla

                         Tiberius Gemellus

Livilla = M. Vinicius = Rubellius   Nero   Cn Domitius = Agrippina = **CLAUDIUS**
          Julia   Blandus   Ahenobarbus the Younger
                                                                    = Valeria
                 Domitia = Passienus =   Messalina
                           Crispus   = Aelia
                                                                     Paetina

Poppaea = (L. Domitius = Octavia Ti Claudius Cn Pompeius = Claudia = Faustus Cornelius
Sabina | Ahenobarbus)   Caesar   Magnus   Antonia   Sulla Felix
          NERO   Britannicus

    Claudia
    Augusta   Key
                                  ---------- indicates adoption

that would have been more or less familiar to Polybius more than 150 years earlier, even if on a more lavish scale. A wax model of Augustus, not the body itself, was propped up on the *rostra* while Tiberius delivered the funeral address. The procession featured images not only of Augustus' ancestors but also of great Romans of the past, including Pompey and Romulus, as if Augustus had been the descendant of them all. After the cremation, Livia – now called Augusta, because Augustus had formally adopted her in his will – rewarded with the sum of a million sesterces the man who swore that he had seen Augustus soaring to heaven. Augustus was now a god.

The emperor in his human form remained enigmatic to the last. Among his final words to his assembled friends, before a lingering kiss with Livia, was a characteristically shifty quotation from a Greek comedy: 'If I have played my part well, then give me applause.' What kind of act had he been playing all those years? they were supposed to wonder. And where was the real Augustus? And who wrote his lines? Those questions remain. How Augustus managed to recast so much of the political landscape of Rome, how he managed to get his own way for more than forty years, and with what support, is still puzzling. Who, for example, made the decision about his (or Livia's) official image? What kind of discussions, and with whom, lay behind the new scheme for army service and pensions? How far was he simply lucky to have survived so long?

Nonetheless, the broad framework he set out for being an emperor lasted for more than 200 years – or, to put it another way, for the rest of the period covered by this book. Every later emperor we shall meet *was* or at least impersonated Augustus. They used the name Augustus among their imperial titles, and they inherited his personal signet ring, which is supposed to have passed down the line from one to the next. This was no longer his original favourite, the sphinx. Over the decades he had changed the design, first to a portrait of Alexander the Great and finally to a portrait of himself. Augustus' head, in other words, and his distinctive features became the signature of each of his successors. Whatever their idiosyncrasies, virtues, vices or backgrounds, whatever the different names we know them by, they were all better or worse reincarnations of Augustus, operating within the model of autocracy he established and dealing with the problems that he left unresolved.

It is to some of the problems facing this series of new Augusti that we now turn – starting with another death.

CHAPTER TEN

·

FOURTEEN EMPERORS

The men on the throne

ON 24 JANUARY 41 CE, almost thirty years after the first Augustus had died in his bed and eighty-five years after the death of Julius Caesar, there was another violent assassination in Rome. This time the victim was the emperor Gaius – or, to give him his full name, Gaius Julius Caesar Augustus Germanicus – who four years earlier had succeeded his great-uncle, the elderly Tiberius, to the throne. He was the second in the series of fourteen emperors, not counting three short-lived claimants in one brief period of civil war through 68 and 69 CE, who ruled Rome in the almost 180 years between the death of Augustus and that of the emperor Commodus, who was assassinated in 192 CE. These include some of the most resonant names in Roman history: Claudius, who replaced Gaius and was given a starring role as a scholarly and shrewd observer of palace politics in the novels of Robert Graves *I, Claudius* and *Claudius the God*; Nero, with his reputation for family murder, lyre playing, Christian persecution and pyromania; Marcus Aurelius, the 'philosopher-emperor', whose philosophical *Thoughts* is even now a bestseller; and Commodus, whose exploits in the arena were re-created, not wholly inaccurately, in the movie *Gladiator*. They also include those who, despite all the ingenuity of modern biographers, survive as little more than names: the elderly Nerva, for example, who held power for just eighteen months at the end of the first century CE.

Tiberius
14 CE – 37 CE

Gaius (Caligula)
37 CE – 41 CE

Claudius
41 CE – 54 CE

Nero
54 CE – 68 CE

Three short-
term emperors
– Galba, Otho
and Vitellius
– between the
death of Nero
and the accession
of Vespasian.

Vespasian
69 CE – 79 CE

Titus
79 CE – 81 CE

Domitian
81 CE – 96 CE

Nerva
96 CE – 98 CE

Trajan
98 CE – 117 CE

Hadrian
117 CE – 138 CE

Antoninus Pius
138 CE – 161 CE

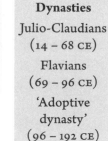

Marcus Aurelius.
161 CE – 180 CE

Lucius Verus.
Joint ruler with
Marcus Aurelius
161 CE – 169 CE

Commodus
180 CE – 192 CE

Dynasties

Julio-Claudians
(14 – 68 CE)

Flavians
(69 – 96 CE)

'Adoptive
dynasty'
(96 – 192 CE)

The murder of Gaius is one of the best-documented events in this whole period of Roman history, and it certainly gives us the most detailed account to survive of any emperor's fall. It is told over thirty modern pages, as an elaborate digression within an encyclopaedic history of the Jews, written some fifty years after the event by Titus Flavius Josephus – a leading Jewish rebel against the Romans in the 60s CE (under the name of Joseph ben Matthias) who changed sides, politically if not religiously, and ended up almost a writer-in-residence at the Roman court. For Josephus, Gaius' murder was divine punishment visited upon an emperor who had scorned the Jews and even erected a statue of himself in the Temple. But to judge from the circumstantial details, in retelling the story, he had on his desk a memoir of what happened in January 41 CE written by someone close to the action.

Josephus' account of the assassination is richly revealing about the new world of politics that followed the first Augustus, from the palace intrigues, through the empty slogans of the old senatorial elite and the problems of succession, to the perils of being an emperor on the throne. What is more, the various assessments, both ancient and modern, of Gaius' faults and failings, of what lay behind his murder and of what followed it point to important questions: about how the reputation of Roman emperors was created, about how their success or failure was, and is, judged and – even more fundamentally – about how far the character and qualities, marriages and murders, of the individual rulers help us understand the broader history of Rome under imperial rule.

So how was Gaius killed, and why?

What went wrong with Gaius?

The emperor Tiberius, who took over from his adoptive father Augustus, apparently seamlessly, in 14 CE, grew increasingly reclusive over the last decade of his rule, spending most of his time on the island of Capri, only remotely in touch with the capital. When Gaius was acclaimed emperor on Tiberius' death in 37 CE, he must have seemed like a welcome change. Just twenty-four years old, he had as good a claim to the throne as any Julio-Claudian could hope for. His mother, Agrippina, was the daughter of Julia, and so the granddaughter of Augustus in his direct bloodline. His father, Germanicus – once tipped as a future emperor before his early, and predictably suspicious, death – was both a grandson of Livia and a great-nephew of Augustus. It was thanks to his parents that Gaius ended up with the embarrassing nickname Caligula ('Bootikins'), by which he is now better known. They had taken him as a young child on military campaigns and dressed him up in a miniature

68. This bust presents Gaius in military guise, wearing an elaborate breastplate. Around his head is a wreath of oak-leaves, the *corona civica* (or civic crown), traditionally awarded to Romans who saved the lives of their fellow citizens in battle.

soldier's uniform, including some trademark miniature army boots (*caligae* in Latin).

His assassination, after just four years on the throne, by three soldiers from the Praetorian Guard, was as bloody and messy as Caesar's. In the ancient world, murder was rarely possible from a safe distance. Killing usually meant getting up close and often spilling a lot of blood. As both Caesar and Gaius found, anyone in power was most at risk from those who were allowed to come closest to them: from wives and children, bodyguards, colleagues, friends and slaves. Yet the contrast between the two assassinations is striking too, and a sign of changed times between the Republic and the rule of the emperors. It was fellow senators who stabbed Caesar, at a public meeting, in full view, as they were presenting a petition. Gaius was hacked to pieces at home, all alone in a deserted corridor, by some of the crack troops who were supposed to ensure the regime's home security. And when his wife came with her baby daughter to find the body, they too were eliminated.

The emperor, Josephus explains, had been watching some performances on the Palatine Hill at the annual festival held there in memory of the first Augustus, timed to coincide with the wedding anniversary of the first imperial couple. At the end of the morning's show, he decided to skip lunch – another version claims that he was feeling slightly nauseous after overindulging the night before – and to go on his own from the theatre to his private baths. As he walked down a passage between two of the properties that were part of the growing 'palace complex' (already far more extensive than Augustus' relatively modest accommodation), the three praetorians, NCOs in our terms, attacked him. A personal grudge reputedly drove the leader, Cassius Chaerea. He had often acted as the emperor's agent, torturer and enforcer, but Gaius in return is supposed to have repeatedly and publicly mocked his effeminacy ('girlie' was one of the favourite taunts). This was Chaerea's revenge.

There may also have been some higher principles driving the plot and more widespread support for it among soldiers and senators. Or so the many stories told of Gaius' villainies suggest. His incest with his sisters and his mad plans to make his horse a consul have become notorious. His vanity building projects have been placed somewhere on the spectrum between an affront to the laws of nature and ludicrous display. (Imagine him, as more than one ancient writer pictures the scene, prancing on horseback along a roadway constructed on top of a bridge of boats across the Bay of Naples, wearing the breastplate of Alexander the Great ...) His valiant soldiers were disgracefully humiliated by being made to hunt for seashells on a French beach. And his gleeful menace directed at the long-suffering Roman aristocracy became legendary. On one famous occasion he was caught bursting into laughter at a palace dinner party when he was reclining next to the two consuls. 'What's the joke?' one asked politely. 'Just the thought that I would only have to nod and your throats would be cut on the spot,' came the reply. Someone else would have wielded the knife if Chaerea had not.

Whatever the exact motives for the assassination, however, this was a new politics: a hit squad operating behind closed doors and a dynastic murder that demanded that the victim's immediate family should share his fate. No one had gone after Julius Caesar's wife. It also revealed that, despite Augustus' largely successful attempts to remove the Roman legions from politics, the few soldiers stationed in the city could wield an enormous amount of power if they chose. In 41 CE it was not just that a group of disaffected praetorians killed one emperor; the Praetorian Guard immediately installed his successor. The emperor's most intimate personal bodyguard, a small private militia of Germans, chosen because their barbarity was thought to be a guarantee against corruption, also played a bloody part in what happened next.

As soon as news of the murder leaked out, the Germans proved their brutal, thuggish loyalty. They ran through the Palatine, killing anyone they suspected of involvement in the plot. One senator was slaughtered because his toga was splattered with animal blood from a religious sacrifice earlier in the day, which gave the impression that he might have been involved in the emperor's killing. And they terrorised the people who were still mingling in the theatre after the emperor had left. These remnants of the audience were barricaded in, until a kindly doctor intervened. He had come there to treat those who had been wounded in the aftermath of the assassination, and he engineered the evacuation of the innocent bystanders by sending them off on the pretext of picking up medical supplies.

Meanwhile, the senate met in the Temple of Jupiter on the Capitoline Hill, the great symbolic monument of the Republic, and exchanged fine words about the end of political slavery and the return of liberty. It was a hundred years, they calculated, since freedom had been lost – presumably thinking that the deal arranged in 60 BCE by Pompey, Caesar and Crassus, as the Gang of Three, was the turning point – and so it was a particularly auspicious moment to reclaim it. The consul Gnaeus Sentius Saturninus delivered the most stirring speech. He was too young, he admitted, to remember the Republic, but he had seen with his own eyes 'the evils with which tyrannies fill the state'. A new dawn had come with the murder of Gaius: 'No despot is set over you now who can get away with ruining the city … what recently nurtured the tyranny was nothing other than our inaction … Weakened by the pleasure of peace we learned to live like slaves … Our first duty now is to give the highest possible honours to those who have killed the tyrant.' This sounded impressive but proved hollow. All the time Saturninus spoke, he was wearing his usual signet ring, which loyally featured the head of Gaius. One observer, spotting the inconsistency between the words and the jewellery, went up and tore it off his finger.

The whole performance was in any case too late. The Praetorian

Guard, who had a low view of the capabilities of the senate and no desire to return to the Republic, had already picked a new emperor. The story was that, terrified by the violence and commotion, Gaius' uncle the fifty-year-old Claudius had hidden himself down another dark alley. But he was quickly discovered by the praetorians and, though fearing he too was about to be killed, was hailed as emperor instead. His blood relationship with Livia and Augustus made him as plausible a candidate as anyone, and he was conveniently on the spot.

Edgy negotiations, careful publicity and awkward decisions followed. Claudius gave each of the praetorians a vast handout: 'the first emperor to use bribery to secure the loyalty of the soldiers', carped the biographer Suetonius, as if Augustus had not done much the same thing. The senators gave up any idea of Republican liberty and were soon demanding no more than that Claudius should formally accept the throne from them, while most of them quickly scuttled off to the safety of their country estates. Instead of receiving 'the highest possible honours', Chaerea and one of his fellow assassins were executed, the new emperor's advisors sternly arguing that, while the deed had been a glorious one, disloyalty should nevertheless be punished to discourage any repetition. Claudius continued to claim that he was a reluctant ruler, thrust into power against his will. Maybe that was true, but a parade of reluctance has often provided a useful cover for ruthless ambition. It was not long before sculptors across the Roman world were going with the times and were busy recarving redundant portraits of Gaius to give them passable versions of the features of his old uncle, the new emperor.

These events are a vivid snapshot of the politics of Roman autocracy almost thirty years after the death of Augustus. The senate's ineffective posturing over the restoration of the Republic serves only to prove that the old system of government was gone for good, little more than a nostalgic fantasy conjured up by those who had never experienced it. As Josephus hints, anyone who could loudly advocate a return to Republican rule while sporting the emperor's portrait on his ring did not understand what Republican rule was about. The confusion and violence that followed the assassination not only shows how easy it was for a peaceful morning of theatrical performance to turn into a bloodbath but also points to all kinds of different political views between senate, soldiers and ordinary people. The majority of the rich and privileged were celebrating the death of a tyrant. The poor were instead lamenting the murder of their hero. Josephus singles out for scorn the folly of the women, children and slaves who 'were reluctant to accept the truth' and joyfully believed the false rumours that Gaius had been patched up and was walking around the Forum. It is clear enough that those who were pleased to see him out of the way did not agree on what should happen next. Many more did not want to see their emperor assassinated at all.

Those differences of opinion challenge orthodoxies and raise some bigger historical questions. Was Gaius really as monstrous as he has been consistently painted? Had the ordinary people, as Josephus suggests, been taken in by an emperor reputed to make extravagantly

69. The slightly awkward appearance of this portrait of Claudius, especially in the hair, is due to an identity change. A head of Gaius has been recut into a head of his successor. It is a nice symbol of the erasure of the previous regime, while also hinting that there was less difference between individuals than we like to think.

generous gestures to the crowds – on one occasion, it was said, standing on top of a building in the Forum and literally throwing money down at the bystanders? Maybe they had. But there are some strong reasons to be suspicious about many of the standard tales of Gaius' wickedness that have we have inherited.

Some of these tales are simply implausible. Leaving aside his histrionics in the Bay of Naples, could he really have built a huge bridge in Rome from the Palatine Hill to the Capitoline Hill of which no sure trace remains? Almost all our stories were written years after the emperor's death, and the most extravagant look weaker the more they are examined. The one about the seashells may well go back to a confusion around the Latin word *musculi*, which can mean both 'shells' and 'military huts'. Were the soldiers actually dismantling a temporary camp and not on a shell hunt? And the first surviving reference to incest is found only at the end of the first century CE, while the clearest evidence for it seems to be his deep distress at the death of his sister Drusilla, which is hardly clinching proof of sexual relations. The idea of some modern writers that his dinner parties came close to orgies, with his sisters 'underneath' him and his wife 'on top', rests simply on a mistranslation of the words of Suetonius, who is referring to the place settings – 'above' and 'below' – at a Roman dining table.

It would be naive to imagine that Gaius was an innocent and benevolent ruler, horribly misunderstood or consistently misrepresented. But it is hard to resist the conclusion that, whatever kernel of truth they might have, the stories told about him are an inextricable mixture of fact, exaggeration, wilful misinterpretation and outright invention – largely constructed after his death, and largely for the benefit of the new emperor, Claudius, whose legitimacy on the throne depended partly on the idea that his predecessor had been rightly eliminated. As it was in the interests of Augustus to vilify Antony so it was in the interests of the Claudian regime, and of those under the new emperor who wanted to distance themselves from the old, to pile abuse on

Gaius, whatever the truth. To put it another way, Gaius may have been assassinated because he was a monster, but it is equally possible that he was made into a monster because he was assassinated.

But suppose – ignoring all suspicions – that the stories are entirely accurate, that the ordinary people had been merely gullible and that Rome had been under the rule of a mad sadist somewhere between a clinical psychopath and a Stalin. The truth is that, beyond making it absolutely clear that emperors had become a permanent fixture, the killing of Gaius had no significant impact on the long history of imperial rule at all. That was one thing the assassins of 41 CE had in common with the assassins of 44 BCE, who killed one autocrat (Julius Caesar) only to end up with another (Augustus). For all the excitement generated by the murder of Gaius, the suspense, the uncertainty of the moment and the flirtation with Republicanism, as brief as it was unrealistic, the end result was another emperor on the throne who was not all that unlike the one he had replaced. Claudius may have had a better and far more bookish posthumous reputation than Gaius; for it was not so obviously in the interests of his adopted son and successor, Nero, to damn his memory. But scratch the surface, and he too has a grim record of cruelty and criminality (35 senators, out of a total of about 600, and 300 equestrians put to death during his rule, according to one ancient tally), and he filled the same slot in the Roman power structure.

That is one message of the recarving of the portraits of the old emperor. Economic good sense must in part have driven the clever alterations. Any sculptor who had nearly finished a head of Gaius in January 41 CE would not have wanted to see his time and money wasted with a useless portrait of a deposed ruler; far better to recast it quickly into the likeness of the new man on the throne. Some of the changes may also have been a form of symbolic elimination. Romans often tried to strike from the record those who had fallen from favour, demolishing their houses, pulling down their statues and erasing their names from public inscriptions (often with crude chisel marks, which serve mainly to draw attention to the names they wanted forgotten). But another underlying point, much like the message of Augustus and the ravens, is that emperors were more similar to one another than they were different, and that it took only some superficial adjustments to turn one into the next. Assassinations were minor interruptions to the grander narrative of imperial rule.

'Good emperors' and 'bad emperors'?

The standard story of the almost two centuries of autocracy between Tiberius and Commodus, those fourteen emperors across three imperial dynasties, focuses on the virtues and vices of the man on the throne, and on his abuse and use of autocratic power. It is hard to imagine Roman history without Nero 'fiddling while Rome burned' (more precisely, irresponsibly playing his lyre while the city was destroyed in a vast blaze in 64 CE), bungling an attempt to murder his mother by drowning her in a collapsible boat (a peculiar combination of ingenuity, cruelty and absurdity) or torturing Christians, as if they were to blame for the great fire, in the first of a sporadic series of violent Roman reactions to the new religion. But Nero is only one of a wide repertoire of different versions of imperial sadism.

The emperor Commodus, dressed as a gladiator and threatening the senators in the front-row seats of the Colosseum by waving the head of a decapitated ostrich at them, is often taken to sum up the ludicrous sadism of corrupt autocracy. One eyewitness, describing the incident, admits that he was terrified but, at the same time, so dangerously close to laughter that he had to pluck some laurel leaves from the wreath he was wearing and stuff them in his mouth to stifle the giggles. The antics of the reclusive Tiberius in his swimming pool on the island of Capri, where boys ('little fishes') were reputedly employed to nibble

at his genitals underwater, point to the exploitative sexuality of imperial power – the scenes being gleefully re-enacted in Bob Guccione's
1970s film *Caligula*. Even more chilling is the story of how Domitian
turned sadism into a solitary pastime. He is said to have shut himself
up alone in his room, whiling away the hours torturing flies by killing them with his pen. 'Is there anyone in there with the emperor?'
someone once asked. 'Not even a fly' was one courtier's sharp reply.

There are occasional examples of outstanding imperial virtue too.
The philosophical *Thoughts* of the emperor Marcus Aurelius, cliché
as much of it is ('Do not act as if you were going to live 10,000 years.
Death hangs over you'), still finds many admirers, buyers and advocates today, from self-help gurus to former US president Bill Clinton.
The heroic common sense of Vespasian, Domitian's father, deserves
to be as well known. Coming to the throne in 69 CE after the extravagant Nero, he was reputed to be a shrewd manager of the imperial
finances, right down to putting a tax on human urine, a key ingredi-
ent in the ancient laundry and cloth-processing industry. He almost
certainly never uttered the snappy quip on the subject, '*Pecunia non
olet*' ('Money doesn't smell'), often attributed to him, but it captures
just the right spirit. He was also renowned for puncturing imperial
pretensions, including his own. 'That serves me right for being a silly
old man and wanting a triumph at my age,' he is supposed to have said
at the end of his triumphal procession in 71 CE, after he had been on
his feet all day in a bumpy chariot, at the age of sixty-one.

These emperors are some of the most vividly drawn characters in
the Roman world. But all the intriguing circumstantial details, from
the swing of their togas to their bald patches, can deflect us from the
more fundamental questions already glimpsed underneath the story of
Gaius. How far it is useful to see Roman history in terms of imperial
biographies or to divide the story of the empire into emperor-sized
(or dynasty-sized) chunks? How accurate are the standard images
of these rulers that have come down to us? What exactly did the

emperor's character explain? How much difference, and to whom, did the qualities of the man on the throne make?

Ancient biographers, historians and political analysts certainly believed that it made a great deal of difference, hence their focus on the flaws and failings, hypocrisies and sadism of the Augusti, and occasionally on their sturdy patience or tolerant good humour. Suetonius, in his series of biographies *The Twelve Caesars*, ranging from Julius Caesar to Domitian, including the three short-lived claimants of 68 to 69 CE, gives pride of place to the kind of revealing personal anecdotes that I have just quoted, and he lavishes attention on the diagnostic minutiae of his subjects' eating habits, style of dress, sex life and clever sayings, from jokes to last words. It is here that we read of Tiberius' acne, Claudius' recurrent indigestion and Domitian's habit of going swimming with prostitutes.

Even the far more cerebral Publius Cornelius Tacitus relished such personal details. In his account of the first two imperial dynasties, ending with Domitian, Tacitus, a successful senator and cynical historian, offers the most hard-hitting analysis of political corruption to survive from the ancient world – albeit written from the safe distance of the reign of Trajan in the early second century CE. He certainly had an eye for the big picture. The first sentence of his *Annales* (or *Chronicles*), a history of the Julio-Claudian emperors from Tiberius to Nero, runs simply 'From the very beginning, *kings* have ruled the city of Rome': '*Urbem Romam a principio reges habuere.*' In just six Latin words, it was a direct challenge to the ideological foundations of the regime and the insistence of the Augusti that they were not a monarchy in the old sense. But Tacitus regularly rests his case on the character and the crimes of the individuals on the throne. He embellishes his description, for example, of the attempted murder of Nero's mother, Agrippina, in the collapsible boat into a ghastly baroque tale, including one horrible detail of human naivety and imperial ruthlessness. While Agrippina swam gamely to the shore, her drowning maid tried to save her own skin by shouting out that *she* was the emperor's mother: the desperate lie only ensured her instant slaughter at the hands of Nero's henchmen.

Much of the great tradition of modern writing on the Roman emperors has been framed in similar terms, around imperial characters good and bad. The words of Edward Gibbon, whose *History of the Decline and Fall of the Roman Empire* was published in instalments from 1776, have had enormous influence on the views of generations of later historians. Before broaching the main theme of his title, Gibbon briefly reflects on the earlier period of one-man rule between Tiberius and Commodus, and he singles out for praise the emperors in the second century CE. His memorable aphorism, crafted with typical eighteenth-century self-confidence, is still much quoted: 'If a man were called to fix the period in the history of the world, during which the condition of the human race was most happy and prosperous, he would, without hesitation, name that which elapsed from the death of Domitian to the accession of Commodus' – that is, what many since have called the period of the 'good emperors': Nerva, Trajan, Hadrian, Antoninus Pius, Marcus Aurelius and Lucius Verus.

These were rulers, Gibbon goes on, whose characters and authority 'commanded involuntary respect' and who 'delighted in the image of liberty'. Their only regret, he concludes, must have been the knowledge that some unworthy successor ('some licentious youth or some jealous tyrant') would soon appear to ruin everything, as their predecessors had almost all done in the past: 'the dark unrelenting Tiberius, the furious Caligula, the feeble Claudius, the profligate and cruel Nero … and the timid inhuman Domitian'.

It is a magisterial way of summing up almost two centuries of Roman history. Gibbon lived in an age when historians made judgements 'without hesitation' and were prepared to believe that the Roman world might have been a better place to live than their own. It is also deeply misleading, for several reasons. The various rulers were not easy to fit into any standard, stereotypical image. Gibbon himself concedes – in lines that are now rarely quoted, because they spoil the splendid certainty of the aphorism – that one of his favourites, Hadrian, could be vain, capricious and cruel, as much a jealous tyrant as an excellent prince. Gibbon must have known the story of how Hadrian had his architect put to death over a disagreement about building design; if true, it is a piece of imperial abuse worthy of Gaius.

And some of the modern admirers of the gentle philosopher-emperor Marcus Aurelius would be less admiring if they reflected on the brutality of his suppression of the Germans, proudly illustrated in the scenes of battle that circle their way up his commemorative column that still stands in the centre of Rome; though less famous,

70. A typical scene of Roman violence from Marcus Aurelius' column. The bound German prisoners are lined up and executed one by one. The head lying on the ground, next to its body, is a particularly gruesome touch.

it was clearly intended to rival Trajan's and was carefully built just a little taller (see plate 10).

There are also all the problems of sorting fact from fantasy that we find in the various stories about the villainies of Gaius. The many ancient tales of imperial transgression certainly offer unforgettable insights into Roman anxieties, suspicions and prejudices. How exactly Roman writers imagined that bad emperors revealed their badness can tell us an enormous amount about Roman cultural assumptions and morality more generally, from the particular frisson that attached – and still does – to sex in swimming pools, to the more surprising objection to cruelty to flies (probably a sign that there was nothing so trivial in the world that Domitian would not make a hobby out of hurting it). But as evidence for the reality of imperial rule, they remain a mixture of accurate reporting, exaggeration and guesswork that it is almost always impossible to untangle.

What went on behind the closed doors of the palace was usually secret. Some facts leaked out, some pronouncements were made in public, but for the most part conspiracy theories flourished. It did not take much to turn a nearly tragic boating accident into a bungled murder attempt (how, anyway, did Tacitus know about the foolish gambit of Agrippina's servant?). And what we would call urban myths abounded. More or less identical anecdotes and apparently spontaneous bons mots turn up in the biographies of different rulers. Was it Domitian or was it Hadrian who wryly observed that no one would believe there was a plot against an emperor until he was found dead? Maybe both of them did. Maybe Domitian coined it and Hadrian repeated it. Or maybe it was a convenient cliché about the dangers of high rank that could be put into the mouth of almost any ruler.

More generally, the politics of regime change had a major influence on how each emperor went down in history, as imperial careers and characters were reinvented to serve the interests of those who followed them. The basic rule of Roman history is that those who were assassinated were, like Gaius, demonised. Those who died in their beds, succeeded by a son and heir, natural or adopted, were praised as generous and avuncular characters, devoted to the success of Rome, who did not take themselves too seriously.

These are the considerations that have recently encouraged a few brave, revisionist attempts to rehabilitate some of the most notorious imperial monsters. A number of modern historians have presented Nero in particular more as a victim of the propaganda of the Flavian dynasty, starting with Vespasian, which succeeded him, than as a self-obsessed, mother-killing pyromaniac who reputedly started the great fire of 64 CE not just to enjoy the spectacle but also to clear land for building his vast new palace, the Golden House. Even Tacitus admits, the rehabilitators point out, that Nero was the sponsor of effective relief measures for the homeless after the fire; and the reputed extravagance of his new residence, with all its luxuries (including a revolving dining room), did not prevent the parsimonious Vespasian and his sons from taking over part of it as their home. Besides, in the twenty years after Nero's death in 68 CE at least three false Neros, complete with lyre, appeared in the eastern parts of the empire, making a bid for power by claiming to be the emperor himself, still alive despite all the reports of his suicide. They were all quickly eliminated, but the deception suggests that in some areas of the Roman world Nero was fondly remembered: no one seeks power by pretending to be an emperor universally hated.

This historical scepticism is healthy. But it misses the bigger point: that whatever the views of Suetonius and other ancient writers, the qualities and characters of the individual emperors did not matter very much to most inhabitants of the empire, or to the essential structure of Roman history and its major developments.

It probably did matter to some members of the metropolitan elite, the emperor's advisors, the senate and the palace staff. Day-to-day dealings with the teenaged Emperor Nero may well have been rather more trying than those with Claudius before him or Vespasian after. And the absence of Tiberius, in his retreat on Capri, or of Hadrian on one of his many travels around the Roman world (he was an inveterate tourist, more often abroad than at home) must have had an impact on administration for those directly concerned – including at one point Suetonius, who worked briefly in Hadrian's secretariat.

Outside that narrow circle, however, and certainly outside the city of Rome, where the effects of an individual emperor's generosity could trickle down to the man or woman in the street, it can hardly have

71. Part of the decoration of Nero's Golden House. The surviving sections, mostly preserved within the foundations of the later Baths of Trajan, are impressive, but do not quite match up to the written descriptions of it. Despite various optimistic claims, no certain trace of its revolving dining room has been discovered. It may well be that much of the decoration that has been preserved, and that made such an impact on Renaissance artists (who dug down specially to copy it), came from the service quarters of the palace.

made much difference who was on the throne, or what their personal habits or intrigues were. And there is no sign at all that the character of the ruler affected the basic template of government at home or abroad in any significant way. If Gaius or Nero or Domitian really were as irresponsible, sadistic and mad as they are painted, it made little or no difference to how Roman politics and empire worked behind the headline anecdotes. Beneath the scandalous tales and stories of sodomy (which obscure as much as they enliven), away from the carefully constructed aphorisms of Gibbon, there was a remarkably stable structure of rule and – as we shall see – a remarkably stable set of problems and tensions across the whole period. It is those that we need to understand in order to make sense of imperial rule, not the individual idiosyncrasies of the rulers. After all, no horse was ever really made consul.

Changes at the top

That is not to say that everything remained the same between 14 and 192 CE. There was an enormous expansion over that period in the palatial headquarters of imperial power; the staff of imperial administration grew out of all recognition; and the infrastructure became far more complicated. And, by the early second century CE, the emperor began to look very different to his subjects.

The first Augustus had made a great show (and it was partly a show) of living more or less on a par with traditional Roman aristocrats. Within decades, though, the emperors were living in a style of luxury and extravagance that was unmatched in the Western world. The Roman town of Pompeii gives a clear sense of the scale of this change. In the second century BCE the biggest house in Pompeii (which we now know as the House of the Faun, after the bronze statue of a dancing faun or satyr found there) roughly equalled the size of the palaces of some of the kings in the eastern Mediterranean who had grabbed, or been given, parts of the territory conquered by Alexander the Great. In the second century CE, the 'villa' (as it is now euphemistically known) that Hadrian built at Tivoli, a few miles from Rome, was bigger than the town of Pompeii itself. And there he re-created for himself a miniature Roman Empire, with replicas of the greatest imperial monuments and treasures – from Egyptian waterways to the famous temple of Aphrodite in the town of Cnidos, with its even more famous nude statue of the goddess.

In between, the couple of houses that Augustus had occupied on the Palatine Hill had grown to be a full blown palace. Nero was the most notorious of the first emperors for extravagant domestic building. His Golden House incorporated state-of-the-art luxury and engineering, but the size was just as striking. The residential quarters and parkland together stretched, so it was said, across half the city, almost as if centuries later the Palace of Versailles had taken over the centre

72. A sculpture of a crocodile, giving an Egyptian flavour, set beside an ornamental pool in Hadrian's villa at Tivoli. This villa was even more extravagant than Nero's Golden House. Hadrian got away with it, when Nero did not, largely because his development was relatively hidden in the countryside, and did not appear to take over the city of Rome itself.

of Paris. It prompted some clever graffiti from its critics. 'All Rome is becoming a single house. Flee to Veii, citizens,' one wag scrawled. He was looking back to the proposal made centuries before, after the invasion of the Gauls in 390 BCE, that the Romans should abandon their city and set up home in what had been an enemy Etruscan town. But controversial as Nero's 'invasion' of Rome was, his grand construction projects set the pattern for the future.

By the late first century CE, the emperors were enjoying newly acquired luxurious suburban estates around the edge of most of the city (combinations of palace and pleasure parks know as *horti*, or 'gardens'), and they had more or less taken over the whole of the Palatine Hill for their central headquarters, or 'palace' (from 'Palatine'). This now included audience chambers, official dining rooms, reception suites, offices, baths, and accommodation for family, staff and slaves – and right at its back door, symbolically close, was the bogus 'Hut of Romulus', where Rome had once begun. The palace was not only widely visible, on many storeys, towering over the city. It had completely taken over land on the Palatine that for centuries had been the favourite place for senators to live. It was here that Cicero had his main city house, as did Clodius and many other of the leading players in the politics of the Roman Republic. There could hardly be a clearer symbol of the change in the balance of power in Rome than that the best remains of those old Palatine houses are now found buried in the foundations of the later palace, or that the elite families, finding themselves pushed out of their district of choice, tended to migrate to the Aventine Hill, which in Rome's early days had been the stronghold of radical plebeians.

Hand in hand with the expansion of the imperial palace went an expansion of the imperial administration at the central hub of the empire. Little is known in any detail about how the first Augustus' staff was organised, but it was probably an expanded version of the household of any leading senator of the previous century: large numbers of slaves and ex-slaves, acting in every capacity from cleaners to secretaries, with family and friends as advisors, confidants and sounding boards. That is certainly the impression given by the occupants of a large communal tomb (a so-called *columbarium*, or 'dovecote'), discovered in 1726 on the Appian Way. This originally contained the ashes of more than a thousand of the slaves and ex-slaves of Livia, with small plaques recording their names and jobs. Those that survive give a snapshot of her staff: they included five doctors and a medical supervisor, two midwives (presumably for the rest of the household), a painter, seven seamstresses (or menders), a bedroom attendant (*capsarius*, possibly the ancient equivalent of 'handbag carrier'), a caterer and a eunuch (function unspecified). This looks like the slave staff that any aristocratic lady might have had, but on a vastly expanded scale. Where they all lived is something of a mystery. They can hardly have fitted into the imperial couple's Palatine houses and presumably must have been lodged elsewhere.

By the time of Claudius, thirty years later, there was an administrative organisation attached to the emperor on a completely different scale and level of complexity. A series of departments or bureaux had been established to deal with different aspects of administration: separate offices for Latin correspondence and Greek correspondence, another to handle petitions to the emperor, another accounts, another to prepare and organise the legal cases judged by the emperor. They were largely staffed by slaves, many hundreds of them, and headed by divisional managers, who were at first usually ex-slaves – reliable administrators, whose loyalty to the emperor could more or less be guaranteed. But when the immense power that these men wielded became something of a cause célèbre with the traditional elite, members of the equestrian class replaced them as managers. The senators never enjoyed being upstaged by a powerful servile underclass prancing around (as they would have seen it) above their station.

This looks very much like a modern civil service, but in one important sense it was not. There is no sign of the clearly defined hierarchies below the divisional managers or of the grading of posts, the qualifications and examinations that we now associate with the modern Western or ancient Chinese idea of the civil service. So far as we can tell, it was still based on the structure of the old-fashioned slave household, such as Cicero's, even if vastly magnified. But it also points to another aspect of the emperor's job that often gets forgotten among all the tales of luxury and excess: the paperwork.

Most Roman rulers spent longer at their desks than at the dinner table. They were expected to work at the job, to be seen to exercise practical power, to respond to petitions, to adjudicate disputes throughout the empire and to give verdicts in tricky legal cases, right down to those that from the outside (though not to the parties involved, no doubt) appear relatively trivial. On one occasion, so a long inscription explains, the first Augustus was asked to pass judgement on a brawl in Cnidos, where the famous Aphrodite came from, on the southwestern coast of modern Turkey. It was a nasty local fight that had ended with one thug being killed by a falling chamber pot accidentally dropped by a slave from the upper window of the house that the 'victim' was attacking. Who was guilty, Augustus had to decide, the assailant or the pot dropper or his owner?

It was the support of the emperor's increasingly large staff that made it possible to deal with many cases like this, with the sacks of letters arriving in the palace post room and the streams of envoys that turned up, all expecting an imperial answer or audience. In that sense, it *was* rather like a modern civil service: for it must often have been a team of slaves and ex-slaves who read the documents, advised the emperor on the appropriate course of action and no doubt drafted many of the decisions and replies. Realistically, a good proportion of the letters 'from the emperor' received by local communities in the provinces and proudly put on display inscribed in permanent form in marble or bronze can hardly have been more than nodded through by him and stamped with his seal. But maybe that did not matter much to the recipients.

The majority of those who lived in the provinces, or even in Italy, had only the vaguest idea, if any, of what the imperial palace was like or how the emperor's administration operated. Only a tiny number would ever have seen the living emperor. They would, however, have seen his image over and over again, on the coins in their purses and in his portraits that continued to flood the Roman world. The atmosphere was not so different from that of a modern dictatorship, with the ruler's face peering out from every shopfront, street corner and government department. It even occasionally was converted into edible form, stamped into the biscuits distributed at religious sacrifices, as a few of the surviving biscuit moulds make clear. In fact, the second-century CE scholar, teacher and courtier Marcus Cornelius Fronto, in a letter to his grandest pupil, Marcus Aurelius, treated the spread of imperial images as a source of pride, even if he was sniffy about the artistic talents on display in the spontaneous initiatives of the ordinary people. 'In all the banks, shops, bars, gables, colonnades, windows everywhere,' he wrote, 'portraits of you are on public display, even if they are badly painted and modelled and carved in crude, almost worthless style.'

The emperor's face was ubiquitous, but it could be represented very differently. Only those with their eyes half shut could have failed to spot a dramatic change near the beginning of the second century CE in how the ruler looked. With the accession of Hadrian in 117 CE, after more than a hundred years of imperial portraits with no trace of facial hair (only a little stubble, if they were supposed to be in mourning), emperors started to be portrayed with full beards, a trend that lasted throughout the rest of the century and well after the period covered by this book. It is a guaranteed way of dating all those imperial heads that now line museum shelves: if they are bearded, they are after 117 CE.

This change cannot have been merely a whim of fashion or, as one ancient writer predictably speculated, a device for Hadrian to cover

73. The head of Hadrian in gilded bronze, with his characteristic facial hair. It was once on loyal display in a town in North Italy (Velleia, near modern Parma).

his spots. But the reason for it remains puzzling. Was it an attempt to emulate the Greek philosophers of the past? Hadrian was a well-known admirer of Greek culture, as was the philosophical Marcus Aurelius. So was it part of an attempt to intellectualise Roman imperial power, to re-present it in Greek terms? Or did it point in the opposite direction, harking back to the tough military heroes of earliest Rome, even before the era of Scipio Barbatus in the early third century BCE, when to sport a beard seems already to have been something remarkable in a Roman? It is impossible to know, and no ancient writing that survives ever explains the new beards. But, at the very least, they hint that within the palace someone was thinking hard about the imperial image, right down to the facial hair, and, for whatever reason, was prepared to make a break from tradition.

Important, and visible, as some of these developments were, the basic structures of imperial power, as the first Augustus had formulated them, remained in place throughout the rule of these fourteen emperors, no matter who was on the throne: Tiberius near the beginning of the first century CE would not have found it difficult to slip into the

imperial shoes of Commodus near the end of the second. They all
continued to blazon the title 'Augustus', amid a string of other often
very similar names. It has always taken a sharp eye to distinguish
Caesar Publius Aelius Traianus Hadrianus Augustus from the man
who was emperor after him, Caesar Titus Aelius Hadrianus Antoninus
Augustus Pius, the pair better known as Hadrian and Antoninus Pius.
To their face they were all called Caesar. 'Hail, Caesar, those about
to die salute you', as gladiators occasionally shouted to the emperor
before fights, would have been a form of address appropriate to each
and every one of them.

They all continued to follow the Augustan precedent in building
their way into power, in flaunting their generosity to the people and
in displaying their military prowess – or they were much criticised if
they did not. Vespasian's most famous construction, the amphitheatre
inaugurated under his son Titus in 80 CE, cleverly combined all three
aims. Eventually known as the Colosseum, from a colossal statue of
Nero that stood close by and lasted long after Nero's end, this was
simultaneously a massive building project (it took almost ten years
to finish, using 100,000 cubic metres of stone), a commemoration of
his victory over Jewish rebels (the booty from the war paid for it)
and a conspicuous act of generosity to the Roman people (the most
famous popular entertainment venue ever). It was also a criticism of
his predecessor, pointedly built on the site that had once belonged to
Nero's private park.

But the fourteen emperors were also heirs to the problems and tensions that Augustus bequeathed. For the 'Augustan template', though
enduringly solid in some respects, was in others a precarious balancing act. It had left some issues perilously unresolved. In particular,
Augustus had never solved the problem of succession to imperial
power. He had left the role of the senate and the relationship between
the emperor and the rest of the elite highly contested. And, more
generally, awkward questions remained about how the power of the

ruler of the Roman world was to be defined and represented. How, for example, did the parade of *civilitas* or the idea that he was simply the 'first among equals' ('*primus inter pares*', in the Latin slogan) fit with vast imperial honours and the emperor's nearly divine status? Exactly how close to a god was the Roman ruler?

All emperors and their advisors had to grapple with these dilemmas, which lie just below the surface of many of the lurid anecdotes. Several of the stories of the poisoning of imperial heirs, for example, point to the uncertainty of the rights of succession. The bantering insults of Gaius to his long-suffering consuls reflect the edgy relationship between senate and ruler. So it is to these defining conflicts of imperial power that we now turn: the succession, the senate and the status of the emperor, divine or not. They are as important to our understanding of how Roman imperial politics worked as the mammoth building schemes, military campaigns and generous benefactions; far more important than all the curious stories about crime, conspiracy or horses as consuls.

Succession

The murder of Gaius was a particularly bloody case of regime change, but the transmission of imperial power in Rome was often murderous. Despite the impressive survival rate of the emperors (fourteen rulers in almost 200 years is one testament to stability), the moment of succession was fraught with violence and surrounded by allegations of treachery. Vespasian in 79 CE was the only emperor in the first two dynasties to die without any rumours of foul play surfacing. Gaius, Nero and Domitian met obviously violent ends. There were rumours of murder surrounding the deaths of all the others. The names, dates and details change, but the story remains the same. Some said that Livia poisoned Augustus to ease Tiberius on to the throne; Tiberius was widely believed to have been poisoned or smothered to make way for Gaius; Agrippina is supposed to have dispatched her husband Claudius with some poisoned mushrooms in her successful bid to make her son Nero emperor; and some said that Domitian had a hand in the early death of Titus – contrary to a hopeful story in the Talmud which claims that after Titus destroyed the Temple in Jerusalem, a gnat flew into his nostril and gradually ate away his brain.

Many of these stories must be fiction. It takes a lot to believe that the elderly Livia would have painstakingly smeared poison on figs still growing on a tree, then tricked her husband into eating them. But true or not, together they underline the uncertainty and danger in the transmission of power. The message was that succession almost never happened without a struggle or a victim. This was a pattern projected back to the myths of the early kings too: they enjoyed long reigns, but only two of the seven died natural deaths. Why was it so difficult? And what solutions did the Romans find?

The first Augustus intended to make one-man rule permanent and to keep it in the family. But the series of deaths among those marked out as his heirs and the lack of any surviving sons from his marriage to Livia dogged his plans. Succession throughout the first dynasty continued to be fraught, as different claims from different sides of the Julio-Claudian family tree clashed. But the problems were bigger than that, and they would not have disappeared even if the imperial couple had produced half a dozen healthy boys.

Augustus was trying to invent from scratch a system of dynastic succession, against the background of a fluid set of Roman rules about the inheritance of status and property. Crucially there was no presumption in Roman law that the firstborn son would be the sole or principal heir. The standard modern system of primogeniture is a fail-safe mechanism for removing any doubt about who should succeed, although – by making the order of birth the only criterion – it risks some decidedly unsuitable incumbents on the throne. In Rome, the eldest male child of the emperor would have had a certain advantage in trying to follow his father, but no more than that. A successful claim to power also rested on behind-the-scenes manoeuvres, on the support of key interest groups, on being groomed for the part and on the careful manipulation of opinion. It also depended on being in the right place at the right time. The only reliable way to guarantee a peaceful transition was to have the new emperor on the spot to take over the old Augustus' signet ring as he breathed his last, with no awkward gap. That is what the rumour-mongers realised: most of the allegations of poisoning under the Julio-Claudians present the murder not as part of a plot to spring some new candidate into power but as an attempt to get the timing right and to ensure a seamless takeover for the man already marked out as the likely successor.

These uncertainties about how to establish a legitimate claim to rule also help to explain the peculiarly murderous image of the Roman imperial court, where danger seems to have lurked on every fig and such an atmosphere of suspicion prevailed that Domitian is said to have had the palace walls lined with reflecting stone so that he could see who was coming up behind. Without any agreed system for the transmission of power, every relative counted as a potential rival of the emperor or of his likely heir – and it followed that those in the penumbra of the imperial family found themselves in a very perilous position indeed. Many of the stories may well be more fantasy than fact; the Roman elite was not by nature particularly cruel and ruthless, even if that is the image they have in film and fiction. What *was* ruthless was the fundamental logic of imperial succession. Tacitus captures that, with characteristic cynicism, in describing the events of the beginning of Nero's reign in 54 CE. 'The first death under the new emperor,' he starts, implying that there were many more to follow, was that of Marcus Junius Silanus Torquatus, the governor of Asia. He was a man of no ambition whatsoever, so shamelessly apathetic,

Tacitus explains, that Gaius had aptly nicknamed him the Golden Sheep. But his death was inevitable, and the reason obvious: 'He was a great-grandson of Augustus.'

There were alternative routes to power. One was exactly what the first Augustus had tried to preclude: elevation by the army. In 41 CE the Praetorian Guard in Rome had played the leading part in putting Claudius on the throne. In 68 CE, to quote Tacitus again, 'the secret of imperial rule was revealed, that an emperor could be made somewhere other than Rome'. 'Somewhere other than Rome' is a euphemism for 'by the legions in the provinces', as each of the four rival claimants to replace Nero was backed by army units from different provinces. Within eighteen months, Vespasian was raised to power in the East, with no connection by birth to the Julio-Claudian dynasty. It is clear, however, that he and his supporters felt that military force alone was not enough to secure his position. Despite the down-to-earth image he later projected, at the beginning of his rule widespread reports of the miracles he had worked underpinned his claims to the throne. In Egypt, just before his proclamation as emperor, he is supposed to have restored sight to a blind man by spitting on his eyes and to have cured another man's withered hand by standing on it. Whatever carefully manipulated display lay behind these reports (and whatever the uncanny similarity with a far better known miracle worker of the first century CE), eyewitnesses are said to have vouched for the miraculous cures years later, long after Vespasian's death.

The praetorians continued to influence imperial succession; certainly, no one would have been able to hold on to the throne if the troops in the city actively opposed him. But in the period up to 192 CE they never again engineered quite such an open coup as they had in 41 CE, nor in that period did the legions in the provinces ever again create an emperor. That is partly because from the end of the first century CE – after a brief interlude of relatively unproblematic succession in which Vespasian had been followed by his two natural sons – an alternative route to the throne was devised, which appeared to get round some of the earlier difficulties: adoption.

Adoption in Rome had never been principally a means for a childless couple to create a family. If anyone just wanted a baby, they could easily find one on a rubbish heap. Adoption among the elite had always been a means to ensure the transmission of status and property and the continuance of the family name in the absence of surviving sons. Those adopted were more likely to be distinguished adolescents or young adults than babies, whose high risk of death made them an unwise investment. That is how Scipio Aemilianus, for example, the friend of Polybius and conqueror of Carthage in 146 BCE, the natural son of another famous Roman commander, Aemilius Paullus, ended up in the Scipio family.

It was not at all surprising that Augustus and his successors in the Julio-Claudian dynasty used adoption, as other elite families sometimes did, to mark out their favoured heir among the wider group of relatives. Hence Augustus adopted his grandsons and, when they died, did the same thing with Livia's natural son, Tiberius; Claudius likewise adopted his wife's son, Nero. But from the end of the first century CE there was a new pattern. When Domitian was assassinated in 96 CE, the senate offered the throne to the elderly and childless Nerva – a safe pair of hands presumably. Between Nerva and Marcus Aurelius heirs to the throne were selected and adopted without obvious concern for family relationships. Some had no link to the existing emperor by blood or marriage at all, or only a remote one, and they came from further afield. Trajan, the first such adoptee, was originally from Spain; the families of others came from either there or Gaul. They were the descendants of early Roman settlers abroad, who had probably married into the local communities, rather than from the indigenous population. But, in a way that dramatically fulfilled the Roman project of incorporation, they made the point that the emperor could come from the provinces of the empire.

This new system, which operated for most of the second century CE, was sometimes presented as a major shift in the ideology of political power, almost a meritocratic revolution. Gaius Plinius Caecilius Secundus (now called 'Pliny the Younger', to distinguish him from his uncle 'the Elder') justified the procedure in precisely those terms, in a speech delivered to the emperor Trajan: 'When you are about to hand control of the senate and people of Rome, the armies, the provinces, the allies to one man alone, would you look to the belly of a wife to produce him or search for an heir to supreme power only within the walls of your own home? ... If he is to rule over all, he must be chosen from all.' Tacitus, also writing during the rule of Trajan, echoes those sentiments in a speech he put into the mouth of Servius Sulpicius Galba, one of the claimants who briefly held power after the death of Nero. Just a few days before his death, elderly and without an heir, Galba looked for someone outside his family to adopt as a successor. Tacitus' words ostensibly justify that decision in 69 CE; but they really belong to the world of imperial adoption in his day: 'Under Tiberius and Gaius and Claudius,' he makes Galba say, 'we Romans became the inheritance of just one family ... Now that the Julio-Claudian dynasty is over, adoption will select only the best. For to be descended and born from emperors is pure chance, and is rated no more highly.'

These are fine words, and they suggest a new style of reflection on the nature of the emperor's power and qualities. In practice too, the adoptive system occasionally worked smoothly. On the death of Nerva in 98 CE, Trajan's succession was so guaranteed that the new emperor did not even return to Rome from Germany for more than a year. But it was not the perfect solution that some of the glowing ancient accounts make it seem. To read between the lines, it is clear that the praetorians had pressured Nerva into adopting Trajan (Pliny's speech lets out rather awkwardly that Trajan had been 'forced' on the old man), and the legions massed with Trajan on the Rhine might well have been a factor too. And when Trajan died, almost twenty years later, whatever really happened, the reported machinations are very much on the Julio-Claudian model: there were rumours of poisoning, the adoption of Hadrian was announced only at the very last minute, and some suspected Plotina, Trajan's wife, of manipulating the succession in Hadrian's favour and concealing the death until all arrangements were in place.

Besides, despite the splendid meritocratic rhetoric, adoption was still treated as a second-best means of succession. When Hadrian wrote a little poem in honour of Trajan, he preferred to call him the descendant of Aeneas rather than the son of Nerva – a fantasy of genealogy that perhaps also hints at Trajan's overseas origin. Pliny ended his fulsome speech in praise of Trajan with hopes that the emperor would in due course have sons and that his successor would indeed come from 'the belly of a wife'. And when Marcus Aurelius was the first emperor for more than seventy years to produce a son and heir who survived childhood, that son succeeded him without there being any pretence of searching for the best man for the job. The outcome was disastrous. Commodus' assassination in 192 CE was followed by the intervention of the praetorians and of rival legions from outside Rome and by another round of civil war, which marked the beginning of the end of the Augustan template of imperial rule.

Roman emperors and their advisors never solved the problem of succession. They were defeated in part by biology, in part by lingering uncertainties and disagreements about how inheritance should best operate. Succession always came down to some combination of luck, improvisation, plotting, violence and secret deals. The moment when Roman power was handed on was always the moment when it was most vulnerable.

Senators

Another problem that dogged the history of the fourteen emperors over the first two centuries CE, and one that preoccupied ancient writers above anything else, was the relationship between the men on the throne and the senators, and the question of how the senate was to operate under an autocracy. Senators were essential to the running of the empire. Among their number were most of the emperor's friends, advisors, confidants, dinner guests and drinking partners – as well as the men who, second only to his own family, were likely to become his successful rivals, vociferous opponents and assassins. Augustus had attempted a careful balancing act, combining extra privileges for the senate and a parade of *civilitas* with an attempt to reconfigure the old Republican institution into something closer to an arm of administration in his new regime.

It was a fragile compromise, which left the political role of the senate under an all-powerful autocrat awkwardly ill defined. Soon after the first Augustus' death, Tiberius exposed the problem when, in a surprise return to more old-fashioned ways, he attempted to get the senators to take decisions on their own, and they repeatedly refused to do so. According to Tacitus, when the emperor insisted on one occasion that they should all vote in an open ballot, himself included, one sharp senator summed up the issue with presumably mock deference: 'Could you tell me in what order you will cast your vote, Caesar?' he asked. 'If you go first I shall have something to follow. If you go last of all, I fear I might find myself inadvertently on the wrong side.' Tiberius is said to have interpreted all this as insufferable servility on the senate's part, and every time he left their meetings he used to declare in Greek, 'Men fit for slavery!' If so, he failed to see that the free senate he claimed to want was incompatible with his own power.

Roman accounts of this period, largely written from a senatorial point of view, make much of the stand-offs or open hostility between emperor and senators. Gloomy tallies are recorded, accurately or not, of senators executed or forced to suicide under every emperor, and notorious examples singled out. Most reigns are supposed to have started off with conciliatory noises from the emperor to the senate before in several cases degenerating into open hostility between the ruler and some sections of the elite. In his first speech to the assembled senators, Nero insisted that they 'would keep their ancient privileges', a promise that to some looked decidedly hollow only a few years later. Hadrian began with fine words about having no senator put to death without trial, though it was not long before four ex-consuls were executed after no more than a rumour of a plot against the new ruler. Tacitus is not the only ancient historian to conjure up an atmosphere of deadly suspicion between the Palatine and the senate house.

Even the most discreet of the dissidents among the senators were always at risk from informers, who were said to have made their fortunes out of leaking to the emperor the names of those who were less than loyal. Others did not bother with discretion but publicly paraded their opposition to the fawning and the flattery of their class and to the ridiculous excesses of the emperor in power. In the reign of Nero, for example, the high-principled Publius Clodius Thrasea Paetus stormed out of the senate after listening to a letter from the emperor justifying the (eventually successful) murder of his mother, refused to take the annual votes of loyalty to the emperor and showed a definite disinclination to applaud Nero's stage performances. As a result of these and other 'crimes', he was tried for treason *in absentia*, found guilty and forced to suicide. Tacitus had his doubts about how useful these self-advertising protests were. Of one of Thrasea's gestures, he writes: 'He managed to put himself in danger, without opening up the path to liberty for the others.'

In this political context, the image of Brutus and Cassius as the upholders of the free Republic and senatorial power, and as opponents of autocracy, could become a powerful symbol of dissidence. As we have seen, there was no realistic chance of turning the clock back to the 'liberty' (for some) of earlier times. The senate bungled their opportunity to gain some control in 41 CE. Almost thirty years later, in 69 CE, when Vespasian, who had just been declared emperor, was still abroad, they did not even make the attempt but (in Tacitus' account, at least) sat down in the new emperor's absence to settle old scores among themselves. By this point, anyway, the idea of the Republic had become for many little more than harmless nostalgia, a version of 'the good old days' and a source of famous anecdotes about traditional Roman virtues. Even as early as the rule of Augustus, the historian Livy could get away with being a well-known partisan of Pompey the Great, Julius Caesar's eventual enemy; Augustus merely teased him.

Nevertheless, a public admiration for Caesar's assassins could in some cases be a death sentence for a senator. Under Tiberius, in 25 CE the historian Aulus Cremutius Cordus starved himself to death after being tried for treason. His crime was to have written a history that praised Brutus and Cassius and to have called Cassius 'the last of the Romans'. The book itself was burnt. The long poem on the civil war between Caesar and Pompey by Marcus Annaeus Lucanus ('Lucan'), which presents them as both terribly flawed and recognises true virtue only in the diehard Republican Cato, escaped that fate, and still survives. But those views cannot have been entirely unconnected to the poet's part in an alleged plot against Nero and his subsequent suicide.

The emperor's power to humiliate as well as to harm was also a major theme of disapproval. Gaius' 'joke' about being able to execute the consuls at the nod of his head and Commodus' performance with the poor decapitated ostrich are only two of a string of stories about quixotic emperors terrifying or ridiculing senators in all kinds of ingenious ways.

The historian Lucius Cassius Dio, whose vast compendium covered the story of Rome from Aeneas until his own day in the early third century CE, described some of the most memorable incidents.

As a senator under Commodus, he was an eyewitness to some of the emperor's extravagant gladiatorial spectacles, but he also tells of one of the strangest exercises in imperial menace, dreamt up by Domitian in 89 CE. The story was that the emperor invited a group of senators and knights to a dinner party, where to their horror they found on arrival that the whole decor was black, from the couches to the crockery and the serving boys. Each guest's name was inscribed on a slab like a tombstone, and all evening the emperor's conversation never strayed from the topic of death. They were all convinced that they would not live to see the next day. But they were wrong. When they had returned home and the expected knock on the door came, instead of a killer they found one of the emperor's staff laden with gifts from the party, including their own name slab and their own personal serving boy.

It is hard to know what to make of this story or where Dio picked it up. If it is based in fact, it is tempting to wonder whether a quirky fancy-dress party lies behind it (the spendthrift Roman elite are known to have enjoyed elegantly coloured-coded meals) – or even some philosophical display on the part of the emperor ('Eat, drink and be merry, for tomorrow you die' was a favourite theme in Roman moralising). But Dio certainly tells it as an example of the emperor's sadistic games at the expense of the senate and of the endemic conflicts between the ruler and the rest of the elite. This is a classic tale of Roman fear, fed by paranoia, suspicion and distrust. The message was that no invitation to dinner with the emperor was ever likely to be quite what it seemed.

There is, however, a very different side to this picture of the relations between senate and emperor. After Cicero, the best-known Roman letter writer is Pliny the Younger, with ten books of surviving letters to his name: 247 letters in the first nine books and more than 100 in the tenth, all documenting his senatorial career under the emperors Nerva and Trajan, with some backward glances to Domitian. Books 1 to 9 are letters to various friends, much more crafted pieces of writing than Cicero's, artfully ordered and probably extensively edited to hang together as a coherent self-portrait. Book 10 is a contrast, maybe not so much reworked, consisting entirely of letters between Pliny and Trajan. Most of them were exchanged after Trajan sent Pliny out in 109 CE as his special envoy to govern the province of Bithynia on the Black Sea. Pliny regularly wrote back home to consult the emperor on administrative queries or to keep him up to date, typically on such matters as local finances, overambitious building schemes or how Trajan's birthday was to be celebrated in the province. That was an important piece of protocol, even where reputedly down-to-earth emperors such as Trajan were concerned.

Throughout the collection, Pliny presents himself as the kind of cultured and conscientious public servant that Augustus must have dreamed of in a senator. He was an orator and advocate, largely making his name in the court that specialised in disputed inheritances. His political career, which started under Domitian and continued under later emperors, included major administrative responsibilities – for army financing and the Tiber waterway – as well as the still standard sequence of political offices. It was when he formally entered his consulship, in 100 CE, that he made the speech to Trajan that covers, among many other things, the subject of children and adoption.

Pliny's letters are not free from complaints and annoyance: he clashes with his fellow advocate Regulus, whose character he systematically assassinates throughout the correspondence, pouring scorn not least on the man's eyepatch and make-up; and he gets cross in a rather humourless way when fellow senators start spoiling their senatorial voting papers with smutty jokes. But overall the letters offer a sunny, and slightly self-congratulatory, image of senatorial life. Pliny writes of his pleasure at taking dinner with the emperor (no tombstones here), his patronage of his home town in northern Italy, including the gift of a library, his support of his friends and clients, his literary pursuits and his amateur historical interests; his reply to a letter from his friend Tacitus in fact gives us the only eyewitness account to survive of the eruption of Vesuvius in 79 CE (as a young man Pliny had been staying nearby at the time of the disaster, and years later the historian, researching that portion of his histories, asked him for his recollections). He was even on friendly terms with someone who cherished portrait busts of Brutus and Cassius, at no apparent risk to his own safety.

The most striking thing about Pliny's career is its success, across different reigns and dynasties, from the assassinated Domitian, who first noticed and promoted him, through the elderly Nerva, to the adopted military man Trajan. This pattern was not unusual. In one of his letters he describes a dinner party held by Nerva, probably in 97 CE. Conversation fell to one of Domitian's most vicious supporters, who had recently died. 'What do you think he would be doing if he had survived?' asked the emperor, with possibly faux naivety. 'He would be dining with us,' replied one of the clear-headed guests. The point was that it took only a little readjustment, and some appropriate vilification of the last man on the throne, to continue as a welcome guest at the new emperor's dining table, still creeping up the ladder of senatorial power. Even Tacitus, a particularly vitriolic critic of Domitian, admitted that his own career had prospered under his hated rule. It is another sign that the characteristics of individual emperors did not matter so much as the biographical tradition tries to insist.

So how to explain the difference between these two images of senatorial life, between gentlemanly collegiality and an atmosphere of terror, between the relaxed and self-confident Pliny and those senators who found themselves the victims of the emperor's cruel whims, or hit squad? Were there two very different types of senator: on the one hand an unlucky, and maybe tiresome, few who refused to go along with the system, took the emperor's jokes and displays far too seriously, made their opposition known and paid for it; on the other, the largely silent majority of men who were grateful to serve and prosper in the limelight of the imperial court, whoever the emperor was, were prepared to vote for book burning when required and did not think celebrating the emperor's birthday or overseeing the dredging of the Tiber beneath them?

In part, there probably were. Over the first two centuries CE, senators gradually changed anyway. Many more came, as Pliny did, from new or relatively new families, and increasingly from provinces abroad. They may have been far less invested in some fantasy of the Republican past, far less touchy about some of the more irritating examples of the emperor's whim and happy to get on with the job. It is also clear that the most unbending opposition to emperors tended to run in families, a tradition of dissidence handed down from father to son, and sometimes to daughter. Thrasea Paetus' son-in-law, Quintus Helvidius Priscus, followed in his footsteps and suffered much the same fate; he insisted, for example, on addressing the emperor Vespasian as just plain 'Vespasian' and on one occasion in the senate heckled him almost to tears.

It was not, however, quite as simple as that. Pliny was not blithely unaware of what had happened to some of the emperor's opponents while he himself prospered during the rule of Domitian. In fact, his letters are carefully arranged repeatedly to highlight his close relationship with Domitian's victims. One of these memorably records the grave illness of an old lady called Fannia ('a constant fever and a cough that is getting worse'), who was none other than the daughter of Thrasea Paetus and the widow of Helvidius Priscus. It provides Pliny with the opportunity to praise her noble career among a family of senatorial dissidents and to emphasise his support for them ('My services were theirs in good times and bad; I comforted them in exile and avenged them when they returned'). This does not entirely square with his success under Domitian, and an unflattering interpretation would cast Pliny as the guilty collaborator, back-pedalling under Trajan's new regime and inventing a record of support for the opposition. But there was something more to it than that.

Most Roman senators chose a mixture of collaboration and dissidence, which the first Augustus' awkward compromise between senatorial power and senatorial service made almost inevitable. The outspoken opponents of the regime were no doubt men and women of trenchant principles, but also blind – bloody-minded, we might say – to the careful balancing act and delicate choreography that in practice gave the relationship between emperor and senate its fragile stability. The majority of the senators were different: more realistic, less stubborn and less confident in their own moral judgement. In the evenings, among friends, they may well have entertained one another with those horror stories of humiliation and the abuse of power that we still read. They no doubt warmed to the heroic opposition of martyrs in the cause of freedom. But, by and large, like Tacitus and most other ancient historians, they fought their battles in the past, against emperors whom it was now safe to demonise. In the day, like Pliny, they got on with the job of being senators – as most of us would.

Oh dear, I think I'm becoming a god ...

One of the big questions that lay behind many of the clashes between the emperor and his senatorial opponents was how the power of the ruler of the known world, and of his family, was to be defined, described and understood. The idea that the emperor was simply 'first among equals' was at one end of a wide spectrum of possibilities, and the status of a god, or something very close to it, was at the other. Helvidius Priscus tactlessly stuck out for the former by refusing to use Vespasian's imperial titles. Thrasea Paetus objected to the extension of divine honours not just to emperors but also to their female relatives. He staged one of his public absences from the senate in 65 CE when the vote was taken to declare honours for Poppaea Sabina, Nero's wife who apparently died after her husband kicked her in the stomach while she was pregnant (whether tragic accident or terrible domestic abuse is still, fruitlessly, debated). Among those honours, she was declared a goddess. It was too much for Thrasea Paetus to take.

Poppaea, however, was not the first. She joined several other female members of the imperial family who had been added to the Roman pantheon since Julius Caesar had been declared a god in 42 BCE. In addition to the first Augustus, and Claudius in 54 CE, the new deities formally decreed by the senate were Gaius' sister Drusilla, followed by Livia 'Augusta', as she then was, and Poppaea's baby daughter, Claudia, who had been deified in 63 CE after her death at the age of just four months. Official deification entitled them all to a temple and priests and to receive sacrifices. There is no surviving trace of any temple for little Claudia, but according to Dio, a temple was soon dedicated to Poppaea under the title 'Venus Sabina'.

The idea of a tiny baby becoming a goddess must have outraged more than the diehard dissidents at Rome. But we have already seen that it had long been the practice in many places of the ancient Mediterranean world to represent overwhelming political power using language and imagery cast in divine terms. The kings who followed Alexander the Great in the eastern part of the Mediterranean, like the Roman generals who took their place, had been offered festivals on the model of religious festivals and used epithets shared with the gods (such as 'Saviour'). This was one logical way of making sense of men who had far transcended ordinary human power and of finding an existing category into which such superhuman people might more or less fit. The representation of the successful general as Jupiter in the ceremony of triumph and Cicero's attempt to reinterpret his loss of Tullia in terms of deification are other examples of the flexibility of a polytheistic religion such as Rome's.

It is largely the legacy of the two main monotheisms of the ancient world – Judaism and its offshoot Christianity – that has encouraged us to see the invention of new gods, the adjustment and the extension of the pantheon and the fluidity of the boundary between humans and gods as faintly ludicrous. Christians, in particular, both ridiculed the very notion that the obviously human emperor was divine and occasionally paid with their lives for their refusal to give him any kind of religious honour. But that is not to say that the divine status of the emperor was unproblematic for pre-Christian Romans or that there were no debates and disagreements about just how godlike the human ruler, let alone his family, was. It was another awkward balancing act bequeathed to his successors by Augustus, who straddled the boundary between the human and the divine with greater success than some of those who followed.

Some imperial claims to divine status were always thought undeniably wrong. For most inhabitants of the Roman Empire, it would have been a crass category mistake and a hyperbolic affront for an emperor to declare himself a living god, as if there were no difference between himself and Jupiter. The Romans were hardly stupid: they knew the difference between bona fide Olympians and a living emperor. If it is true (rather than a vicious slur) that Gaius turned the Temple of Castor and Pollux in the Forum into the vestibule of his residence on the Palatine above and sat there between the statues of the gods to enjoy the worship of anyone who chose to give it, then that was a memorable symbol of imperial megalomania and it broke all the official protocols of imperial worship. It was likewise an abuse of power for an emperor to attempt to stretch the official Roman pantheon to accommodate dead babies, boyfriends and even favourite sisters; Hadrian was no better on this score than Nero or Gaius in having his young male companion, Antinous, made a god after his mysterious death by drowning in the Nile in 130 CE. The theology of the emperor and the imperial family was far more subtle than this and has to be seen in two parts: first the divine status of the living emperor, second that of the dead.

Throughout the Roman world, the living emperor was treated *very like* a god. He was incorporated into rituals celebrated in honour of the gods, he was addressed in language that overlapped with divine language, and he was assumed to have some similar powers. Augustus' name, for example, was included in the wording of some religious litanies. Runaway slaves could claim asylum by clinging to a statue of the emperor, just as to a statue of a god. At the town of Gytheum, near Sparta in the Peloponnese, a surviving inscription lays out in great detail the procedures for a regular festival to be held over several days, with processions around the town, musical contests and sacrifices, honouring a pair of local benefactors, the ruling emperor, Tiberius, and various members of his family, the Republican general Titus Quinctius Flamininus, as well as the traditional Olympian deities.

There may well have been many people, especially far outside the city of Rome, for whom the emperor was about as remote, and powerful, a figure as an Olympian deity, and who did not see much difference between the two. But wherever the formal details were spelled out, a careful distinction was drawn between the emperor and the Olympians. In Gytheum, for example, and elsewhere, a technical but crucial difference was expressed. The animal sacrifices were to be performed *to* the traditional gods, but they were performed *on behalf of* or *for the protection of* the living emperor and his family; the emperor, in other words, was still under the protection of the Olympian gods rather than being their equal. In Rome, it was usually the *numen,* or the 'power', of the living emperor that received sacrifice, not the emperor himself. More widely, the package of honours offered to the imperial family in the Greek world were known as *isotheoi timai*: that is, honours equivalent (*iso-*) to those of the gods (*theoi*), but not identical. It was always transgressive to ignore the difference between the gods and the living emperor, however *godlike* he might be.

It was not the same when they were dead. Following the pattern of Julius Caesar, the senate might choose to incorporate a dead emperor or one of his close relations into the official pantheon; for it was a decision that was, formally at least, in the hands of the senate and a posthumous power over their ruler that some senators must have enjoyed. In this case the distinction between gods and emperors was negligible; there were priests and temples, sacrifices carried out to them, not on their behalf, and some wonderful surviving images that literally put the imperial gods in the Olympian heavens (see plate 20). But the differences were not entirely eroded. Roman writers, intellectuals and artists repeatedly wondered about the nature of the transition from emperor to god and how someone who had been a human being one day was divine the next. In a way reminiscent of the modern Catholic Church's requirement of authenticated miracles in making a new saint, they claimed to ask for proof or witnesses; the appearance of a comet apparently demonstrated the apotheosis of Julius Caesar, but the stories of Livia's suspiciously large cash reward to the senator who was prepared to say that he had seen Augustus ascend to heaven suggest some uncertainty about the process.

The transition was fraught enough to prompt jokes and satire. According to Suetonius, Vespasian continued his down-to-earth line in self-deprecating wit right up until his last words: 'Oh dear, I think I'm becoming a god ...' The whole process of becoming, or not becoming, a god is the theme of a long skit probably written in the mid 50s CE by Lucius Annaeus Seneca – Nero's one-time tutor and later victim, reputedly on the margins of a conspiracy against him, and forced to a difficult suicide. He was so old and desiccated that, according to another ghastly set piece from Tacitus, he found it hard to get enough blood to flow from his slashed arteries. The subject of his skit is the attempt of the emperor Claudius to be admitted to the company of the gods. We find him, just having died (last words: 'Oh dear, I think I've shat myself ...'), limping up to heaven to join the gods. Things look promising at first, especially when Hercules is the first deity to greet him, quoting Homer, which impresses the dead emperor. But when the adjudication of his case begins, the divine Augustus, giving his maiden speech in the heavenly senate (the implication is that deified emperors are rather low in the pecking order), holds up Claudius' vicious cruelty against him: 'This man, fellow senators, who looks to you as if he couldn't hurt a fly, used to kill people as easily as a dog squats.' And there is a dark reference to those thirty-five senators put to death.

There is no doubt that, in real-time Roman politics, Claudius was made a god; he had priests and a temple, the remains of which have been excavated. But in this fantasy he fails the test, and a tailor-made punishment is devised for him. Given his known passion for gambling, he is to spend eternity shaking dice in a bottomless dice shaker. Or

74. The base of the (lost) column of Antoninus Pius shows the apotheosis of the emperor and his wife Faustina. It is in many ways an awkward image. Though they are represented going up to heaven together, Faustina died twenty years before her husband. The winged creature transporting them seems a rather desperate attempt to conjure up the processes by which emperors became gods.

that is exactly what would have happened, had not the emperor Gaius appeared from nowhere, claimed Claudius as his slave and handed him over to one of his staff to work for eternity as a very junior secretary in the imperial legal department. This is a nice glimpse into the new bureaucracy of the imperial regime, with all its specialist departments. It is a hilarious example of the way dead rulers were safer and easier targets than their living counterparts. It sends up the whole unlikely process by which a human emperor became a manifest god. And, in fantasy, it upturns the assassination with which this chapter started. Claudius may have become emperor, but here Gaius has the last laugh.

CHAPTER ELEVEN

·

THE HAVES AND
HAVE-NOTS

Rich and poor

RICH ROMANS HAD a lifestyle that was luxurious by any standards, ancient or modern. The emperor, with his palatial residences, acres of parkland, the occasional revolving dining room (how well these worked, or by what mechanism, is another question), jewelled walls and consumption on a scale that mesmerised most Roman observers, was at the very top of the spectrum, outbidding even the super-rich. His fortune was founded on the proceeds of vast imperial estates, across the Roman world, that passed from one ruler to the next and included mines and industrial properties as well as farms; on the blurred lines between the finances of the state and of the emperor himself; and, so it was sometimes alleged, on various forms of extractions, such as forced legacies, if ready cash ran short (see plate 13).

But many well-off inhabitants of the empire also led lives of privileged comfort. Vociferous Roman disapproval of 'luxury' and admiration of the simple, old-fashioned peasant life coexisted, as they often do, with massive expenditure and luxurious habits. Disapprovers always need something to disapprove of; and, in any case, the distinction between exquisite good taste (mine) and vulgar ostentation (yours) is necessarily a subjective one.

Pliny the Younger – whose uncle 'the Elder' was one of the most strident critics of extravagance, in everything from one-legged tables to wearing several rings on the same finger – described his own country villa, a few miles outside Rome, in one of his letters. It was, he explained, 'fit for purpose and not too expensive to maintain'. Despite that modest description, it was actually a vast pile, with dining rooms for use in different seasons, a private bathing suite and swimming pool, courtyards and shady porticoes, central heating, ample running water, a gymnasium, sunny lounges with picture windows overlooking the sea, and garden hideaways where Pliny, who was not a man for raucous fun, could escape the noise of the parties on those rare days when the slaves took a holiday.

All over the empire the rich paraded their wealth in large and expensive accommodations for themselves, measured not by floor area but by the number of tiles on the roof (to qualify as a local councillor, one law states, you needed to have a house with 1,500 roof tiles). And they indulged in the many pleasures that money could buy, from silks to oriental spices, skilled slaves to pricey antiques. They also paraded their wealth in sponsoring amenities for their local communities. The emperor had a monopoly on public building in Rome, but in the towns of Italy and the provinces, the elite, both men and women, built themselves into prominence in much the same way.

Pliny was typical in ploughing some of his money into construction projects in his home town of Comum in northern Italy, including a new public library, which cost a million sesterces to construct (that is the equivalent of the minimum fortune required to be a senator). His elderly friend Ummidia Quadratilla, who died around 107 CE, did similar things in her home town south of Rome. Though Pliny wrote her up as a tough old lady with a fondness for board games, surviving inscriptions show that she also sponsored a new amphitheatre and temple, and restored the theatre and funded a public banquet ('for the local council, the people and the women') in celebration of the new facilities. As far away as the small town of Timgad in North Africa, originally established on the edges of the Sahara in 100 CE as a settlement of veteran Roman soldiers, one local married couple around 200 CE were building themselves a mini-palace on at least two floors, not so grand as Pliny's villa but still equipped with multiple dining rooms, a private bathhouse, internal gardens, fancy water features, expensive mosaic floors and central heating for the cold African winters. And they sponsored a huge new temple and a splendid new market, decorated with a dozen statues – of themselves.

Money could not protect the rich from all the discomforts and harsher sides of ancient life. Although in Rome the emperor lived at a safe remove from the masses, and the wealthy tended to favour one or two areas in particular (the Palatine Hill before the imperial palace encroached is an obvious example), for the most part ancient cities were not zoned as modern cities are. Rich and poor lived side

75. A moody reconstruction of Pliny's palatial villa by the architect Karl Friedrich Schinkel (1841). It has been a favourite scholarly pastime for centuries to take Pliny's own description of the place (*Letters* 2, 17) and to try to re-create an image or plan of it.

76. The town of Timgad in modern Algeria, looking across the ruins of the city to a large temple sponsored by the rich couple with their mini-palace. Timgad is one of the most evocative Roman sites in the world, with everything from a very smart set of public lavatories to one of the few libraries actually to survive from antiquity.

by side, large houses with many tiles sharing the same streets and districts with tiny hovels. The Romans had no Mayfairs or Fifth Avenues. Travel in a curtained sedan chair, carried by a team of hefty slaves, might have protected a few ladies and gentlemen from the worst aspects of the public highway in any big city of the empire. But the lack of any organised refuse collection, the use of the road as a public lavatory (with the contents of chamber pots chucked on all comers from upper-floor windows, as the poet Juvenal pictures the scene, probably with some satiric exaggeration) and the noise and congestion of carts and carriages fighting for space in streets often too narrow for two-way traffic would have been at the very least an assault on the senses of rich and poor alike, and sometimes dangerous. Although it is often claimed that, among notable pieces of Roman enlightenment, wheeled transport was banned from city streets during the daytime (as if in some modern pedestrian precinct), this applied at most to heavy transport, or the ancient equivalent of juggernaut lorries. And that itself, as Juvenal also complains, could make the noise at night almost intolerable for anyone of any rank: 'it would even steal sleep from a drowsy emperor'.

Germs were no respecters of wealth either. Those rich enough to have secluded country properties had a chance of escaping the periodic epidemics of sickness that blighted all cities, especially Rome, and they made an effort to find relatively mosquito-free places to spend their summer months. A better diet might also have helped the more prosperous to withstand illnesses that those on subsistence rations could not. But the same diseases, and much the same dirt, killed the children of rich and poor alike. And anyone who went to the public baths – and that certainly included on occasion even those who had their own bathing suites at home – risked becoming a victim of those breeding grounds of infection. One sensible Roman doctor got it absolutely right when he wrote that baths were to be avoided if you had an open wound, otherwise deathly gangrene was likely to be the result.

In reality, even in the imperial palace, emperors were killed by disease more often than by poison. For more than a decade from the mid 160s CE, much of the Roman Empire suffered a pandemic, very likely smallpox apparently brought back by soldiers serving in the East. Galen, the most acute and prolific medical writer of the ancient world, discussed individual cases and gave detailed eyewitness descriptions of the symptoms, including a blistering skin rash and diarrhoea. Quite how devastating this outbreak was is still intensely debated. Firm evidence is scanty, and deaths are variously estimated at between 1 per cent and an almost impossibly high 30 per cent of the total population. But in 169 CE the emperor Lucius Verus, who from

161 CE had ruled jointly with Marcus Aurelius, was almost certainly one of the victims.

There was some even-handedness, then, in these few, largely biological, aspects of misfortune. Yet for the most part the great divide in the Roman world was between the haves and the have-nots: between the tiny minority of people with substantial surplus wealth and a lifestyle somewhere on the scale between very comfortable and extravagantly luxurious, and the vast majority of even the non-slave population, who at best had a modest amount of spare cash (for more food, for an extra room, for cheap jewellery, for simple tombstones), and at worst were destitute, jobless and homeless.

About the privileged – the haves – of the Roman world we know a great deal. They were the authors of almost all the literature to survive from antiquity. Even writers like Juvenal, who sometimes cast themselves as among the socially disadvantaged, were actually well off, despite their complaints about cascading chamber pots. And it is the rich who leave by far the biggest footprint in the archaeological record, from grand houses to new theatres. Across the empire, they amounted at a generous estimate to 300,000 people in all, including comparatively wealthy local bigwigs as well as the plutocrats in the big cities – and a rather larger total if you add in their other household members. Assuming that the population of the empire in the first two centuries CE was somewhere between 50 and 60 million, what were the living conditions, the lifestyles and the values of the overwhelming majority, the 99 per cent of Romans?

Elite Roman writers were mostly disdainful of those less fortunate, and less rich, than themselves. Apart from their nostalgic admiration of a simple peasant way of life – a fantasy of country picnics, and lazy afternoons under shady trees – they found little virtue in poverty or in the poor or even in earning an honest day's wages. Juvenal is not the only one to write off the priorities of the Roman people as 'bread and circuses'. Fronto, the tutor of Marcus Aurelius, makes exactly the same point when he writes of the emperor Trajan that 'he understood that the Roman people are kept in line by two things beyond all else: the corn dole and entertainments'. Cicero turned his scorn on those who worked for a living: 'The cash that comes from selling your labour is vulgar and unacceptable for a gentleman … for wages are effectively the bonds of slavery.' It became a cliché of Roman moralising that a true gentleman was supported by the profits of his estates, not by wage labour, which was inherently dishonourable. Latin vocabulary itself captured the idea: the desired state of humanity was *otium* (not so much 'leisure', as it is usually translated, but the state of being in control of one's own time); 'business' of any kind was its undesirable opposite, *negotium* ('not *otium*').

Those who became wealthy from nothing were equally the objects of snobbish derision, as jumped-up arrivistes. The character of Trimalchio, the nouveau riche ex-slave in Petronius' *Satyricon* who has made his fortune trading everything from bacon and perfume to slaves, is a simultaneously engaging and ghastly fictional parody of a man with more cash than good taste, who repeatedly gets proper elite behaviour slightly wrong. He keeps his own slaves in rather too vulgar designer uniforms (the porter at Trimalchio's front door is dressed in green with a red belt and spends his time shelling peas into a silver bowl); the walls of his house are boastfully decorated with paintings that tell the story of his career, from the slave market to his current splendour, under the protection of Mercury, the god of moneymaking; and the dinner party he hosts is an impossible combination of every Roman fancy food, from dormice, prepared in honey and poppyseeds, to wine that was well over a hundred years old, vintage 121 BCE, 'when Opimius was consul'. The ignorant Trimalchio presumably does not realise that the name of the diehard conservative who in 121 BCE had 3,000 supporters of Gaius Gracchus put to death is hardly an auspicious name for a vintage, even if wine lasted that long anyway.

The prejudices are obvious, and they tell us more about the world of the writers than of their subjects – especially if, as some modern critics have suggested, Petronius' parody of the elite lifestyle was meant to make his elite readers wonder quite how different they really were from this vulgar ex-slave. The big question is whether, and how, we can re-create a picture of the lives of ordinary Romans that they themselves might have recognised. If surviving literature produces these disdainful caricatures, where else can we turn?

Degrees of poverty

The 50 million or so inhabitants of the Roman Empire did not fall into one single category. Roman society was not divided simply into a small group of the very rich and the rest, a fairly undifferentiated mass, struggling on the breadline. Among those who must count as the non-elite there were different degrees of privilege, status and money, and they included plenty of 'ordinary' or 'middling' types as well as the very poor. It proves much easier to get a glimpse into the lives of some of these types than of others.

The majority of the 50 million would have been peasant farmers, not the fantasy creations of Roman writers but smallholders across the empire, struggling to grow enough to feed themselves in some years, doing better, with a small surplus to sell, in others. For these families, Roman rule made little difference, beyond a different tax collector, a bigger economy into which to sell their produce and a wider range of trinkets to buy if they had any spare cash. In Britain, for example, so far as we can tell from the archaeological traces, there was little significant change in the lives of peasant farmers over more than a millennium, from the end of the Iron Age immediately before the successful Roman invasion in 43 CE, through the Roman occupation, and into the Middles Ages. But there is almost no evidence surviving for the attitudes, aspirations, hopes or fears of these farmers and their families. The only ordinary people in the Roman world we can get to know in that sense, or whose style of life we can begin to reconstruct, are those who lived in the towns and cities.

There was certainly extreme urban poverty. Roman laws expressly forbade any squatting in tombs: 'Anyone who so wishes may prosecute a person who lives or makes his dwelling in a tomb', one Roman legal opinion runs. The implication is that there were homeless people, whether locals or foreigners, citizens, new immigrants or runaway slaves, doing exactly that, camping out in the grand tombs of the

77. This cartoon captures one view of the impact of Roman power on ordinary peasants in the provinces. They are living life in round huts just as they always have done, but can put on an act of embracing Roman culture when, occasionally, required.

aristocracy that lined the roads into most big cities of the empire. Others, it seems, preferred to put up lean-to huts against any convenient wall, from arches to aqueducts, which according to other laws could be demolished if they were judged to be a fire risk or charged a rent if not. The outskirts of many Roman towns may have been not far different from those of modern 'Third World' cities, covered in squatter settlements or shanty towns populated by the nearly starving and those who begged as much as worked for their living. Roman moralists make numerous references to beggars – often to the effect that they are better ignored – and a series of paintings in Pompeii depicting life in the local Forum includes a cameo scene of a hunched beggar, with dog, being handed some small change by a posh lady and her maid, who are not obeying the moralists' advice.

There is, in fact, rather less evidence for this kind of borderline destitution than we might expect. But the reasons for that are clear. First, those with nothing leave very few traces in the historical or archaeological record. Ephemeral shanty towns do not leave a permanent imprint in the soil; those buried with nothing in unmarked graves tell us much less about themselves than those accompanied by an eloquent epitaph. But second, and even more to the point, extreme poverty in the Roman world was a condition that usually solved itself:

78. A drawing of one of the now very faded scenes illustrating life in the Forum, from the House of Julia Felix in Pompeii (first century CE). This is a rare image of interaction between rich and poor in the Roman world. The bearded beggar is unmistakably 'down and out', semi-clad, only in rags, and with a dog for company.

79. The well-preserved apartment block which stood next to the splendour of the Capitoline Hill in Rome. Now it is overshadowed by the huge Victor Emmanuel monument (visible behind) and overlooked by most passers-by.

its victims died. Those without some support mechanism could not survive. Even the corn dole in the city of Rome, the descendant of Gaius Gracchus' initiative in the 120s BCE, did not provide that. It certainly underlined the responsibility of the state for the basic food of its citizens. But the beneficiaries were a large but still limited and privileged group, of about 250,000 male citizens in the first and second centuries CE, who received enough to keep about two people in bread. The dole was not a safety net for all comers.

Many more people occupied the next rungs up on the ladder of wealth, and they have left clearer traces of their lives. There is still a wide spectrum of privilege and comfort. At one end were those with a relatively secure livelihood, often from manufacturing, producing and selling anything from basic bread to fancy clothing; they were families living in several rooms, sometimes above the shop or workshop, possibly with a couple of slaves, even if (as was often the case) they were ex-slaves themselves or the children of ex-slaves. A particularly intimate view of lifestyle at this level comes from a cesspit excavated underneath a small block of retail units and apartments in the town of Herculaneum, Pompeii's neighbour, also destroyed by the eruption of Vesuvius in 79 CE. The contents of the cesspit, still being analysed, are what came down directly from the simple lavatories of the modest flats above, having already passed through the digestive tracts of the roughly 150 residents. It was a varied and decent diet: among other things, they were eating fish, sea urchins (fragments of the spikes survive), chicken, eggs, walnut and figs (the pips go straight through intestines, undigested). Those living on upper floors also used the lavatories as rudimentary waste-disposal units, to get rid of broken glass and crockery, as well as accidentally dropping their gemstones down them. These were people who had some money to spend, household utensils to spare and jewellery to lose.

At the other end of the spectrum were those in a much more precarious position – men, women and children with no permanent trade or particular skill, who must have tried to pick up casual work in bars and restaurants or the sex industry, as porters or hauliers at the docks or as navvies on building sites. Plenty of such labour was needed. One rough and ready estimate, calculating the total quantity of staples – oil, wine and grain – that must have been imported to keep a million people in the city of Rome alive, reckons that it would have taken more than 9 million single 'porter loads' to get the stuff from ship to shore, in sacks or amphorae, each year. Those loads alone would have provided enough work for 3,000 men for about 100 days. But it was seasonal, hence the use of free labourers on a casual basis rather than slaves, and it meant an uncertain livelihood. Many of these people must have often gone hungry; telltale lesions in surviving skeletons (especially in their teeth) point to various forms of malnutrition affecting not only the very poorest in the city. They would have lived in the ancient equivalent of hostels, renting by the hour, or sharing a single room with several others and sleeping in shifts. They would probably not even have enjoyed many of the entertainments often supposed to have been the staple and the passion of the Roman poor. The seating capacity of the Colosseum, vast as it seems, was around 50,000, which in a city of a million probably means that the audience for gladiatorial shows and bloody beast hunts was relatively upmarket. It was not made up of these people, who, if they only fell one rung lower, would have been camping in a tomb or in a squatter settlement.

The huge multistorey apartment blocks (*insulae*, or 'islands) common in Rome and its port of Ostia symbolise this hierarchy among the more ordinary Romans and capture the spectrum from the reasonably comfortable to those only barely hanging on. Insulae provided rented accommodation at a high density, which is how such a large population managed to cram into a relatively small area in the city of Rome. They were attractive investment opportunities for their owners and provided a job for ruthless rent collectors. The epitaph of one tenant, Ancarenus Nothus, an ex-slave who died at the age of forty-three and whose ashes were buried in a shared tomb just outside the walls of Rome, hints at common complaints in some simple lines of verse, as if spoken from the afterlife: 'I'm no longer worried that I shall die of hunger / I'm rid of aching legs and getting a deposit for my rent / I'm enjoying free board and lodging for eternity.' But even if the landlord came down heavily on all of them, some tenants lived much more comfortably than others.

The basic logic was always that the lower down in the building you lived, the more spacious and expensive your accommodation was, and the higher up in the building, the cheaper, pokier and more dangerous, with no facilities for cooking or washing and no means of escape in the (frequent) event of a fire. As Juvenal jokes, someone living at the top ('with nothing to keep him from the rain but the roof tiles') was simply the last one to die if a blaze started further down. The logic is exactly the reverse of that of the modern apartment block with its luxury penthouses, and it is perfectly illustrated in one of the best-preserved insulae in the city of Rome, still visible just underneath the Capitoline Hill and within a few metres of the shining temples that once stood there (literally shining: by the end of the first century CE the Temple of Jupiter was roofed with gilded tiles). In this block, shops with living accommodation on a mezzanine occupied the street level. The first floor, or piano nobile, contained a few spacious apartments; by the fourth floor, which still survives, there were a series of small bedsits, though each probably housed a family rather than a single person; and above, it must have been worse. The city's lack of zoning meant that some of the grandest public celebrations on the Capitoline took place within a stone's throw of what was on its upper floors a slum.

It is the world of the people who occupied these blocks, and others like them, that is the theme of the rest of this chapter. Realistically, it will be more the world of those on the lower floors than those on the upper: the more disposable income that people had, the more evidence they have left for us. We will look at the world of work, of leisure, of culture and of anxiety: not just where and how the non-elite lived but also how they faced the inequality of Roman life, what fun they enjoyed and what resources they had against adversity of all kinds, from petty crime to pain and sickness.

The world of work

Cicero and most of the elite professed to despise wage labour. But for the majority of the urban inhabitants of the Roman world, as now, their job was the key to their identity. It was usually tough. Most people who needed a regular income to survive (and that was most people) worked, if they could, until they died; the army was an exception in having any kind of retirement package, and even that usually involved working a small farm. Many children worked as soon as they were physically capable, whether they were free or slave. Skeletons of the very young have been discovered in excavations with clear signs in their bones and joints of hard physical labour; one particular cemetery just outside Rome, near an ancient laundry and textile works, contains the remains of young people who obviously had years of heavy work behind them (showing the effects of the stamping and the treading needed in the treatment of cloth, rather than of skipping and ball games). Children are even commemorated as workers in their epitaphs. Modern sensibilities might hope that the simple tombstone in Spain of a four-year-old child, shown carrying his mining tools, was put up in memory of some young local mining mascot. Most likely he was an active worker.

Only the offspring of the rich spent their youth learning grammar, rhetoric, philosophy and how to make speeches – or the less meaty syllabus, from reading and writing to spinning and music, offered to girls. Child labour was the norm. It is not a problem, or even a category, that most Romans would have understood. The invention of 'childhood' and the regulation of what work 'children' could do only came fifteen hundred years later and is still a peculiarly Western preoccupation.

Their tombstones make clear how important work was to the personal identity of ordinary Romans. Whereas Scipio Barbatus, and

80. This rather battered memorial is one of the few tombstones apparently to commemorate a child worker. In his hands the four-year-old holds a basket and a pick, similar to objects found in excavations at the Spanish mining sites.

81. The tombstone of a 'dyer of purple'
from North Italy. Underneath his portrait
are the tools of his trade, including scales,
phials and hanging skeins of wool.

others like him at the top of the social hierarchy, emphasised the
political offices they had held or the battles they had won, many more
people blazoned what they did as a job. More than 200 occupations
are known in this way from the city of Rome alone. Men and women
(or whoever commissioned their memorials) often summarised their
careers in just a few words and images, with a job description and some
recognisable symbols of their craft. Gaius Pupius Amicus, for example,
an ex-slave and by trade a dyer of 'purple' – a notoriously expensive
dye, extracted from tiny shellfish and according to law used only to
colour cloth worn by senators and the emperor – proudly described
himself as a *purpurarius* and had various items of his craft equipment
carved on the stone. Other tombs displayed sculptured panels depicting the deceased in action at their job, from midwives and butchers
to a particularly splendid seller of poultry.

Occasionally the whole tomb was designed even more ambitiously,
to display the craft of the dead person, as if to equate the man or

woman with the job itself. In the late first century BCE one enterpris-
ing baker was responsible for a large memorial to himself and his
wife in a prime position just outside the Roman city walls. Marcus
Vergilius Eurysaces was likely an ex-slave, and – to judge from the
scale of the tomb, 10 metres high – he had made a large amount of
money from his business. The inscribed epitaph describes him as
a 'baker and contractor', which points at the very least to a chain
of bakeries and probably some lucrative public contracts for bread
supply. The whole edifice is constructed in the shape of bread-making
equipment, and around the top, where on official monuments you
would expect a sculpted frieze depicting something like a religious
procession or a triumph, there are instead scenes from the working
life in one of Eurysaces' bakeries; a figure in a toga directing operations is presumably meant to be the man himself. If Eurysaces knew of
Cicero's disparaging words on the nature of trade and of wage labour,
then this tomb would be the equivalent of two fingers put up to such

82. A marble relief showing a poultry seller's stall from Ostia,
perhaps from a tomb or perhaps a shop sign. The man second from
the left seems to be drumming up trade, and behind the counter
a woman is serving customers. The stall is constructed from cages
(containing a couple of rabbits), on which a pair of monkeys sits.

snobbery. Equally, a passing aristocrat might well have thought that there was a touch of Trimalchio about it.

But more than individual identity was at stake here. There were communal and social aspects too, as trades and crafts provided a

83. The tomb of Eurysaces the baking contractor; dating to the first century BCE, it was preserved because it was built into a tower of the later city walls. The strange roundels on the façade almost certainly represent the kneading machines used in large scale bakeries.

context for joint activities among their workers, for promotion of the interests they held in common and for a shared sense of identity. All across the empire, local trade associations (*collegia*) flourished, with members who were both slave and free, a combination reflecting the usual mixture of statuses in most kinds of work. In one *collegium* based just outside Rome, rules drawn up in the second century CE stipulated that any slave member who was granted his freedom had to donate 'an amphora of good wine' to the others, presumably for the celebratory party. Sometimes they had impressive headquarters, usually a defined administrative structure, rules and regulations, entry fees and annual subscriptions, and they could act as political pressure groups, talking shops, dining clubs and burial insurance agencies. For one element of the members' subscription to the association regularly went towards guaranteeing them a decent funeral, which may partly account for the prominence of job descriptions on epitaphs. You were buried as a carpenter, in a funeral paid for by carpenters.

These were a long way from guilds in the medieval sense; they did not set qualifications for practising particular crafts or impose what was effectively a closed shop. Nor were they exactly the ancient version of a trades union or business cartel – although it seems, from a surviving ruling of the provincial governor there, that the bakers of Ephesus, in what is now Turkey, did cause a riot in the middle of the second century CE by going out on strike, and Petronius has one of his characters in the *Satyricon* complain that the bakers (again) are in league with the local officials to keep the bread prices high. But at some point an historic stake in Roman society was invented for these associations. There was a tall, but important, story that it was the second king of Rome, Numa, who first established them, to include the builders, bronze workers, potters, goldsmiths, dyers, leather processers and musicians. Whoever dreamt this up, and it *was* a dream, was giving the craftsmen and their organisations a genealogy that went back almost as far as it was possible to go in Roman history.

Evidence for the public profile of trades and workers can still be found at Pompeii. The electoral slogans visible even now on the walls of the town, the temporary painted signs urging the voters to back this or that candidate in the elections to the local council, provide one example. These are not unlike modern political posters, though they are rather more standardised, usually taking the form of a simple sentence along the lines of 'Crescens asks for Gnaeus Helvius Sabinus as aedile'. Variations on the theme include a few traces of negative campaigning ('The little thieves ask for Vatia as aedile' was presumably much the same as saying 'Don't vote for Vatia'); but there is also a series of notices that give a candidate the backing of a particular group of tradesmen, including the bakers, carpenters, chicken keepers, laundry workers and mule drivers. How formal this backing was is uncertain. We should not necessarily imagine some official vote of endorsement by the local association, though that might have been the case. But at the very least some of them had got together to decide that *as laundry workers* (or whatever ...) they were supporting one candidate rather than another.

Pompeii also allows us a rare view into the working environment of some of these people, in particular into the laundries. Roman laundry work and textile processing (a combination conventionally known as 'fulling') was not a glamorous trade. One of the staple ingredients in this process was human urine, which was the source of the joke attributed to the emperor Vespasian about money not smelling. And the young skeletons found in the cemetery near the textile works outside Rome show the intense stresses and strains of the physical labour involved. But one of the many fulleries in Pompeii gives an alternative picture of the industry, for the consumption of the fullers themselves. Decorating the working areas where the men – and it was mostly men – pummelled and processed the cloth, in whatever foul-smelling mixture they used, were paintings of exactly those elaborate and messy processes going on. It was these paintings that the men saw – a version of what they were doing reflected back to them in a sanitised, even glamorised, form – as they went about their long days' work (see plate 18).

Cicero's rivals may have mocked him, incorrectly or not, for being the son of a laundry proprietor. But in this laundry at Pompeii, as in many others, no doubt, across the empire, the launderers were offered an image of the nobility of labour, a pride in its execution and a sense of belonging, that Cicero would never have dreamt of.

Bar culture

Elite Romans were often even more dismissive – and anxious – about what the rest of the population got up to when they were *not* working. Their keenness for shows and spectacles was one thing, but even worse were the bars and cheap cafés and restaurants where ordinary men tended to congregate. Lurid images were conjured up of the types of people you were likely to meet there. Juvenal, for example, pictures a seedy drinking den at the port of Ostia patronised, he claims, by cut-throats, sailors, thieves and runaway slaves, hangmen and coffin makers, plus the occasional eunuch priest (presumably off duty from the sanctuary of the Great Mother in the town). And writing later, in the fourth century CE, one Roman historian complained that the 'lowest' sort of person spent the whole night in bars, and he picked out as especially disgusting the snorting noise the dice players made as they concentrated on the board and drew in breath through their snotty noses.

There are also records of repeated attempts to impose legal restrictions or taxes on these establishments. Tiberius, for example, apparently banned the sale of pastries; Claudius is supposed to have abolished 'taverns' entirely and to have forbidden the serving of boiled meat and hot water (presumably to be mixed, in the standard Roman fashion, with wine – but then why not ban the wine?); and Vespasian is said to have ruled that bars and pubs should sell no form of food at all except peas and beans. Assuming that all this is not a fantasy of ancient biographers and historians, it can only have been fruitless posturing, legislation at its most symbolic, which the resources of the Roman state had no means to enforce.

Elites everywhere tend to worry about places where the lower orders congregate, and – though there was certainly a rough side and some rude talk – the reality of the normal bar was tamer than its reputation. For bars were not just drinking dens but an essential part of everyday life for those who had, at best, limited cooking facilities in their lodgings. As with the arrangement of apartment blocks, the Roman pattern is precisely the reverse of our own: the Roman rich, with their kitchens and multiple dining rooms, ate at home; the poor, if they wanted much more than the ancient equivalent of a sandwich, had to eat out. Roman towns were full of cheap bars and cafés, and it was here that a large number of ordinary Romans spent many hours of their non-working lives. Pompeii is again one of the best examples. Taking account of the still unexcavated parts of the town and resisting the temptation (as some archaeologists have not) to call any building with a serving counter a bar, we can reckon that there were well

84. Looking out from a typical Roman bar, in Pompeii. A counter faces the street with large bowls, from which food or drink could be served to takeaway customers. The steps on the left acted as a display stand for more food.

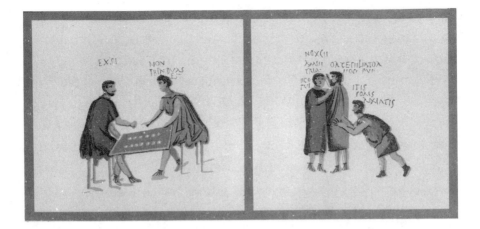

85. A brawl in a bar over a game of dice. In this nineteenth-century
copy of some of the paintings from the Bar of Salvius in Pompeii,
the argument starts in the left–hand panel. '*Exsi*' shouts one of the
players, 'I've won, I'm out', while his opponent disputes the throw.
In the next scene, the landlord, on the right, is not only telling
them to get out, but man-handling them towards the door.

over a hundred such places there, for a population of perhaps 12,000
residents, and travellers passing through.

They were built to a fairly standard plan: a counter facing the pavement, for the 'takeaway' service; an inner room with tables and chairs
for the eat-in, waiter service; and usually a display stand for food and
drink, as well as a brazier or oven for preparing hot dishes and drinks.
In a couple of cases at Pompeii, in the same way as in the fullery,
their decoration includes a series of paintings depicting scenes – part
fantasy, part real – of life in the bar itself. There is not much evidence
of the terrible moral turpitude that Roman writers feared. One image
shows the wine supplies being delivered in a large vat, another some
snacks being consumed underneath sausages and other delicacies
strung from the ceiling. The 'worst' signs are one full-on image of sex
(hard to make out now because some modern moralist has defaced it),
a number of graffiti along the lines of 'I fucked the landlady' (whether

statement of fact, boast or insult is impossible to say) and several paintings which show customers playing dice games, presumably for money, snorting or not. On the walls of one bar, where speech bubbles accompany the pictures to flesh out what is going on, the game is leading to a fight and to some decidedly ungentlemanly language. After a disputed throw ('It was a two, not a three'), the landlord has to intervene: 'If you want to fight, get outside,' he is saying, as landlords always do, while the pair start to foul-mouth each other ('Scumbag, I had the three, I won', 'No, come on, cocksucker, I did').

Gambling and board games were one of the most extreme cases of Roman elite double standards. Some of the loftiest aristocrats were keen gamers. According to Suetonius, the emperor Claudius was such an enthusiast that he wrote a book on dice games and had his carriage specially adapted so that he could continue playing on the move, while the first Augustus was so addicted to gaming – but so mindful of the purses of his friends – that he would simply give his guests large quantities of cash to use as their stake (though Suetonius hints at his own disapproval when he observes that Augustus did not seek to deny his habit, and compares it archly to another of the emperor's supposed hobbies: deflowering virgins). Board games were not only a man's pastime, either. They were a favourite recreation of the elderly Ummidia Quadratilla too – whether played for money or not, Pliny does not say. But, as Juvenal observes, on this occasion pointing a well-directed finger at Roman hypocrisy, when the ordinary people indulged in these games, the elite were outraged and thought it 'a disgrace'.

One of their main objections was that dicing was a gateway to crime. The brawl depicted in the Pompeian bar points to that on a very small scale; on a grander scale, the prominence of 'dicers' (*aleatores*) among Catiline's followers suggested a connection with conspiracy and treason. But, in the heads of the rich and powerful, the destabilising effect of gambling was a major factor too. In a world where the hierarchy of wealth had always directly correlated with political power and social status, the possibility, however remote, of the established order being upturned by money that was obtained solely by chance was dangerously disruptive. The riches of Trimalchio were bad enough; the idea that a fortune might be obtained by a throw of the dice was far worse. So there were attempts to control gambling among the general population, to restrict it to particular times or occasions and to limit the legal responsibility for recovering the debts incurred. This legislation had about as much effect as the restrictions on bars. Gaming boards are found all over the Roman world. Those that survive are in durable stone and come from tombs, bars and army barracks or are carved into pavements and into the steps of public buildings – presumably intended as an amusement for people with time on their hands.

Dice games had different names and were played by different rules and on different designs of board. No one has ever managed to reconstruct quite how any of these games worked in detail (it is rather like trying to figure out how to play Monopoly without the instructions or any of the pieces or the cards). But, despite that, one common type of board offers some memorable glimpses of the atmosphere of play and the attitudes of the players. These boards were made for a game that clearly involved moving pieces across thirty-six points, arranged in three rows of twelve, each row divided into two groups of six. But taking the place of the 'squares' that are usually found on a modern board are letters of the alphabet, and the players moved their pieces from letter to letter. The letters are often carefully arranged to read as words, so that the boards proclaim some snappy slogans: in six words of six letters each. These were some of the mottoes of bar culture and of the gamers themselves.

A few are slightly dourly moralising, reflecting on the downsides of the very activity that the boards were designed for. 'The nasty dots on the dice compel even the skilled player to play by luck' (*INVIDA PUNCTA IUBENT FELICE LUDERE DOCTUM*) or 'The board is a circus. Retire when you're beaten. You don't know how to play' (*TABULA CIRCUS BICTUS RECEDE LUDERE NESCIS*). More are triumphalist in a very Roman way, even if they hark back to rather old triumphs. 'The Parthians have been slaughtered, the Briton conquered, play on, Romans' (*PARTHI OCCISI BRITTO VICTUS LUDITE ROMANI*), as one board probably of the third century CE proclaims. Others stress a down-to-earth popular hedonism, referring to the races in the Circus Maximus ('The circus is packed, the people shout, the citizens are having fun', *CIRCUS PLENUS CLAMOR POPULI GAUDIA CIVIUM*) or to even simpler pleasures of life. On the steps of the Forum at Timgad, one board sums it all up with 'Hunting, bathing, gaming, laughing: that's living' (*VENARI LAVARE LUDERE RIDERE OCCEST VIVERE*).

These slogans undercut some of the stern disapproval of the Roman elite, capturing the banter and zest of bar life, the pleasure that ordinary people could take in being Roman (from circuses to conquest), and a no-nonsense view of what amounted to good living and contentment. It was with slogans like these that the average Pompeian laundry

86. Another variant on 'The Circus is packed ...' Here the last line (now broken on the right) reads IANUAE TENSAE – 'the doors are heaving'.

worker sat down in the evening in his local bar, with a glass or two of wine (mixed with hot water), a friend, a board and some dice – and dreamt about gambling his way into a better life.

One or two did get lucky. A scrawled graffito at Pompeii records the delight of one winner at his gaming victory in a nearby town: 'I won at Nuceria, playing dice, 855 1/2 denarii. Honestly, it's true.' It was, as the excitement of the scrawler makes clear, an almost unbelievable win and a substantial sum; at four sesterces to the denarius, it amounted to almost 4,000 sesterces, or roughly four times the annual salary of a Roman soldier. It must have made a big difference to the winner. He cannot have been desperately poor in the first place. As the shrewd Augustus realised, gambling always required a stake and, even in the bars and on street corners, was the pastime of those with a bit of spare cash. Presumably a win of this size would have meant improved lodgings, new clothes, faster transport (500 sesterces would buy a new mule) and better food and wine (one sesterce, according to a surviving Pompeian price list, would buy a glass, or pitcher, of the best Falernian vintage, four times the cost of the local plonk). But, whatever the paranoia of the elite, none of this was likely to undermine the foundation of the social order.

Putting up and making do

Four thousand sesterces was, in any case, a rare win and beyond the dreams of most small-time gamblers in local bars. Even the simplest slogans on the game boards would have been aspirational for some. 'Hunting, bathing, gaming, laughing' might have been basic pleasures for those in country towns like Timgad, but for the men and women on the street in Rome, hunting was only a dream. For those at the top of an insula block, the races – as in 'The Circus is packed ...' – would have been a rare treat (though more within reach than the gladiatorial shows: the capacity of the Circus Maximus, the main race track, at 250,000, was five times that of the Colosseum). Even those living at the more comfortable, lower levels of the insulae would have faced, in our terms, a risky future; their comfort was always precarious. Some modern historians have even speculated that the popularity of games of chance among ordinary Romans had something to do with the close match to the structure of their lives. For most of the Roman people, life was always a gamble, and making money not far short of a lottery.

To be living adequately at one moment was no guarantee for the next. Those who were making a small profit today could be derailed tomorrow, by some illness that would prevent them from working, by the regular floods or fires that would wreck their homes. The grandeur of the remains of the city of Rome – and its nineteenth-century flood defences, which have largely prevented devastating inundations – can deflect our attention from the natural disasters that repeatedly fell upon the place, and unequally on the rich and the poor, even though they often lived as close neighbours. A few metres of extra height, up the slope of a hill, would have given a rich house protection from floods that inundated the nicer apartments in low-lying insulae. Fire could be a problem for anyone; in a terrible blaze in 192 CE Galen lost the contents of his lock-up storeroom near the Forum, including some of his medical writing, doctor's instruments, medicines and other valuables (as we learn from the manuscript of his essay on the subject that was rediscovered only in 2005). But it was a particular problem in a high-rise block, especially when the residents tried to cook or keep warm with unstable braziers on the upper floors.

Petty, and not so petty, crime might regularly have left any of these people without their savings, their precious possessions, their clothes or the tools of their trade. Then as now, the rich with their guard dogs and the equivalent of security systems (in the shape of slaves) complained most loudly about house crime and street robbery. The poor were the main victims. Some of the stories preserved in handwritten papyrus documents discovered in Roman Egypt – often even more immediate and informal than the public pronouncements inscribed on stone elsewhere in the empire – give personal accounts of the everyday crime, violence and thuggery that was endemic. One man, for example, complains of a group of lads attacking his house, beating him up ('on every limb of my body') and walking off with some of his clothes, including a tunic and a cloak, a pair of scissors and some beer. Another claims that some ne'er-do-well who owed him money had turned up at his house and attacked his pregnant wife, who had miscarried and was now 'in danger of her life'. More than 3,000 miles away, in the town of Bath (then Aquae Sulis) in the province of Britain, other inscribed records point to persistent thieving of clothes and accessories, from rings to gloves and (especially) cloaks.

There were few resources, and almost no regular public services, to mitigate these crises. In the city of Rome, by the first century CE there was a small and rudimentary fire service, but it was equipped with only a few blankets and pails of water and vinegar to douse the flames and relied more on demolition of the surrounding properties to break the blaze – which was a good idea, unless you lived in one of those properties. And there was no police force to whom crimes could be reported or through whom redress could be sought. Most victims of crime would have relied on their own strong arms or friends, family or local vigilantes to get even with the person they believed responsible. There was no system for dealing effectively, through official channels, with ordinary wrongdoing, only a cycle of rough justice and brutal retaliation. The unfortunate pregnant wife who miscarried after her assault might have been a victim of just that, despite the tear-jerking account by her apparently innocent aggrieved husband. The story of one Roman shopkeeper hints at the start of another cycle. One dark evening he had pursued a thief who had stolen a lamp from near his counter. In the struggle that followed, the thief got out a whip and set about lashing the shopkeeper, who retaliated – and in the process knocked out one of the assailant's eyes.

The sophisticated edifice of Roman law, despite its extraordinary expertise in formulating legal rules and principles, deciding issues of responsibility and determining rights of ownership and contract, had little impact on the lives of those below the elite and offered little help for their problems. When they tried to use it, the system was sometimes simply overloaded. We do not know how far the complaints of those ordinary victims in Roman Egypt ever progressed, although they were aimed at officials in the province in the hope of some legal action. But we do know, from another papyrus document, that at the beginning of the third century CE one governor of Egypt (the prefect, as he was called there) had received in just three days in a single place more than 1,800 petitions from those wanting to press cases or complaints. The majority of them must have been brushed under the carpet.

Most of the time, the official institutions of the law were not interested in the problems of the ordinary people, or vice versa. Occasionally, Roman academics and specialists in the law looked at the misfortunes of the poor as knotty case studies; they agreed, for example, that the shopkeeper had not acted unlawfully, provided the thief really had used his whip first. And even more occasionally, especially in matters of inheritance and civil status, ordinary people found it worth obtaining a legal ruling. At Herculaneum, for example, several documents have been discovered that were written on wax tablets (the pen scratches are still visible on the wood that lay under the original wax) and record a number of witness statements taken in a tricky, and now baffling, local dispute. The question turned on whether a woman from the town had been born a slave or free. Like most people in the Roman world, she had no formal proof of status, and in this case (the result is unknown) someone had the time, contacts and cash to take the issue to the very top in Rome itself. But in general the law was out of the reach of most of the population, who, as we shall soon see, often looked on trials and legal processes more as a threat to be feared than as a possible protection.

So, if not to the law, where did the ordinary people look for help, beyond family and friends? Often it was to 'alternative' support systems, to the gods, to the supernatural and to those, such as cheap fortune tellers, who claimed to have access to knowledge about the future and the outcome of problems – and about whom the elite were predictably sniffy. The only reason we know about the cloak crime in Roman Bath is because people went to the sacred spring of Sulis, the local goddess, and inscribed a curse on the thief on small lead tablets and cast them into the water. Many of these tablets have been discovered, with their angry or desperate messages: 'Docilianus son of Brucerus to the most holy goddess Sulis, I curse whoever stole my hooded cloak, whether man or woman, slave or free, that the goddess Sulis inflict death on him and not let him sleep or have children now or in the future until he brings my cloak to the temple of her divinity', as one runs, typical of many.

One of the alternative resources, and one of the strangest documents to have survived from classical antiquity, takes us directly into the specific problems and anxieties that afflicted the lives of the men and women on the ancient street. Titled *The Oracles of Astrampsychus,* after a legendary ancient Egyptian magician (with whom it had nothing to do whatsoever), and claiming (implausibly) in its introduction to have been written by the philosopher Pythagoras and to have been the secret behind the success of Alexander the Great, it is in fact an off-the-peg fortune-telling kit, dating probably to the second century CE, centuries after either Pythagoras or Alexander. It consists of a numbered list of ninety-two questions that someone might want to ask of a fortune teller, plus a list of more than a thousand possible answers. The idea was that the questioner chose the question that best represented his or her problem and gave its number to the fortune teller, who by following the kit's instructions – which involve a good deal of mumbo jumbo, choosing more numbers, taking away the number you first thought of and so on – was eventually directed to the single right answer out of the thousand.

Whoever compiled the *Oracles* thought those ninety-two questions summed up the problems that were most likely to send people to the cheap local clairvoyant. One or two may suggest some relatively upmarket customers: 'Will I become a senator?' was hardly a concern for many – though it may have been the kind of fantasy question that 'Will I marry a handsome prince?' has been in the modern world, posed by those unlikely to meet, still less marry, a member of any royal family. Most of the questions focus on much more ordinary anxieties. Some, predictably, are about health, marriage and children. Number 42, 'Will I survive the illness?', must have been a common choice, though it is interesting that 'Have I been poisoned?' also appears on the list, a suspicion obviously not restricted to the imperial house. Number 24, 'Is my wife having a baby?', is nicely balanced by the guilty query 'Will I soon get caught as an adulterer?' and by 'Will I rear the baby?', pointing to the ancient dilemma of whether to expose a newborn. It is clear also that slaves were among the intended customers ('Will I be freed?' and 'Will I be sold?') and that travel was seen as one of life's pressing dangers ('Is the traveller alive?' and 'Will I sail safely?'). But the main preoccupation is money and livelihood, appearing in question after question: 'Will I be able to borrow the money?', 'Will I open a workshop?', 'Will I pay back what I owe?', 'Are my belongings going to be sold at auction?', 'Will I inherit from a friend?' The law, when it is present, tends to be a looming menace: from 'Am I safe from prosecution?' to 'Will I be safe if someone informs on me?'

The complicated system could produce good, bad and ambivalent answers to all these questions. Assuming that the customers took the responses seriously (and some might have been as sceptical as many horoscope readers now), 'You won't be caught as an adulterer' was obviously rather better than 'You will be caught as an adulterer, but not for some time'. 'You haven't been poisoned, but you have been bewitched' would merely have raised another anxiety, while 'The traveller is alive, he is on his way' would in most circumstances have been cause for celebration. Throughout, there is a lingering tone of resignation about the responses: 'Wait', 'Not yet', 'Be patient' and 'Don't expect it' are repeated words of advice.

This is a tone also captured in the only genre of mainstream Roman literature that can claim an origin outside the world of the elite: the animal fable. The most famous of these stories were attributed to Aesop, supposedly a Greek slave from centuries earlier, who still gives his name to many modern collections of them (*Aesop's Fables*). But in Rome another key figure, who adapted earlier versions and composed new ones, with a specifically Roman spin, was Phaedrus, an ex-slave from the imperial household who wrote during the reign of Tiberius, in the early first century CE. Many of these stories sharply encapsulate the inequities of Roman society and the point of view from the bottom up, by pitting the little animals of the world, such as foxes, frogs and sheep, against the creatures of power, in the shape of lions, eagles, wolves and hawks.

Very occasionally the underdog manages to win. A mother fox, for example, recovers her babies, which a mother eagle had snatched as food for her own young; the fox starts a fire, and the eagle releases the cubs to rescue her own brood. But usually the dice are stacked against the powerless. In one story, a cow, a goat and a sheep go into partnership with a lion, but when they together capture a large, tasty stag, the lion takes it all and refuses to share. In another, a crane puts her head down the throat of a wolf to remove a bone on which the animal was choking but is cheated of the promised reward (wasn't it enough, the wolf demands, that she did not get her head bitten off?). Overall, the message is a striking contrast with the optimistic fantasies of gambling. The only real option, many of these fables insist, is to put up with one's lot. The frogs ask Jupiter to give them a king, and he gives them a log; when they ask for a better one, they are given a snake, which eats them up. A little jackdaw, who dresses himself up in fine feathers as a grand peacock, is rejected as an imposter by the peacocks and rejected again, this time as a bird getting above himself, when he tries to return to the jackdaws. It is the Trimalchio story in a very different guise and from a very different point of view.

One thing is for certain: there is no help for any of these poor creatures in the forces of the law. That is horribly demonstrated in the story of a swallow returning from abroad, who had built her nest in the wall of a courtroom and hatched seven eggs there. A serpent came along while the mother was away and devoured all the nestlings. The law might protect the rights of some, so the fable's moral runs, but not of the poor young swallows, whose murder took place under the judges' noses.

Swallows and serpents

Given the huge gulf between the haves and the have-nots in the Roman world, why was there not more open social and political conflict? How was it that in the city of Rome, the emperor and a few thousand of the wealthy, plus their slave staff, managed to monopolise acres of land, including sprawling mansions and spacious pleasure parks around the city's edge, when close to a million people were crammed into the space left over? Why, to put it in terms of the fable, did the swallows not rise up in revolt against the serpents?

One answer is that there was probably more conflict than is recorded, even if it was for the most part guerrilla warfare rather than outright revolt: rotten eggs thrown at the curtains of passing sedan chairs rather than coordinated assaults on the gates of the imperial palace. Roman writers did not have much of an eye for moderate levels of unrest. But emperors were certainly anxious about the kind of reception they would receive when they went to public games and spectacles. And, although public order did not repeatedly break down under the rule of the emperors as it had in the conflicts of the late Republic, there is evidence of occasional violent riots in Rome and in other towns of the empire. The main cause was disruption to the food supply. In 51 CE Claudius was pelted with bread in the Forum (an odd weapon in a food shortage, you might think) and had to be smuggled into the palace by a back door. At roughly the same time, in Aspendus in modern Turkey, one local official only narrowly escaped being burned alive by an angry crowd protesting against the landowners who had locked their grain away, intending it for export. But food was not the only issue.

In 61 CE, a leading senator was murdered by one of his slaves, and the senate decided to follow the traditional rules for such a crime, which insisted that all of the victim's slaves be put to death along with the guilty party (the threat of such a punishment was meant to encourage slaves to inform on one another). On this occasion, there were 400 of them altogether, all innocent. The people took to the streets in outrage at the severity of what was proposed and in a display of solidarity between the slaves and the free population, many of whom would have once been slaves themselves. But even though a significant number of senators were on the side of the rioters, the emperor Nero brought the troops in to prevent trouble and had the sentence carried out.

Another answer is that, despite the vast disparities of wealth, the disdain of the elite for the less fortunate, and the glaring double standards, there was a greater cultural overlap between the rich and at least the 'middling' people of Rome, or those on the lower floors of the insula blocks, than we might imagine. Scratch the surface, and the two cultures prove to be more permeable than they first seem, the outlook of the swallows not always so drastically different from the outlook of the serpents.

We have already seen some hints of that. The speech bubbles in the bar and the cleverly written epitaphs (sometimes composed as poetry, with all the complex rules governing that in Latin) suggest a world where the ability to read and write was taken for granted. There have been endless, inconclusive debates in recent years about exactly how many of the inhabitants of the Roman Empire were literate. Across the Roman world as a whole, country and town, the number may have been very low, well under 20 per cent of adult men. But it must have been much higher than that in urban communities, where many small traders, craftsmen and slaves would have needed some level of basic literacy and numeracy to function successfully in their jobs (taking the orders, counting the cash, organising deliveries and so on). There are indications too that 'functional literacy' of that sort gave even the 'middling' people some stake in what we would think of as high classical culture.

There are more than fifty quotations from the poetry of Virgil scrawled as graffiti on the walls of Pompeii. That certainly does not mean that the *Aeneid* or his other poems were widely read in their entirety. The majority of the quotes are of the first words of the first book of the *Aeneid* ('*Arma virumque cano*', 'Arms and the man I sing') or the first words of the second book ('*Conticuere omnes*', 'Everyone fell silent') – lines that had probably become as quotable as 'To be or not to be'. And many of them might have been the work of rich lads, for whom Virgil was a school textbook; it is a fallacy to imagine that only the poor write on walls. But it would be implausible to suppose that all of these scrawlings had a rich pedigree.

The signs are that, even if in bite-sized chunks, Virgil's poetry was one shared cultural commodity, to be quoted, adapted and even used for jokes and play. The façade of one Pompeian laundry was decorated with a scene taken from the story of the *Aeneid*, showing the hero Aeneas leading his father and son from the wreckage of Troy, on their way to found the new Troy in Italy. Just nearby some joker scrawled, in a parody of the famous first line of the poem, '*Fullones ululamque cano, non arma virumque*' – 'The fullers and their owl I sing, not arms and the man' (referring to the bird that was a trade mascot of the laundry business). It was hardly high culture, but it does point to a shared frame of reference between the world of the street and the world of classic literature.

An even more striking case of that is found in the decoration of a bar designed in the second century CE in the port town of Ostia. The main theme of the painting is the standard ancient line-up of Greek philosophers and gurus traditionally grouped under the title of 'The Seven Sages': they include Thales of Miletus, the sixth-century BCE thinker famous for claiming that water was the origin of the universe, and his rough contemporaries Solon of Athens, an almost legendary lawgiver, and Chilon of Sparta, another early luminary and intellectual. Some of the paintings have not survived, but originally the full seven would have been there, shown seated on elegant chairs and carrying scrolls. But there was a surprise. For each of them was accompanied by a slogan not on their specialist subjects of politics, science, law or ethics – but on defecation, and running along a familiar scatological theme (see plate 15).

Above Thales ran the words 'Thales advised those who shit hard to really work at it'; above Solon, 'To shit well Solon stroked his belly'; and above Chilon, 'Cunning Chilon taught how to fart without making a noise.' Beneath the Sages there was another row of figures, all sitting together on a communal multiseater lavatory (a normal arrangement in the Roman world). They too are uttering lavatorial mottoes: for example, 'Jump up and down and you'll go quicker' and 'It's coming'.

One way of explaining this is as an aggressive popular joke against elite culture. The ordinary boys in the bar were enjoying some scatological fun against the pillars of the elite intellectual establishment, by seeing their wisdom in terms of the lavatory. And that must be one side of it: bringing high thoughts down to the level of defecation. But it was more complicated than that. These slogans do not only assume a literate audience, or at least enough literates among the customers to be able to read the slogans to the non-literates. In order to devise and to get the joke here you also had to know something about the Seven Sages; if Thales of Miletus meant absolutely nothing to you, then his advice on defecation was hardly funny. In order to take a swipe against the pretensions of intellectual life, you had to have some knowledge of it.

There are many ways to imagine the life in this bar: the rowdy guffawing at the lavatorial humour, the occasional discussion about what exactly Chilon's claim to fame was, the bantering with the landlord, the flirtation with the waiting staff. The customers would have come for all kinds of reasons: to get a good, hot meal, to enjoy an evening in jollier and warmer surroundings than they had at home or simply to get drunk. Some would have been the sort to dream of the riches that came with a lucky throw of the dice. Others would have believed that it was better to put up with your lot in life rather than lose the little extra you had on the gaming board. Many would have resented the arrogance and disdain, the double standards and the lifestyle of their rich neighbours; lack of zoning in Roman cities may have had its equitable side, but it also meant that the poor constantly had their noses rubbed in the privilege of others.

What all would have agreed, both rich and poor, was that to be rich was a desirable state, that poverty was to be avoided if you possibly could. Just as the ambition of Roman slaves was usually to gain freedom for themselves, not to abolish slavery as an institution, so the ambitions of the poor were not radically to reconfigure the social order but to find a place for themselves nearer the top of the hierarchy of wealth. Apart from a very few philosophical extremists, no one in the

Roman world seriously believed that poverty was honourable – until the growth of Christianity, which we shall explore further in the next chapter. The idea that the rich man might have a problem entering the kingdom of heaven would have seemed as preposterous to those hanging out in our Ostian bar as to the plutocrat in his mansion.

CHAPTER TWELVE

·

ROME OUTSIDE ROME

Pliny's province

IN 109 CE, Pliny the Younger left Italy and his lavish country villa to travel for at least four weeks, over almost 2,000 miles, to the province of Bithynia. Lawyer, advocate and ex-consul, then in his late forties, he was the new provincial governor, appointed by the emperor Trajan, with a special mandate to look into the condition of the cities there. His was a large territory, stretching along much of the southern shore of the Black Sea and covering more than 15,000 square miles, including the rump of Mithradates' old kingdom of Pontus. As his companion, Pliny took his third wife, Calpurnia, some twenty-five years his junior (there were no living children from any of his marriages). She went home a couple of years later, on receiving news of the death of her grandfather. Pliny never returned to Italy. The likelihood is that he died in post not long after Calpurnia left.

What Pliny did as governor is known from roughly a hundred surviving letters he exchanged with the emperor during his time in Bithynia, on the organisation and administration of the province, on legal disputes, urban regeneration, financial management and imperial protocol. Whoever selected and edited these for public circulation (for they are certainly not the random contents of Pliny's filing cabinet) was concerned to present him as a safe pair of hands, a man of probity with an eye for detail who took the business of provincial administration seriously. He often comes across as a bit too good to be true.

The letters show him scrupulously inspecting the finances of the local towns, reporting to the emperor on the state of their public services and asking for architects and engineers to be sent from Rome. Pliny was worried about the state of the aqueduct at Nicomedia, the baths at Claudiopolis and the theatre and gymnasium at Nicaea; even the 6-metre-thick walls in this new gymnasium were not structurally sound, he suspected, but a specialist opinion was needed. At Nicomedia he considered establishing a local fire brigade, though Trajan advised against the plan, on the revealing grounds that such organisations could turn into political pressure groups, and suggested simply providing some firefighting equipment instead. Pliny fretted too about how to punish slaves who had tried to enrol in the army, which was strictly open to the freeborn only, about whether the town council of Nicaea should be allowed to appropriate the property of anyone who died without making a will and about whether Trajan would mind having his statue put up in a building where human remains were buried.

Any advice from the emperor would have taken at least two months to get back to Pliny, even assuming an instant turnaround at the palace end. But Trajan did regularly reply, and an occasional tone of irritation suggests that the letters were dictated or drafted by the man himself rather than simply passed across the desk of some underling. Of course, he growls, he would not mind the proximity of human remains to his statue; how on earth could Pliny ever have imagined that he would take that as an insult?

It would probably have surprised both Pliny and Trajan to discover that 2,000 years later the most famous of their exchanges is to do with an apparently insignificant, but awkward and time-consuming, new religious group: the Christians. Pliny admitted that he was not sure how to handle them. To start with he had given them several opportunities to recant and executed only those who would not do so ('their stubbornness and unbending obstinacy certainly ought to be punished'). But then many more names were brought to his attention, as people started to settle old scores by accusing their enemies of being Christian. Pliny continued to allow those under investigation to recant, so long as they proved their sincerity by pouring wine and incense in front of statues of the emperor and the true gods. But in order to find out what was at the bottom of all this, he had two Christian slave women tortured and questioned (in both ancient Greece and Rome, slaves were allowed to give legal evidence only under torture) and concluded that Christianity was 'nothing other than a perverse and unruly superstition'. He still wanted Trajan to confirm that this had been the right method of approach. And that is more or less what the emperor did, though he added a note of caution: 'Christians should not be sought out,' he wrote, 'but if they are accused and found guilty, they must be punished.' This is the earliest surviving discussion of Christianity outside Jewish or Christian literature.

The contrast with Cicero's letters sent from Cilicia 150 years earlier could hardly be starker. For Cicero, the province presented the opportunity for military exploits and offered dreams of Alexander the Great – and it was a man's world (in the Republic, governors' wives seem to have been expressly prohibited from accompanying their husbands abroad). He paints a picture of uncertainty and disorganisation that, for all his good intentions, he could only mitigate, not solve. And that was combined with persistent, low-level exploitation of the local population by many of the Roman provincial staff, including Caesar's assassin Brutus, whose high political principles did not apply to all: he had been trying to extract 48 per cent interest from the unfortunate Cypriots. Pliny appears to have had no aspiration to armed heroics, and he was there with his wife, though what young Calpurnia spent her time doing we can only guess. His province comes across as an ordered place, where good financial practices were enforced and corruption sniffed out, where the local amenities were high on the governor's agenda and disputes were resolved within a clear legal framework.

It would be wrong to take this contrast entirely at face value. Dispatches back to the emperor are almost bound to have had a different flavour, and give a different impression, from letters like Cicero's, to close friends and confidants. Besides, some of the specific legal framework within which Pliny was operating went back to the era of Cicero; for it was Pompey who had established the regulations for the new province after his defeat of Rome's long-standing enemy Mithradates in the 60s BCE, and Pliny on several occasions refers back to them explicitly (as the *lex Pompeia*, or 'Pompeian code'). And even Cicero occasionally turned his attention to the irregularities going on in the provincial towns. Nevertheless, there was a new style of government in the provinces from the reign of Augustus onwards, and Pliny's correspondence captures this well.

There was a new clarity of command. Pliny had gone out to Bithynia with specific instructions from Trajan, and he knew exactly to whom he should report. It is clear too that the emperor could make decisions about matters in the provinces, right down to detailed questions on particular buildings in particular towns, in a way that the senate of the Republic never had. Some rogue governors might have liked to behave as mini-autocrats, acting on their own initiative, laying down their own law and living a lavish lifestyle, largely out of touch with the capital; and not all of them were entirely loyal to the man on the throne. There was, however, a new sense that governors were officials directly answerable to a higher authority back in Rome. As we shall see, the palace administration, although several weeks' journey from many provinces, had ways of keeping track of what these officials were up to far from home.

This was a new world of 'Rome outside Rome', and Pliny is a good guide to it. His letters raise questions about how far the empire under the emperors was different from the empire under the Republic, whether for the governed or the governing, victors or victims. They point to wider dilemmas over official relations with the Christians, which eventually became one of the most divisive conflicts across the Roman world, and hint at many important issues in the infrastructure of imperial rule at this period, from the role of soldiers in provincial administration to the organisation of official transport. But Pliny had his blind spots too.

He had little eye for any general sources of opposition to the Romans or for the commercial opportunities of this huge empire, and none at all for the cultural differences between his province and his home. No one would guess from the correspondence that the main language of his province was Greek, not Latin. Trajan at one point does pass an opinion on Greek fitness regimes: 'Greeklings,' he writes, meaning the Greek-speaking provincials, 'do love their gymnasia.' But the closest Pliny comes to remarking on cultural variety is when he deems Christianity 'a perverse and unruly superstition' and tries to get to the bottom of its rituals and ceremonies.

The province of Bithynia and Pontus, as it was technically known, was a world away from Rome, with a dazzling and sometimes 'exotic'

87. The snake god Glycon is vividly imagined in this second-century CE sculpture. Lucian's sceptical skit on the cult of the god tells of a range of unbelievable stunts that he pulled off for a gullible crowd.

mix of Greek and other local traditions, as some other ancient writers were keen to underline. The essayist and satirist Lucian – himself a striking example of cultural hybridity, being a Roman citizen from Syria whose first language was Greek – devoted a whole skit to an unforgettably weird new oracle that emerged in the province just fifty years after Pliny's death. It featured a prophetic snake with a human head and was hugely popular, attracting the attention of elite Romans from the emperor Marcus Aurelius down. Lucian ridiculed it as a moneymaking fraud, with a homemade puppet at its centre.

For historians now, one of the most pressing questions of the Roman Empire is precisely how cultural differences and oddities of this kind were debated, how 'Roman' those outside Rome and Italy became and how people in the provinces related their traditions, religions, languages and, in some cases, literatures to those of the imperial power – and vice versa. Pliny does not seem to have been the slightest bit interested in this.

The boundaries of empire

The expansion of the empire by the first Augustus had come to an abrupt end in 9 CE when, in the course of stabilising Roman conquests in Germany, the Roman commander Publius Quinctilius Varus lost most of three legions at the Battle of the Teutoburg Forest, just north of the modern town of Osnabrück. It was a defeat that ranked in Roman imagination with the disaster at Cannae during the war against Hannibal, and lurid stories were told of how captured soldiers were sacrificed in barbaric rituals and how the gales and pouring rain made the massacre worse. It was said that the helpless Romans could not fire their arrows, throw their javelins or even wield their soaking shields. In the end, the casualties came to not far short of 10 per cent of the Roman armed forces; the remains of some of them, plus their pack animals, have recently been discovered on the site, including skulls with traces of deep head wounds. The victorious enemy was a German rebel, Arminius ('Herman the German', as he is now affectionately known), a man who had served in the Roman army and whom Varus had trusted as a loyal friend; Arminius tricked Varus into the ambush after saying that he was going off to raise local support for the Romans. As on other occasions, the most effective opponents of the legions were those whom the Roman themselves had trained.

Augustus had been planning to expand Roman territory into eastern Germany beyond the river Rhine. Clear signs of his intentions have been discovered over the past twenty years in the excavations of a half-finished Roman town, at Waldgirmes, 60 miles east of the river; its central Forum was already constructed, complete with a gilded statue of the emperor on horseback. It was never finished because after the disaster Augustus gave up plans for more conquests, withdrew westwards and at his death left instructions that the empire should not be extended any further.

Those instructions were not, however, quite so simple. For, as we have seen, Augustus also left a template for imperial power that was founded on conquest and on traditional Roman military prowess. And he bequeathed to his successors, and to the Roman people, a vision of the Roman Empire extending over the whole world. Could Jupiter's prophecy in Virgil's *Aeneid*, that the Romans would have power 'without limit', be conveniently shelved just because of a single disaster? That was hardly the spirit of Cannae.

For the next 200 years, until the end of the second century CE, those two incompatible visions of empire – consolidation versus expansion – coexisted surprisingly easily. There were a few additions to Roman territory. Claudius, for example, compensated for his decidedly unmilitary image by taking the credit for conquering Britain and celebrated the event with a triumphal procession in 44 CE, the first in almost thirty years. This had considerable symbolic value. It

88. The head of the gilded horse from Waldgirmes – here seen
in conservation – is a clear sign that before the military reverse
in 9 CE the town was being planned as a major centre, with a
full complement of characters (including Augustus himself on
horseback). The town has been excavated in its half-finished state.

was the first Roman conquest in those strange lands that lay beyond
the Ocean (otherwise known, in this case, as the English Channel)
and turned Julius Caesar's temporary foray on to the island a hundred
years earlier into permanent occupation. But it was hardly expansion
on a grand scale, and over the next decades it proceeded northwards
to Scotland very slowly indeed. The careful assessment by the geog-
rapher Strabo, writing in the early first century CE, of the viability of
annexing Britain is in fact a telling illustration of a newly cautious
imperial culture. After reviewing the characteristics of the Britons
(tall, bandy-legged and weird) and the resources of the island (including grain, cattle, slaves and hunting dogs), he argues that the cost of

the garrison would outweigh any tax revenue that would accrue. But Claudius needed the kudos.

Only Trajan's campaigns led to any significant expansion of the empire: through 101 and 102 CE he conquered Dacia, part of what is now Romania, in the operations that are depicted in detail on his column; between 114 and 117 CE he invaded Mesopotamia and went beyond, as far as modern Iran. This was the furthest east that Roman power was ever formally to extend, but not for long. Within days of coming to the throne in 117 CE, Hadrian abandoned most of the territory. The success was celebrated in a peculiarly bizarre triumphal procession. As Trajan had died on the way home, an effigy took his place in the triumphal chariot – and anyway, the conquered lands had already been handed back.

Many obstacles slowed down foreign conquests. The instructions of Augustus were one thing, but few posthumous wishes hold as

89. On Trajan's column the army appear as an efficient military machine, as much concerned with logistics as with slaughter. Here the troops are engaged in clearing forests in Dacia, their fort behind them.

much weight as the dead had hoped for while alive. The end of the competitive Republican political culture was more important. The emperors, who claimed the glory of military success whether they participated in the fighting or not, were mainly competing with their dead predecessors: a much less intense rivalry than that between, say, Sulla and Marius or Pompey and Caesar. This went hand in hand with a growing sense that the empire might in practical terms have boundaries, even if the extravagant prophecy in the *Aeneid* was never forgotten. That did not mean a fixed frontier in a precise sense. There was always a fuzzy zone where Roman control faded gradually into non-Roman territory, and there were always peoples who were not formally part of the provinces of the empire but nevertheless did what the Romans told them to, on the old model of obedience. That is why modern maps that claim to plot the edges of the empire in a simple line can be more misleading than helpful. But edges were gradually becoming less fluid and more important, as the wall constructed in northern Britain on the orders of Hadrian suggests.

Hadrian's Wall, as we call it, stretched for more than 70 miles, right across the island from one coast to the other. Its construction was an enormous investment of military man-hours – but it is surprisingly hard to know what exactly it was for. The old idea that it was a defensive structure to keep the 'barbarians' out is unconvincing. It is true that the one ancient writer to mention its construction – an anonymous biographer and fantasist writing at the end of the fourth century CE (though for some unknown reason he pretends to be writing a century earlier) – refers to Hadrian 'separating' Romans and barbarians. But it could hardly have deterred any reasonably spirited and well-organised enemies who were keen to scale it, especially as much of it was built only of turf, unlike the solid stone sections that star in most photographs. Without a walkway along the top, it was not even well designed for surveillance and patrol purposes. But as a customs barrier, which is one recent suggestion, or as an attempt to control the movement of people more generally it seems a more hefty construction than was necessary. What it asserts is Roman power over the landscape while also hinting at a sense of ending. It may be no coincidence that other, rather less dramatic walls, banks and fortifications were developed in other frontier zones at roughly the same period, as if to suggest that the boundaries of Roman power were beginning to take a more physical form.

No one, however, who looked around Rome and many other cities of the empire could possibly have guessed that the project of world conquest had been dampened. Images of Roman victory and barbarian defeat were everywhere. Diplomatic deals with inconvenient neighbours were greeted with spectacular displays, as if they had been achieved by force of arms. After a rather inglorious peace agreement with Tiridates, the king of Armenia, Nero persuaded him in

90. Hadrian's Wall, whatever its original purpose, still clings to the tops of hills in north England. It was probably more symbolic than a defensive barrier; it could not have been hard to scale. But it surely represented some kind of boundary marker.

91. A classic image of Roman military power. The first Augustus, on the left, with an eagle at his feet (a symbol of the legions) is paired with a figure representing 'Victory' on the right. Between them is a suit of armour that was a trophy of military victory (Fig. 41) and squashed beneath a naked prisoner, his arms bound behind his back. This is one of a series of sculpted panels, depicting Roman emperors and their empire, from a sanctuary in honour of the Augusti at Aphrodisias in modern Turkey.

66 CE to travel the thousands of miles to Rome to receive his crown from the emperor himself – who was dressed up in the costume of a triumphing general and is reputed to have covered the whole of the Theatre of Pompey in gold leaf for the day, to make it literally dazzling. Victories in defensive wars against internal enemies, rebels and invaders were commemorated as if they were glorious military achievements fought on Rome's terms. The Column of Marcus Aurelius, for example, finished in 193 CE and towering those careful few metres above its Trajanic rival, celebrates campaigns that were a successful but extremely costly response to a German invasion. And everywhere there were statues of emperors in splendid suits of armour, and images of conquered, bound and trampled barbarians. Perhaps that was the easiest way to reconcile the conflicting legacy of the first Augustus: art and symbol could usefully compensate for the fact that in real life there was less trampling of barbarians now going on.

The management of empire

In practice, if not in the Roman imagination, the empire of the first two centuries CE became less a field of conquest and pacification and more a territory to be managed, policed and taxed. Scipio Aemilianus and Mummius would have been amazed to discover that the cities of Carthage and Corinth that they devastated in 146 BCE had been refounded, on Julius Caesar's initiative, as settlements of veteran soldiers and by the end of the first century CE were two of the most prosperous towns in a very different sort of Roman world.

This was the result not of any imperial grand plan but of a gradual process of change, a series of minor adjustments and shifts. So far as we can tell, even under the rule of the emperors there was hardly any such thing as a general policy for running the empire or an overarching strategy of military deployment. The directive of Augustus against further conquest in general was a rare intervention of that sort. Although major construction projects such as Hadrian's Wall must have been the result of some decision at a high level, for the most part the emperor's involvement was on the pattern of Trajan's in Bithynia, dealing with issues as and when they came up. The emperor did represent a new tier in the structure of command, but his role was largely a reactive one; he was not a strategist or forward planner. Pliny, in other words, was not the nervous fusspot that he sometimes seems to modern readers of his letters, bombarding the boss with questions on all kinds of trivia. He was following the logic of Roman imperial administration, that you got no decision from the emperor unless you asked him for one.

Whether or not the government of the provinces was better or fairer in the first two centuries CE than it had been in the last century of the Republic depended on who or where you were. It is too easy to compare the diligent Pliny with Cicero or, even more obviously, the extortionate Verres and to claim, on the basis of some entirely unrepresentative (or misrepresented) individuals, a vast improvement.

Some things no doubt did improve. There was a gradual move away from the big companies of tax collectors, whose incentive had always been to extract as much cash from the provincials as possible. The system remained very mixed and the *publicani* continued to play a part, but much more of the collecting was made the responsibility of the locals, which was also the cheapest option. In most provinces too, a specialist financial officer, or *procurator*, appointed by the emperor looked after the imperial estates and had a watching brief over the tax collection. He and his staff of slaves and ex-slaves from the imperial household (the *familia Caesaris*, as it was known) could also keep an eye on what the governor was up to and are known sometimes to have blown the whistle back in Rome. But the truth is that, on the ground, the standard of government was as varied as it ever had been.

Trials for extortion and malpractice in the provinces continued, which may equally well be a sign of the persistent flouting of the law as of its proper enforcement. Many kinds of day-to-day exploitation of the provincials were simply taken for granted. The emperor Tiberius summed up the basic ethics of Roman rule rather well when he said, in reaction to some excessive profits turned in from the provinces, 'I want my sheep shorn, not shaven'. It was out of the question that provincial fleeces should be left as they were. One regular irritant was the need to provide transport and lodgings for Roman officials. The governor's staff did not have their own fleet of official vehicles. The courier taking the post to Rome or the governor travelling from city to city was expected to requisition transport on the spot: horses, mules and carts. A small fee was payable, but the locals had no choice but to provide what was asked. Unsurprisingly, a large number of Roman hangers-on tried to take advantage of this rather than make their own costly and inconvenient arrangements. Pliny gave his wife an official travel voucher so that she could get back to Italy quickly when her grandfather died. He felt the need after the event to confess this bending of the rules to Trajan, but he did it all the same.

The new method of appointing governors might have led to some more responsible candidates. This was now directly, or indirectly, in the hands of the emperor rather than the result of a mixture of drawing lots and political chicanery in the senate. But the emperor's criteria for choice were not only, and maybe not often, the ability of the candidate or the interests of the provincials. If Trajan really had wanted a careful administrator to look into the problems of local government in Bithynia, then in Pliny he got his man. But it was a common joke, and possibly true, that Nero had appointed his friend Marcus Salvius Otho, a man who shared many of the emperor's enthusiasms, to be the governor of the province of Lusitania, in modern Portugal and Spain, simply so that he could more easily enjoy his affair in Rome with Otho's ex-wife, Poppaea. Even if appointments were usually made on less whimsical grounds, there is no sign of any training or briefing for the job, beyond a few instructions (*mandata*) given by the emperor. We can only wonder how on earth a new governor managed, when he had been sent to some remote northern province he had never visited, whose native language he did not understand, whose strange customs he had heard rumours of, where he knew no one but a wary *procurator* – and which he was supposed to manage for anything up to five years or so. From his point of view, it must have seemed a journey into the dark unknown.

What is certain is that the Romans made hardly any attempts, even during this more leisurely phase of imperial control, to impose their cultural norms or to eradicate local traditions. They did try to stamp out the Druids in Britain. The reports of the human sacrifice they practised may have been hugely exaggerated, and in any case it was a ritual not entirely unknown in Rome, but it was not something the Roman authorities were prepared to tolerate in these strange foreign priests. There was also the special case of the Christians. But those were exceptions. The eastern half of the empire continued largely to operate in Greek, not Latin. Local calendars were not much adjusted, apart from occasionally realigning to the life cycle of the emperor or celebrating his achievements. Travelling around the empire meant not just crossing time zones in our sense but moving between entirely different ways of calculating dates or hours of the day (how anyone managed their diary is a mystery). Local traditions flourished in everything from clothing (trousers and Greek cloaks) to religion. It was a world full of gods and of festivals in a vast variety, whose strangeness lost nothing in the telling. The oracular snake with a human head does not look quite so odd when seen against the Egyptian Anubis, part jackal and part human, or the so-called Syrian Goddess, also satirised by Lucian, whose rituals were supposed to have involved participants climbing up huge stone phalluses at the goddess's sanctuary.

Romans may well not have wanted to impose any such norms. But even if that had been their aim, they did not have the manpower to achieve it. A reasonable estimate is that across the empire at any one time there were fewer than 200 elite Roman administrators, plus maybe a few thousand slaves of the emperor, who had been sent out from the imperial centre to govern an empire of more than 50 million people. Pliny refers just to his deputy (*legatus*) and the *procurator*. So how did they do it?

The army was one answer. Over the first few decades of the rule of the emperors, soldiers were recruited increasingly from outside Italy (the provincials were in practice guarding the empire), were more and more stationed towards the edges of the Roman world (safely away from Rome, on the Augustan model) and became heavily involved in administrative as well as front-line jobs. This is vividly illustrated by the letters and documents, recovered over the past forty years, from excavations at the small army base of Vindolanda, just south of Hadrian's Wall, which housed one unit of the wall's Roman garrison. Originally scratched on wax, and preserved by the still faint traces on the surviving wood underneath, they date to the early second century

CE. This is the other side of the Roman world, but they are roughly contemporary with the correspondence of Pliny and Trajan.

The documents give a very different impression of Roman barracks life from the usual image of an exclusively male, highly militarised regime. To be sure, they include hints at armed skirmishes and some dismissive comments about the natives. Where Trajan referred to 'Greeklings [*Graeculi*] loving their gymnasia', some soldier from the wall referred to 'Little Brits [*Brittunculi*, a similarly patronising diminutive] throwing their javelins without getting on horseback'. But it is the everyday domestic and the housekeeping side of Vindolanda that is especially interesting. One letter is an invitation to a birthday party from the camp commandant's wife to a female friend, and – despite legal prohibitions on marriages for serving soldiers in the ranks – the discovery in the excavations of a significant number of women's and children's leather shoes confirms the presence of women on the base. Of course, shoes cannot tell us what exactly their wearers were doing or how permanent a fixture they were. But it looks very much as if family life was going on here.

Equally telling is a 'strength report', a register of the soldiers on the base and those off on other duties. More than half of the 752 were absent or unavailable for work. Of those, 337 were at a neighbouring camp, 31 were sick (eye inflammation being a bigger problem than wounds) and almost 100 were busy with other responsibilities: 46 were 300 miles away in London as the governor's bodyguard; one or more had been assigned to an unspecified 'office'; and several centurions (NCOs) were on business in other parts of the country. This fits perfectly with one of Trajan's worries in his letters to Pliny: too many soldiers were off doing other things and were absent from their units.

The other answer to how the Romans managed is that the local populations played a big part in running the empire, through the towns and cities across the Roman world that Rome either supported or founded. The city (*polis*) had been the defining institution in Greece and the East long before the coming of Rome, and it remained so afterwards, sometimes with a considerable injection of Roman cash. The emperor Hadrian, for example, sponsored massive building programmes in Athens. In the north and west of the empire, where this had not been the case, the foundation of towns from scratch, on a Roman model, was the most significant impact of Roman conquest on the provincial landscape.

This was exactly what Augustus' forces had been doing at Waldgirmes before the emperor gave the orders for retreat. And many of the towns of modern Britain, including London, owe their sites to Roman choices and planning. Some were more successful than others. There must be a sad story behind the Mediterranean-style, outdoor swimming pool in the Roman baths at Viriconium (modern Wroxeter, near the English–Welsh border), which did not survive many frosty winters and soon became the town's rubbish dump. And the habits of urban life would have meant little or nothing to the majority of the population, who continued to live, as they always had done, in the country. But in the West, as well as the East, a network of more or less self-governing towns came to be the foundation of Roman administration. Only when things were thought to be going wrong did someone like Pliny interfere in them. It was urbanisation on an unprecedented scale.

The provincial – or 'native' – elites living in these towns acted as the crucial middlemen between the Roman governor, with his tiny staff, and the provincial population at large. It was through them that much taxation was raised and that an acceptable degree of loyalty, or at least absence of trouble, was ensured. It was probably some of them too who met that nervous new governor as he took his first steps in the province. The details of these arrangements and encounters would have been very different in different parts of the empire. The literary salons of Roman Athens had almost nothing in common with the beer gardens of Roman Colchester. But the same underlying logic operated across the empire: pre-existing local hierarchies were transformed into hierarchies that served Rome, and the power of local leaders was harnessed to the needs of the imperial ruler.

In Britain, a native ruler by the name of Togidubnus was a classic case of this. He had been on the Roman side when the Claudian forces invaded in 43 CE and was likely some sort of ally before that, for remote and rural as Britain was, there had been links between its aristocracy and mainland Europe since at least the time of Caesar's invasions in the 50s BCE. Togidubnus may or may not have been the owner of the large villa near Chichester now known rather grandly as Fishbourne Roman Palace; the connection is pure guesswork. But he was certainly given Roman citizenship and with it the new Roman name of Tiberius Claudius Togidubnus. And there is clear evidence that he continued to act as a local source of authority in the pacified areas of the new province.

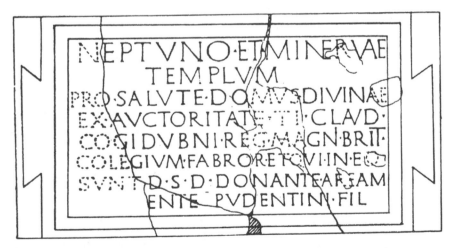

92. This first-century CE inscription from Chichester, in southern England, records the dedication of a temple to Neptune and Minerva, 'for the welfare of the imperial house' (literally the 'divine house'). The temple was erected under the authority of Tiberius Claudius Togidubnus, here restored as Cogidubnus (the spelling is uncertain).

What originally lay behind this system of government was at least as much simple necessity as ideological vision. Outside the areas of active fighting, Romans were simply too few in number to govern in any other way. But the character of imperial rule was increasingly defined by its collaboration with the elite of the subject peoples. They in turn increasingly identified their interests with the Romans, both culturally and politically; they came to feel that they had a stake in the Roman project, as insiders rather than outsiders; and some of the most successful in due course took a place, as Roman citizens, in the central government of Rome. For these men and their families, the experience of Roman rule was partly the experience of *becoming Roman.*

Romanisation and resistance

The historian Tacitus has some characteristically shrewd, and cynical, things to say about this process of Romanisation, as it is now often called. They come in the short biography he wrote of his father-in-law, Gnaeus Julius Agricola, who served as the governor of Britain from 77 to 85 CE, an unusually long period. Most of Tacitus' account concerns Agricola's successful military operations in the province, his exten-sion of Roman power northwards into Caledonia (Scotland) and the jealousy of the emperor Domitian, who refused him the honour and glory he deserved for his success. The biography is as much a critique of autocracy as it is a eulogy of Tacitus' distinguished relative: the overriding message is that the imperial regime allowed no place for traditional Roman virtue and military prowess. Occasionally, how-ever, Tacitus turns to the civilian aspects of Agricola's government of the province.

Some of the topics are fairly routine and would not have looked out of place in the letters of Pliny, who was a friend of Tacitus' in the literary circles of early second-century CE Rome. Agricola is praised for keeping his household under tight control ('as hard a job for many as actually governing the province'). He also sorted out some of the abuses in army requisitioning, and he put money into enhancing the towns of Britain with new temples and Roman-style public buildings. It is rather more surprising to discover that he had a local education policy too: he made sure that the sons of the leading provincials were educated in the 'liberal arts' (literally 'the intellectual pursuits suited to the free') and in the Latin language. And soon, as Tacitus put it, the Britons were dressing up in togas and taking their first steps on the path to vice, thanks to porticoes, baths and banquets. He sums this up in a pithy sentence: 'They called it, in their ignorance, "civilisation", but it was really part of their enslavement' ('*Humanitas vocabatur, cum pars servitutis esset*'). This has been hugely influential, for better or worse, in modern attempts to understand how the Roman Empire worked.

In one respect it is the sharpest analysis there is of Roman government in the western part of the empire (but not the East: no official from Rome would have dreamt of instructing the Greeks in 'civilisation' like this). However snobbish Tacitus was about the naive ignorance of these poor provincials, who have left no written account of their perspective on these transactions, however cynical he was about slavery masquerading as sophistication, he saw straight through to the connection between culture and power and realised that by becoming Roman the Britons were doing the conquerors' work for them. But in other ways Tacitus' comments give a seriously misleading impression of what was going on.

For a start, if Agricola really did promote an organised programme of education in the way Tacitus suggests, inculcating Roman habits into the upper echelons of British society, he was the only provincial governor, so far as we know, to do that. Romanisation was not usually something that was imposed directly from above. It was much more a consequence of the provincial elites opting in to a version of Roman culture. It was bottom up rather than top down. Tacitus would no doubt have objected that, given the balance of military and political power which was so overwhelmingly in Rome's favour, it was not exactly a free choice. That is true. But nonetheless, on a practical day-to-day level, the relatively well-off urban population of the provinces became the agents of their own Romanisation, not the objects of a concerted Roman campaign of cultural reprogramming or a civilising mission.

The evidence of archaeology makes it clear that they opted for new Roman forms in everything from architecture and town planning, through crockery and kitchenware, to fabrics, food and drink. There are a few choice Roman items found buried in British graves even before the conquest of 43 CE; and as early as the beginning of the first century BCE, the same Greek visitor to Gaul who had been shocked to find enemy heads pinned up outside huts also spotted that – despite what Caesar had to say about local distaste for the grape – the richer locals had started to quaff imported wine, leaving traditional Gallic beer to the less well off. By the beginning of the second century CE, there were rather fewer beer gardens and rather more wine bars in Roman Colchester; or that, at least, is what the surviving fragments of the jars used to transport the wine suggest. And for the first time, at the start of another long tradition whose origins lie in the Roman Empire, a substantial quantity of wine was being made in what is now France, outperforming the Italian vintages.

There was a dynamic combination of forces at work here: on the one hand, the power of Rome made Roman culture an aspirational goal; on the other, Rome's traditional openness meant that those who wished to 'do it the Roman way' were welcome to do so – and, of course, it suited the stable maintenance of Roman rule that they should. The main beneficiaries (or victims, as Tacitus saw it) were the wealthy. But they were not the only ones to create a Roman identity for themselves.

A surprising glimpse into a different way of becoming Roman

comes from the potteries of southern Gaul, which during a boom in the first and second centuries CE produced on an industrial scale some of the most characteristic 'Roman' shiny red tableware. The names of many of the individual potters have been preserved on rosters and lists found at the pottery site. There are still arguments about exactly how to read them, but they appear to be a mixed bag of both characteristically Latin names (Verecundus, Iucundus) and Celtic ones (Petrecos, Matugenos). This is not so on the pots themselves: when these same men came to stamp their names into the plates and bowls that would be put on sale as their handiwork, many of them Romanised. Petrecos called himself Quartus; Matugenos became Felix. There may have been a narrowly commercial incentive here. Customers buying Roman-style pottery produced in southern Gaul might have been attracted by an authentically Roman maker's name. But it is also possible that, for the public face of their trade, these successful but relatively humble craftsmen saw themselves as at least partly Roman and embraced one version of Romanness.

Version is the right way to put it. For another problem with Tacitus' analysis is that it implies a simple opposition between 'native' and 'Roman' cultures or a single spectrum along which degrees of Romanness could be plotted: Togidubnus the wine-drinking new Roman citizen much further along the line than Petrecos the potter, who used a Latin soubriquet on his work but may have been resolutely Celtic in many other respects. In fact, the interaction between Rome and other cultures in the empire is striking for the variety of forms it took and for the very diverse hybrid versions of Roman (and sometimes 'not-Roman') culture that were the result. Across the Roman world, all kinds of different cultural amalgams emerged from particular local attempts to embrace, to accommodate or to resist the imperial power.

The signs of these range from the images of Roman emperors in the province of Egypt, all presented as if they were traditional Egyptian pharaohs, to the flamboyant sculpture on the façade of the Temple of Sulis Minerva in the Roman town of Bath in southern England. In some respects, this is as clear a case of Romanisation as you could wish. It was part of a classical temple built to a design unknown in Britain before the Roman conquest; it was put up in honour of a Celtic deity, Sulis, now seen as the equivalent of the Roman Minerva; and it includes various elements, from the oak-leaf roundel to the supporting figures of Victory, drawn directly from the traditional Roman repertoire. But at the same time it is a glaring example of a provincial culture either failing or, perhaps better, refusing to become Roman.

The most remarkable case of this kind of interaction is found in the provinces of the Greek world, where an extraordinary literary

93. Portrait of Trajan in the guise of a pharaoh, from the Temple of Hathor at Dendera, Egypt. How Roman or Egyptian this is depends on the eyes of the viewer: was it Trajan assimilated into Egyptian culture, or inserting himself into the conventions of the provincial community?

94. At Bath, there is a gap between the rigidly classical framework in this façade, and the bearded central figure. This has been thought to be a Celtic image of the snake-haired classical Gorgon, but the Gorgon was female where this appears to be male. Or was it the face of the Ocean?

and cultural renaissance was one result of what we would now call the 'colonial encounter'. In the early period of Roman military expansion overseas, starting in the third century BCE, Roman literature and visual art developed in dialogue with Greek models and predecessors. The poet Horace exaggerated when, in the late first century BCE, he summed up the process as one of simple cultural takeover: 'Greece, once conquered, conquered her savage victor and brought culture into the rough land of Latium' (better in Latin: '*Graecia capta ferum victorem cepit et artes intulit agresti Latio*'). It was a much more complicated interrelationship than that, as Horace's own poetry shows, which is a distinctively Roman combination of homage to Greek culture, ambitious transformation of Greek literary models and celebration of Latin traditions. But, all the same, he had a point.

In the Roman Empire of the first two centuries CE, the encounter took a different turn. It was not simply that many Greeks, like many Britons, adopted such habits as Roman-style bathing and watching gladiatorial fights. The transformation of local culture in the East was nothing like as radical as in the West, but sophisticated Greeks did not necessarily look down their noses at brutish Roman blood sports. There is clear evidence that Greek theatres and stadia were adapted for both gladiators and wild beast hunts; traces of the fixing for the nets intended to keep the audience safe from the animals are one clear sign. But the most striking development was an outpouring of literature in Greek, in which the power of Rome either hovers in the background or is directly addressed – in playful satire, passive resistance, curiosity or admiration. The quantity of this material is huge. The vast majority of all the ancient Greek literature that has survived comes from this period of imperial rule. To give a sense of scale, the work of just one of these writers – Plutarch, the second-century CE biographer, philosopher, essayist and priest of the famous Greek oracle at Delphi – extends to as many modern pages as all the surviving work of the fifth century BCE put together, from the tragedies of Aeschylus to the history of Thucydides.

Greek writing of the empire ranges from elaborate praise of Roman rule to obvious exercises in denial. In 144 CE, for example, Publius Aelius Aristides, better known as a hypochondriac who wrote several volumes on his illnesses, delivered his *Speech in Honour of Rome* in front of the emperor Antoninus Pius. It may have gone down well on the day, but it now makes a fairly sickening read, even for those used to probing between the lines of panegyric. Rome has surpassed all previous empires, bringing peace and prosperity to the whole world: 'may all the gods and their children be called upon to grant that the empire and the city itself flourish forever and do not come to an end until stones float on the sea'. At roughly the same time, Pausanias was writing the ten volumes of his *Guidebook to Greece* (or *Periegesis*), in which he gives Roman rule exactly the opposite treatment: silent eradication. Whatever his story was (we know next to nothing about Pausanias' life), as he guides his travellers around the monuments, sights and customs of Greece, from Delphi to the southern Peloponnese, he simply omits to mention most of the buildings on his route erected by Romans or with Roman money. This was not so much a guidebook in the modern sense but a literary attempt to turn the clock back and to re-create an image of a 'Rome-free' Greece.

It is, however, the prolific Plutarch who made the most systematic attempt to define the relationship between Greece and Rome, to dissect their differences and similarities and to wonder what a *Greco-Roman* culture might be. In his volumes of essays – on subjects as diverse as how to listen to lectures, how to tell a flatterer from a friend and the customs of his sanctuary at Delphi – he explores the details of religion, politics and traditions that distinguished (or united) the two cultures. Why, he wondered, did the Romans start the beginning of a new day at midnight? Why did Roman women wear white in mourning? But it is his *Parallel Lives* that is especially revealing, a series of pairs of biographies – twenty-two pairs still surviving – made up of the life story of one Greek and one Roman figure, with a short comparison at the end. He puts together two founding fathers, Romulus with the equally legendary Greek Theseus; two great orators, Cicero with the Athenian orator Demosthenes; two famous conquerors, Julius Caesar with Alexander the Great; and a pair of equally famous traitors, Coriolanus with his contemporary the glamorous but unreliable Athenian Alcibiades.

Modern historians have tended to break up the pairs and to read them as individual life stories. That is to miss Plutarch's point entirely. These were not just biographies. They were a concerted attempt to evaluate the great men (and they were all men) of Greece and Rome against each other, to think about the relative strengths and weaknesses of the two cultures and about what it meant to be 'Greek' or

'Roman'. They were nicely ambivalent: putting the Roman subjects into the same league as the ancient Greek heroes and – to see it from the other perspective – making the characters from the ancient Greek past comparable to those who then ruled the world. In a way, this was the fulfilment of a project sketched out 250 years earlier by Polybius, who as a Greek hostage in Rome and friend of the Scipios had been the first to attempt that cross-cultural political anthropology of Rome and its empire and to try to explain systematically why Greece had lost to Rome.

Free movement

The cultural interaction that defined the Roman Empire was not something that took place only within peoples' heads, whether humble potters or ancient theorists. And it was not merely a matter of different local accommodations to the power of Rome, although that was an important part of it. There were also massive movements of peoples and goods across the empire, which intensified this cultural diversity while bringing enormous profits to some and making victims out of others. This was a world in which people could, as never before on this scale, make their homes, their fortunes or their graves thousands of miles away from where they were born; in which the population of Rome relied on basic food grown at the edges of the empire; and in which trade distributed new tastes, smells and luxuries – spices, ivory, amber and silks – from one end of the Mediterranean to the other and beyond, and not only to the super-rich. Among the precious possessions of a fairly ordinary house in Pompeii was a delicate ivory figurine made in India; and a document from Vindolanda shows that quantities of pepper, from the Far East, were being sold to the garrison there.

The routes into Italy from the rest of the empire were an important axis of this movement. Everything that Rome wanted was sucked into the metropolis. People were one of those commodities. Packed as the city was, the human death rate – from malaria and infections, as well as the other regular dangers to ancient life – meant that there was always the room, and the need, for more. Some of them were slaves, picked up in war or now more likely the victims of an unsavoury trade of people trafficking that made the margins of the Roman world a dangerous place to live. Others must have migrated to the city with hopes and aspirations or out of desperation. Their stories are largely lost to us; but the short epitaph of a young man called Menophilos, who died in Rome, had come 'from Asia' and was skilled in music ('I never uttered offensive words, and I was a friend of the Muses'), hints at the innocent ambitions of some of those who thought that the streets of the capital were paved with gold.

95. An Indian figurine, and no doubt precious possession, found in a house at Pompeii. How it travelled from India is a mystery. Maybe it was brought back directly by a trader with the East, or maybe it came through various hands, thanks to a series of indirect connections between Rome and the outside world.

The natural products of empire, its luxuries and curiosities, also flooded to Rome and signalled the city's status as an imperial power. Balsam trees of Judaea were paraded in the triumphal procession of 71 CE. Exotic animals captured in Africa, from lions to ostriches, were slaughtered in the arena. Luscious coloured marbles, quarried in remote locations across the Roman world, decorated the theatres, temples and palaces in the capital. The images of trampled barbarians were not the only things to stand for Roman domination. So too did

96. Hadrian's Pantheon with the exotic Egyptian columns supporting the porch. It is a deceptive building. Although in its present form it was built by Hadrian, the bronze letters across the gable proclaim that it was the work of Augustus' colleague Marcus Agrippa. He certainly was behind an earlier version of the temple, but Hadrian's new build was entirely new – and his reference to Agrippa was public piety.

the colours of the floors on which the Romans walked in the grandest buildings of their city: these stones amounted to an assertion – and a map – of empire.

They also hint at the enormous effort, time and money that the emperors were prepared to devote to displaying their control over their distant possessions. To take just one example: supporting the porch of the emperor Hadrian's Pantheon, finished in the 120s CE, were twelve columns, each 40 Roman feet high (roughly 12 metres) and carved from a single block of Egyptian grey granite. This is not to modern eyes a spectacular material, but it was an extremely prestigious stone used in many imperial projects, partly because it was found only in one faraway place, 2,500 miles from Rome, Mons Claudianus (the 'Mountain of Claudius', named after the emperor who first sponsored work there) in the middle of the eastern Egyptian desert. It was only with immense difficulty and a huge investment of labour and cash that columns of this size could be quarried and transported to Rome in one piece.

Excavations at Mons Claudianus over the past thirty years have revealed a military base, small villages for the quarry workers and a supply and transport centre; and they have turned up many hundreds of written documents, often scratched on recycled broken pieces of pottery (a workable alternative to wax tablets), that give a hint of the organisation and its problems. The provision of food and drink was only the first. There was a complicated supply chain of everything from wine to cucumbers, which did not always work ('Please send me two loaves of bread, for no grain has come up here for me so far,' reads one begging letter), and water was rationed (one document is a water distribution list that numbers 917 people working in the quarries). The work was laborious. Every one of the Pantheon columns would have taken three men well over a year to hack out and trim down, and occasionally, as some of the documents attest, a half-prepared monolith would crack and they would have to start again. Transport

97. The site of Mons Claudianus, where the famous grey granite (granodiorite) for the Pantheon columns was quarried; 30 miles away in the desert another quarry, Mons Porphyrites, was the source of the porphyry also used in major Roman building projects. These were literally military operations, serving the construction needs of the Roman state.

was the next hurdle, especially as the quarries were almost 100 miles from the Nile. One letter on papyrus from Mons Claudianus begs a local official to send grain supplies, as the quarries had a column of 50 Roman feet (weight: 100 tons) ready to go, but the food for the pack animals to get it to the river was running out. Even in the case of the Pantheon, it is clear that not everything went to plan: some slightly awkward design features of the finished building make it seem likely that Hadrian's architects had banked on getting twelve 50-foot columns but had to adjust at the last minute when twelve 40-foot columns were all that the quarry could provide.

The stone transported from Mons Claudianus is an unusual case of the movement of goods around the Roman world. It was largely in the hands of the imperial administration, backed up by soldiers; and is hard not to suspect that it was intended in part as a display of Rome's ability to pull off the virtually impossible – a *reductio ad absurdum* of Roman power. But in many other markets, from absolute staples to more affordable luxuries, trade and profits boomed in the empire. Vivid snapshots survive of men who struck it very lucky in all sorts of commercial enterprise. One papyrus of the mid second century CE lists the goods, with their cash value, which came on a single ship from southern India to Egypt, presumably destined for Rome. It was worth, after tax, more than 6 million sesterces, the equivalent of a decent senatorial estate in Italy at the time (Pliny had bought a large but slightly run-down property, plus land, for 3 million), and the cargo included a hundred or so pairs of elephant tusks, boxes of oils and spices and very likely vast quantities of pepper. A man called Flavius Zeuxis was not quite in that league, but his epitaph, found in the ancient textile town of Hieropolis in what is now southern Turkey, boasts that over his career he made seventy-two journeys around Cape Malea, at the southern tip of the Peloponnese, on his way to Rome to sell his fabric. It is not clear whether his seventy-two trips were single or return voyages, but either way this was a lifetime's achievement worth parading.

Beyond these individual entrepreneurs, the bigger picture is revealed in the much less glamorous but even more impressive facts and figures of basic supply. A little hill on the bank of the river Tiber in Rome, now known as Monte Testaccio ('Broken Pot Mountain'), conjures up better than anything else the scale of the trade in staple foodstuffs that kept the million people who lived in the city alive, and the network of transport facilities, shipping, warehousing and retailing required to sustain it. Despite its appearance, this is not a natural hill at all but the remains of a man-made Roman rubbish dump, the broken fragments of 53 million containers of olive oil, pottery amphorae with a capacity of about 60 litres each. These had almost all been imported from southern Spain over a hundred years or so, from the mid second to the mid third century CE, and had been dumped as soon as the oil was decanted. This was one part of an enormous export trade that changed the economy of that part of Spain into an agricultural monoculture (nothing but olives and more olives) and delivered to the city of Rome just some of what it needed to survive. At a rough estimate, that basic requirement amounted to 20 million litres of olive oil per year (for lighting and cleaning, as well as cooking), 100 million litres of wine and 250 tons of grain. Almost all of this came to Rome from outside Italy.

The mobility of empire, however, was not restricted to the axis between the metropolitan centre and the rest of the Roman world. One of the main developments in the empire of the first two centuries CE was that it became a territory through, around and within which people moved, often bypassing Rome; the traffic did not simply flow between centre and periphery. There are many ways of tracking this

98. Monte Testaccio is one of the most surprising hills, and rubbish dumps, in the world – being made up almost entirely of broken amphorae, which once carried Spanish olive oil. They could not be re-used because the oil seeped into the fabric of the vessel and turned rancid.

movement. The most up-to-date involves looking at the evidence of human skeletons, particularly their mouths, in ever more precise ways. Modern scientific analysis has shown how the distinctive imprint of the climate, water supply and diet of the growing child leaves traces in the teeth of the adult, giving hints about where any particular dead person grew up. The studies are still very provisional, but they seem to show that a substantial proportion of the urban population of, for example, Roman Britain grew up in a different climatic region from the one in which they died – whether that was the warm south coast of Britain versus the chilly north or the balmy south of France, is so far hard to tell.

Some of those journeys can be traced in the stories of the people who ended up near Hadrian's Wall. The picture often conjured up of a miserable bunch of soldiers from sunny Italy being forced to endure the fog, frost and rain of northern Britain is very misleading. The garrison was largely made up of forces recruited in equally foggy places across the English Channel, in what are now Holland, Belgium and Germany. But at all levels of the Wall community, individuals came from much further afield, even from the opposite ends of the empire. These range from Victor, an ex-slave of a cavalry soldier, whose tombstone identifies him as a 'Moor', to one of the grandest Romans in the province, Quintus Lollius Urbicus, the governor of Britain between 139 and 142 CE. Thanks to some lucky survivals we can still identify both the building work he sponsored in northern Britain and the family tomb he commissioned at the other end of the Roman world, in his home town (of Tiddis, as it is now called) in northern Algeria.

Most evocative of all is the story of a man from Palmyra in Syria, Barates, who was working near Hadrian's Wall in the second century CE. It is not known what brought him the 4,000 miles across the world (probably the longest journey of anyone in this book); it may have been trade, or he may have had some connection with the army. But he settled in Britain long enough to marry Regina ('Queenie'), a

99. The figure of Regina on her tombstone is similar to many found in Palmyra. But the Latin text beneath explains that 'Barates the Palmyrene put this up for Regina, ex-slave and wife, aged thirty, of the Catuvellaunian tribe'. It is not made absolutely explicit, but she had almost certainly been *his own* slave. The production of the memorial is an interesting puzzle. Did Barates provide a sketch of what he wanted to some local sculptor? Or was there a craftsman at South Shields already familiar with this style?

British woman and ex-slave. When she died at the age of thirty, Barates commemorated her with a tombstone, near the Roman fort of Arbeia, modern South Shields. This depicts Queenie – who, as the epitaph makes clear, was born and bred just north of London – as if she were a stately Palmyrene matron; and underneath the Latin text, Barates had her name inscribed in the Aramaic language of his homeland. It is a memorial which nicely sums up the movement of peoples and the cultural mix that defined the Roman Empire, and raises even more tantalising questions. Who did Queenie think she was? Would she have recognised herself as that Palmyrene lady? And what would this couple have thought about the 'Rome' in whose world they lived?

They create desolation and call it peace

There was certainly some strong opposition to aspects of Roman rule. Integration, mobility, luxuries and commercial profit were only one side of the story of the empire. The other side included disobedience and tax dodging, passive resistance and popular protests, often aimed as much at the local elites as at the Romans. But open, armed rebellion against Roman 'occupation' seems to have been rare over the first two centuries CE. Some brave, though ultimately always doomed, rebels against the invincible power of Rome have become the legendary heroes and heroines of modern nations, whether 'Herman the German' or Boudicca, whose regal bronze statue stands proudly outside the Houses of Parliament on the banks of the river Thames. And the fortress of Masada, where in 73 CE 960 Jewish rebels opted for suicide rather than submission at the end of a long siege, is now an Israeli national monument. But these are the exceptions. The Roman Empire does not appear to have been an empire of insurrection.

That impression may be slightly misleading. Roman authorities, like many modern states, had a vested interest in writing off principled political rebellion as if it were treachery, riot or simple crime. It is impossible to know the aspirations of the so-called bandits who troubled Roman governors in many parts of the world or to pinpoint where exactly the boundary lay between highway robbery and ideological dissidence. And when the Jews in Jerusalem took to violence in the reign of Claudius after a Roman soldier exposed himself in the Temple, was that just a riot? Or should it be seen as the spark of an incipient rebellion, quashed by the Roman authorities in the province at the cost of thousands of Jewish lives? Besides, emperors hungry for military glory could find it convenient to represent the suppression of internal insurrection as if it were external conquest in the old tradition. The arch erected to commemorate the triumph of Vespasian and Titus over the Jews in 71 CE, before the final Roman victory at Masada, offers no clue that the victory was against armed internal rebels, not a foreign foe.

The rebellions that we know about were not the work of high-principled, or narrow-minded, nationalists. Getting rid of the Romans was never the same as an independence movement in the modern sense. Nor were they driven by an excluded underclass or religious zealotry. Religion often confirmed the aspirations of the rebels and provided unifying rituals and symbols – from the messianic hopes of the Jews to the human sacrifices reputedly carried out by Arminius in the Teutoburg Forest – but rebellions were not specifically religious uprisings. They were usually led by the provincial aristocracy and were

100. The arch near the Roman Forum to commemorate the victory of Vespasian and Titus over the Jews. This sculpted panel in the passage through the centre of the arch shows the triumphal procession, with the menorah that had come to Rome as part of the spoils carried aloft.

a sign that the relationship of collusion between the local elites and the Roman authorities had broken down. To put it another way, they were the price the Romans paid for their dependence on collaboration. Rebellions were usually sparked by some isolated inflammatory or offensive act on the part of the Romans which upset the delicate balance of power.

The Jewish revolt, which began in 66 CE, stemmed largely from divisions in the ruling class in Judaea and the mutual distrust between them and the Roman authorities. The governor's order to flog and crucify a number of Jews in the province, who were also Roman citizens, was one powerful provocation. Most of the best-known rebel leaders in other parts of the world had very close connections with the Roman administration. Arminius, who massacred Varus' legions in 9 CE, and Julius Civilis, who led another German rebellion in 69 and 70 CE, were both Roman citizens and ex-soldiers in the Roman army, as well as being members of the local aristocracy. Even the uprising of Boudicca in Britain in 60 CE fits this pattern.

Boudicca, or Buduica (we do not know exactly how to spell the name, but neither, presumably, did she), was not an inveterate enemy of Rome but part of a family of elite collaborators. She was the widow of Prasutagus, a leader of the Britons in eastern England and a Roman ally: a Tiberius Claudius Togidubnus on a more modest scale. On his death, he left half his tribal kingdom to the emperor and half to his daughters, a sensible division intended to ensure peaceful continuity. In this case, according to Roman writers, it was the behaviour of some Romans in taking possession of the bequest that was the spark to the rebellion. They moved in with determined, or heedless, brutality: soldiers plundered the property of Prasutagus, raped his daughters and flogged his widow. In reaction, Boudicca raised her supporters and went on the attack.

As usual in these rebellions, short-term success on the part of the insurgents and terror on the part of the Romans was followed sooner or later by a resounding Roman victory. Boudicca's militia instantly destroyed three Roman towns in the new province, burning them to the ground and cruelly killing the inhabitants. One Roman historian, mingling fantasy – one hopes – with misogyny and patriotism, refers to Boudicca's soldiers hanging up the enemy women, cutting off their breasts and sewing them into the victims' mouths, 'to make them look as if they were eating them'. But as soon as the news reached the governor of the province, who was fighting 250 miles away in Wales, he marched straight back and wiped out the British insurgents. Tacitus gives a boastful but highly implausible figure of 80,000 British casualties, as against just 400 Romans; Boudicca took poison and according to one tall story lies buried somewhere near Platform 10 of King's Cross railway station in North London.

What Boudicca's aims were we can only guess. Her true story is clouded by ancient and modern mythmaking. For Roman writers, she was a figure simultaneously of horror and of fascination. A warrior queen, intersex, barbarian Cleopatra: 'very tall in stature, with a manly physique, piercing eyes and harsh voice, and a mass of red hair falling to her hips', as she was described centuries later by someone who could not possibly have known what she looked like. In Britain over the past few centuries she has not only been turned into a national heroine, on the optimistic assumption that her more unsavoury aspects were Roman propaganda; she has also been reinvented as the ancestor of the British Empire that one day outstripped ancient Rome. 'Regions Caesar never knew / Thy posterity shall sway' is the message carved on the plinth of her statue by the Thames: empire to – even bigger – empire.

No word from Boudicca or from any of the other rebels has come down to us. The closest we have to such a perspective are the multivolume Jewish histories by Josephus, the one-time insurgent against the Romans, who wrote his self-serving account of the rebellion that ended in the siege of Masada from the comfort of his study in Rome.

101. The statue of Boudicca (or 'Boadicea' as she is known here, in the Latin form of her name) on the Thames Embankment in London, by Thomas Thorneycroft. It is a wonderful image of a warrior queen, but almost every detail is archaeologically inaccurate, including the deadly scythes fixed to the chariot wheels. Started in the 1850s the sculpture was not put on public display, after much debate about where it should be placed, until 1902.

Whether as traitor, asylum seeker or far-sighted politician, he had taken up residence there under the protection of the emperor Vespasian. But that is a very special and very partial case. The histories of Tacitus and other Roman writers do feature long speeches from many of the most prominent opponents of Roman rule. In them, Boudicca denounces the immoral luxuries of Roman 'civilisation' and the effeminacy of the Romans while lamenting the lost *libertas* of the Britons – a loss symbolised by the rape of her daughters and her own flogging. Julius Civilis in Germany rouses his followers by comparing Roman rule to slavery rather than alliance and lists the unfair exactions imposed by the imperial power. Most memorably of all, in Tacitus' biography of his father-in-law, one of Rome's enemies, as part of a set-piece speech delivered before he enters battle with Agricola, challenges Roman rule and what it adds up to. The Romans, he insists, are the robbers of the world, insatiable for domination and profit. And in a much-quoted phrase that still hits home, he sums up the Roman imperial project: 'they create desolation and call it peace', '*solitudinem faciunt, pacem appellant*'.

These local rebels almost certainly did not utter any such fine phrases on the eve of battle. And the Roman historians who coined them could not possibly have known what was said on those occasions in any case and would have dreaded the thought of living under a Boudicca. But they knew exactly what the political objections to Roman rule might be and how to express it. While we must regret not being able to read the authentic views of the provincial dissidents of the empire, the idea that Roman writers could imagine what it was like to be in opposition to their own imperial power is perhaps even more important, and it is a distinguishing feature of Roman culture and power. At the end of the first century BCE, the historian Sallust, looking back, saw Rome's destruction of Carthage and Corinth in 146 BCE as a turning point towards Roman decadence and could try to reconstruct some of King Jugurtha's views of the Romans (as power hungry, corrupt and irrationally opposed to monarchy). A century or so later Tacitus and others imagined in vivid detail what the script of those provincials who rebelled against Rome might be. No one has ever framed a better critique of Roman imperial power than the words put into the mouths of rebels against Rome by Roman writers themselves.

Christian trouble

The problems with understanding the conflicts between the ancient Romans and the troublesome Christians are the exact opposite. The victory of Christianity, which in the fourth century CE became the 'official' religion of the Roman Empire, ensured that there is an enormous amount of surviving evidence, argument and self-justification from Christian Roman writers and almost nothing from their traditional, 'pagan' Roman opponents outlining their objections to the new religion. The letters between Pliny and Trajan amount to one of the most loquacious non-Christian discussions of the new religion to survive. The Christian texts of the third, fourth and fifth centuries CE are some of the most extreme examples ever of the rewriting of history to fit the agenda of the winners. They construct a triumphalist history of Christianity as victorious both against its pagan rivals, despite cruel persecution by the Roman state, and against all the internal variants ('heresies', as later Christians defined them), which challenged what came to be Christian orthodoxy.

The truth is that for two centuries after the crucifixion of Jesus sometime in the early 30s CE, Christianity is hard to pin down. It started as a radical Jewish sect, but how and when it became clearly separated from Judaism is impossible to say. It is not even certain when 'Christians' started regularly to use that name for themselves; it may originally have been a nickname applied by outsiders. They were for many years small in number. The best estimate is that by 200 CE there were around 200,000 Christians in the Roman Empire, of between 50 and 60 million people, though they may have been more visible than that figure suggests, as they were overwhelmingly concentrated in towns; the word 'pagan' was their term for anyone who was not a Christian or a Jew, and it implied anything from 'outsider' to 'rustic'. And they held a whole variety of views and beliefs about the nature of god and of Jesus and about the basic tenets of Christian faith that were gradually, and with great difficulty, pared down to the range of Christian orthodoxies (still not a single one) that we know today. Was Jesus married with children? What exactly happened at the crucifixion? Did he die or not?, many wondered, not unreasonably.

From time to time in the first two centuries CE, Roman authorities punished the Christians. There was at this period no general or systematic persecution; there was no sign of that until the mid third century CE. In practice, most of the early generations of Christians lived untroubled by the intervention of the state. Yet they were occasionally scapegoated, as when Nero decided to shift the blame for the great fire of Rome in 64 CE on to them. They were plausible candidates perhaps, as some Christians were prophesying that the world would shortly end in flames. The letters between Pliny and Trajan suggest that there was some Roman legislation that, whether explicitly or implicitly, outlawed the religion, though we know no more than that. Pliny's uncertainty and puzzlement are reflected on some other occasions when Romans chose to punish Christians in different parts of the empire, from Gaul to Africa.

One particularly revealing moment is described, in the account of her own trial, by a Christian woman who was sent to be killed by wild beasts in the amphitheatre in Roman Carthage in 203 CE. Vibia Perpetua, a newly converted Christian, was aged about twenty-two, married and with a young baby, when she was arrested and brought before the *procurator* of the province, who was acting in place of the governor who had recently died. Her memoir is the most lengthy, personal and intimate account by a woman of her own experiences to have survived from the whole of the ancient world, dwelling on her anxieties about her child and the dreams that she experienced in prison before she was sent to the beasts. Even in this account the frustration of her interrogator comes across, and his keenness to get her to recant. 'Have pity on the white hairs of your father, have pity on your tiny baby,' he urged her. 'Just make a sacrifice for the well-being of the emperor.' 'I will not do so,' she replied. 'Are you a Christian?' he asked, now putting the formal question. When she said she was – 'Christiana sum' – she was sentenced to death. The *procurator* was obviously baffled, and so it seems was the crowd who watched her die in the amphitheatre. Roman blood sports obeyed a rather strict set of rules. It was animals and criminals and the slave underclass who met their deaths, not young mothers. In fact 'the crowd shuddered at the sight', when they saw that Perpetua's fellow martyr Felicitas had breasts dripping milk. So why on earth were the Romans doing this?

Whatever the letter of the law or the precise circumstances of any individual trial, there was an irreconcilable clash between traditional Roman values and Christianity. Roman religion was not only polytheistic but treated foreign gods much as it treated foreign peoples: by incorporation. As far back as the takeover of Veii in the early fourth century BCE, Rome had regularly welcomed the gods of the conquered. There were from time to time controversies and anxieties about this; the priests of the Egyptian goddess Isis found themselves expelled from the city of Rome on more than one occasion. But the basic rule was that as the Roman Empire expanded, so did its pantheon of deities. Christianity was, in theory, an exclusive monotheism, which rejected the gods who for centuries had guaranteed the success of Rome. In practice, for every Perpetua who went bravely, or in Roman eyes stubbornly, to her death, there were probably hundreds of ordinary Christians who chose to sacrifice to the traditional gods, cross their fingers and ask for forgiveness later. But on paper there could be no accommodation.

The same was true, in a sense, of Judaism. But to a remarkable and in some ways unexpected degree, the Jews managed to operate within Roman culture. For the Romans, Christianity was far worse. First, it had no ancestral home. In their ordered religious geography, Romans expected deities to be *from* somewhere: Isis from Egypt, Mithras from Persia, the Jewish god from Judaea. The Christian god was rootless, claimed to be universal and sought more adherents. All kinds of mystical moments of enlightenment might attract new worshippers to (say) the religion of Isis. But Christianity was defined entirely by a process of spiritual conversion that was utterly new. What is more, some Christians were preaching values that threatened to overturn some of the most fundamental Greco-Roman assumptions about the nature of the world and of the people within it: that poverty, for example, was good; or that the body was to be tamed or rejected rather than cared for. All these factors help to explain the worries, confusion and hostility of Pliny and others like him.

At the same time, the success of Christianity was rooted in the Roman Empire, in its territorial extent, in the mobility that it promoted, in its towns and its cultural mix. From Pliny's Bithynia to Perpetua's Carthage, Christianity spread from its small-scale origins in Judaea largely because of the channels of communication across the Mediterranean world that the Roman Empire had opened up and because of the movement through those channels of people, goods, books and ideas. The irony is that the only religion that the Romans ever attempted to eradicate was the one whose success their empire made possible and which grew up entirely within the Roman world.

Citizens

So was Christianity really a Roman religion? Yes and no. For it obviously depends on what we mean by 'Roman' – a malleable and elusive adjective that can be used in many senses, from political control to style of art, from place to period of time. The right answer to the question of how many 'Romans' lived in 'Roman Britain' could well be 'about five', if we mean only those born and bred in Rome. It could equally well be 'around 50,000', if every single soldier plus the small staff of the imperial administration, including slaves, are all deemed to count. It would be more like '3 million' if we reckon that all the inhabitants of the Roman province were now in a way Roman, even though most of them, outside the towns, would probably not have known where in the world Rome was and would have had no more direct contact with Roman power than the occasional bit of loose change in their pockets.

One important definition still rested in Roman citizenship. For an increasingly large number of the inhabitants of the empire, becoming Roman meant becoming a Roman citizen. Throughout the provinces in the first two centuries CE, there were many ways in which this happened. Non-citizens who served in the Roman army were made citizens when they completed their terms of service; local officials in towns across the empire were more or less automatically granted Roman citizenship; whole communities or individuals (like Tiberius Claudius Togidubnus) were made citizens for special services they had rendered; and slaves of Roman citizens wherever they lived became Roman citizens if and when they were freed. There were none of the tests or examinations that we have come to associate with acquiring citizenship, no saluting the flag, swearing loyalty or paying a fee. Citizenship was a gift, and by 200 CE, according to the best recent estimate, roughly 20 per cent of the free population had become citizens. To put it another way, there were probably at least 10 million provincial Roman citizens.

Citizenship brought with it all kinds of specific rights under Roman law, covering a wide range of topics, from contracts to punishments. The simple reason that, in the 60s CE, Saint Peter was crucified while Saint Paul enjoyed the privilege of being beheaded was that Paul was a Roman citizen. For a few, citizenship was the first step in joining the elite of the central Roman government, on a journey that even led to the senate and imperial palace. Several emperors in the second century CE had origins outside Italy, from Trajan, whose family came from Spain, to Septimius Severus, who ruled between 193 and 211 CE and was the first emperor from Africa.

More and more senators were also of provincial origin. They included Lollius Urbicus, the governor of Britain from North Africa; Agricola, whose family came from southern Gaul; and many more, who proudly displayed their achievements in the capital ('the fifth man ever to enter the senate from the whole of Asia') in inscriptions in their home towns. Some emperors promoted the trend. In his speech in 48 CE which advocated admitting to the senate men from northern Gaul ('hairy Gaul', as the Romans called it), Claudius explicitly justified the proposal by looking back to Rome's openness to foreigners from its earliest days and forestalling one obvious objection: 'If anyone concentrates on the fact that the Gauls gave Julius Caesar, now a god, such trouble in war for ten years, he should consider that they have also been loyal and trustworthy for a hundred years since then.' By the end of the second century CE more than 50 per cent of the senators were from the provinces. They were not drawn evenly from different parts of the empire (none came from Britain), and some of them, like the first 'foreign' emperors, may have been the descendants of earlier Italian settlers in the provinces rather than 'native', but not all, or even most. In effect, the provincials were now ruling Rome.

That does not mean the governing classes of Rome were part of some warm, liberal cultural melting pot. In our terms, they were relatively race blind. The reason that we can still debate the ethnic origins of the African emperor Septimius Severus is that ancient writers made no comment on them. But the Roman elite were certainly snobbish about senators from the provinces. People joked about them not being able to find their way to the senate house. Even Septimius Severus is supposed to have been so embarrassed by his sister's bad Latin accent that he sent her back home. And Claudius' speech arguing in favour of admitting 'hairy Gauls' to the senate was prompted by widespread senatorial objections to the proposal. Yet, at least by the second century CE, at the centre of the Roman world were a substantial number of men and women who saw the empire from both sides, who had two homes – Roman and provincial – and who were culturally bilingual.

Gaius Julius Zoilos

It is with the story of one of those bilinguals that we end this chapter. Gaius Julius Zoilos is not a familiar name. He was no Polybius, Scipio Barbatus, Cicero or Pliny; he has left no writing (except a few words on stone) and is never once mentioned in the surviving literature of the Roman world. But different periods of Roman history are captured by different kinds of people. Zoilos, an ex-slave, imperial agent and wealthy benefactor of his home town, stands for many of the themes of the Roman Empire. At the same time he is a powerful reminder of those many Roman life stories that are almost hidden from history and are still being pieced together.

All we know about Zoilos has been revealed in excavations, mostly over the past fifty years, of the small Roman town of Aphrodisias, in what is now southern Turkey, which must have been his original – and final – home. His elaborate tomb has been discovered there, which gives a glimpse of his appearance, though tantalisingly most of his face has not survived. He is mentioned in a letter from the future emperor Augustus, written in 39 or 38 BCE and inscribed on stone by the Aphrodisians in their city centre: 'You know how fond I am of my Zoilos' are the exact words. And building projects that Zoilos sponsored in the town, from a new stage at the theatre to a major restoration of the main temple, blazoned his name as benefactor and philanthropist. From all these it is possible to reconstruct the outline of his career.

He was almost certainly born free, just plain Zoilos, sometime in the first half of the first century BCE but was taken into slavery – likely by pirates or people traffickers but possibly as a prisoner of war in one of the many conflicts of the period. He ended up in Rome as a slave, and agent, of Julius Caesar, who gave him his freedom and with it Roman citizenship and the Roman name of Gaius Julius Zoilos. He went on to work closely with the first Augustus, who knew him well enough to claim fondness, before returning to his home town as an extremely wealthy man, probably enriched by the booty from Caesar's campaigns, which trickled down even to slaves and ex-slaves. There he built himself into prominence in the traditional way and at his death, probably sometime in the reign of Augustus, was given a monumental tomb at public expense. If an epitaph found in Rome

102. A reconstruction of the sculpture of Zoilos' tomb, with the best preserved figure of the man himself (left). On the left hand side of the sculpture he appears in markedly Roman idiom (orating and clad in a toga). On the right hand side he is very much the Greek.

to a 'son of Zoilos' refers to his son (there were other men called Zoilos in the Roman world), then some of his family did not return to Aphrodisias with their father. For this 'Tiberius Julius Pappus, son of Zoilos' is commemorated as the head librarian of the emperor's libraries in the mid first century CE, through the reigns of Tiberius, Gaius and Claudius.

It is Zoilos' tomb at Aphrodisias that captures the culture of empire best, a vast square pile decorated with an elaborate sculptured frieze around its base, which even in the fragments that survive features Zoilos more than once, in crucially different guises. On the best-preserved side of the monument were two images of the dead man, clearly named, being crowned. On the left, he is being honoured by the very Roman figures of Virtus, with her shield, and Honos ('Manly Heroism' or 'Prestige'). On the right, it is the turn of his local 'people' and his 'city'. But it is the differences between the two outfits of Zoilos that are the key. On the left he is dressed in a distinctively Roman toga, one arm is raised as if to address an audience, and in the other hand he probably held a scroll. On the right he is shown in a Greek cloak, or chlamys, with a characteristically Greek hat on his head.

The monument underlines Zoilos' success, his wealth, his social mobility and his mobility across the Roman world. But most of all it shows him creating his identity in two very different forms, here seen side by side. In the culture of the Roman Empire, it was possible to be both Greek and Roman.

EPILOGUE

·

THE FIRST ROMAN MILLENNIUM

IN 212 CE the emperor Caracalla decreed that all the free inhabitants of the Roman Empire, wherever they lived, from Scotland to Syria, were Roman citizens. It was a revolutionary decision, which removed at a stroke the legal difference between the rulers and the ruled, and the culmination of a process that had been going on for almost a millennium. More than 30 million provincials became legally Roman overnight. This was one of the biggest single grants of citizenship – if not *the* biggest – in the history of the world.

For centuries, defeated enemies had become Romans. Slaves had been granted Roman citizenship at the same time as their freedom. And, as time went on, provincials in vast numbers, both soldiers and civilians, were made citizens as a reward for loyalty, service and collaboration. This was not entirely without controversy or conflict. Not all of those who were given citizenship wanted it. Some Romans did not conceal their suspicion of outsiders, citizens or not ('I can't bear a city full of Greeks', as the satirist Juvenal voices the complaint). And the desire of some of Rome's Italian allies to gain the citizenship from which they felt excluded partly drove one of the bloodiest wars in Roman history, the so-called Social War in the early first century BCE. But the underlying pattern is clear. Caracalla in 212 CE completed a process that in Roman myth Romulus had started a thousand years earlier – that is, according to the conventional date, in 753 BCE. Rome's founding father had been able to establish his new city only by offering citizenship to all comers, by turning foreigners into Romans.

Why Caracalla chose to take this step, at precisely this moment, has puzzled historians ever since. He was the second ruler in a new dynasty that came to power after the assassination of Commodus on 31 December 192 CE. In the first civil war at Rome since the brief conflict after the death of Nero in 68 CE, different units of the army, including the Praetorian Guard and legions in the provinces, attempted to install their own candidate on the throne. One of these was Lucius Septimius Severus, originally from Leptis Magna in North Africa, who marched into Italy backed by the army he had been commanding on the river Danube. His first years as emperor, until 197 CE, were spent eliminating the opposition. Caracalla was his son and heir, who ruled from 211 CE – and was officially known as Marcus Aurelius Antoninus. For, in a ludicrous twist on the use of adoption in imperial succession and in a desperate gambit for legitimacy, Septimius Severus arranged for himself and his family to be retrospectively adopted by the long-dead emperor Marcus Aurelius. 'Caracalla' was a nickname taken from the particular style of military cloak (*caracallus*) that he often wore.

Caracalla is not remembered as a far-sighted, radical reformer. He is best known as the sponsor of the largest set of public baths then built in Rome, whose towering brick walls still provide the impressive backdrop for a summer, open-air opera season. But that hardly hints at the bloodier aspects of his reign. This started in 211 CE with the murder of his younger brother and rival, Geta. In a tawdry replay of the fratricide that marked the origin of the city of Rome, Caracalla apparently engaged a posse of soldiers to finish the young man off as he cowered in his mother's arms. It ended when Caracalla was just twenty-nine years old, in 217 CE, with assassination by one of his bodyguard, who took advantage of a private moment when the emperor was relieving himself by the roadside to plunge the knife in. The commander of the Praetorian Guard at the time, Marcus Opellius

Macrinus, followed him briefly on to the throne. Probably implicated in the assassination, Macrinus was the first Roman emperor who was not by birth a senator.

This inglorious career of Caracalla has often suggested that there must have been sinister, or at least self-interested, motives behind the citizenship decree. Many historians, including Lucius Cassius Dio and Edward Gibbon, have suspected that it was prompted by a need to raise money, for these new citizens would automatically have become liable for Roman inheritance tax. If so, this was an extremely cumbersome way of going about it. There was no need to give citizenship to more than 30 million people if all you wanted to do was increase tax revenue.

Whatever lay behind it, this decree changed the Roman world forever, and that is why my story of Rome closes here, at the end of the first Roman millennium. The big question that had guided politics and debate for centuries, about the boundary between the Romans and those they ruled, had been answered. After a thousand years, Rome's 'citizenship project' had been completed and a new era had begun. It was not an era of peaceful, multicultural equality, though. For no sooner had one barrier of privilege been removed than another was put up in its place, on very different terms. Citizenship, once granted to all, became irrelevant. Over the third century CE, it was the distinction between the *honestiores* (literally 'the more honourable', the rich elite, including veteran soldiers) and the *humiliores* (literally 'the lower sort') that came to matter and to divide Romans again into two groups, with unequal rights formally written into Roman law. It was, for example, only *honestiores* who were exempted, as all citizens once had been, from particularly cruel or degrading punishments, such as crucifixion or flogging. The 'lower sort' of citizens found themselves liable to the kind of penalties that had previously been reserved for slaves and non-citizens. The new boundary between insiders and outsiders followed the line of wealth, class and status.

The citizenship decree was only one element in a wide series of transformations, disruptions, crises and invasions that changed the Roman world beyond recognition in the third century CE. The second Roman millennium – which did not finally end until Constantinople, the capital of the Roman Empire in the East by the sixth century CE, fell to the Ottoman Turks in 1453 CE – was grounded on entirely new principles, on a new world order and, for most of the time, on a different religion. The autocratic regime established by the first Augustus had been based in a political language and institutions that went back as far as anyone could trace in the first millennium of Roman history, and what I have called the Augustan template of imperial rule provided a relatively stable political framework for almost two hundred years after Augustus' death in 14 CE. But if the emperor Tiberius, who succeeded the first Augustus, could have slipped fairly comfortably into the imperial shoes of Commodus at the end of the second century CE, he would not have understood what it was to be an emperor a few decades further on. Rome in its second millennium was effectively a new state masquerading under an old name. Whether this millennium was one long, slow period of decline; a series of patchy cultural and political changes which eventually transformed the ancient world into the medieval; or an extraordinarily dynamic era of art, architecture and cultural reflection depends on your point of view.

Historians now often talk about 'the crisis' of the third century CE. What they mean is the process by which, after the assassination of Commodus in 192 CE, the Augustan template collapsed. The number of emperors is one obvious sign of that. In the nearly 180 years between 14 and 192 CE – apart from the single brief interlude of civil war after the death of Nero, when there were three unsuccessful claimants to the throne – there were just fourteen emperors. In the hundred years between 193 and 293 CE there were more than seventy (the list is elastic depending on how many unmemorable co-emperors, usurpers or 'pretenders' you decide to include). But, more to the point, any attempts to keep the legions out of the process of making emperors dramatically failed. Almost all the men who claimed the throne in the middle of the third century CE did so with the backing of one army unit or another. It was more or less continuous civil war. And there were flagrant subversions of traditional claims to power. For Septimius Severus to announce that he and his family had been adopted as heirs by an emperor who had died more than ten years earlier strained even the most flexible Roman standards of adoption.

At the same time, the city of Rome was eclipsed as the centre of power. Emperors were not often there but hundred of miles away with their armies. They did not have the time, incentive or cash to follow the Augustan model of leaving their mark on the city in brick and marble or of acting as popular benefactors. After the vast baths that Caracalla constructed in the 210s CE, there were hardly any major imperial building projects in the capital for eighty years, until the emperor Diocletian built his even bigger set of public baths in the 290s (large parts of which still stand outside Rome's main railway station). The absence of emperors from Rome also hastened the decline of the senate. There was no place for *civilitas* between emperors and senators, for delicate consultation or even for walkouts and stubborn protests by high-minded and unrealistic senators when the man on the throne was not in sight. Emperors increasingly ruled remotely, by decree or by letter, and without reference to the senate. The elevation to the throne of Macrinus, who was not a senator (and more such emperors followed), was another sure indication that the senate could be bypassed.

What lay behind these changes, and what was cause and what was effect, remains fiercely debated. Invasions by more efficient and often substantially 'Romanised' groups of 'barbarians' from outside the empire played a part. So too did the effects of the widespread plague in the late second century CE, which even on moderate estimates of its death toll must have seriously undermined Roman manpower. So too did the delicate balance of the Augustan template, with its failure to establish clear rules for succession and its awkward compromises between emperor and senate. Once flouted, it crumbled. But whatever the causes, the new Rome that emerged from 'the crisis' of the third century CE was strikingly different from anything that we have been exploring in Rome's first millennium.

The city of Rome irrevocably lost its place as the capital of the empire and fell to invaders on three occasions in the fifth century CE, for the first time since its sack by the Gauls 800 years earlier. The Roman world came to be controlled from regional capitals, such as Ravenna and Constantinople, modern Istanbul. The western and eastern parts of the empire were governed separately. And, after periods of coordinated persecution of the Christians in the later third century CE, the universal empire decided to embrace the universal religion (or vice versa). The emperor Constantine, the founder of the city of Constantinople in the early fourth century CE, was the first Roman emperor to formally convert to Christianity, baptised on his deathbed in 337 CE. Constantine did, in a way, follow the Augustan model of building himself into power, but what he built was churches.

Not everything changed in this new Rome, and certainly not all at once. The population of the city, Christian or not, were still enjoying spectacles in the Colosseum, probably wild beast hunts rather than gladiators, until well into the fifth century CE, and emperors in Constantinople sponsored popular entertainments on the old model of benefaction, often in the form of chariot racing. But many of the political continuities were superficial or even misunderstood. As a gesture to tradition, Constantinople was given its own senate house, but it was a building for an institution that had become a fossil. When an admittedly rather muddled commentator tried to explain the name of this building in the eighth century CE, he decided that it must have been built by a man called 'Senatus'.

In the city of Rome, the best indication of the changed world is the arch erected in 315 CE in honour of the emperor Constantine's victory over one of his internal rivals. It still stands, preserved because it was once built into a Renaissance fortress, between the old Roman Forum and the great amphitheatre of the Colosseum. At first glance it looks entirely traditional, harking back to the arches erected in honour of many military victories in Rome and copied in imperial memorials ever since, from the Arc de Triomphe in Paris to the Wellington Arch at Hyde Park Corner in London. It is decorated with an array of scenes that celebrate Constantine's authority in an idiom familiar from the first two centuries of autocratic power in Rome. The emperor is shown doing battle against barbarian enemies, addressing his troops, pardoning captives, sacrificing to the traditional gods, being crowned

103. The Arch of Constantine. Almost all the sculpture visible on this façade came from earlier monuments. That includes the roundels above the side arches, which are Hadrianic, and the rectangular panels on the attic level, which come from a monument of Marcus Aurelius. The standing barbarians, also at the attic level, are Trajanic.

by Victory and giving handouts to the people. All this could have been carved 150 years earlier.

In fact, much of it was. Apart from a few modest panels, all these sculptures had been prised or hacked off earlier monuments that commemorated Trajan, Hadrian and Marcus Aurelius. The faces of the original emperors were roughly recut in the likeness of Constantine, and the pieces were reassembled for display on the new arch. It was a costly and destructive exercise in nostalgia. For a few ancient onlookers, it may have succeeded in placing the new emperor in the illustrious tradition of the old. But, more than anything, this careful refabrication points to the historical distance between the first millennium of ancient Rome, which is the subject of my *SPQR*, and Rome's second millennium, which is a story for another time, another book – and another writer.

And so to end

I have spent a good deal of the past fifty years of my life with these 'first millennium Romans'. I have learnt their languages as well as I can. I have read a good deal of the literature they have left us (no one has read it all), and I have studied some of the hundreds of thousands of books and papers written over the centuries about them, from Machiavelli and Gibbon to Gore Vidal and beyond. I have tried to decipher the words they carved into stone, and I have dug them up, quite literally, on wet, windy and unglamorous archaeological sites in Roman Britain. And I have wondered for a long time about how best to tell Rome's story and to explain why I think it matters. I have also been one of those 5 million people who each year queue to step inside the Colosseum. I have let my children be photographed there, for a fee, with the chancers who ply their trade dressed up as gladiators. I have bought them plastic gladiator helmets, and, turning a blind eye to the cruelties of the modern world, I have reassured them that we do not do anything as cruel as that now. For me, as much as for anyone else, the Romans are a subject not just of history and inquiry but also of imagination and fantasy, horror and fun.

I no longer think, as I once naively did, that we have much to learn directly *from* the Romans – or, for that matter, from the ancient Greeks, or from any other ancient civilisation. We do not need to read of the difficulties of the Roman legions in Mesopotamia or against the Parthians to understand why modern military interventions in western Asia might be ill advised. I am not even certain that those generals who claim to follow the tactics of Julius Caesar really do so in more than their own imaginations. And attractive as some Roman approaches to citizenship may sound, as I have tried to explain them, it would be folly to imagine that they could be applied to our situation, centuries later. Besides, 'the Romans' were as divided about how they thought the world worked, or should work, as we are. There is no simple Roman model to follow. If only things were that easy.

But I am more and more convinced that we have an enormous amount to learn – as much about ourselves as about the past – by *engaging with* the history of the Romans, their poetry and prose, their controversies and arguments. Western culture has a very varied inheritance. Happily, we are not the heirs of the classical past alone. Nevertheless, since the Renaissance at least, many of our most fundamental assumptions about power, citizenship, responsibility, political violence, empire, luxury and beauty have been formed, and tested, in dialogue with the Romans and their writing.

We do not want to follow Cicero's example, but his clash with the bankrupt aristocrat, or popular revolutionary, with which I started this book still underlies our views of the rights of the citizen and still provides a language for political dissent: '*Quo usque tandem abutere, Catilina, patientia nostra?*' The idea of 'desolation' masquerading as 'peace', as Tacitus put into the mouths of Rome's British enemies, still echoes in modern critiques of imperialism. And the lurid vices that are attributed to the most memorable Roman emperors have always raised the question of where autocratic excess ends and a reign of terror begins.

We do the Romans a disservice if we heroise them, as much as if we demonise them. But we do ourselves a disservice if we fail to take them seriously – and if we close our long conversation with them. This book, I hope, is not just *A History of Ancient Rome* but part of that conversation with its Senate and People: *SPQR*.

FURTHER READING

The bibliography on the history of Rome is more than any one person could master. What follows are suggestions for exploring further the topics I have discussed, directions to some of the more out-of-the-way texts and sources that I have mentioned, including some personal favourite contributions to the subject, new and old. Under specific chapters I first note important thematic studies before identifying the source of particular arguments or pieces of information which might otherwise be hard to track down.

General

Almost all the ancient literature I draw on is available in good modern translation. The volumes of the Loeb Classical Library (Harvard University Press) include all but a handful of mainstream classical authors, with a Greek or Latin text and facing English translation. The series of Penguin Classics is more selective and does not include the original Greek or Latin but is more affordably priced. Increasingly, texts are available free online. The most useful sites are *Lacus Curtius* (http://penelope.uchicago.edu/Thayer/E/Roman/home.html) and the *Perseus Digital Library* (www.perseus.tufts.edu/hopper/collections). Both include a mixture of the original language and translations, and often have both. I give pointers here mainly to translations not available in these standard series.

Ancient inscriptions and papyri can be harder to track down. Their original texts are often included in huge ongoing collections, which began to be compiled in the nineteenth century (and, in what was then a gesture to easy understanding across different modern countries, were written entirely in Latin). The main collection (the *Corpus Inscriptionum Latinarum*) also has a website, http://cil.bbaw.de/cil_en/index_en.html. It is technical, but now mostly available in English. The website of the Oxford Centre for the Study of Ancient Documents (www.csad.ox.ac.uk/) gives a glimpse into the vivid evidence that can come from papyri. Some smaller collections of translations of these documents, chosen by period or theme, are available, noted below.

Anyone who has the nerve to write about a thousand years of Roman history follows in the footsteps of distinguished predecessors. The beginning of Edward Gibbon's *The Decline and Fall of the Roman Empire* remains one of the most memorable accounts of the first two centuries CE; the abridged version edited by David Womersely (Penguin, 2000) is in a handy single volume with a good introduction but omits substantial sections in this period. Two useful multi-authored series cover the period of *SPQR*. The Routledge History of the Ancient World includes two especially relevant volumes: T. J. Cornell, *The Beginnings of Rome: Italy and Rome from the Bronze Age to the Punic Wars (c. 1000–264 BC)* (1995), and Martin Goodman, *The Roman World, 44 BC–AD 180* (2nd edition, 2011). In the Edinburgh History of Ancient Rome (Edinburgh UP), note Nathan Rosenstein, *Rome and the Mediterranean 290 to 146 BC: The Imperial Republic* (2012), Catherine Steel, *The End of the Roman Republic 146 to 44 BC: Conquest and Crisis* (2013), J. S. Richardson, *Augustan Rome 44 BC to AD 14: The Restoration of the Republic and the Establishment of Empire* (2012) and, picking up more or less where I stop, Clifford Ando, *Imperial Rome AD 193 to 284* (2012). The relevant weighty parts – volumes 7.2 to 11 – of the *Cambridge Ancient History* (Cambridge UP, 2nd edition, from 1990 on) include even more detailed accounts and analysis. On a more succinct scale, I have learned a lot from Christopher Kelly, *The Roman Empire: A Very Short Introduction* (Oxford UP, 2006), Simon Price and Peter Thonemann, *The Birth of Classical Europe: A History from Troy to Augustine* (Viking, 2011), Brian Campbell, *The Romans and Their World: A Short Introduction* (Yale UP, 2011), Greg Woolf, *Rome: An Empire's Story* (Oxford UP, 2013) and Peter Garnsey and Richard Saller, *The Roman Empire: Economy, Society and Culture* (Bloomsbury, 2nd edition, 2014). All these underlie my discussion throughout this book.

Most aspects of Roman religion can be followed up in Mary Beard, John North and Simon Price, *Religions of Rome* (Cambridge UP, 1998), and I have discussed the details and history of the ceremony of triumph in my *The Roman Triumph* (Harvard UP, 2007). The essays in *The Cambridge Economic History of the GrecoRoman World*, edited by Walter Scheidel, Ian Morris and Richard P. Saller (Cambridge UP, 2007), offer up-to-date discussion of the economy and demography of the Roman world, though all population estimates in *SPQR* should be taken for what they are: (rough) estimates.

For general reference, *The Oxford Classical Dictionary*, edited by Simon Hornblower, Antony Spawforth and Esther Eidinow (Oxford UP, 4th edition, 2012, and online), includes reliable entries on hundreds of classical people, places and topics (a good present for anyone interested in the history of Rome). For maps, the *Barrington Atlas of the Greek and Roman World*, edited by Richard J. A. Talbert (Princeton UP, 2000), is the gold standard, and also available cheaply as an app. Free online, *Orbis*, the rather ponderously subtitled "Stanford Geospatial Network Model of the Roman World", allows you to plot routes and distances across the Roman world and shows the time and money it would have taken to get from A to B (http://orbis.stanford.edu/). All my journey times are based on this. For anyone planning a visit to ancient sites in Rome, the guidebook to take is Amanda Claridge, *Rome: An Oxford Archaeological Guide* (Oxford UP, 2nd edition, 2010).

Prologue

The essay by a Roman doctor (Galen) is translated by Vivian Nutton in *Galen: Psychological Writings*, edited by P. N. Singer (Cambridge UP, 2014). The technical data from the Greenland ice cap are presented by, for example, S. Hong et al. in 'Greenland ice', *Science* 265 (1994), and by C. J. Sapart et al. in 'Natural and anthropogenic variations', *Nature* 490 (2012). The cesspit in Herculaneum has a share of the limelight in Andrew Wallace-Hadrill, *Herculaneum: Past and Future* (Frances Lincoln, 2011).

Chapter 1

My favourite modern biography of Cicero is still Elizabeth Rawson, *Cicero: A Portrait* (Allen Lane, 1975; reprint, Bristol Classical Paperbacks, 1994). *The Cambridge Companion to Cicero*, edited by Catherine Steel (Cambridge UP, 2013), is a good guide to more up-to-date approaches. There is an astute discussion of Cicero's rhetoric against Catiline in Thomas Habinek, *The Politics of Latin Literature: Writing, Identity, and Empire in Ancient Rome* (Princeton UP, 1998). The Greek historian resident in the second century BCE was Polybius, who takes a leading part in Chapter 5. John R. Patterson, *Political Life in the City of Rome* (Bloomsbury, 2000) is a succinct guide to exactly that. For the conditions of Roman urban life at this period, John E. Stambaugh, *The Ancient Roman City* (Johns Hopkins UP, 1988) is a useful introduction.

Cicero 'the lodger' is put in the mouth of Catiline by Sallust, *War against Catiline* 31; his joke about the rats is found in his *Letters to Atticus* 14, 9; his abject self-pity when in exile is captured in his letters to his wife collected in Book 14 of his *Letters to Friends*, while the boastful fragments of his poem on his consulate are largely preserved in his treatise *On Divination*. The line '*O fortunatam natam ...*' is targeted by Juvenal, *Satires* 10, 122, and by Cicero's admirer Quintilian, *Handbook on Oratory* 11, 1, 24, while defended, for example, by Sander M. Goldberg, *Epic in Republican Rome* (Oxford UP, 1995). The letter to Lucceius is *Letters to Friends* 5, 12; the Greek poet whom Cicero hoped would take on his consulship is Archias, who features in Chapter 6. Alvaro Sanchez-Ostiz analyses the bilingual fragments of the speeches on papyri in 'Cicero graecus', *Zeitschrift für Papyrologie und Epigraphik* 187 (2013). The echoes of '*Quo usque ...*' are explored by Andrew Feldherr in 'Free spirits', *American Journal of Philology* 134 (2013); the story of Manlius is told, and his speech concocted, at Livy, *History* 6, 11–20; and Catiline's cameo appearance comes at *Aeneid* 8, 666–70. The calculations of the money supply are clearly explained by Keith Hopkins in 'Taxes and trade', *Journal of Roman Studies* 70 (1980), with more general reflections on the use of coins in ancient historical argument by Christopher Howgego, *Ancient History from Coins* (Routledge, 1995). The allegation that Cicero turned the conspiracy to his advantage is made in Ps-Sallust, *Invective against Cicero* 2. The medieval and Renaissance traditions of Catiline are the subject of Patricia J. Osmond, 'Catiline in Fiesole and Florence', *International Journal of the Classical Tradition* 7 (2000).

Chapter 2

R. Ross Holloway, *The Archaeology of Early Rome and Latium* (Routledge, 1994), Christopher J. Smith, *Early Rome and Latium: Economy and Society c. 1000–500 BC* (Oxford UP, 1996) and G. Forsythe, *A Critical History of Early Rome: From Prehistory to the First Punic War* (Univ. of California Press, 2005) are useful introductions to the period of this and the next chapters. T. P. Wiseman brilliantly (if, in the end, unconvincingly) discusses the mythology of Romulus and Remus in *Remus: A Roman Myth* (Cambridge UP, 1995) and explores related themes in the earliest history of the city in *Unwritten Rome* (Exeter UP, 2008); the story of Troy at Rome is the theme of Andrew Erskine, *Troy Between Greece and Rome: Local Tradition and Imperial Power* (Oxford UP, 2003). Livy's account is dissected by G. Miles, *Livy: Reconstructing Early Rome* (Cornell UP, 1997). Emma Dench's *Romulus' Asylum: Roman Identities from the Age of Alexander to the Age of Hadrian* (Oxford UP, 2005) is a sophisticated discussion of the role of foundation legends in Roman identity.

Cicero as the new Romulus is one theme in Ann Vasaly, *Representations: Images of the World in Ciceronian Oratory* (Univ. of California Press, 1993); 'Romulus of Arpinum' is a sneer in Ps-Sallust, *Invective against Cicero* 7. The case for the bronze wolf as a medieval work is put by Anna Maria Carruba, *La Lupa capitolina: Un bronzo medievale* (De Luca, 2007). Cicero's version of the foundation legend is in *On the State* 2, 4–13. The tragedy on the Rape of the Sabines was by Ennius; the one line can be found in volume 1 of the Loeb collection *Remains of Old Latin* (Harvard UP, 1935). Juba's calculations are recorded by Plutarch, *Romulus* 14; the passage of Sallust's *History* (Book 4, 67) is translated by Patrick McGushin in Sallust, *The Histories* 2 (Oxford UP, 1992); the inheritance of Romulus is the view of an early Roman historian, quoted by Aulus Gellius, *Attic Nights* 13, 23, 13; and Ovid's jokes are at *Love Lessons* 1, 101–34. What little is known about Egnatius is included in *The Fragments of the Roman Historians*, edited by T. J. Cornell (Oxford UP, 2014); Dionysius gives his view of Romulus' reaction in *Roman Antiquities* 1, 87; Horace's reflections on civil war are in *Epode* 7. P. S. Derow and W. G. Forrest discuss 'An inscription from Chios' in *Annual of the British School at Athens* 77 (1982); it is now in the Archaeological Museum at Chios. A translation of Claudius' speech is included in David C. Braund, *Augustus to Nero: A Sourcebook on Roman History 31 BC–AD 68* (Croom Helm, 1985; reprint, Routledge, 2014). The words of the king of Macedon (preserved in an inscription) are cited in Michel Austin, *The Hellenistic World from Alexander to the Roman Conquest: A Selection of Ancient Sources in Translation* (Cambridge UP, 2nd edition, 2006); Juvenal's scorn is found in his *Satires* 8; the 'crap' of Romulus is a quip in Cicero's *Letters to Atticus* 2, 1. The hut of Romulus was seen by Dionysius (*Roman Antiquities* 1, 79) and is discussed by Catharine Edwards in *Writing Rome* (Cambridge UP, 2006). The debates on the date of the origin of Rome are a major theme in Denis Feeney, *Caesar's Calendar: Ancient Times and the Beginnings of History* (Univ. of California Press, 2007). For the 'fate of Romulus' as a threat, see Plutarch, *Pompey* 25. Dionysius mentions Romus and Odysseus in *Roman Antiquities* 1, 72, 5 and refers to the tomb of Romulus at 1, 64, 4–5; the embassy from Delos is discussed by Andrew Erskine in 'Delos, Aeneas and *IG* XI.4.756', *Zeitschrift für Papyrologie und Epigraphik* 117 (1997). Dionysius' attempt to make sense of 'Aborigines' is in *Roman Antiquities* 1, 10. For the learned Varro's discussion of the Septimontium, see his *On the Latin Language* 6, 24. The hut at Fidenae is described by Rosanna Cappelli, *Fidene: Una casa dell'età del ferro* (Electa, 1996). The wattle and daub in the Forum is reanalysed by Albert J. Ammerman, 'On the origins of the Forum Romanum', *American Journal of Archaeology* 94 (1990). Various interpretations of the black stone are found in Festus, *On the Significance of Words* 184L (no convenient translation) and Dionysius, *Roman Antiquities* 1, 87 and 3, 1.

Chapter 3

The Roman Historical Tradition: Regal and Republican Rome, edited by James H. Richardson and Federico Santangelo (Oxford UP, 2014), is an important collection of essays on this and the early Republican period. The working of the Roman calendar is the main theme of Jörg Rüpke, *The Roman Calendar from Numa to Constantine: Time, History and the Fasti* (Blackwell, 2011). For an introduction to Etruria, see Christopher Smith, *The Etruscans* (Oxford UP, 2014), and *The Etruscan World*, edited by Jean MacIntosh Turfa (Routledge,

2013). The central role of *libertas* throughout Roman history is recently discussed by Valentina Arena, *Libertas and the Practice of Politics in the Late Roman Republic* (Cambridge UP, 2012). The later debates around the story of Lucretia are analysed in Ian Donaldson, *The Rapes of Lucretia: A Myth and Its Transformation* (Oxford UP, 1982).

G. Dumézil, *Archaic Roman Religion* (Chicago UP, 1970) proposes the 'excrement interpretation' of the Forum inscription. One classic statement of nineteenth-century scepticism on the Roman kings can still be found in Ettore Pais, *Ancient Legends of Roman History* (Dodd, Mead, 1905). Fabius Pictor's population estimate is quoted at Livy, *History* 1, 44. A translation of the letter to Teos is given in Beard, North and Price, *Religions of Rome*, volume 2 (see *General*, above), along with further details on the Antium calendar. Livy dismisses the idea of Numa being a pupil of Pythagoras at *History* 1, 18. The bronze for the decoration of St John Lateran is documented in John Franklin Hall, *Etruscan Italy: Etruscan Influences on the Civilizations of Italy from Antiquity to the Modern Era* (Indiana UP, 1996). The Latin names in early Etruria are discussed by Kathryn Lomas, 'The polis in Italy', in *Alternatives to Athens: Varieties of Political Organization and Community in Ancient Greece*, edited by Roger Brock and Stephen Hodkinson (Oxford UP, 2002). The François Tomb is the subject of one chapter in Peter J. Holliday, *The Origins of Roman Historical Commemoration in the Visual Arts* (Cambridge UP, 2002). Wiseman in *Unwritten Rome* (see *Chapter 2*) sceptically reviews the evidence for the large houses near the Forum. Pliny's complaints about the *Cloaca Maxima* are in his *Natural History* 36, 104. For Martial's quips on Lucretia, see his *Epigrams* 11, 16 and 104, and for Augustine's reflections, see *City of God* 1, 19. Pliny, *Natural History* 34, 139 hints that Lars Porsenna held power in Rome. The phrase 'getting rid of kings' is borrowed from John Henderson's article with that title in *Classical Quarterly* 44 (1994), which scrutinises the surname 'Rex'. Livy, *History* 7, 3 refers to the nail in the Capitoline temple, and 2, 5 to the formation of the Tiber's island. The Greek theorist is again Polybius. Mortimer N. S. Sellers discusses later appropriations of the Roman ideal of liberty in 'The Roman Republic and the French and American Revolutions', in *The Cambridge Companion to the Roman Republic*, edited by Harriet I. Flower (Cambridge UP, 2014).

Chapter 4

In addition to useful chapters in *A Companion to the Roman Republic,* edited by Nathan Rosenstein and Robert MorsteinMarx (Blackwell, 2007), the conflicts in early Republican Rome are the theme of *Social Struggles in Archaic Rome: New Perspectives on the Conflict of the Orders,* edited by Kurt A. Raaflaub (Univ. of California Press, 1986). A careful overview of office holding in the early Republic is given by Christopher Smith, 'The magistrates of the early Roman Republic', in *Consuls and Res Publica: Holding High Office in the Roman Republic,* edited by Hans Beck et al. (Cambridge UP, 2011). The structures of Republican political life in general are the subject of C. Nicolet, *The World of the Citizen in Republican Rome* (Univ. of California Press, 1980).

The 'chief praetor' is mentioned at Livy, *History* 7, 3; the translation 'colonels' I have borrowed from T. P. Wiseman (in *Remus;* see *Chapter 2*). The suspicious burnt layer in the Forum and elsewhere is noted by Filippo Coarelli in *Il Foro Romano* 1 (Quasar, 1983) and *Il Foro Boario dale origini alla fine della repubblica* (Quasar, 1988). The Tomb of the Scipios on the Appian Way is the theme of Filippo Coarelli, 'Il sepolcro degli Scipioni', in his *Revixit Ars: Arte e ideologia a Roma* (Quasar, 1997). The sarcophagus of Barbatus is well analysed by Harriet I. Flower, in *The Art of Forgetting: Disgrace and Oblivion in Roman Political Culture* (Univ. of North Carolina Press, 2011), who disposes of the common idea that his epitaph is a much later composition; translations of the main epitaphs from the family mausoleum are available online, at www.attalus.org/docs/cil/epitaph.html (see also Livy, *History* 10 for the context of Barbatus' career). Duris' comments on Sentinum are quoted by Diodorus Siculus, *Library of History* 21, 6. For Roman barbers, see Varro, *On Country Matters* 2, 11. An up-to-date analysis of the work of Fabius Pictor is included in *The Fragments of Roman Historians,* edited by T. J. Cornell (see *Chapter 2*); the exploit of the Fabii is described by Livy, *History* 2, 48–50; Coriolanus is carefully scrutinised by Tim Cornell, 'Coriolanus: Myth, History and Performance', in *Myth, History and Culture in Republican Rome,* edited by David Braund and Christopher Gill (Exeter UP, 2003). A glimpse of ancient dentistry is offered by D. J. Waarsenburg, 'Auro dentes iuncti', in *Stips Votiva,* edited by M. Gnade (Allard Pierson Museum, 1991). The Loeb collection *Remains of Old Latin*, volume 3 (Harvard UP, 1938), assembles the fragments of the Twelve Tables, but the most up-to-date edition is in *Roman Statutes*, edited by M. H. Crawford (Institute of Classical Studies, 1996). The irritated lawyers are mentioned by Aulus Gellius, *Attic Nights* 20, 1. On the conversion of the Roman senate to a permanent body, see T. J. Cornell, 'Lex Ovinia and the emancipation of the senate', in *The Roman Middle Republic: Politics, Religion and Historiography*, edited by C. Bruun (Institutum Romanum Finlandiae, 2000). The baseline for the archaeology of Veii is still J. B. Ward-Perkins, 'Veii: the historical topography of the ancient city', *Papers of the British School at Rome* 29 (1961), with now Roberta Cascino et al., *Veii, the Historical Topography of the Ancient City: A Restudy of John Ward-Perkins's Survey* (British School at Rome, 2012). Propertius' view is found at *Elegies* 4, 10. On a possible circuit wall earlier than the fourth century, see S. G. Bernard, 'Continuing the debate on Rome's earliest circuit walls', *Papers of the British School at Rome* 80 (2012). The tragedy on Sentinum is by Lucius Accius; its extant fragments are in *Remains of Old Latin* 2 (Harvard UP, 1936). The Esquiline tomb is discussed by Holliday, *The Origins of Roman Historical Commemoration* (see Chapter 3). The 'Upper' and 'Lower' Seas are referred to by Plautus, *Menaechmi* 237 and Cicero, *Letters to Atticus* 9, 5. The Roman impact on the landscape is well emphasised by Nicholas Purcell, 'The creation of the provincial landscape', in *The Early Roman Empire in the West*, edited by Thomas Blagg and Martin Millett (Oxbow, 1990).

Chapter 5

Modern debates on Roman imperialism go back to William V. Harris's classic study *War and Imperialism in Republican Rome, 327–70 BC* (Oxford UP, 2nd edition, 1985), which puts a strong case for aggressive Roman expansion. The work of Arthur Eckstein – for example, *Mediterranean Anarchy, Interstate War, and the Rise of Rome* (Univ. of California Press, 2006) – offers an alternative view, which in many ways I have followed in this book; even more powerful is J. A. North's brief essay 'The development of Roman imperialism', in *Journal of Roman Studies* 71 (1981). The cultural origins of Roman literature and the interaction between the Roman and Greek worlds are explored by Erich S. Gruen in *Culture and National Identity in Republican Rome* (Cornell UP, 1992) and very differently by Andrew Wallace-Hadrill in *Rome's Cultural Revolution* (Cambridge UP, 2008). Brian C. McGing, *Polybius* (Oxford UP, 2010) is a succinct introduction to the historian; Polybius' main analysis of Roman politics is found in Book 6 of his *Histories*. Useful discussions of the Roman wars against the Carthaginians and of their major players include A. E. Astin, *Scipio Aemilianus* (Oxford UP, 1967), Adrian Goldsworthy, *The Fall of Carthage: The Punic Wars 265–146 BC* (Cassell, 2003), and *A Companion to the Punic Wars*, edited by Dexter Hoyos (Blackwell, 2011). Philip Kay discusses economic aspects of Roman imperialism in *Rome's Economic Revolution* (Oxford UP, 2014). Roman funerals and commemoration are the subject of Harriet I. Flower, *Ancestor Masks and Aristocratic Power in Roman Culture* (Oxford UP, 1999). Important contributions to the debates on the popular element of Roman politics include John North, 'Democratic politics in Republican Rome', in *Studies in Ancient Greek and Roman Society*, edited by Robin Osborne (Cambridge UP, 2004), Fergus Millar, *The Crowd in the Late Republic* (Michigan UP, 1998), Henrik Mouritsen, *Plebs and Politics in the Late Roman Republic* (Cambridge UP, 2001) and Robert Morstein-Marx, *Mass Oratory and Political Power in the Late Roman Republic* (Cambridge UP, 2004).

The warlike Muse is imagined by Porcius Licinius, quoted in Aulus Gellius, *Attic Nights* 17, 21. Aemilianus' tears are described by Polybius, *Histories* 38, 21–22. The story of Pyrrhus' stunt with the elephants is told by Plutarch, *Pyrrhus* 20; the rams are discussed by Sebastiano Tusa and Jeffrey Royal, 'The landscape of the naval battle at the Egadi Islands', *Journal of Roman Archaeology* 25 (2012). A translation of the surviving fragments of Ennius' epic on Rome (the *Annales*, or *Chronicles*) is included in volume 1 of the Loeb collection *Remains of Old Latin* (Harvard UP, 1935); Livy's 'quotation' from Maharbal is at *History* 22, 51. The reality of the Battle of Cannae is discussed by Victor Davis Hanson in *Experience of War: An Anthology of Articles from MHQ, the Quarterly Journal of Military History* (Norton, 1992); Aemilius Paullus' quip on battles and games is quoted by Polybius, *Histories* 30, 14, while Polybius' advice to Aemilianus is recorded by Plutarch, *Table Talk* 4. Cato's jibe about the elderly Greeks is mentioned by Polybius, *Histories* 35, 6, and the story of the unfortunate crow by Cassius Dio, *Roman History* 36, 30. Polybius notes the Roman habits of Antiochus Epiphanes at *Histories* 26, 1, and Valerius Maximus tells the anecdote about Scipio Nasica in his *Memorable Deeds and Sayings* 7, 5. Jupiter's prophecy is scripted at *Aeneid* 1, 278–79. A translation of the inscription from Teos is given in Robert K. Sherk, *Rome and the Greek East to the Death of Augustus* (Cambridge UP, 1984); the Spanish mines are discussed in Kay's *Rome's Economic Revolution*; the vocabulary of empire is a theme in John Richardson, *The Language of Empire: Rome and the Idea of Empire from the Third Century BC to the Second Century AD* (Cambridge UP, 2011); and the idea of obedience is stressed by Robert Kallet-Marx, *Hegemony to Empire: The Development of the Roman Imperium in the East from 148 to 62 BC* (Univ. of California Press, 1996). The trick of Laenas is described by Polybius, *Histories* 29, 27; the Greek ambassador who fell down the sewer was Crates of Mallos (Suetonius, *On Grammarians* 2); and jokes about bad Roman accents in Greek are recorded by, for example, Dionysius, *Roman Antiquities* 19, 5. For the inscription of Lucius the mercenary, see Sherk, *Rome and the Greek East*; and for the Cossutii, Elizabeth Rawson, 'Architecture and sculpture: the activities of the Cossutii', *Papers of the British School at Rome* 43 (1975). The establishment of Carteia is noted by Livy, *History* 43, 3, and the presence of 'prostitutes' by the surviving 'Summary' of the lost Book 57 of his *History*. The historian Lucius Annaeus Florus compared later spoils to 'the cattle of the Volsci' (*Epitome* 1, 13). The awkward 'happy ending' is in Terence's *Hecyra*; the relevant plays of Plautus are *The Persian* and *The Little Carthaginian*, and one joke about 'barbarising' is in the prologue of the *Asinaria* ('Comedy of asses'). Many of Cato's bons mots are collected in Alan E. Astin, *Cato the Censor* (Oxford UP, 1978); the insistence of standing up at the theatre is mentioned by Valerius Maximus, *Memorable Deeds and Sayings* 2, 4.

Chapters 6 and 7

Rome in the Late Republic: Problems and Interpretations by Mary Beard and Michael Crawford (Duckworth, 2nd edition, 2000) is a brief account of the main issues of this period; Tom Holland's *Rubicon: The Triumph and Tragedy of the Roman Republic* (Little, Brown, 2003) is an excellent popular history. One of the sharpest analyses of socio-economic changes in the late Republic remains the first chapter of Keith Hopkins, *Conquerors and Slaves* (Cambridge UP, 1978). The major characters of these chapters have attracted modern biographies, although (apart from Cicero; see *Chapter 1*) there is almost never enough material to tell a life story in the conventional sense. That said, Robin Seager, *Pompey the Great* (Blackwell, 2nd edition, 2002) is a careful political account of Pompey's career; Adrian Goldsworthy, *Caesar: Life of a Colossus* (Yale UP, 2006) offers a clear outline of what we know of Julius Caesar, and W. Jeffery Tatum, *The Patrician Tribune: Publius Clodius Pulcher* (Univ. of North Carolina Press, 1999) of what we know of Cicero's great adversary; Barry Strauss, *The Spartacus War* (Simon and Schuster, 2009) is a reliable popular overview of Spartacus and his slave uprising. Note that I refer to Pompey, Caesar and Crassus as the 'Gang of Three', though they are more commonly now known by the spuriously formal title 'The First Triumvirate'.

The fullest account of the destruction of Carthage is Appian, *Punic Wars*; its archaeology is discussed by Serge Lancel, *Carthage: A History* (Blackwell, 1995). Polybius, *Histories* 38, 20 records the suicide of Hasdrubal's wife, and Pliny, *Natural History* 18, 22 highlights the works of Mago. Corinthian bronze is discussed at Pliny, *Natural History* 34, 7. Key anecdotes about Mummius are found in Polybius, *Histories* 39, 2 (gaming boards) and Velleius Paterculus, *History of Rome* 1, 13 ('new for old', also reprised in a much later collection of Roman jokes, the *Philogelos*). His spoils are discussed by Liv Yarrow, 'Lucius Mummius and the spoils of Corinth', *Scripta Classica Israelica* 25 (2006). For Cato's stunt with the figs, see Plutarch, *Cato the Elder* 27. Polybius cites the view that the Romans now aimed at extermination for its own sake at *Histories* 36, 9. Virgil references Mummius at *Aeneid* 6, 836–37; Velleius Paterculus, *History of Rome* 2, 1 reflects on the abandonment of virtue. Maria C. Gagliardo and James E. Packer provide an up-to-date discussion of Rome's first permanent stone theatre in 'A new look at Pompey's Theater', *American Journal of Archaeology* 110 (2006). Plutarch's *Tiberius Gracchus* is the source of many of the details of, and comments on, his life: the first political bloodshed since the monarchy (20), the story of Tiberius' 'conversion' (8), 'masters of the world' (9), Aemilianus' Homeric quotation (21). Alessandro Launaro, *Peasants and*

Slaves: The Rural Population of Roman Italy (200 BC to AD 100) (Cambridge UP, 2011) is an important recent discussion of the demography and agricultural history of Italy, though D. W. Rathbone, 'The development of agriculture in the "Ager Cosanus" during the Roman Republic', *Journal of Roman Studies* 71 (1981), remains one of the clearest introductions to the problems; 'fighting for their own displacement' is the phrase of Keith Hopkins in *Conquerors and Slaves*. On the rituals of Roman elections, see Hopkins, 'From violence to blessing', in *City States in Classical and Medieval Italy*, edited by A. Molho et al. (Franz Steiner, 1991). Cicero's reference to *partes* is at *On the State* 1, 31, and his huffing and puffing over the secret ballot is at *On the Laws* 3, 34–35. Juvenal, *Satires* 10, 81 coined 'bread and circuses'. The Roman food supply is clearly discussed by Peter Garnsey, *Food and Society in Classical Antiquity* (Cambridge UP, 1999); see also, for the Thessaly inscription, Garnsey and Dominic Rathbone, 'The background to the grain law of Gaius Gracchus', *Journal of Roman Studies* 75 (1985). The outburst of Frugi is recorded by Cicero, *Tusculan Disputations* 3, 48, Gaius' turning away from the *comitium* and demolition of the seating by Plutarch, *Gaius Gracchus* 5 and 12, the exchange with the consul's attendants and the carving on the Temple of Concord by Plutarch, *Gaius Gracchus* 13 and 17. Modern theories of the emergency powers act are fully discussed by Gregory K. Golden, *Crisis Management During the Roman Republic: The Role of Political Institutions in Emergencies* (Cambridge UP, 2013). Gaius' words on the affair of Teanum are quoted by Aulus Gellius, *Attic Nights* 10, 3 (as are Cato's earlier complaints about the consul dissatisfied with his supply arrangements). P. A. Brunt, 'Italian aims at the time of the Social War', in his *The Fall of the Roman Republic* (Oxford UP, 1988), and H. Mouritsen, *Italian Unification: A Study in Ancient and Modern Historiography* (Institute of Classical Studies, 1998) are major interventions on different sides of the question of motivation for the Social War. The friezes from Fregellae are discussed by F. Coarelli, 'Due fregi da Fregellae', *Ostraka* 3 (1994), and Praeneste by Wallace-Hadrill in *Rome's Cultural Revolution* (see *Chapter 5*). For the Social War as a civil war, see Florus, *Epitome* 2, 18; for 'seeking citizenship', Velleius Paterculus, *History of Rome* 2, 15 and for 'wolves', 2, 27. Publius Ventidius Bassus, the general who appeared on both sides of the triumph, features in Valerius Maximus, *Memorable Deeds and Sayings* 6, 9. The siege of Pompeii is documented in Flavio Russo and Ferruccio Russo, *89 a.C.: Assedio a Pompei* (Edizioni Scientifiche Italiane, 2005); the heads in Sulla's atrium are mentioned by Valerius Maximus, *Memorable Deeds and Sayings* 3, 1; the new low in the quotation of Greek is referred to by Appian, *Civil War* 1, 94; the dictator's death and epitaph are at Plutarch, *Sulla* 36–38. Catiline's misdeeds in the proscriptions are recorded by Plutarch, *Sulla* 32. The evidence on Spartacus is collected in Brent D. Shaw, *Spartacus and the Slave Wars: A Brief History with Documents* (Bedford/St Martins, 2001). Cicero refers to the problems at Pompeii in his speech *In Defence of Lucius Sulla* 60–62; the story of the comic at Asculum is told by Diodorus Siculus, *Library of History* 37, 12.

The activities of Verres in Sicily are the subject of Cicero's final speech *Against Verres* 2, 5. Gaius' sharp words are recorded by Plutarch, *Gaius Gracchus* 2. Both the Penguin and Loeb editions of Cicero's *Letters* are arranged in roughly chronological order; although this loses the logic of the original book division and demands a different numbering system, it makes the material from particular periods of his career (including his provincial governorship) easy to access. His philosophical treatise on provincial rule is *Letters to his Brother Quintus* 1.1. The law of Gaius can be found in *Roman Statutes*, edited by M. H. Crawford (see *Chapter 4*), and in a full study by A. Lintott, *Judicial Reform and Land Reform in the Roman Republic: A New Edition, with Translation and Commentary, of the Laws from Urbino* (Cambridge UP, 1992). The Roman *equites* are discussed by P. A. Brunt, 'The *equites* in the late Republic', in his *The Fall of the Roman Republic*, and *publicani* by Nicolet, *The World of the Citizen in Republican Rome* (see *Chapter 4*). The senator who returned to his province in exile is mentioned by Valerius Maximus, *Memorable Deeds and Sayings* 2, 10. The slogan 'Rome for sale' goes back to Sallust, *War Against Jugurtha* 35, 10. The impact of Marius' army reforms and the 'private' armies of the late Republic are one theme of a classic essay by Brunt, 'The army and the land', in *The Fall of the Roman Republic*. The death of Marius is described by Plutarch, *Marius* 45. Cicero's speech advocating Pompey's command is known by two titles, *On the Command of Pompey* and *In Support of the Manilian Law*. The old pirate is conjured up by Virgil, *Georgics* 4, 125–46; Valerius Maximus, *Memorable Deeds and Sayings* 6, 2 quotes the phrase 'kid butcher'. F. W. Walbank discusses 'The Scipionic legend' in *Proceedings of the*

Cambridge Philological Society 13 (1967). Horace *Odes* 2, 1 pinpoints 60 BCE as a key turning point; Cato's remark is quoted by Plutarch, *Pompey* 47; the notebook is joked about, sardonically, in Cicero, *Letters to Atticus* 4, 8b. The fate of Crassus' head is mentioned by Plutarch, *Crassus* 33; Cicero's unsuccessful plea on behalf of Clodius' murderer is his *In Defence of Milo*. The absence of wine is noted in Julius Caesar's *Commentaries on the Gallic War* 2, 15 and 4, 2, the position of the Druids at 6, 13–16. Catullus' reference is in his *Poems* 11; the 'crimes' of Caesar are stressed by Plutarch, *Cato the Younger* 51 and Pliny, *Natural History* 7, 92. The Greek visitor who saw the heads was Posidonius, quoted by Strabo, *Geography* 4.4. Peticius is mentioned by Plutarch, *Pompey* 73; the story of Soterides is explained by Nicholas Purcell, 'Romans in the Roman world', in *The Cambridge Companion to the Age of Augustus*, edited by Karl Galinsky (Cambridge UP, 2005). Cato's lurid death is described by Plutarch, *Cato the Younger*, 68–70. The incident at the Lupercalia is examined by J. A. North, 'Caesar at the Lupercalia', *Journal of Roman Studies* 98 (2008). For jokes about the short-term consul, see Cicero, *Letters to Friends* 7, 30 and Macrobius, *Saturnalia* 2, 3.

Chapter 8

Good introductions to some of the main topics include Jane F. Gardner, *Women in Roman Law and Society* (Croom Helm, 1986), Florence Dupont, *Daily Life in Ancient Rome* (Blackwell, 1994), *Life, Death and Entertainment in the Roman Empire*, edited by D. S. Potter and D. J. Mattingly (Univ. of Michigan Press, 1999), *Roman Women*, edited by Augusto Fraschetti (Univ. of Chicago Press, 2001), *The Cambridge World History of Slavery*, volume 1, edited by Keith Bradley and Paul Cartledge (Cambridge UP, 2011), Christian Laes, *Children in the Roman Empire: Outsiders Within* (Cambridge UP, 2011) and Henrik Mouritsen, *The Freedman in the Roman World* (Cambridge UP, 2011).

The twenty-five books on the Latin language (some of which survive) are by Marcus Terentius Varro; Cicero's jokes are one theme in my *Laughter in Ancient Rome: On Joking, Tickling, and Cracking Up* (Univ. of California Press, 2014). Susan Treggiari sees things from the side of Cicero's female relations in *Terentia, Tullia and Publilia: The Women of Cicero's Family* (Routledge, 2007). The story of the dinner with Caesar is told in *Letters to Atticus* 13, 52; Gore Vidal's essay is in his *Selected Essays* (Abacus, 2007). The classic study of Roman marriage is Susan Treggiari, *Roman Marriage: Iusti Coniuges from the Time of Cicero to the Time of Ulpian* (Oxford UP, 1993); Claudia's epitaph is included in Mary R. Lefkowitz and Maureen Fant, *Women's Life in Greece and Rome* (Duckworth, 3rd edition, 2005). The tough line of Egnatius Metellus is highlighted by Valerius Maximus, *Memorable Deeds and Sayings* 6, 3; Livia's wool working is mentioned in Suetonius, *Augustus* 73, Volumnia Cytheris by Cicero, *Letters to Atticus* 10, 10 and 16, 5. Marilyn B. Skinner, *Clodia Metelli: The Tribune's Sister* (Oxford UP, 2011) attempts to reconstruct Clodia's career; the tricky court case is what we know as *In Defence of Caelius*. The problems of Verres' dinner are discussed by Catherine Steel, 'Being economical with the truth: what really happened at Lampsacus?', in *Cicero the Advocate*, edited by J. Powell and J. Paterson (Oxford UP, 2004). Cicero's reference to women's weakness is at *In Defence of Murena* 27, the joke about tying his son-in-law to a sword at Macrobius *Saturnalia* 2, 3. Glimpses into the marriage of Quintus and Pomponia are at *Letters to Atticus* 5, 1 and 14, 13. Marriage age is discussed in Brent D. Shaw, 'The age of Roman girls at marriage', *Journal of Roman Studies* 77 (1987). Terentia's view of an old man's infatuation is reported by Plutarch, *Cicero* 41; Cicero's quip is praised by Quintilian, *Handbook on Oratory* 6, 3. Evidence for ancient contraception is collected by John M. Riddle, *Contraception and Abortion from the Ancient World to the Renaissance* (Harvard UP, 1994). The letter from the husband in Roman Egypt is included in Jane Rowlandson, *Women and Society in Greek and Roman Egypt: A Sourcebook* (Cambridge UP, 1998). Issues of life expectancy and family relations are discussed in Richard P. Saller, *Patriarchy, Property and Death in the Roman Family* (Cambridge UP, 1997). House ownership is the theme of Elizabeth Rawson, 'The Ciceronian aristocracy and its properties', in her *Roman Culture and Society* (Oxford UP, 1991). Andrew Wallace-Hadrill, *Houses and Society in Pompeii and Herculaneum* (Princeton UP, 1994) explores the layout of the Roman house; Pliny, *Natural History* 36, 5–6 discusses Scaurus' house; and the problem of luxury is highlighted in Catharine Edwards, *The Politics of Immorality in Ancient Rome* (Cambridge UP, 2002). The Antikythera wreck is documented in *The Antikythera Shipwreck: The Ship, the Treasures, the Mechanism*, edited by N. Kaltsas et al. (National Archaeological Museum, Athens, 2012). The Sestii are a case study in John H. D'Arms, *Commerce and Social Standing in Ancient Rome* (Harvard UP, 1981). The bright idea of slave uniforms is mentioned in Seneca, *On Mercy* 1, 24, slave runaways in Cicero's *Letters to Friends* 5, 9; 5, 10a; 13, 77 and *Letters to Atticus* 7, 2. Tiro is a major focus of my 'Ciceronian correspondences', in *Classics in Progress: Essays on Ancient Greece and Rome*, edited by T. P. Wiseman (Oxford UP, 2006), and his collection of Cicero's jokes is criticised by Quintilian, *Handbook on Oratory* 6, 3. Greg Woolf, 'Monumental writing', *Journal of Roman Studies* 86 (1996), discusses the explosion of writing. The *ménage à trois* is described in the long epitaph of Allia Potestas, translated in Lefkowitz and Fant, *Women's Life in Greece and Rome*.

Chapter 9

The Cambridge Companion to the Age of Augustus, edited by Karl Galinsky (see *Chapters 6 and 7*), is a good introduction to this period, as is *Caesar Augustus: Seven Aspects*, edited by Fergus Millar and Erich Segal (Oxford UP, 1984). *Augustus*, edited by Jonathan Edmondson (Edinburgh UP, 2009), is a collection of some of the best recent essays on the emperor. Paul Zanker, *The Power of Images in the Age of Augustus* (Univ. of Michigan Press, 1988) transformed our understanding of the art and architecture of the period. The period of civil war following the death of Caesar is the subject of Josiah Osgood, *Caesar's Legacy: Civil War and the Emergence of the Roman Empire* (Cambridge UP, 2006). Jane Bellemore, in *Nicolaus of Damascus* (Bristol Classical Press, 1984), gives a translation of the surviving sections of his early biography of Augustus (or see www.csun.edu/~hcfii004/nicolaus.html). Alison Cooley's *Res Gestae Divi Augusti* (Cambridge UP, 2009) translates Augustus' own account of his life, with a full discussion.

The best modern analysis of the details of Caesar's assassination is in T. P. Wiseman, *Remembering the Roman People* (Oxford UP, 2009). The stories of Octavian's early brutality and the 'banquet of the twelve gods' are told by

Suetonius, *Augustus* 27 and 70. Decapitation is the subject of Amy Richlin's 'Cicero's head', in *Constructions of the Classical Body*, edited by James I. Porter (Univ. of Michigan Press, 2002); Seneca's *Suasoriae* (*Pleas*) 6 and 7 give a flavour of the rhetorical exercises on the subject of Cicero's death. Appian, *Civil War* 4 is a good source of anecdotes about the proscriptions. Josiah Osgood, *Turia: A Roman Woman's Civil War* (Oxford UP, 2014) explores the female bravery commemorated on the epitaph; Judith Hallett brings the sling bullets from Perugia to life in '*Perusinae glandes*', *American Journal of Ancient History* 2 (1977). Cleopatra's departure is noted by Cicero, *Letters to Atticus* 14, 8. The disapproving account of Cleopatran luxury is Pliny, *Natural History* 9, 119–21; Plutarch, *Antony* 50 reports his treatment of Alexandria as if it were Rome; and there is plenty of sensible discussion of Antony and Cleopatra in C. B. R. Pelling, *Plutarch: Life of Antony* (Cambridge UP, 1988). The 'below stairs' source is mentioned by Plutarch, *Antony* 28. Konstantinos L. Zachos, 'The *tropaeum* of the sea-battle at Actium', *Journal of Roman Archaeology* 16 (2003), analyses the monument. The story of ravens is told in Macrobius, *Saturnalia* 2, 4. Debates at the funeral are reported by Tacitus, *Annals* 1, 9. Price and Thonemann, *The Birth of Classical Europe* (see *General*) stress Augustus' abolition of *nothing*. For the importance of *civilitas*, see Andrew Wallace-Hadrill, 'Civilis princeps', *Journal of Roman Studies* 72 (1982); for the chameleon and the sphinx, Julian *Saturnalia* 309 and Suetonius, *Augustus* 50. The display of 'maps' is discussed by Claude Nicolet, *Space, Geography, and Politics in the Early Roman Empire* (Univ. of Michigan Press, 1991), with Pliny, *Natural History* 3, 17. Jas Elsner emphasises the importance of building in the *Res Gestae* in 'Inventing imperium', in *Art and Text in Roman Culture*, edited by Elsner (Cambridge UP, 1996). The inscription on the calendar of Asia is translated in Sherk, *Rome and the Greek East* (see *Chapter 5*). One attempt to calculate the total cost of the Roman army is by Keith Hopkins, 'Taxes and trade' (see *Chapter 1*). The senate is discussed by P. A. Brunt in 'The role of the senate', *Classical Quarterly* 34 (1984); the defeat of the Romans in Germany is the subject of Peter S. Wells, *The Battle That Stopped Rome* (Norton, 2004). Egnatius Rufus and other opponents are discussed by K. A. Raaflaub and L. J. Samons II, 'Opposition to Augustus', in *Between Republic and Empire: Interpretations of Augustus and His Principate*, edited by Raaflaub and Mark

Toher, problems of succession by *The Julio-Claudian Succession: Reality and Perception of the "Augustan Model"*, edited by A. G. G. Gibson (Brill, 2013). Livia's role is fully documented in Nicholas Purcell's 'Livia and the womanhood of Rome', in *Augustus*, edited by Jonathan Edmondson.

Chapter 10

Important overviews of the rulers and the political life of Rome during the first two centuries of the empire include Fergus Millar, *The Emperor in the Roman World* (Bristol Classical Press, revised edition, 1992), P. A. Brunt, *Roman Imperial Themes* (Oxford UP, 1990), R. J. A. Talbert, *The Senate of Imperial Rome* (Princeton UP, 1984) and Keith Hopkins, *Death and Renewal* (Cambridge UP, 1985), especially Chapter 3. The biographical approach remains popular, despite the fragile factual base. Nevertheless, Aloys Winterling, *Caligula: A Biography* (Univ. of California Press, 2011) and Edward Champlin, *Nero* (Harvard UP, 2003) are interesting for their revisionist stances on two 'monstrous' emperors. I have also used the gratifyingly sober accounts of *Claudius* by Barbara Levick (Routledge, 1993), *Nero: The End of a Dynasty* by Miriam T. Griffin (Routledge, revised edition, 1987) and *Hadrian: The Restless Emperor* by Anthony R. Birley (Routledge, 1997).

The assassination of Gaius is analysed by T. P. Wiseman, *The Death of Caligula* (Liverpool UP, 2nd edition, 2013), translating and analysing Josephus' account in his *Jewish Antiquities* 19. Eric R. Varner, *Mutilation and Transformation: Damnatio Memoriae and Roman Imperial Portraiture* (Brill, 2004) discusses the recarving of portrait statues. The ancient source for most lurid anecdotes about Gaius is Suetonius' biography: the mistranslated passage about sex at dinner (24), the 'seashells' (46). The victims of Claudius are tallied at Suetonius, *Claudius* 29. Commodus in the amphitheatre provides the opening to my *Laughter in Ancient Rome* (see *Chapter 8*); the 'little fishes' appear in Suetonius, *Tiberius* 44, and the fly killing in Suetonius, *Domitian* 3. There is a story along the lines of '*pecunia non olet*' in Suetonius, *Vespasian* 23; Vespasian's triumphal common sense is quoted by Suetonius, *Vespasian* 12. The set piece with the collapsible boat is at Tacitus, *Annales* 13, 3–7. The sardonic quip about plots is attributed to Domitian at Suetonius, *Domitian* 21 and to Hadrian at *Augustan History* (*SHA*), *Avidius Cassius* 2. The graffiti about the 'Golden House' is quoted by Suetonius, *Nero* 39. Susan Treggiari analyses 'Jobs in the household of Livia' in *Papers of the British School at Rome* 43 (1975). The desk job of the emperor is conjured up by Fergus Millar, 'Emperors at work', in *Government, Society, and Culture in the Roman Empire*, edited by Hannah M. Cotton and Guy M. Rogers (Univ. of North Carolina Press, 2004). Augustus' judgement on the chamber pot case is translated in Sherk, *Rome and the Greek East* (see *Chapter 5*). Sacrificial biscuits are discussed by Richard Gordon, 'The veil of power', in *Pagan Priests: Religion and Power in the Ancient World*, edited by Mary Beard and John North (Duckworth, 1990). Fronto's comment on imperial images is made in his *Letters* 4, 12. Caroline Vout reflects on 'What's in a beard' in *Rethinking Revolutions Through Ancient Greece*, edited by Simon Goldhill and Robin Osborne (Cambridge UP, 2006). The scale, impact and financing of the Colosseum are themes in Keith Hopkins and Mary Beard, *The Colosseum* (Profile, 2005). For the Talmudic story of Titus' death, see *Gittin* 56 B; for Domitian's mirrored walls, Suetonius, *Domitian* 14; for the 'Golden Sheep', Tacitus, *Annales* 13, 1. 'The secret of imperial rule' are the words of Tacitus, *Histories* 1, 4. Vespasian's miracles are mentioned by Suetonius, *Vespasian* 7 and Tacitus, *Histories* 4, 81–82. Hugh Lindsay, *Adoption in the Roman World* (Cambridge UP, 2009) discusses the adoption of imperial heirs and the wider background. Pliny's remarks are from his *Panegyric* 7–8; Galba's speech is scripted in Tacitus, *Histories* 1, 14–17. Hadrian's poem is in the *Palatine Anthology* 6, 332. The story of Tiberius and the sharp senator is reported by Tacitus, *Annales* 1, 74, 'men fit for slavery' at 3, 65 and Nero's first speech at 13, 4. Hadrian's execution of the ex-consuls is alleged by *Augustan History* (*SHA*), *Hadrian* 5. Alain Gowing, *Empire and Memory: The Representation of the Roman Republic in Imperial Culture* (Cambridge UP, 2005) explores exactly that. Cordus is supposed to have pointed out that Livy had praised Pompey (Tacitus, *Annales* 4, 34). For Lucan's death, see Tacitus, *Annales* 15, 70. Domitian's black dinner party is described by Cassius Dio, *Roman History* 67, 9. The conversation at dinner with Nerva is quoted at *Letters* 4, 22; Tacitus' admission is made at *Histories* 1, 1. Cassius Dio, *Roman History* 66, 12 and Suetonius, *Vespasian* 15 mention clashes between Helvidius

Priscus and Vespasian. Pliny reports Fannia's illness at *Letters* 7, 19. Cassius Dio, *Roman History* 63, 26 references the temple of Venus Sabina. The subtlety of emperor worship is a major theme in S. R. F. Price, *Rituals and Power: The Roman Imperial Cult in Asia Minor* (Cambridge UP, 1986), which discusses the inscription from Gytheum; a translation is included in Beard, North and Price, *Religions of Rome*, volume 2 (see *General*). Livia's 'reward' is noted by Cassius Dio, *Roman History* 56, 46, Vespasian's quip by Suetonius, *Vespasian* 23.

Chapter 11

Roman city life and planning are discussed by Stambaugh, *The Ancient Roman City* (see *Chapter 1*), including a chapter on Timgad. Useful overviews of non-elite lives in ancient Rome are given by Jerry Toner, *Popular Culture in Ancient Rome* (Polity, 2009) and Robert Knapp, *Invisible Romans: Prostitutes, Outlaws, Slaves, Gladiators, Ordinary Men and Women ... the Romans That History Forgot* (Profile, 2013). *The Romans*, edited by Andrea Giardina (Univ. of Chicago Press, 1993), includes essays on representative characters of all ranks of Roman society, including the poor. Despite the title, the *Anthology of Ancient Greek Popular Literature*, edited by William Hansen (Indiana UP, 1998), includes translations of plenty of the Roman material I discuss in this chapter. John R. Clarke, *Art in the Lives of Ordinary Romans: Visual Representations and Non-elite Viewers in Italy, 100 BC–AD 315* (Univ. of California Press, 2003) explores popular art. An influential but pessimistic view of levels of literacy is found in William V. Harris, *Ancient Literacy* (Harvard UP, 1991).

One-legged tables and multiple rings are described by Pliny, *Natural History* 34, 14 and 33, 24. Pliny the Younger's villa at Laurentum is described in *Letters* 2, 17 and discussed in a chapter of Roy K. Gibson and Ruth Morello, *Reading the Letters of Pliny the Younger* (Cambridge UP, 2012). The law with specifications on a minimum number of roof tiles is part of a local charter for the town of Tarentum, translated in Kathryn Lomas, *Roman Italy, 338 BC–AD 200: A Sourcebook* (Univ. College London Press, 1996). The rich residents of Timgad are the subject of Elizabeth W. B. Fentress, 'Frontier culture and politics at Timgad', *Bulletin Archéologique du Comité des Travaux Historiques et Scientifiques* 17 (1984). The lack of city zoning, including 'moral zoning', is discussed by Andrew Wallace-Hadrill, 'Public honour and private shame: the urban texture of Pompeii', in *Urban Society in Roman Italy*, edited by Tim J. Cornell and Kathryn Lomas (UCL Press, 1995). Juvenal's complaints are in his *Satires* 3; at most, *plostra* (heavy carts) were banned during the daytime, to judge from regulations going back to Julius Caesar found at Heraclea in southern Italy – the 'Table of Heraclea', translated in *Roman Statutes*, edited by M. H. Crawford (see *Chapter 4*). Fronto's version of 'bread and circuses' is in his *Introduction to History* 17 (part of his series of *Letters*). Cicero's scorn of work is at *On Duties* 1, 150–51. The continuity of the majority of British lifestyles under the Romans is a point forcefully made by Richard Reece in *My Roman Britain* (Oxbow, 1988). Marginal Romans are discussed by John R. Patterson, 'On the margins', in *Death and Disease in the Ancient City*, edited by Valerie M. Hope and Eireann Marshall (Routledge, 2002). For the demand for day labourers, see David Mattingly, 'The feeding of imperial Rome', in *Ancient Rome: The Archaeology of the Eternal City*, edited by Jon Coulston and Hazel Dodge (Oxford Univ. School of Archaeology, 2000); Ancarenus Nothus features in another fine essay in the same volume, 'Living and dying in the city of Rome' by John R. Patterson. Details of the textile works outside Rome are in S. Musco et al., 'Le complexe archéologique de Casal Bertone', *Les Dossiers d'Archéologie* 330 (2008). Work is the theme of S. R. Joshel, *Work, Identity, and Legal Status at Rome: A Study of the Occupational Inscriptions* (Univ. of Oklahoma Press, 1992) and N. Kampen, *Image and Status: Roman Working Women in Ostia* (Mann, 1981). The tomb of Eurysaces is discussed by Lauren Hackforth Petersen, *The Freedman in Roman Art and Art History* (Cambridge UP, 2006). A translation of the rules for the collegium (not in this case a specifically trade organisation) is included in Beard, North and Price, *Religions of Rome*, volume 2 (see *General*). The inscription relating to the bakers' strike is translated in Barbara Levick, *The Government of the Roman Empire: A Sourcebook* (Routledge, 2002). The slogans (and the bar paintings) from Pompeii are discussed in Mary Beard, *Pompeii: The Life of a Roman Town* (Profile, 2008). For laundry workers, see Miko Flohr, *The World of the Fullo: Work, Economy, and Society in Roman Italy* (Oxford UP, 2013). Juvenal's Ostian bar is conjured up in *Satires* 8. Roman gambling in all its aspects is the subject of Nicholas Purcell, 'Literate games: Roman society and the game of alea', in *Studies in Ancient Greek and Roman Society*, edited by Robin Osborne (see *Chapter 5*). Jerry Toner, *Roman Disasters* (Blackwell, 2013) is an accessible book on all the kinds of misfortunes, from flooding to fire, that threatened ordinary Romans. Crimes (and responses to them) in Roman Egypt are documented in technical detail by Benjamin Kelly, *Petitions, Litigation, and Social Control in Roman Egypt* (Oxford UP, 2011) and Ari Z. Bryen, *Violence in Roman Egypt: A Study in Legal Interpretation* (Univ. of Pennsylvania Press, 2013). The case of the woman from Herculaneum (Petronia Justa) is discussed by Wallace-Hadrill, *Herculaneum* (see *Prologue*). Curses from Roman Bath are translated in Stanley Ireland, *Roman Britain: A Sourcebook* (Routledge, 3rd edition, 2008); the *Oracles of Astrampsychus* are translated in *The Anthology of Ancient Greek Popular Literature*, edited by William Hansen. The spirit of Phaedrus' fables is beautifully captured by John Henderson in *Telling Tales on Caesar: Roman Stories from Phaedrus* (Oxford UP, 2001) and *Aesop's Human Zoo: Roman Stories about our Bodies* (Univ. of Chicago Press, 2004); see especially Phaedrus, *Fables* 1, 2; 1, 3 and 1, 28. Riots are attested by Suetonius, *Claudius* 18, Philostratus, *Life of Apollonius* 1, 15 (Aspendus) and Tacitus, *Annales* 14, 42–45 (murder of a senator). For literate culture among ordinary Romans, see Andrew Wallace-Hadrill, 'Scratching the surface: a case study of domestic graffiti at Pompeii', in *L'écriture dans la maison romaine*, edited by M. Corbier and J.P. Guilhembert (Paris, 2011), and Kristina Milnor, *Graffiti and the Literary Landscape in Roman Pompeii* (Oxford UP, 2014). The Bar of the Seven Sages is an important topic in Clarke's *Art in the Lives of Ordinary Romans* and *Looking at Laughter: Humor, Power, and Transgression in Roman Visual Culture, 100 BC–AD 250* (Univ. of California Press, 2007).

Chapter 12

Pliny's exchanges with Trajan in *Letters* Book 10 provide a linking theme in this chapter. The letters are usefully collected by Wynne Williams in *Pliny, Correspondence with Trajan from Bithynia (Epistles X)* (Aris and Phillips, 1990) and the underlying ideology discussed by Greg Woolf, 'Pliny's province', in

Rome and the Black Sea Region: Domination, Romanisation, Resistance, edited by Tønnes Bekker-Nielsen (Aarhus UP, 2006), and Carlos F. Norena, 'The social economy of Pliny's correspondence with Trajan', *American Journal of Philology* 128 (2007). They also touch on one of the most controversial topics in all of ancient history: the rise of Christianity. A particularly illuminating short account of this is in Kelly, *The Roman Empire* (see *General*); the early sections of Diarmaid MacCullough, *A History of Christianity: The First Three Thousand Years* (Penguin, 2010) are also a sensible starting place. *A Companion to the Roman Empire*, edited by David S. Potter (Blackwell, 2006), includes several useful essays on the principles, practice and administration of the empire. The essays of Fergus Millar collected in *Government, Society, and Culture in the Roman Empire* (see *Chapter 11*) are some of the most important contributions to the subject (including discussion of Pliny and Trajan). Levick, *The Government of the Roman Empire* (see *Chapter 11*) offers a vivid glimpse of the rich primary evidence. Martin Goodman's chapter in Garnsey and Saller, *The Roman Empire* (see *General*) considers various forms and locations of resistance to Rome. Greek literature under Rome is the theme of Tim Whitmarsh, *Greek Literature and the Roman Empire: The Politics of Imitation* (Oxford UP, 2002), likewise *Being Greek under Rome: Cultural Identity, the Second Sophistic and the Development of Empire*, edited by Simon Goldhill (Cambridge UP, 2001). The title of this chapter is borrowed from Beard, North and Price, *Religions of Rome*, volume 2 (see *General*); I have also stressed the idea of *becoming Roman*, using the title of Greg Woolf's important study of imperial cultural interactions, *Becoming Roman: The Origins of Roman Provincial Civilization in Gaul* (Cambridge UP, 1998).

Lucian's skit on the oracle is titled *On the False Prophet*, and on Syrian religion *On the Syrian Goddess*. S. von Schnurbein, 'Augustus in Germania and his new "town" at Waldgirmes east of the Rhine', *Journal of Roman Archaeology* 16 (2003), presents the half-finished town. Strabo's assessment of the potential of Britain is at *Geography* 4, 5. The puzzle of Hadrian's Wall is explored in David J. Breeze and Brian Dobson, *Hadrian's Wall* (Penguin, 2000). The quality of provincial government is scrutinised by P. A. Brunt, 'Charges of provincial maladministration under the early principate', in *Roman Imperial Themes* (see *Chapter 10*); Tiberius' view is quoted by Cassius Dio, *Roman History* 57, 10.

Stephen Mitchell discusses 'Requisitioned transport in the Roman Empire' in the *Journal of Roman Studies* 66 (1976). The disreputable reasons for Otho's appointment are alleged by Suetonius, *Otho* 3. A 'world full of gods' is Keith Hopkins's phrase in his engagingly quirky study of Roman religions, *A World Full of Gods: Pagans, Jews and Christians in the Roman Empire* (Weidenfeld and Nicolson, 1999). The infrastructure at Vindolanda is vividly described by Alan K. Bowman, *Life and Letters on the Roman Frontier: Vindolanda and Its People* (British Museum Press, 1998); the documents are online at http://vindo landa.csad.ox.ac.uk/. The shoes are discussed by Caroline Van Driel-Murray, 'Gender in question', in *Theoretical Roman Archaeology: Second Conference Proceedings*, edited by P. Rush (Avebury, 1995), which raises the possibility that some might have belonged to adolescent men. A report on the Wroxeter swimming pool is included in G. Webster and P. Woodfield, 'The old work', *Antiquaries Journal* 46 (1966). Martin Millett's *Romanization of Britain: An Essay in Archaeological Interpretation* (Cambridge UP, 1990) has been hugely influential in countering old ideas of a top-down approach to 'Romanisation'; David Mattingly, *An Imperial Possession: Britain in the Roman Empire* (Penguin, 2006) is a thorough modern overview. The 'bilinguals' of La Graufesenque are discussed in J. N. Adams, *Bilingualism and the Latin Language* (Cambridge UP, 2003), though Alex Mullen offers alternative views in 'The language of the potteries', in *Seeing Red*, edited by Michael Fulford and Emma Durham (Institute of Classical Studies, 2013). Horace's slogan is in his *Epistles* 2, 1; the adjustments for 'Roman' display at a 'Greek' stadium are described by K. Welch, 'The stadium at Aphrodisias', *American Journal of Archaeology* 102 (1998). *The Pantheon: From Antiquity to the Present*, edited by Tod A. Marder and Mark Wilson Jones (Cambridge UP, 2015), is an up-to-date study of the temple; the source of the grey granite at Mons Claudianus and associated documents are reviewed in Roger S. Bagnall and Dominic W. Rathbone, *Egypt from Alexander to the Copts* (British Museum Press, 2004); and the letter on the 50-foot column is discussed by Theodore J. Peña, 'Evidence for the supplying of stone transport operations', *Journal of Roman Archaeology* 2 (1989). The ship from India is the subject of Dominic Rathbone, 'The Muziris papyrus', in 'Alexandrian Studies II in Honour of Mostafa el Abbadi,' special issue, *Bulletin de la Société d'Archéologie d'Alexandrie* 46 (2000); Zeuxis features in Peter Thonemann, *The Maeander Valley: A Historical Geography from Antiquity to Byzantium* (Cambridge UP, 2011); and the trade behind Monte Testaccio is the theme of D. J. Mattingly, 'Oil for export?', *Journal of Roman Archaeology* 1 (1988). *Roman Diasporas: Archaeological Approaches to Mobility and Diversity in the Roman Empire*, edited by Hella Eckhardt (*Journal of Roman Archaeology* supplement 78, 2011), considers how mobility can be measured; Barates and 'Queenie' are discussed by Alex Mullen, 'Multiple languages, multiple identities', in *Multilingualism in the Graeco-Roman Worlds*, edited by Mullen and Patrick James (Cambridge UP, 2012). The best discussion of the numbers of early Christians is Keith Hopkins, 'Christian number', *Journal of Early Christian Studies* 6 (1998); Perpetua's martyrdom is minutely analysed by Thomas J. Heffernan, *The Passion of Perpetua and Felicity* (Oxford UP, 2012). Septimius' treatment of his sister is described at *Augustan History* (*SHA*), *Septimius Severus* 15; Zoilos is discussed in detail in R. R. R. Smith, *The Monument of C. Julius Zoilos* (von Zabern, 1993).

Epilogue

The number of citizens created by Caracalla is carefully calculated by Myles Lavan, 'The spread of Roman citizenship', *Past and Present* 229 (2016) (I am grateful for the preview). An important appraisal of the Arch of Constantine is Jas Elsner, 'From the culture of *spolia* to the cult of relics', *Papers of the British School at Rome* 68 (2000). The misunderstanding of 'senate' is in *Parastaseis*, translated by Averil Cameron and Judith Herrin (Brill, 1984), Chapter 43.

TIMELINE

Entries in [square brackets] refer to events in classical Greek history.

LITERARY FIGURES	DATES	EVENTS	RULERS, PERIODS, WARS
	753 BCE	Traditional date of Rome's foundation	*REGAL PERIOD 753–509*
			1. Romulus
			2. Numa
			3. Tullus Hostilius
			4. Ancus Marcius
	[582	*Birth of Pythagoras on Samos]*	5. Tarquinius Priscus
			6. Servius Tullius
			7. Tarquinius Superbus
	509	Traditional date of foundation of Roman Republic	*ROMAN REPUBLIC 509–44*
	494	First secession of the plebeians	'Conflict of the Orders' (until 287)
	[490	*Battle of Marathon]*	
	451–450	'The Twelve Tables'	'The Decemvirate'
	[399	*Death of Socrates at Athens]*	
	396	Destruction of Veii	
	390	Gallic sack of Rome	
	341	Beginning of Latin War	WARS IN ITALY
	338	Latin League dissolved	LATIN WAR, 341–338
	[334	*Alexander the Great begins his campaigns]*	
	326	Debt enslavement abolished	SAMNITE WARS
			1st, 343–341
			2nd, 326–304
			3rd, 298–290

LITERARY FIGURES	DATES	EVENTS	RULERS, PERIODS, WARS
	[323	*Death of Alexander]*	
	321	Battle of the Caudine Forks	
	312	Construction of Rome's first aqueduct	
	295	Battle of Sentinum	
	290	End of Samnite Wars	
	287	Decisions of the Plebeian Assembly given force of law	
	280	Death of Scipio Barbatus	PYRRHIC WAR, 280–275 Rome v. Pyrrhus of Epirus
	275	Pyrrhus driven back to Epirus	
	264		1st PUNIC WAR, 264–241
Livius Andronicus' first tragedy performed	240		
	218	Hannibal crosses the Alps	2nd PUNIC WAR, 219–202 Rome v. Hannibal
	216	Battle of Cannae	1st MACEDONIAN WAR, 215–205
Plautus active (until 180s)			Rome v. Philip V
Ennius active (until c.169)	204	Arrival of the Great Mother in Rome	
	202	Battle of Zama	
			2nd MACEDONIAN WAR, 200–197 Rome v. Philip V
	190	Scipio Asiaticus defeats Antiochus	SYRIAN WAR, 192–188 Rome v. Antiochus III of Syria
Terence active (until c.160)			
	183	Deaths of Scipio Africanus and Hannibal	
			3rd MACEDONIAN WAR, 172–168
	171	Deputation from Spain, founding of Carteia	Rome v. Perseus
	168	Battle of Pydna, defeat of King Perseus of Macedon	

LITERARY FIGURES	DATES	EVENTS	RULERS, PERIODS, WARS
Polybius active (until c.118)	167	Polybius arrives at Rome as a hostage	
			WAR IN IBERIA, 155–133 Rome v. Celtiberian tribes
	149	Creation of permanent criminal courts	3rd PUNIC WAR, 149–146
	146	Sack of Carthage by Scipio Aemilianus	
		Sack of Corinth by Mummius	
	139	Introduction of the secret ballot	
	133	Conclusion of war in Iberia, most of which Rome now controls	
		Attalus of Pergamum bequeaths his kingdom to Rome	
		Tribunate and assassination of Tiberius Gracchus	
Lucilius' *Satires*, last third of 2nd century			
	129	Death of Scipio Aemilianus	
	125	Fregellae destroyed	
	123	Gaius Gracchus' tribunate	
	122	Gaius Gracchus re-elected as tribune	
		Compensation law passed	
	121	Assassination of Gaius Gracchus	

LITERARY FIGURES	DATES	EVENTS	RULERS, PERIODS, WARS
			WAR WITH JUGURTHA, 118–106
	107	Marius' first consulship, reform of the Roman army and command against Jugurtha	
Cicero born at Arpinum	106		
			SOCIAL WAR, 91–89
	89	Grants of citizenship to Italians	1st MITHRADATIC WAR, 89–85 Rome v. Mithradates VI of Pontus
	88	Sulla is given command against Mithradates	CIVIL WAR, 88–86 Sulla v. Marius
		Mithradates massacres Italians	
	86	Marius' seventh consulship and death	
	85	Sulla negotiates a truce with Mithradates	
	82–81	Sulla's reforms and proscriptions	2nd MITHRADATIC WAR, 83–81
Cicero and Terentia marry	80		
	79	Sulla resigns dictatorship	
	73	Mithradates invades Bithynia	REVOLT OF SPARTACUS, 73–71 — 3rd MITHRADATIC WAR, 73–63
	71	Crassus crushes Spartacus' revolt	
Cicero's speeches *Against Verres*	70	Cicero prosecutes Verres	
		Pompey's first consulship	
	67	Pompey's command against the pirates	

LITERARY FIGURES	DATES	EVENTS	RULERS, PERIODS, WARS
	66	Pompey given command against Mithradates	
First extant letter from Cicero to Atticus	65		
Catullus and Lucretius active (until mid 50s)			
Cicero's speeches *Against Catiline* 1–4	63	Pompey captures Jerusalem	
		Cicero exposes the 'Catilinarian Conspiracy'	
		Pompey defeats Mithradates, arranges settlement in the East	
Cicero's speech *In Defence of Archias*	62	Pompey celebrates triumph	
	60	Gang of Three make compact	
	59	Pompey marries Caesar's daughter, Julia	
	58	Exile of Cicero (until 57)	
	55	Caesar's first landing in Britannia	
		Pompey's Theatre built	
Cicero's *On the State* (54–51)	54	Death of Julia	
	53	Disaster at Carrhae, death of Crassus	
	52	Murder of Clodius ('Battle of Bovillae')	
		Pompey's sole consulship	
Caesar's *Commentaries on the Gallic War*	51	Cicero governor of Cilicia	
	50	Caesar completes conquest of Gaul	
Sallust active	40s		
Cicero joins Pompey in Greece	49	Caesar crosses the Rubicon	CIVIL WARS 49–31 Caesar v. Pompey

LITERARY FIGURES	DATES	EVENTS	RULERS, PERIODS, WARS
CICERO returns to Rome	48	Battle of Pharsalus; death of Pompey in Egypt	
Cicero and Terentia divorce	46	Caesar's triumph	
Cicero marries Publilia; death of his daughter, Tullia	45		
	44	January: Caesar is voted *dictator perpetuus*	
		March: Caesar's assassination	
Cicero assassinated	43	Formation of the Triumvirate of Octavian, Antony and Lepidus	Caesar's assassins v. Caesar's heirs
Horace on losing side at Philippi	42	Battle of Philippi: the Triumvirate defeats Brutus and Cassius	
	41–40	Siege of Perusia	Lucius Antonius v. Octavian
Virgil's *Eclogues*	39		
Livy's *History*, written from 30s BC to AD 17	37	Octavian and Livia marry	
Horace's *Satires* 1	35/4		
	31	Battle of Actium	Octavian v. Mark Antony
	30	Suicide of Antony and Cleopatra; Egypt becomes a Roman province	THE RULE OF THE EMPERORS
			The Julio-Claudian dynasty, 31 BCE–68CE
			Octavian/Augustus 31 BCE–14CE
Propertius, Tibullus and Ovid active	20s		
Virgil writes the *Georgics*, possibly starts work on the *Aeneid*	29	Octavian returns to Italy and celebrates a triple triumph	
	27	Octavian takes the title *Augustus*	
Death of Virgil	19	Parthian standards lost at Carrhae returned to Rome	

LITERARY FIGURES	DATES	EVENTS	RULERS, PERIODS, WARS
	18	First Augustan marriage legislation	
	8	The month 'Sextilis' is renamed 'Augustus' (August)	
Death of Cicero's ex-slave Tiro	4	Augustus formally adopts Tiberius	
	2	Inauguration of the Forum of Augustus	
		Exile of Julia (Augustus' daughter)	BCE
Ovid exiled to Tomis	8 CE		CE
	9	Battle of the Teutoburg Forest	
Strabo active (until c.24)	10s		Tiberius 14–37
Phaedrus and Velleius Paterculus active	20s		
	25	Aulus Cremutius Cordus starves himself to death	
	26	Pontius Pilate governor of Judaea (until 36)	
	29	Death of Livia	
	33	Traditional date for crucifixion of Jesus	
	37		Gaius (Caligula) 37–41
	40	Jewish embassy to Caligula	
Seneca the Younger active	41	Assassination of Caligula	Claudius 41–54
	43	Claudius' invasion of Britannia	
	44	Claudius celebrates his triumph over Britannia	
	48	Claudius' Lyon speech	
Seneca's *Apocolocyntosis*	54		Nero 54–68

LITERARY FIGURES	DATES	EVENTS	RULERS, PERIODS, WARS
	58	Agricola first in Britain (until 62)	
Pliny the Elder, Lucan, Petronius and Persius active	60s		
	60	Boudicca's rebellion	
Birth of Pliny the Younger	61	Lucius Pedanius Secundus is murdered by his slaves	
	64	Great Fire at Rome	
		Traditional date for St Peter's crucifixion in Rome	
Seneca and Lucan commit suicide	65	Traditional date for St Paul's beheading in Rome	
		Conspiracy of Piso against Nero	
Petronius commits suicide	66	King Tiridates in Rome	1st JEWISH REVOLT, 66–73/4
		Thraesea Paetus commits suicide	
	68	Suicide of Nero	
	69	Civil war: 'The Year of the Four Emperors'	CIVIL WAR
			The Flavian dynasty 69–96
	70	Destruction of the Temple at Jerusalem	
	73/4	First Jewish Revolt ends with the fall of Masada	Vespasian 69–79
Josephus begins to circulate the *Jewish War*	c.75	Work begins on Roman villa at Fishbourne	
	77	Agricola governor of Britannia (until 85)	

LITERARY FIGURES	DATES	EVENTS	RULERS, PERIODS, WARS
Death of Pliny the Elder	79	Eruption of Vesuvius, destruction of Pompeii and Herculaneum	Titus (79–81)
Martial, Plutarch and Juvenal active	80s		
	80	Completion of the Colosseum	
	81		Domitian (81–96)
Vindolanda tablets written (until 120)	c.85		
	89	Domitian's nightmare dinner party	
Josephus' *Jewish Antiquities*	93/4		*Dynasty of 'adoptive' emperors 96–192*
	96	Assassination of Domitian	Nerva (96–98)
Tacitus' consulship; *Agricola* written around this time	97	Nerva adopts Trajan	
	98		Trajan (98–117)
Pliny's consulship and *Panegyric* to Trajan	100		
			1st DACIAN WAR, 101–02
			2nd DACIAN WAR, 105–06
Tacitus' *Histories*	109	Pliny governor of Bithynia (until 110)	
Pliny's *Letters* 10 (to Trajan)	110		
	113	Trajan invades Parthia	TRAJAN's CAMPAIGNS in the East, 113–17
Tacitus' *Annales*	117		Hadrian (117–138)
	118	Execution of four ex-consuls	

LITERARY FIGURES	DATES	EVENTS	RULERS, PERIODS, WARS
Suetonius' *Twelve Caesars*	120s	Construction of Hadrian's Wall	
		Construction of Hadrian's Pantheon	
	130	Hadrian's companion Antinous drowns in the Nile	
	138		Antoninus Pius (138–161)
Fronto, Aulus Gellius, Pausanias and Lucian active (until 180s)	140s		
Aristides' *Roman Oration*	144		
Galen active (until 200s)	160s		
	161		Marcus Aurelius and Lucius Verus (161–169)
	167	Smallpox (?) pandemic in Rome and wider empire	
	169	Lucius Verus dies, probably in pandemic	Marcus Aurelius rules alone (169–180)
	180		Commodus (180–192)
	192	Assassination of Commodus	
	193	Five rival claimants to the throne	CIVIL WAR
	196	Septimius Severus becomes sole emperor	*The Severan dynasty 193–235* Septimius Severus (193–211)
Cassius Dio begins his history	c.202		
	203	Execution of Vibia Perpetua in Carthage	
Cassius Dio's consulship	c.205		
	211	Caracalla kills Geta	Caracalla and Geta, then Caracalla rules alone (211–217)
	212	Citizenship extended to all free inhabitants of the empire	

ACKNOWLEDGEMENTS

This book has been fun and poignant in the making. It was the brainchild of my friend and editor, the much-missed Peter Carson, who sadly died before seeing a word of it. I can only hope that he would not be disappointed in the result.

SPQR is the work of about fifty years, and there are more people to thank than can be recognised here. I have recently called for help from friends and colleagues in Cambridge and elsewhere: Cliff Ando, Emma Dench, Chris Hallett, William Harris, Geoff Hawthorn, Myles Lavan, Matthew Leigh, Angus Mackinnon, Neville Morley, John North, Robin Osborne, Jonathan Prag, Joyce Reynolds, James Romm, Brian Rose, Malcolm Schofield, Ruth Scurr, Bert Smith, Peter Thonemann, Jerry Toner and Carrie Vout. Other friends, including Manolo Blahnik, Corrie Corfield, Gary Ingham and Sean Spence, Roger Michel and our holiday companions in July 2015 (Frank Darbell and Jay Weissberg, Celina Fox, Fionnuala and Simon Jervis, Anna Somers-Cocks, Jonathan and Teresa Sumption) have cheered me up in different ways. The commenters on my blog (*A Don's Life*) have as usual been forthright with constructive criticism as the book progressed. Hannah Price gave expert advice on the bibliography in the final stages; Debbie Whittaker's organising genius was indispensable all along, as was her eagle eye in spotting errors of typing, fact and logic.

Many institutions have done more than I could ever have hoped to push this project forward: the Classics Faculty in Cambridge (and its library) has always supported me; Newnham College has tolerated my single-mindedness; the American Academy in Rome generously hosted me for a few weeks' solid work (my thanks, especially, to Kim Bowes); the *Times Literary Supplement* has put up with my absences. Steve Kimberley saved the data on my laptop at a crucial moment. I have seen, and learned, a lot by working with the rigorous academic professionals at Lion Television for a series that is related to, though not based on, this book. My thanks go in particular to Richard Bradley, Johnny

Crockett, Ben Finney, Craig Hastings, Tim Hodge, Chris Mitchell, Marco Rossi and Caterina Turroni. With them I have had the pleasure of exploring parts of the Roman Empire I would never have dreamt of experiencing first-hand. They have opened my eyes.

My publishers have been, as ever, good to work with – and tolerant of my slowness to deliver. Thanks in the UK must go to Penny Daniel, Frances Ford, Andrew Franklin, Valentina Zanca and all the others at Profile and elsewhere who make these books possible; and that includes Emily Hayward-Whitlock on the media side, Juliana Froggatt, who copy-edited with skill and humour, and Lesley Hodgson who tracked down the pictures. Thanks too to Jonathan Harley and James Alexander for meticulous typesetting and page design. In the US, Bob Weil at Liveright was an editor in the grand old tradition. I am more grateful to him than I can say, and to Peter Miller and Will Menaker. George Lucas at Inkwell has looked after me splendidly in New York.

My family have been incredibly tolerant throughout the writing of *SPQR*: Robin Cormack, Zoe and Raphael. Love and thanks go to them, with the hope of calmer waters – and more time off – to come. And thanks go especially to Peter Stothard, who has read and advised, fed and watered me, throughout the process of gestation and writing. If this book were dedicated to anyone, it would be to him. From one Peter to another, thank you both.

LIST OF ILLUSTRATIONS

Colour plates

1 'Cicero Denounces Catiline' (1889) by Cesare Maccari, Palazzo Madama, Rome. Photo © akg-images/Album/Oronoz

2 'Cicero Denounces Catiline', (*c.* 1850) by John Leech, from Gilbert Abbott A Beckett, *The Comic History of Rome* (Bradbury and Evans, 1852). Photo © Posner Library/Carnegie Mellon

3 Top: 'Rape of the Sabines', by N. Poussin (1637–8), Musée du Louvre, Paris. Photo © akg-images/Erich Lessing. Bottom: 'Rape of the Sabines', by P. Picasso (1962), Centre Pompidou. Photo © Succession Picasso/DACS, London 2015/Courtesy akg-images

4 'Tarquin and Lucretia', by Titian (1571), Fitzwilliam Museum, Cambridge. Photo © Lebrecht Music and Arts Photo Library/Alamy

5 'Ficoroni Cista', fourth century BCE, Museo Nazionale Etrusco di Villa Giulia, Rome. Photo (top) © akg-images/De Agostini Picture Lib./G. Nimatallah; (bottom) © akg-images/Nimatallah

6 Tomb painting, third century BCE, from Esquiline hill, Centrale Montemartini, Rome. Photo © The Art Archive/Alamy

7 Scenes from François Tomb, Vulci, fourth century BCE, Torlonia Collection, Rome. Photo courtesy of Soprintendenza per i Beni Archeologici dell'Etruria meridionale

8 The raising of a ship's ram from the First Punic War, off Sicily. Photo © RPM Nautical Foundation

9 Final panel from the series of 'The Triumphs of Caesar' (1484–92) by Andrea Mantegna, Hampton Court Palace, London. Photo Royal Collection Trust © Her Majesty Queen Elizabeth II, 2015/Bridgeman Images

10 Section of the Column of Marcus Aurelius, Rome. Photo © Really Easy Star/Tullio Valente /Alamy

Illustrations

While every effort has been made to contact copyright-holders of
illustrations, the author and publishers would be grateful for information
about any illustrations where they have been unable to trace them, and
would be glad to make amendments in further editions.

INDEX

Figures in *italics* refer to captions

A